LEE KRASNER

LIVING COLOUR

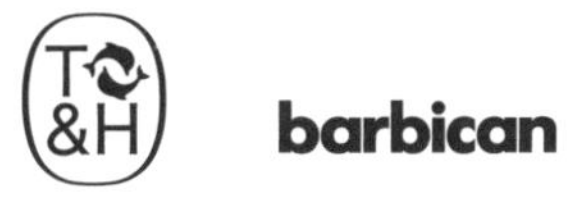

barbican

EDITED BY ELEANOR NAIRNE

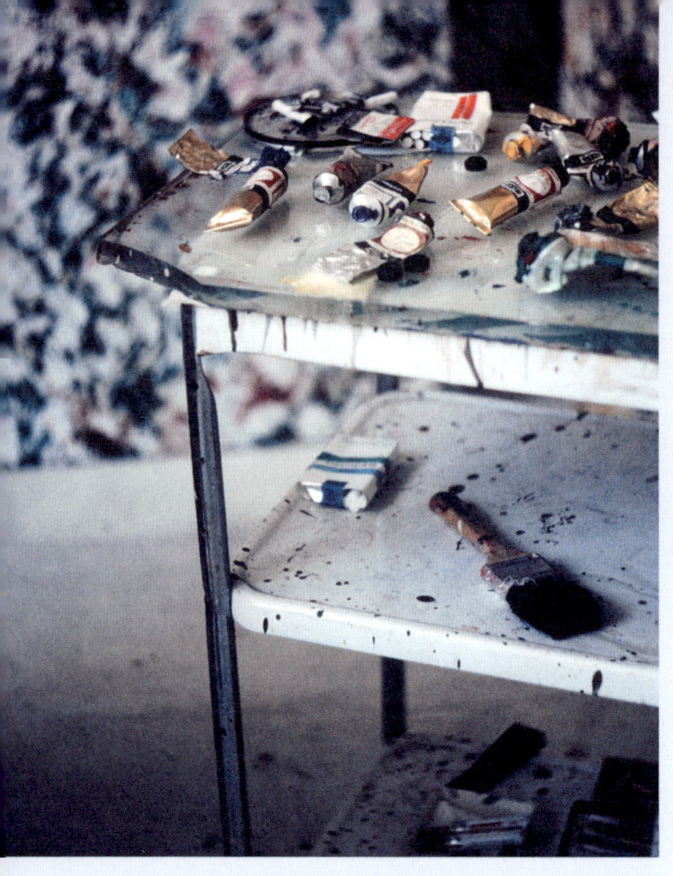

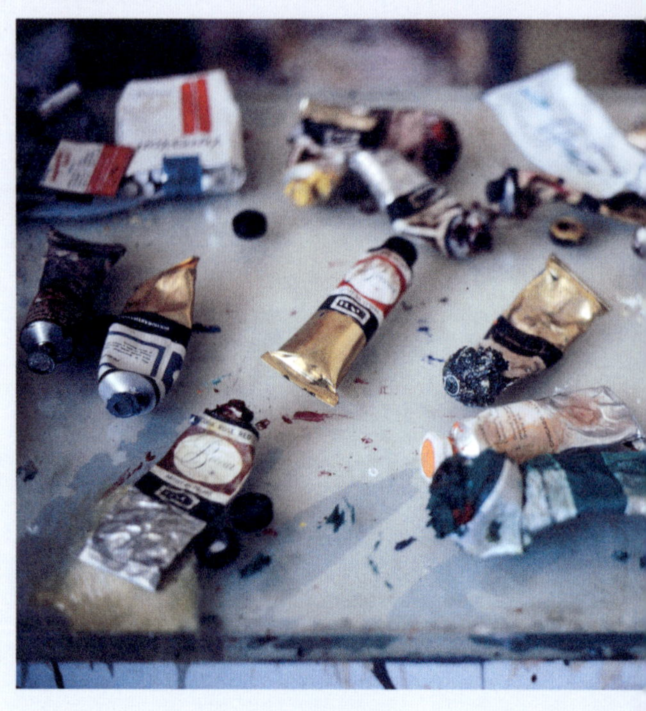

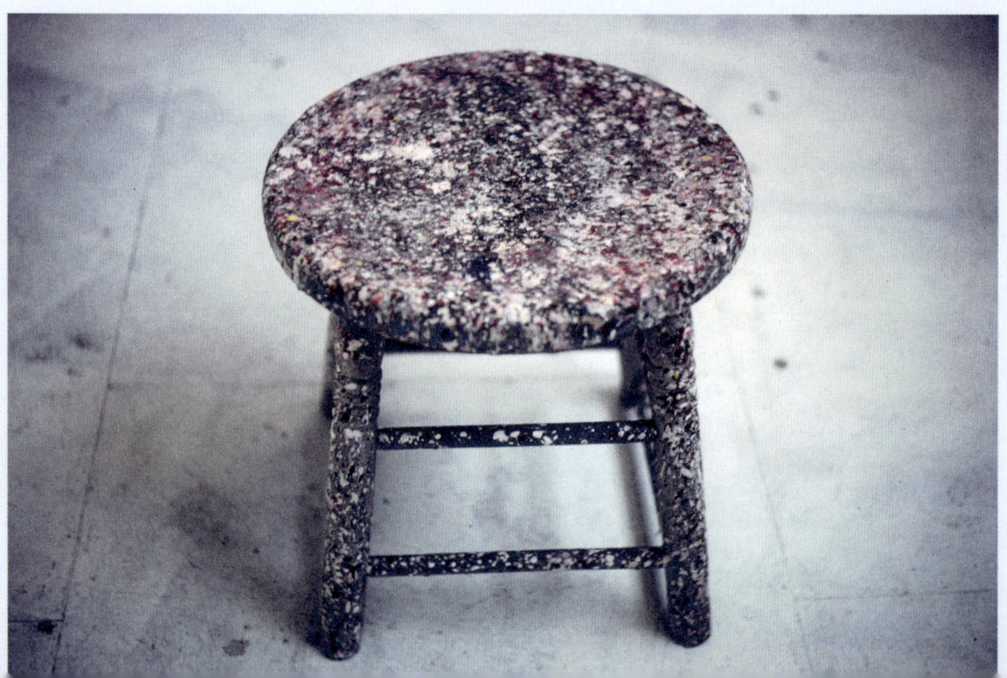

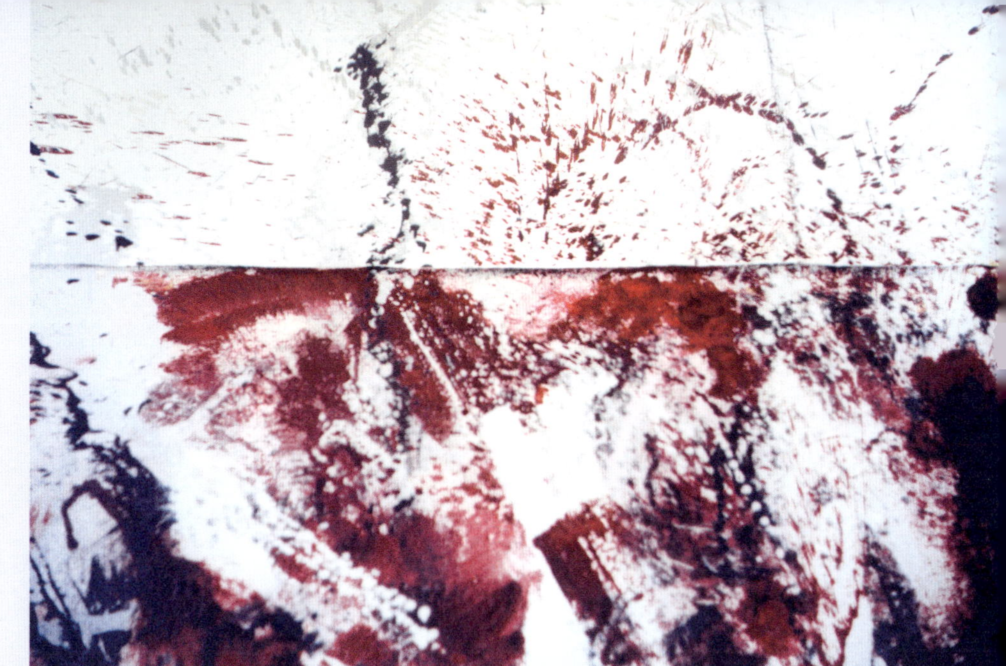

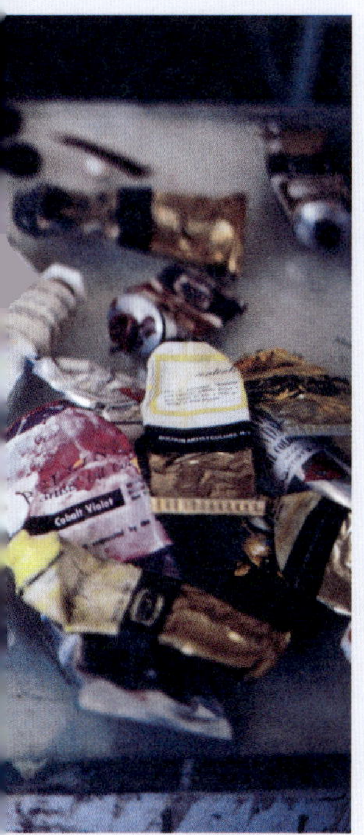

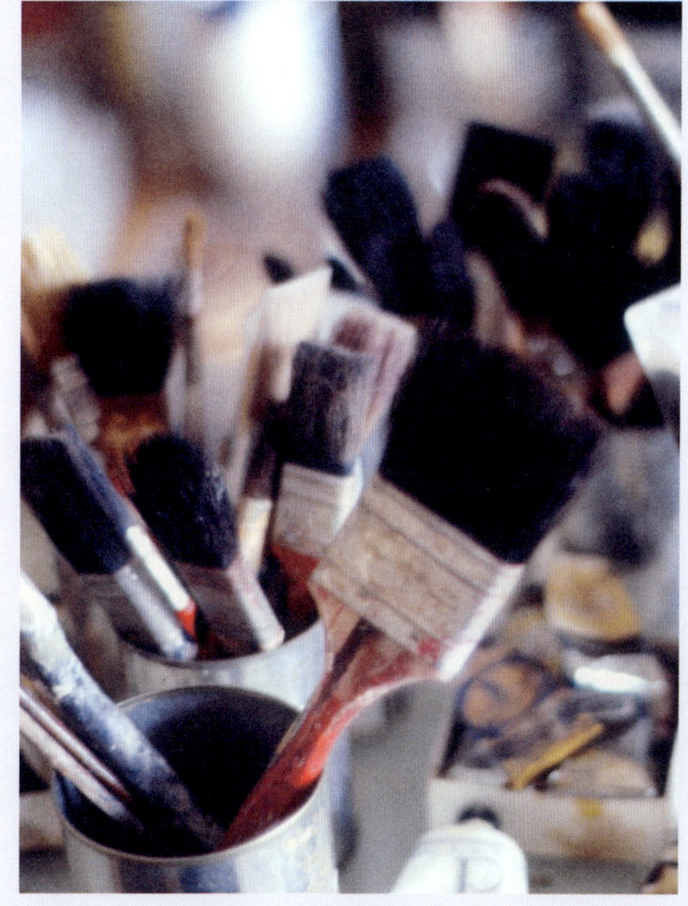

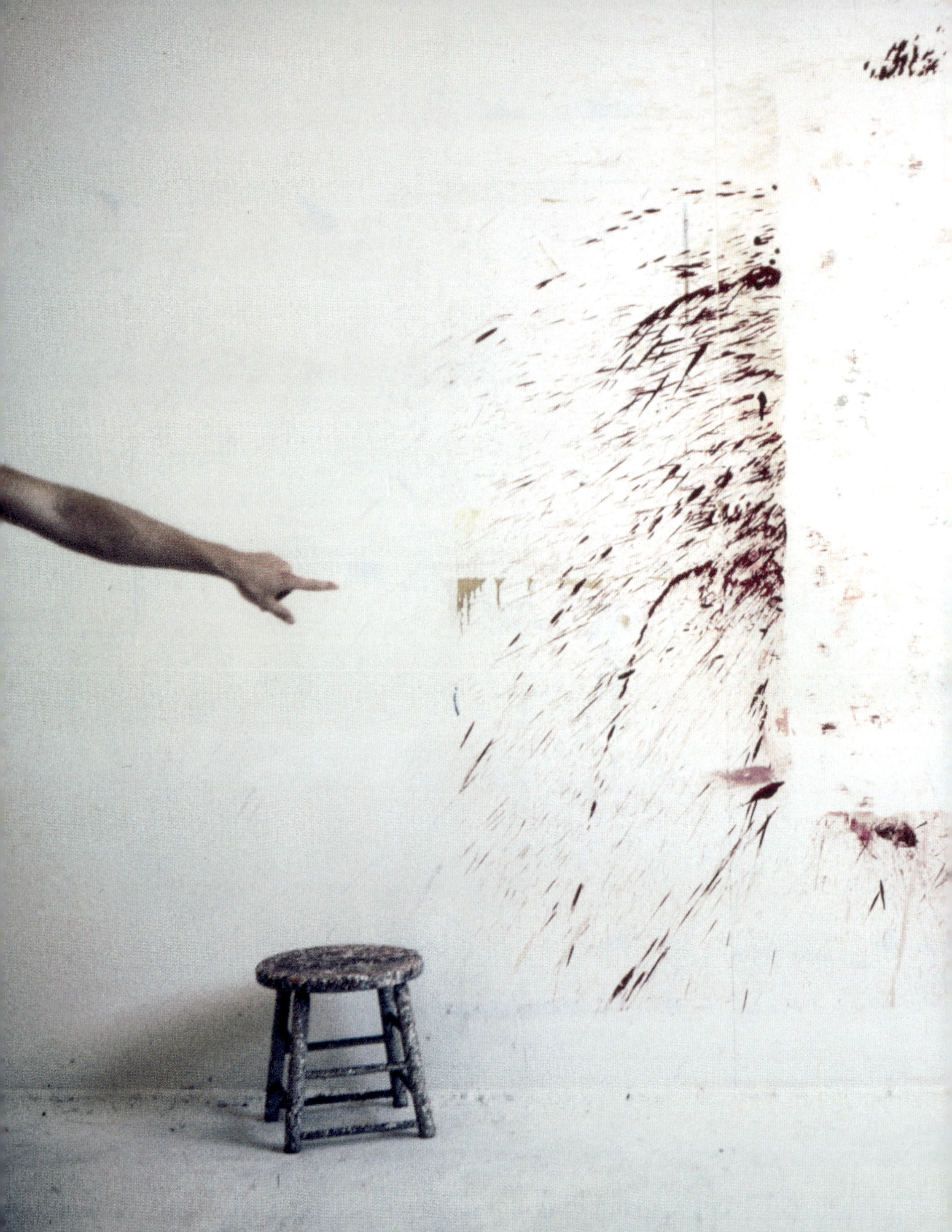

FOREWORD

In 1984 the poet Richard Howard wrote a moving tribute to the artist Lee Krasner, his friend. While acknowledging the tough temperament for which she had become known – her 'clamorous insistence on what she felt, on *what she knew*, to be the truth' – he pointed to the many other 'strands in the web' of her personality that deserved to be remembered.[1] Among them was her capacity for total engagement; as Howard recalled, 'Lee Krasner was the ideal audience for any articulated work of art, she was all there for it, utterly pliant to the demands of vision.'[2]

In today's terminology, we might call this 'presence' – a way of living and working that can be sensed from Krasner's nearly six decades in the studio. She would immerse herself entirely in a cycle of work, and then, just as it threatened to stagnate, she would shift direction. Although she absorbed much from all around her, her primary inspiration came from within; and it is the strength of feeling that she poured into everything she made – from her self-portraits to her 'Little Images', from collages to large-scale abstractions – that brings coherence to her career.

Krasner's work has not always been given the quality of attention it deserves. During her lifetime, she was often marginalized as the suffering spouse of the artist Jackson Pollock; after his death in 1956, she had to cope with the added burden of being the sole executor of his estate. In the 1970s, second-wave feminism revived interest in her career. Yet many of the hyperbolic claims made at the time for Krasner's role in relation to Abstract Expressionism – albeit well-intentioned – have contributed to the difficulty in appreciating her work in a clear light.

A key turning point for Krasner was the survey exhibition organized by Bryan Robertson at the Whitechapel Gallery in London in 1965.[3] It was her first opportunity to review the achievements of her career to date, and the praise she received from journalists on the other side of the Atlantic (many of whom did not realize that she was a woman, let alone Pollock's widow) brought her a degree of critical recognition that was no less welcome for being belated. Since then, she has been the subject of two important retrospectives in the United States: the first curated by Barbara Rose for the Museum of Fine Arts, Houston, the San Francisco Museum of Modern Art and the Museum of Modern Art, New York, in 1983–85; the second curated by Robert Hobbs for Los Angeles County Museum of Art, Des Moines Art Center, the Akron Art Museum and the Brooklyn Museum in 1999–2001. Yet this is the first to be mounted in Europe.

Finally, after more than fifty years, visitors to the Barbican Art Gallery in London, the Schirn Kunsthalle Frankfurt, the Zentrum Paul Klee in Bern and the Guggenheim Museum Bilbao can draw their own conclusions about Krasner's strengths as an artist. Comprised of almost one hundred works, many of which are being brought to Europe for the first time, the exhibition highlights Krasner's extensive artistic training, her early adoption of abstraction, her radical

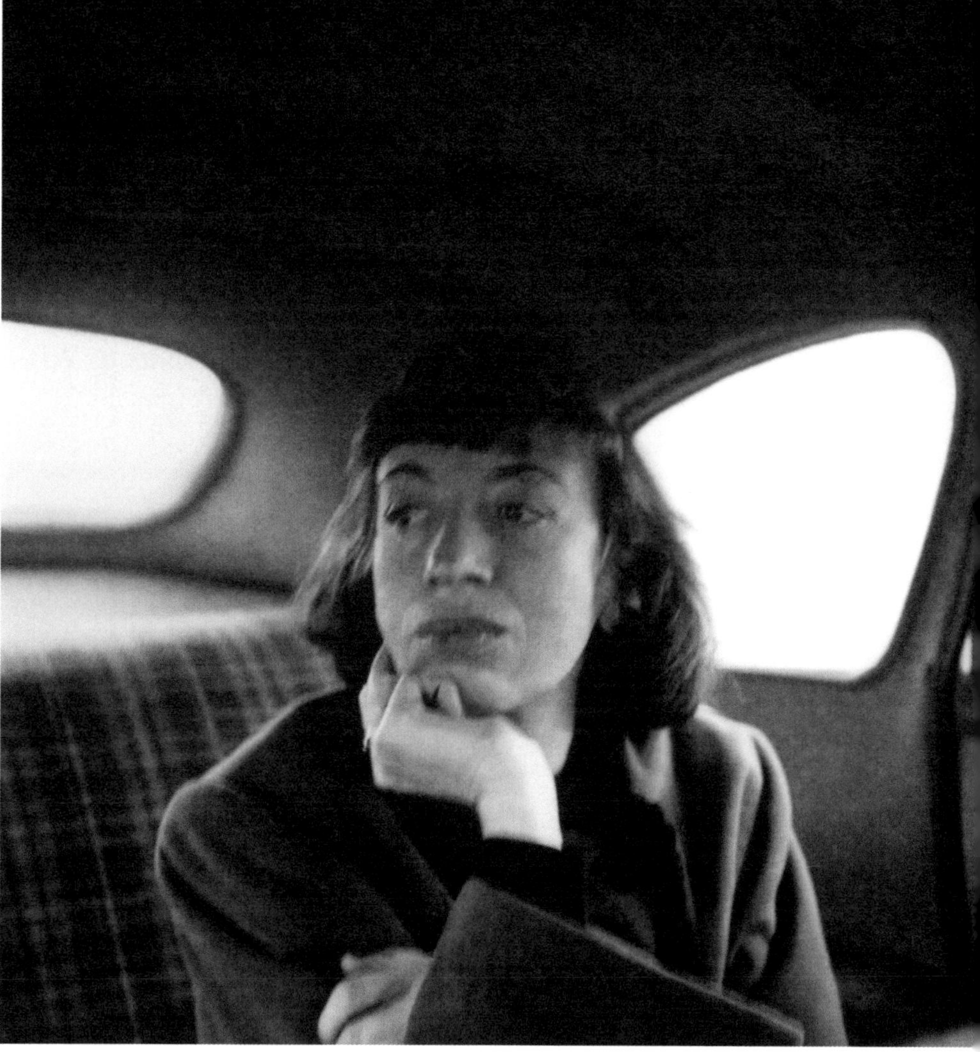

Portrait of Lee Krasner in the back of a car in New York City,
3 January 1949. Photograph by Arnold Newman.

recycling of older work into new, her talents as a colourist, and her powerful explorations of scale and form.

This book offers a timely reassessment of Krasner's work and life, featuring an introductory essay by the curator Eleanor Nairne alongside insightful thematic essays from Katy Siegel, John Yau and Suzanne Hudson. We are delighted to be able to include a previously unpublished interview between Lee Krasner and her biographer, Gail Levin, as well as a fully illustrated chronology, which has been compiled by Jessica Freeman-Attwood. Nairne has edited the book with great care, closely supported at the Barbican by Charlotte Flint.

The project would not have been possible without the warm support of the Pollock-Krasner Foundation, which has been incredibly generous in giving its time and energy to the project's development over the past three years. Our special thanks go to Kerrie Buitrago, Samuel Sachs II, Ronald D. Spencer and Caroline Black – as well as to Charles C. Bergman, who sadly died in 2018, but whose enthusiasm for the project at an early stage was deeply inspiring for the team. Kasmin Gallery has also been critical to the success of the project; in particular, our thanks go to Eric Gleason, who has been a formidable ally from the outset, and to Michal Patchefsky.

We feel privileged to have been able to borrow so extensively from museum collections, and we would like to thank the Albright-Knox Art Gallery, Buffalo; the Flint Institute of Arts, Michigan; the Guild Hall Museum, East Hampton; the Hirshhorn Museum and Sculpture Garden, Washington DC; the Institut Valencià d'Art Modern; the Jewish Museum, New York; the Kunstmuseum Bern; the Los Angeles County Museum of Art; the Metropolitan Museum of Art, New York; the Munson Williams Proctor Arts Institute, Utica; the National Gallery of Art, Washington DC; the National Gallery of Victoria, Melbourne; the Neuberger Museum of Art, Purchase; the Philadelphia Museum of Art; the Pollock-Krasner Foundation, New York; the Reynolda House Museum of American Art, Winston-Salem; the San Francisco Museum of Modern Art; and the Whitney Museum of American Art, New York.

We are also greatly indebted to the private collectors who have supported this exhibition, and we would like to express our sincerest thanks to James Barron, Suzanne Deal Booth, David Dechman and Michel Mercure, Ron Delsener, the Gusford Collection, halley k harrisburg and Michael Rosenfeld, Audrey Irmas, Dr Greg Shannon and family, the Thomson Family Collection, and Bobbi and Walter Zifkin, as well as to the lenders who wish to remain anonymous. We are also grateful to those who helped connect us to works, notably Saara Pritchard, Nicholas Cinque and David Galperin at Sotheby's; Barrett White, Katharine Arnold and Cassi Young at Christie's; and Joshua Holdeman, Janis Gardner Cecil, Angela Nevill and Laura Paulson.

An exhibition of this scale simply would not have been possible without the support of the Terra Foundation for American Art. Its generous contribution to all four iterations of this project has allowed us to organize an exhibition without compromise. The exhibition has further benefitted from sponsorship by tp bennett and Sotheby's, as well as a Jonathan Ruffer Curatorial Research Grant from the Art Fund. We would also like to thank our London Exhibition Circle: Ron Delsener, Kenneth C. Griffin Charitable Fund, Kasmin Gallery, Elizabeth and J. Jeffry Louis, Midge and Simon Palley, and those who wish to remain anonymous.

The project is underscored by considerable research, and we would like to thank all of those who have been such engaging correspondents during its development. In particular, we are grateful to Gail Levin, whose meticulous biography of 2011 shed new light on Krasner; Barbara Rose, who knew Krasner intimately and curated the major 1983–85 retrospective of her work; Ellen G. Landau, whose catalogue raisonné is a gift to any scholar; Robert Hobbs, curator of the second major US retrospective on Krasner; Anne Wagner, who brought new thinking to bear in her book *Three Artists (Three Women)* (1996); Mary Gabriel, for her remarkable contribution to this field with *Ninth Street Women* (2018); Ruth Appelhof, whose memoir on Krasner we await with anticipation; and the authors of the three essays in this book.

A number of individuals have been critical to the staging of this exhibition. Our thanks go to Helen A. Harrison, Director of the Pollock-Krasner House and Study Center, who is a source of special insight into Krasner and her working context; Edith Devaney and David Anfam, who featured Krasner prominently in their outstanding exhibition *Abstract Expressionism* at the Royal Academy in London in 2016–17 and subsequently at the Guggenheim Museum Bilbao in spring 2017; Jason McCoy, gallerist and nephew to Pollock; and John Elderfield, Chief Curator Emeritus at the Museum of Modern Art, New York. The accompanying book has been beautifully designed by A Practice for Everyday Life; the exhibition in London was designed by David Chipperfield Architects.

This project is the result of a remarkable international collaboration. Initiated by the Barbican, it has been curated with Ilka Voermann at the Schirn Kunsthalle Frankfurt, Fabienne Eggelhöfer at the Zentrum Paul Klee and Lucía Agirre at the Guggenheim Museum Bilbao. In London, the exhibition has been organized with the support of Charlotte Flint, Ross Head, Alice Lobb and Peter Sutton; in Frankfurt, our thanks go to Inka Drögemüller, Deputy Director, to Esther Schlicht, Head of Exhibitions, and to Karin Grüning, for the organization of loans; in Bern, we are grateful for the support of Kai-Inga Dost and Edith Heinimann; and in Bilbao, we thank the departments of Exhibitions and Conservation, Communications and Images, General Counsel, Development, Human Resources and Quality, Digital Transformation, and Finance.

Lee Krasner was an artist who, as Richard Howard remembered, felt that 'truth had its claims, and she served them; she observed them'.[4] We hope this exhibition and accompanying book offer a faithful representation of her extraordinary life and work, enabling a new generation internationally to engage with her powerful legacy.

Jane Alison, Head of Visual Arts, Barbican, London
Philipp Demandt, Director, Schirn Kunsthalle Frankfurt
Nina Zimmer, Director, Kunstmuseum Bern / Zentrum Paul Klee
Juan Ignacio Vidarte, Director General, Guggenheim Museum Bilbao

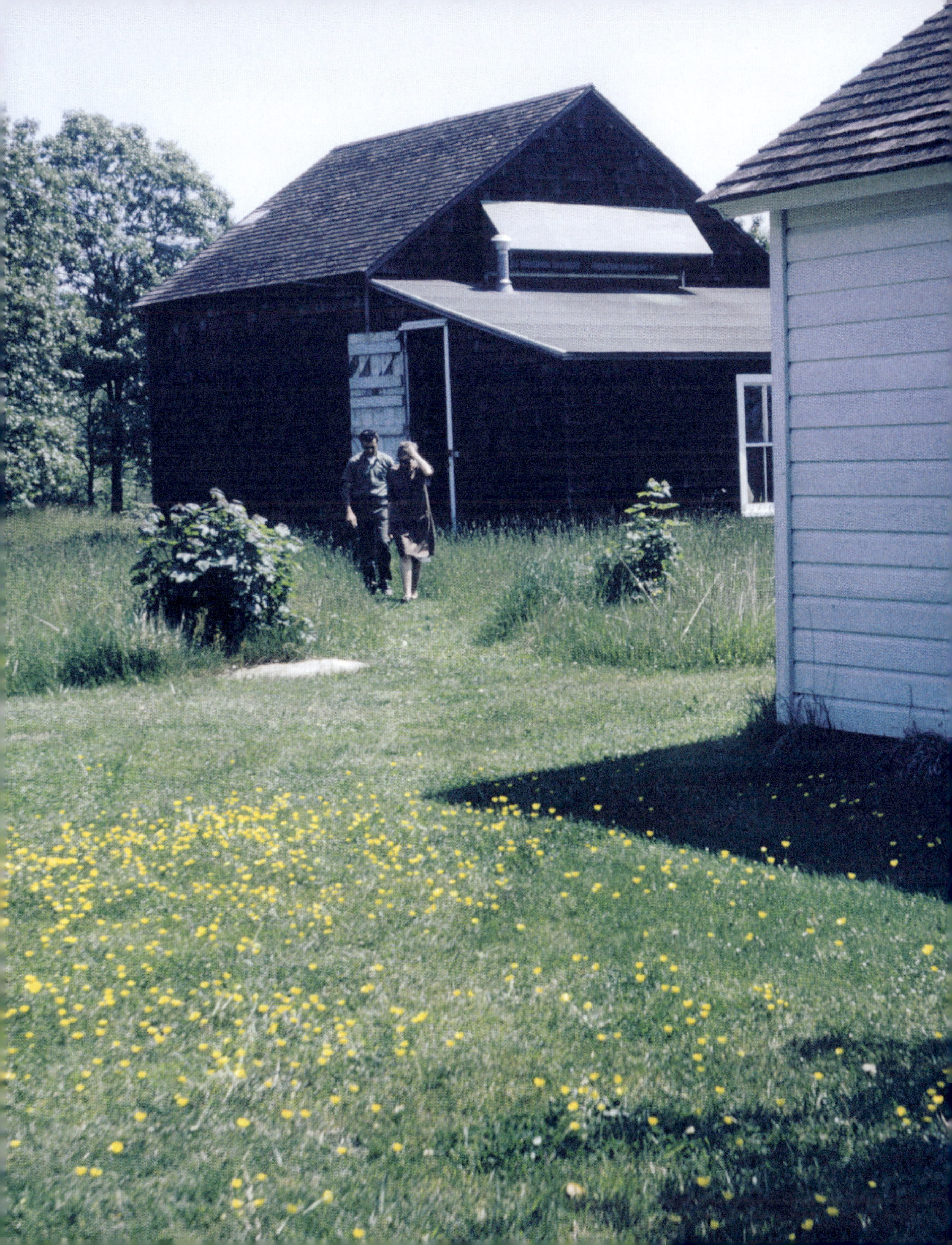

TO BREATHE AND BE ALIVE

I like a canvas to breathe and be alive. Be alive is the point. And, as the limitations are something called pigment and canvas, let's see if I can do it.
Lee Krasner

Lee Krasner was known as a force to be reckoned with. 'She looked you straight in the eye', said the playwright Edward Albee, 'and you dared not flinch.'[1] Albee spoke at her memorial service (along with the writer Susan Sontag and the critic Robert Hughes), which was held at the Metropolitan Museum of Art in New York on 17 September 1984. Becoming and then sustaining herself as an artist had required formidable determination. There was her Orthodox Jewish upbringing, which ran contrary to a bohemian lifestyle in Greenwich Village; the financial precariousness of New York during the Great Depression and the Second World War; and the struggle to be taken seriously as a 'woman painter', which was still largely seen as a contradiction in terms.[2] Not to mention her marriage to Jackson Pollock, whose alcoholism made him an emotionally volatile companion. In 1949 Pollock was brought to international fame with an illustrated article in *Life* magazine that asked, provocatively: 'Is He the Greatest Living Painter in the United States?'[3] There would be no real time to tell, as he died in a car crash (which his lover, Ruth Kligman, survived) in 1956. Through all of this – and three onerous decades as Pollock's widow and executor – Krasner refused to allow her own work to suffer. So it is little wonder that, as Albee recalled, 'Lee was not "easy" – and what a blessing is there; protect us from "easy" women; she demanded the quality she gave, and if she put us on our mettle, she gave us gold in return.'[4]

In an interview with Cindy Nemser in 1973, Krasner declared that 'my painting is so biographical if anyone can take the trouble to read it'.[5] As Anne Wagner has highlighted, her words have bite, but they still offer a clear invitation to consider her work and life in dialogue.[6] The challenge to doing so is that Krasner was a ruthless editor, destroying entire series that she came to dislike. This was partly a very practical measure: with few paintings being sold and having

1   Lee Krasner, c.1938–40

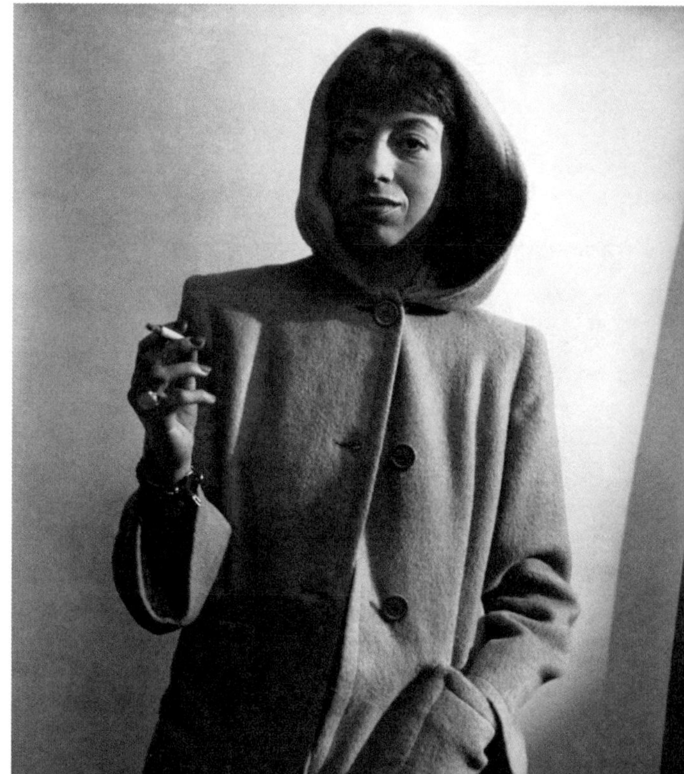

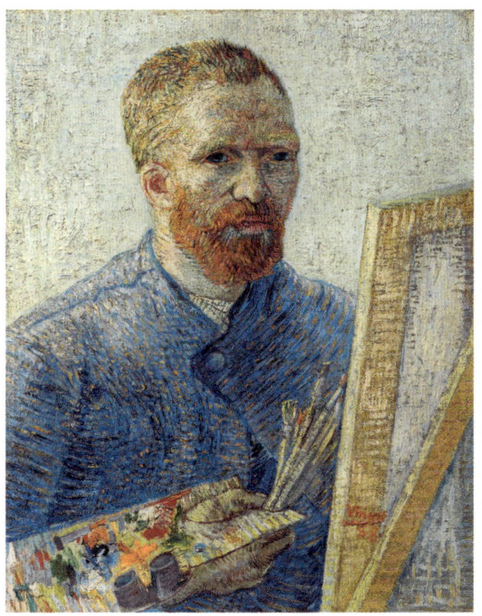

2 Vincent van Gogh, *Self-Portrait as a Painter*, 1887–88

the morning prayer was recited in Hebrew. She later recalled, 'I didn't know what I was saying; I just had to say it or God would strike me dead.'[11] Originally named Lena Krassner, in 1922 she adopted the more American 'Lenore', which later became the more androgynous 'Lee'. It was not uncommon for émigrés to 'translate' their names – her brother, Isak, became 'Irving', while her sister Ides became 'Edith'.[12] Even such natives as Pollock rebranded themselves in New York: when he moved to the city in 1930, he dropped his first name, Paul (presumably because, as John Berger later quipped, 'Jackson Pollock was a name for fighting in the ring. A champ's name').[13] Krasner became Lenore at the same time as she was renouncing religion and chose to attend Washington Irving High – the only school in New York to offer an art course for girls. Graduating at the age of seventeen, she went on to study at the Woman's Art School at Cooper Union and, after a brief spell at the Art Students League, the National Academy of Design.

limited money for materials (let alone storage), it made sense to soak and strip the canvases that she considered less successful in order to reuse them for new work. But it also relates to her refusal to fix on any singular style, which was brave in an era of such 'signature' imagery as that of Franz Kline or Robert Motherwell. As Krasner explained, 'I no sooner settle into something than a break occurs' – a painful process that could be eased by editing, to show herself 'that there's a consistency that holds out'.[7] Krasner was similarly selective in how she spoke to interviewers, who anyway came calling only in the later part of her life.[8] As she did not keep diaries and rarely wrote letters, we have been left with few intimate sources. But what we do know of her life offers a more textured impression of the context in which her work was made and a sense of why it retains such considerable impact today.[9]

Born on 27 October 1908, Krasner arrived almost nine months to the day after her mother was reunited with her father in Brooklyn. They had fled their *shtetl* outside Odessa, in what was then Russia and is now Central Ukraine; records show that 77,544 Russian Jews emigrated to the United States in 1904 (twice that in 1902), seeking asylum from brutal pogroms.[10] As the first child in the family to be born in America, Krasner had a conflicted relationship with her home, where Russian and Yiddish were the primary languages and

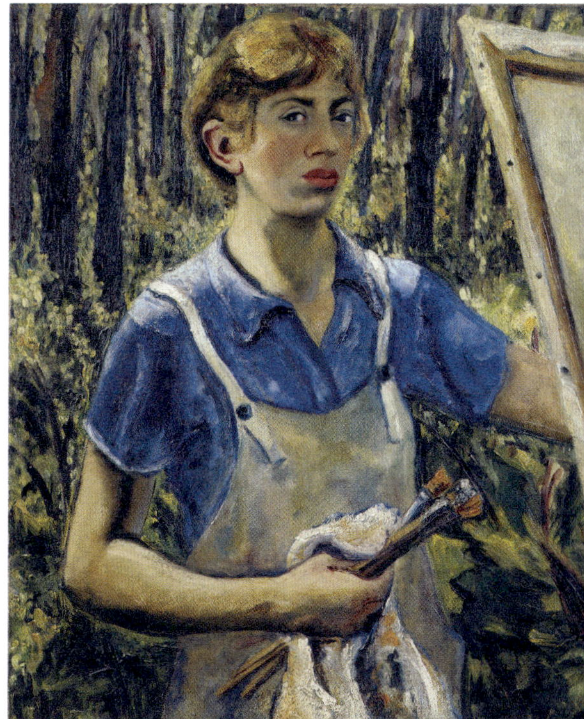

3 *Self-Portrait*, c. 1928

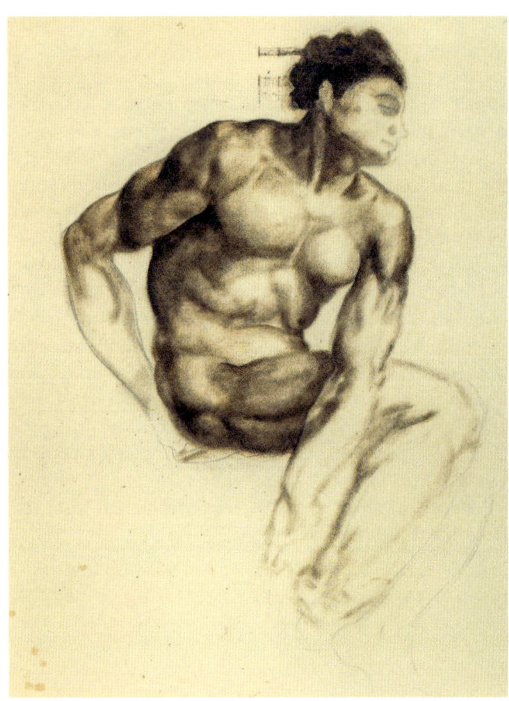

4 *Study from the Nude*, 1933

still).[15] Although she would eventually abandon figuration, she later reflected on the connection to her mature work: 'it [was] clear that my "subject matter" would be myself … The "what" would be truths contained in my own body.'[16]

In the spring of 1932, the Great Depression hit hard and Krasner was forced to leave the National Academy and enroll at the City College of New York, where tuition was free and she hoped to gain a teaching certificate.[17] Working at night as a cocktail waitress at Sam Johnson's in Greenwich Village, she began taking life-drawing classes with Job Goodman. In contrast to her observant family (and in keeping with the newly emancipated 'jazz babies' of the 1920s), Krasner was remarkably relaxed about nudity, working sometimes as a life model for extra income and happily posing naked on the beach with her lover Igor Pantuhoff.[18] This ease found its way into her life studies: as paints were expensive, she worked in Conté crayon, using heavy contrast and soft shading to create a tension between sensuality and muscularity. Goodman had studied at the Art Students League with the Regionalist painter Thomas Hart Benton, who became a mentor to Pollock in the 1930s. Benton was a great admirer of Michelangelo, and Goodman followed suit; so it was

Around the summer of 1928, Krasner began work on a small number of self-portraits, which she hoped would qualify her for promotion to life drawing at the National Academy.[14] Perhaps the most striking of these is *Self-Portrait* (*c*. 1928; fig. 3), painted in oil in the garden of her parents' new home in Greenlawn, Long Island. Nailing a mirror to a tree, she set about capturing her reflection against a woodland backdrop. In her short-sleeved blue shirt and artist's apron, she is the poster image for a 'blue-collar worker', a phrase that had been conceived in the US only a few years earlier, in the mid-1920s. The rag and brushes that she clutches in her left hand (inverted by the mirror) make clear her trade, while her cropped hair lends her look a boyish charm. The composition bears a notable resemblance to *Self-Portrait as a Painter* (1887–88) by Vincent van Gogh (fig. 2), whose work – at least until the inaugural exhibition at the Museum of Modern Art, New York, in November 1929 – Krasner was likely familiar with only in reproduction. Her portrait was perhaps more successful than she intended: when the work was presented to the National Academy's committee, they refused to believe that she could have painted it *en plein air*, calling it a 'dirty trick' (but promoting her

5 *Nude Study from Life*, 1940

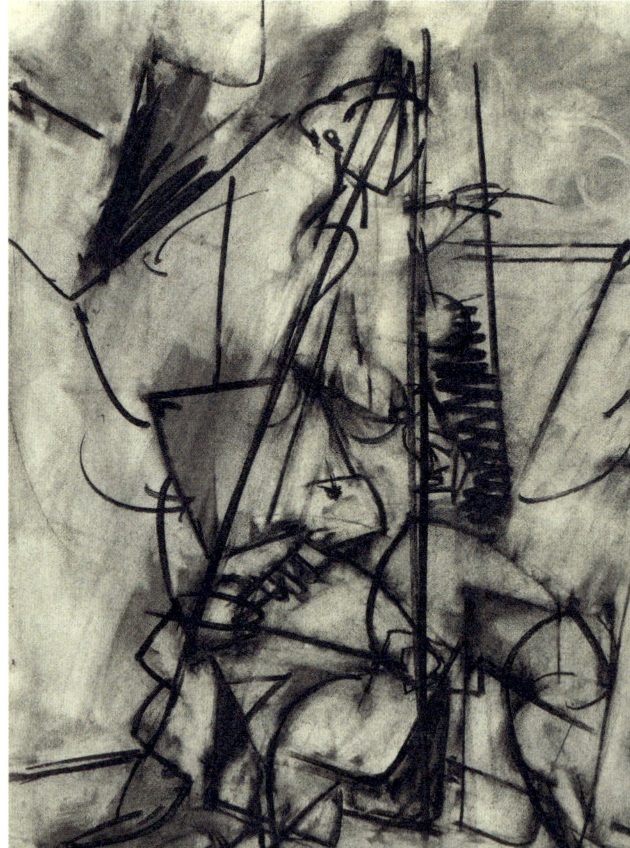

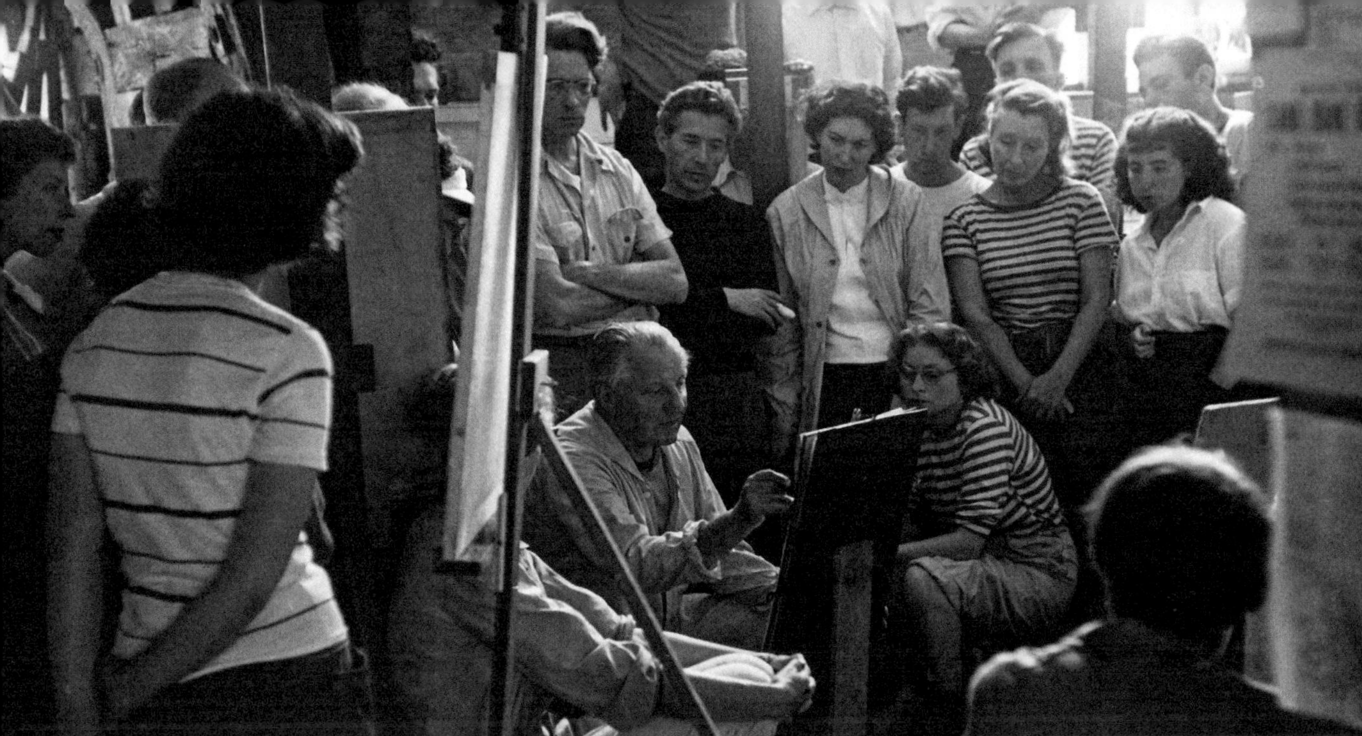

6   A class at Hans Hofmann's summer school, Provincetown,
Massachusetts (Hofmann seated centre), c.1945.

that, unbeknown to the other, both Krasner and Pollock made studies from the Sistine Chapel (fig. 4). By 1937, when Pollock drew his 'Ignudi' (the nude males that Michelangelo incorporated into the chapel's frescoes), Krasner had already gained a scholarship to attend the Hans Hofmann School of Fine Arts and was making the break into exploring Cubist abstraction. Unlike her former teachers, Hofmann was a devoted modernist, who had spent time with Pablo Picasso and Georges Braque in Paris and had taught in Munich before setting up his independent school in New York. It was a far cry from the National Academy, which Krasner deemed a 'sterile atmosphere of ... congealed mediocrity'.[19]

Under Hofmann, Krasner's life drawings took on a new energy, the loosely drawn figures – intersected by sharp lines and abstract shapes – suddenly seeming in dialogue with the space around them. Applying elements of Hofmann's famous 'push and pull' technique, she created the impression of movement through contrasts in form and texture.[20] Krasner was politically active throughout this time, joining debates at the Artists Union, working on murals for the Works Progress Administration (WPA) and picketing the Museum of Modern Art, New York. In 1940 she began to exhibit with the American Abstract Artists, showing work inspired by Piet Mondrian, who joined the group the following year and fast became a friend when they discovered a shared love of boogie-woogie.[21] These influences came together in 1942, when the War Services Project appointed Krasner to supervise the making of twenty department-store window displays, advertising war courses.[22] As part of her research, Krasner joined a number of the classes, including one at City College on explosives.[23] She had recently met Jackson Pollock, when they were both included in John Graham's *American and French Painting* exhibition at McMillen Gallery in New York, and, having been 'just about stunned' by his work, she got him assigned to her project team.[24] Only documentary photographs survive of their designs for window displays, and, as they were collectively produced, it is impossible to account for each artist's contribution. But the dynamic angles and use of montage clearly show the influence of Hofmann, as well as a debt to Russian Constructivism and the Bauhaus – each of which had been featured in *Cubism and Abstract Art,* the pivotal 1936 exhibition at the Museum of Modern Art, New York.[25]

Krasner and Pollock married in 1945 and (with the help of a $2,000 loan from the dealer and art collector Peggy Guggenheim) bought a nineteenth-century farmhouse on Fireplace Road in Springs, Long Island. Krasner had been struggling with a creative impasse – 'a kind of black-out period' – as she adjusted to the idea of working from an internal rather than an external source.[26] Moving to Springs helped her to break with the work she had been making – her 'gray slabs', as she called them – especially once the barn at the farmhouse had been cleared for Pollock, so that she could turn the upstairs bedroom into a studio of her own. It was there, in 1946, that she began creating her 'Little Images'. Positioning a canvas flat on a table or the floor, she would work from above to create layered, jewel-like compositions (fig. 7). Some had a thick impasto, with paint daubed directly from the tube and then worked into with a stiff brush; others were laced with aerial drips of thinned-down paint – oil cut with turpentine in a can. The intimacy of these works may have been inspired by Joan Miró's 'Constellations' series (fig. 8), which Krasner had seen at the Pierre Matisse Gallery in New York the previous year – 'each painting is a little miracle', she had written to her friend George Mercer.[27] Made while fleeing the outbreak of the Second World War (and during a period of literal 'black-out'), Miró's Constellations seem to express a sense of possibility in the face of darkness. Krasner must have been proud of her new work, since she hung a number of them in the guest room at Springs; when the critic Clement Greenberg saw them, she recalled him saying, 'That's hot; it's cooking[!]'[28]

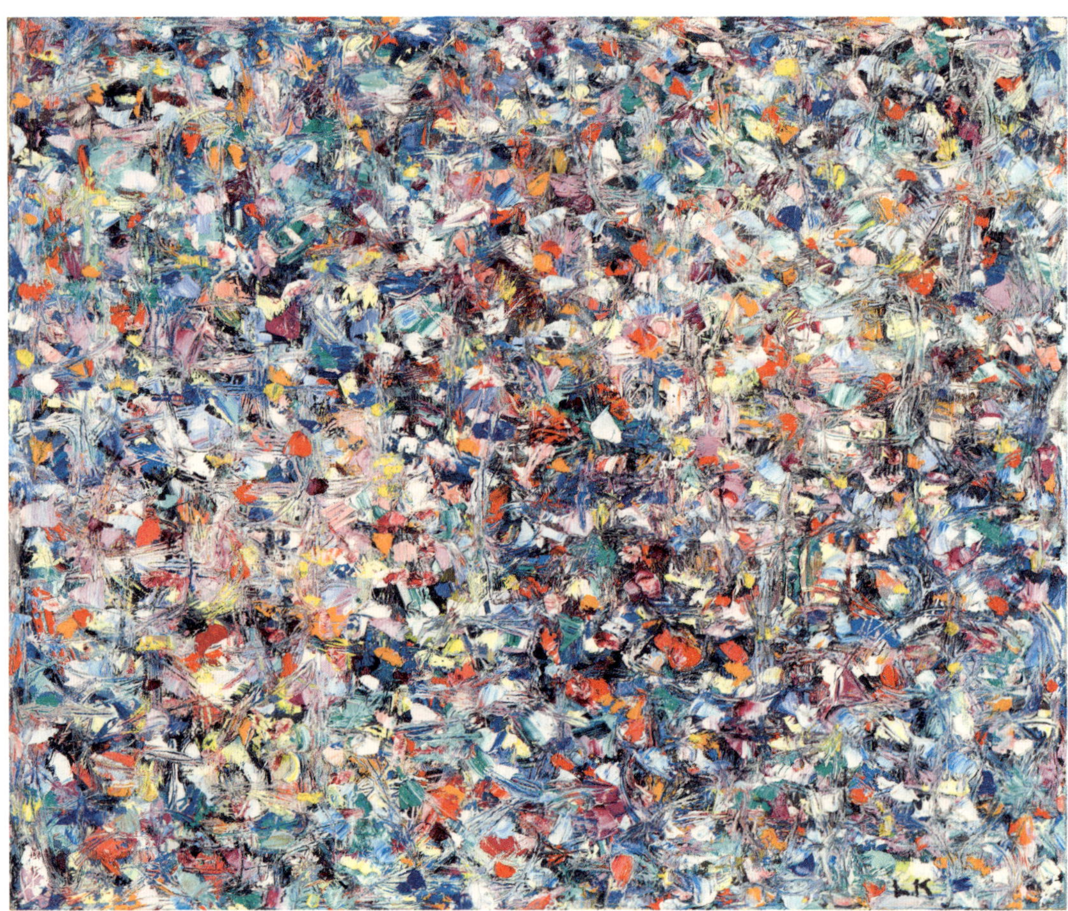

7   *Shellflower*, 1947

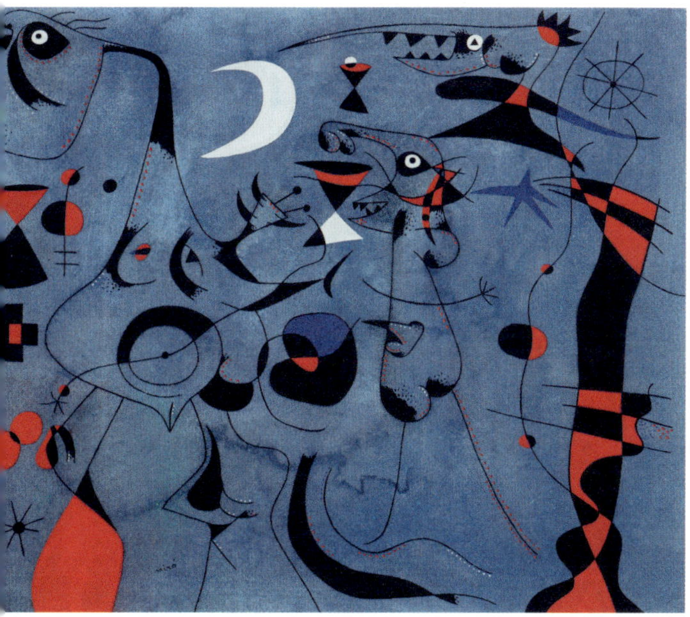

8   Joan Miró, *People at Night, Guided by the Phosphorescent Tracks of Snails*, 1940, from the 'Constellations' series (1939–41)

Even when the bitter winter of 1947 forced Krasner to concede her bedroom studio (she and Pollock could afford to heat only one floor at a time), she continued to work in the living room, salvaging two old wagon wheels and turning them into mosaic tables. She used leftover tesserae from one of Pollock's WPA projects, interspersed with other brilliant fragments she had found: broken glass, shells, costume jewellery, keys. Pollock poured concrete over the tops to set them, and a local welder made the legs. One was exhibited at Bertha Schaefer Gallery, New York, in the exhibition *The Modern House Comes Alive 1948–49*, which brought Krasner her first critical praise: the *New York Herald Tribune* wrote that 'the total effect is … to come right out with it, magnificent.'[29] Perhaps buoyed by this success, she returned to her Little Images. Krasner called the new works 'hieroglyphic': the palette was darker and overlaid with a lexicon of triangles, squares, zig-zags and spirals. Ever resourceful, she even turned the circular wooden board she had used for laying out the mosaics into the painting *Stop and Go* (1949–50). 'Hieroglyphic' is derived from the Greek word for 'sacred carving', and with these new patterns, Krasner may have been recalling Hebrew script, which she had learned to write but not read at the age of five.[30] They may also allude to the unconscious, since Krasner described herself as 'very much interested' in psychoanalysis at this time; Freud wrote of dream interpretation as 'analogous to the decipherment of an ancient pictographic script such as Egyptian hieroglyphs'.[31]

Krasner made her last Little Image in 1950, before another break occurred. Under pressure from Pollock, his dealer Betty Parsons had agreed to give Krasner her first solo exhibition in October 1951. Her new canvases were larger than her Little Images, and mostly populated by a landscape of overlapping oblongs, thinly washed in soft, earthy colours. The works had a subtle, luminous quality, which was cautiously well received by critics: Stuart Preston in the *New York Times* referred to a 'Mondrian formula worked out with feminine acuteness' (whatever that might be), while the artist Robert Goodnough wrote in *ARTnews* of 'journeying through a vast uninhabited land of quiet color'.[32] Krasner was disappointed; as her biographer, Gail Levin, suggests, her hopes may have been unrealistically high after the hype around Pollock's exhibitions. Of the fourteen works exhibited at the Betty Parsons Gallery, only two survive. In 1953 Krasner walked into her studio and found it 'hung solidly with

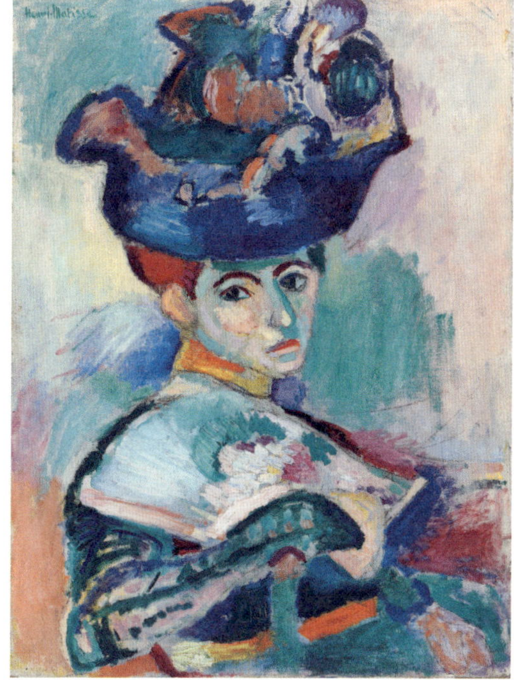

9   Henri Matisse, *Femme au chapeau*, 1905

drawings I couldn't stand', and so began tearing them up.[33] She and Pollock had recently acquired an extra acre of land, and had converted a former outbuilding so that Krasner finally had a proper workspace. She noticed that something exciting was happening amid the shreds on the floor, which led to 'a spurt of collage'.[34] Many of these were layered over her Betty Parsons paintings, with occasional glimpses of the former left exposed. The result was a powerful body of work, highlights of which were exhibited in her second solo exhibition, at Eleanor Ward's Stable Gallery in September 1955.

This time Krasner's work elicited more enthusiastic praise: the artist and critic Fairfield Porter wrote in *ARTnews* that the works made the viewer 'aware of a subtle disorder greater than he might otherwise have thought possible', while Clement Greenberg later referred to the exhibition as 'a major addition to the American art scene of that era'.[35] Collages such as *Burning Candles* (1955) featured more subdued hues and smaller fragments, which climaxed in the high-keyed colours and graphic compositions of such works as *Desert Moon* (1955). Krasner's turn to collage may have been inspired by Henri Matisse, whose work she had always admired, and who exhibited his vibrant new 'cut-outs' as part of his retrospective at the Museum of Modern Art, New York, in November 1951.[36] In a *New York Times* review of the Stable Gallery show, Stuart Preston described Krasner as a 'good noisy

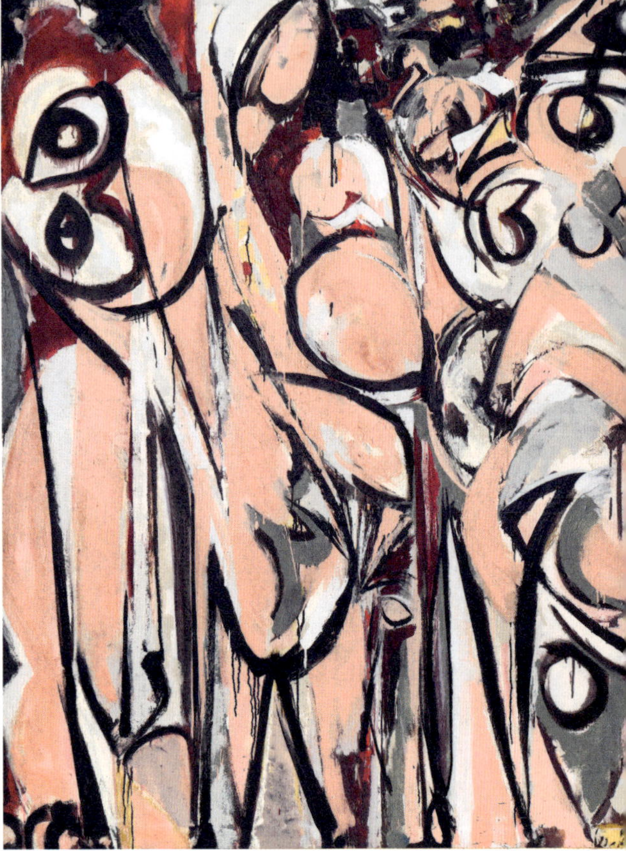

11 *Three in Two*, 1956

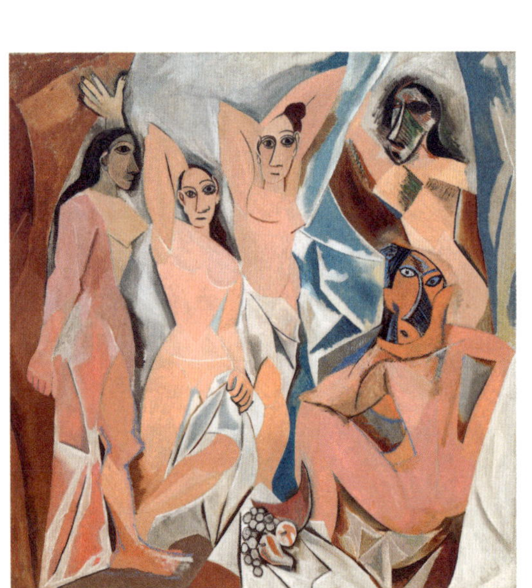

10 Pablo Picasso, *Les Demoiselles d'Avignon*, 1907

colorist' – recalling the decibel metaphor used by Matisse's artist colleagues when, in response to his inclusion of *Femme au chapeau* (fig. 9) in the Salon d'Automne of 1905, they asked, 'What kind of hat and what kind of dress were they that this woman had been wearing which were so incredibly loud in colour?'[37] However, Krasner's frayed edges and visible brushwork meant that the work retained a more organic feel than an entirely 'scissored' collage. In some, like *Bald Eagle* (1955), she incorporated fragments of Pollock's discarded drawings. Perhaps it felt therapeutic to find a use for his abandoned work at a time when, creatively, he was stagnating.[38]

By 1956 Pollock's alcoholism and erratic behaviour had become almost impossible for Krasner to bear. When Pollock turned down an invitation from Paul Jenkins for the couple to visit the painter in Paris, Krasner decided to go alone, using it as an opportunity for a break. Before leaving, she started work on a new painting, *Prophecy*. Looping, fleshy forms dominate the canvas, edged with black and with touches of deep red that accentuate the bodily imagery. 'The painting disturbed me enormously', she recalled.[39] When she showed it to Pollock, he assured her that 'it was a good painting, and said not to think about it, just continue'.[40] It remained on her easel when she travelled for the first time to Europe. In France, she delighted in the Louvre and spent time in Provence. She wrote a letter to Pollock, saying, 'I miss you and wish you were sharing this with me … the painting here is unbelievably bad.'[41] Soon after her return to Paris, a call came from Greenberg to say that Pollock was dead; he had crashed his car into a clump of trees, killing himself and Edith Metzger, a friend of Ruth Kligman, who had survived. Krasner, at just forty-seven, found herself a widow and was thrown into a remorseless period of grief. Not long after Pollock's funeral, she painted three works connected to *Prophecy*: *Embrace*, *Birth* and *Three in Two* (fig. 11). Using the same fleshy colours that characterize the earlier work, she alluded to Picasso's *Les Demoiselles d'Avignon* (1907; fig. 10), creating convulsive scenes of intertwined bodies that felt both erotic and violent. When asked how she managed to paint while grieving, her reply was matter-of-fact: 'Painting is not separate from life. It is one. It is like asking – do I want to live? My answer is yes – and I paint.'[42]

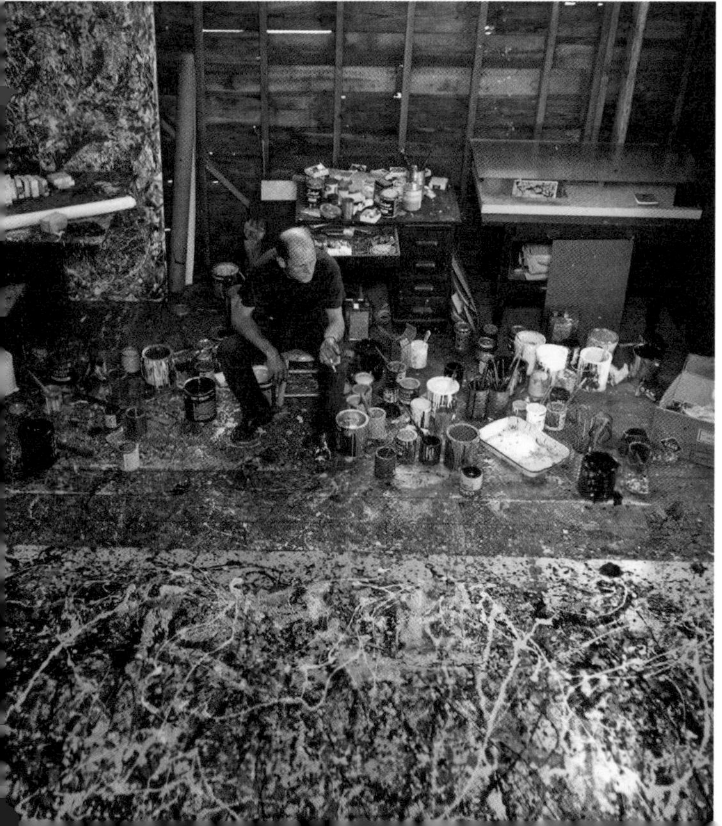

12 Jackson Pollock in his studio in the barn, Springs, 1950. Photograph by Hans Namuth.

In the period after Pollock's death, Krasner decided to move her studio into the barn in Springs. Although it must have been a space loaded with painful memories, it was also the largest working area on the property, with the best natural light, which finally allowed her to work on a larger scale. In 1953 Pollock had laid Masonite boards over his now-legendary wooden floor, which was densely patterned with filigree sprays of his paint (fig. 12); interestingly, he had barely worked after this act of erasure, so the space remained fairly neutral for Krasner's tenancy (fig. 13).[43] She established her own orientation to the barn by tacking her unstretched canvas directly to the wall. During this period, Krasner's mother had also died – 'I wasn't allowed to mourn at my own tempo', she regretted – which caused her to suffer from chronic insomnia.[44] Working at night under artificial light, she refused to use colour, which led to a series of paintings that were predominantly made in raw and burnt umber. The turmoil she was experiencing is conveyed in such a work as *The Eye is the First Circle* (1960), which seethes with the physical energy required for its creation.[45] The title comes from the first line of Ralph Waldo Emerson's essay 'Circles' (1841): 'The eye is the first circle; the horizon which it forms is the second; and throughout nature this primary figure is repeated without end.'[46]

In 1960 Krasner experienced a surge of productivity, making a great number of paintings as part of this series – 'Night Journeys', as her friend the poet Richard Howard called them. They were exhibited at the Howard Wise Gallery, New York, in 1960 and 1962, and were positively received: in the *New York Herald Tribune*, Emily Genauer described the 'highly complex networks of tortured line … through which peer countless agonized eyes', while Stuart Preston wrote in the *New York Times* that '[the paintings] beat with a powerful, even pulse'.[47] The series allowed Krasner to get to grips with an unprecedented size of work and to experiment with the emotive possibilities of a reduced colour palette.[48] In 1963 she took this further with *Another Storm*, a work measuring more than 2 metres (6 ½ ft) in height and 4.4 metres (14 ½ ft) in width, created predominantly in alizarin crimson. The paint is thrust at regular intervals so that the whole, vast canvas seems to reverberate, the strokes of white acting like froth on fast-flowing water. This force abated abruptly that summer, when Krasner fell and broke her right arm. Never one to be discouraged, she taught herself to paint with her left hand, using the fingertips of her right to guide the movements. Applying paint directly from the tube and with her fingertips, she created more tactile works, such as *Through Blue* and *Happy Lady*, which were still large (the latter is almost 1.5 × 2 metres / 5 × 6 ½ ft) and yet seemed to suggest greater intimacy, perhaps because of her closeness to the canvases when they were made.

In 1965 Bryan Robertson organized a retrospective of Krasner's work at the Whitechapel Gallery in London. It was the first time that Krasner had had the opportunity to review the achievements of her career to date; 'the rewarding thing to see for me', she explained in an interview that year, 'is that the break isn't quite as violent as it seems at the time it's taking place.'[49] Robertson had curated a number of critical exhibitions at the Whitechapel, including of Pollock in 1958, of Mark Rothko in 1961 and of Franz Kline in 1964.[50] Krasner's show was densely hung, with smaller works positioned above one another and a few squeezed between the bigger canvases. It must have made a very powerful impression on visitors, especially those who had seen the more spacious hang of Pollock's work seven years earlier. John Russell in the *Sunday Times* called Krasner's show 'exhilarating', while Nigel Gosling wrote in *The Observer* that 'the driving vigour which runs through the largest compositions like sap [is an] enviable birthmark of her time and place.'[51] The success of the exhibition may well have contributed to the confidence with which Krasner returned to her studio. The canvases she made in 1966, such as *Gaea* (fig. 14), continued her use of vibrant colour, but now in somersaulting forms that seem to suggest growth and fertility. In Greek mythology, Gaea is the Earth goddess and mother to all life, which is perhaps what Krasner was referring to when she said: 'I am drawing from sources that are basic.'[52]

The theme of nature had always preoccupied Krasner, and in the early 1970s she began to play with a new kind of biomorphic form. Taking its title from the Greek word for 'rebirth', *Palingenesis* (1971) features a garden of hard-edge forms in lush green and magenta pink (one of Krasner's favourite colours, which Robert Hughes described as 'rap[ping] hotly on the eyeball at 50 paces').[53] The penumbra of white that surrounds each shape gives the impression of collage, harking back to the Stable Gallery exhibition of 1955. This new style could be seen to relate to 'post-painterly abstraction' – a phrase coined by Clement Greenberg for those artists, such as Frank Stella and Ellsworth Kelly, who were inspired by Abstract Expressionism but 'favor[ed] openness or clarity' in their imagery.[54] A key difference was that Krasner refused to use the fast-drying acrylic paints preferred by these artists, with her palette of oils lending her colours a richer, more organic quality.[55] Krasner's new work was exhibited in April 1973 at Marlborough Gallery in New York, where it was met with

effusive reviews. Hilton Kramer wrote in the *New York Times*, for example, that the paintings were 'lyrical expressions of color', offering an 'eloquent simplicity of form'.[56] In 1969 Krasner had made a series of works using gouache on handmade Howell paper, experimenting with the possibility of using just one or two pure pigments. 'I was just mad for doing them', she later explained, 'and they went at quite a clip. Just moved like magic', which might have been what inspired her new purism.[57]

One of Krasner's final bodies of work came about quite by accident. In 1974 Bryan Robertson had come across a portfolio of her Hofmann School drawings that had been languishing in the barn in Springs; Krasner had separated out the ones she wanted to keep, and had brought those she planned to destroy to her Manhattan apartment, where she rediscovered them in 1975.[58]

13 Lee Krasner in her studio in the barn, Springs, 1962. Photograph by Hans Namuth.

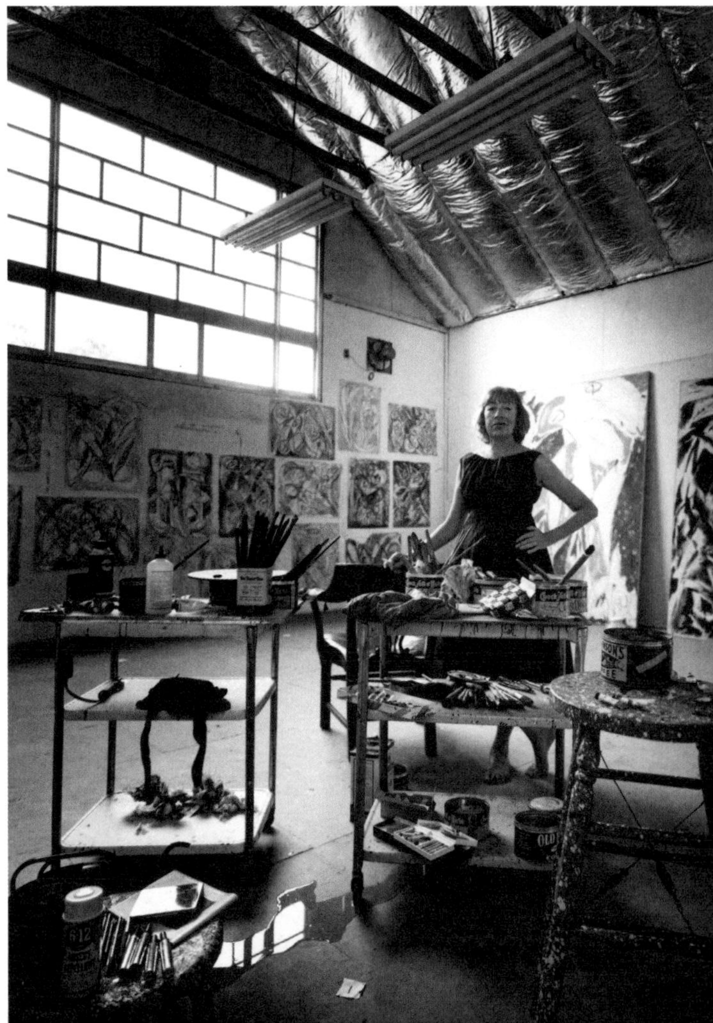

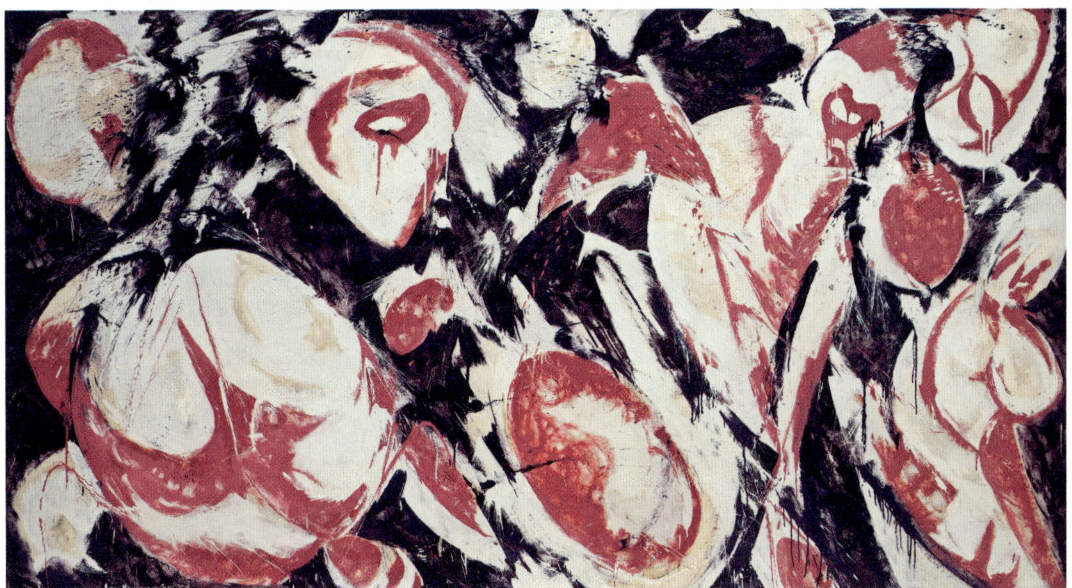

14 *Gaea*, 1966

She decided to use them as raw material for a new series of collages, the first of which she called *Imperative* (1976), in relation to the 'peremptory desire' she felt 'to make them new'.[59] An old friend from Krasner's Hofmann School days, Ray Eames (who was now a successful artist and designer with her husband, Charles), visited the studio in February 1976 and took a series of photographs of Krasner at work. Hofmann had been famed for his overbearing manner in their classes – tearing a student's drawing in two if he wanted to demonstrate a more dynamic arrangement – so they must have taken a particular pleasure in seeing these treasured remnants of their past cut up.[60] Krasner gave the series the elaborate title 'Eleven Ways to Use the Words to See', while the individual works, such as *Past Conditional* and *Future Perfect* (both 1976), were named after verb forms. She also kept a note of the meaning of each work (in the case of the examples just given, it was 'you might have seen' and 'I shall have seen').[61] The titles suggest Krasner's complex relationship to how she saw these forty-year-old drawings; as she explained, 'it's like taking Cubism and carrying it to a totally new dimension. I think it's called Conceptualism.'[62]

A retrospective of Lee Krasner's work opened at the Museum of Fine Arts in Houston on 27 October 1983, her seventy-fifth birthday. The exhibition would travel to the San Francisco Museum of Modern Art and then to the Museum of Modern Art in New York – where Krasner had always longed to have a solo exhibition – but she would not live to see it with her own eyes, as she died on 19 June 1984. Finally, at the very end of her life, she was being given the recognition she so deserved. Yet even she acknowledged that, in some respects, being overlooked had been a 'blessing'.[63] Free from much critical pressure, Krasner had made the work she felt impelled to make; without a coterie of controlling dealers and collectors, she was never forced to repeat herself, but could flow with each new direction as it came to her. 'I painted before Pollock, during Pollock, after Pollock', she once explained, no doubt sick of the endless regurgitation of his name;[64] but her mature work was also paid for by Pollock, in the sense that the sale of his paintings enabled her to be financially independent. This remarkable freedom strengthened her resolve to stay true to her own spirit, which is what connects the many periods of her work so powerfully. Inquisitive, funny and philosophical, she did not resist the cyclical energy that drove her in the studio. She was fond of quoting a line from T. S. Eliot, 'We shall not cease from exploration', and perhaps held in her heart the lines that followed: 'And the end of all our exploring / Will be to arrive where we started / And know the place for the first time.'[65]

Eleanor Nairne

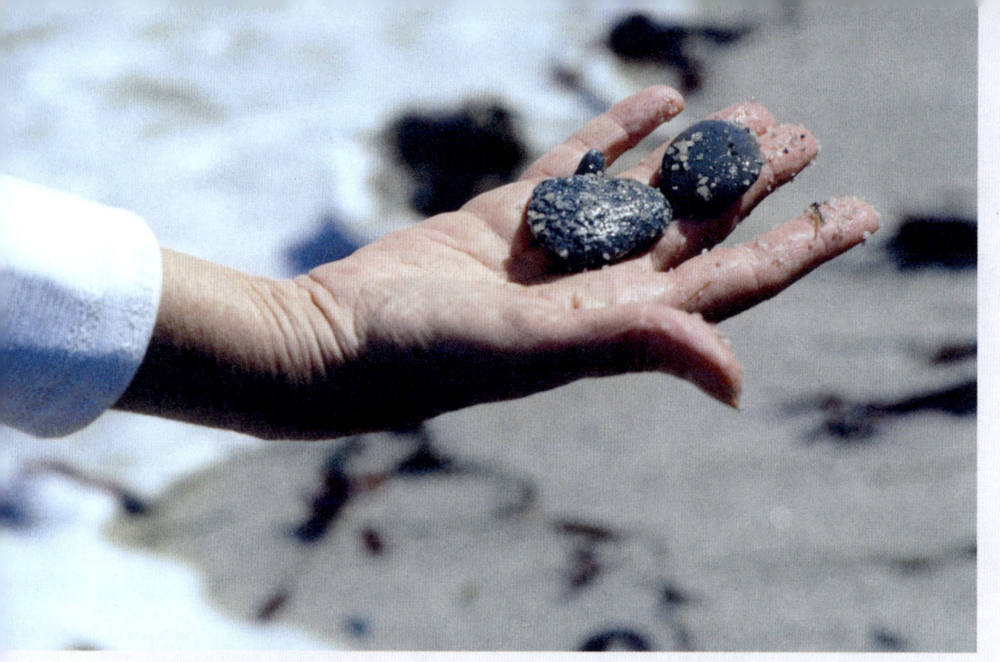
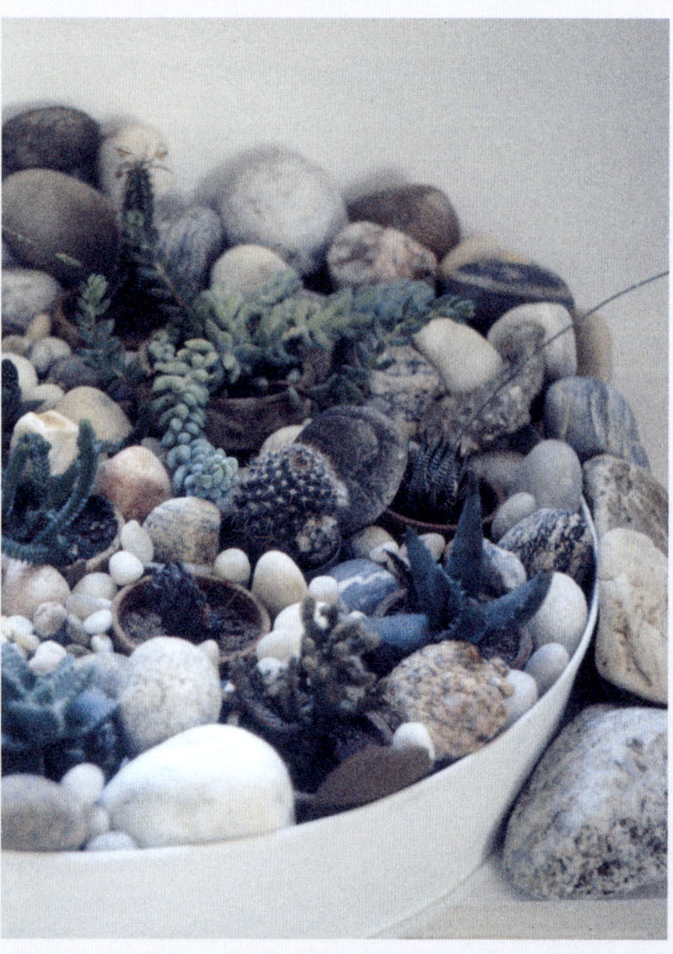
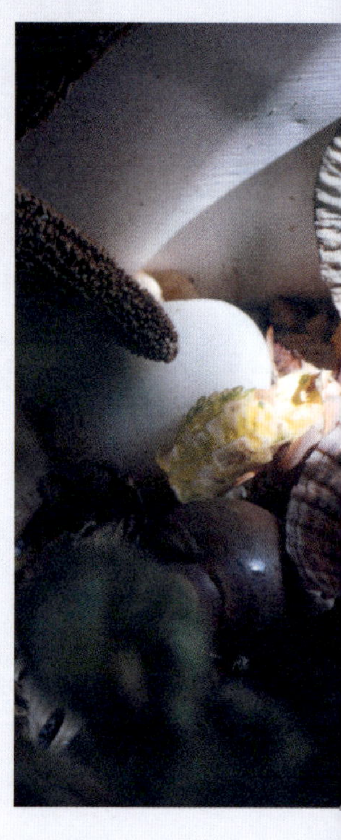

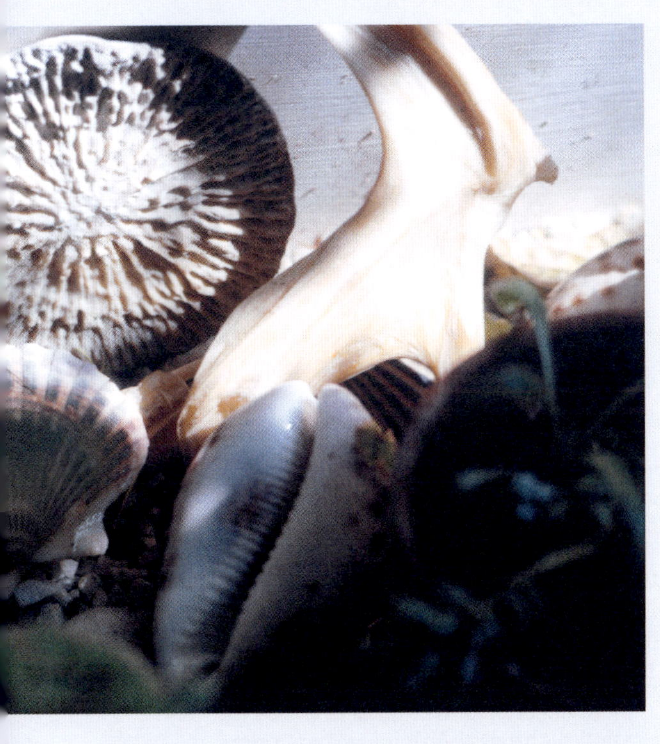

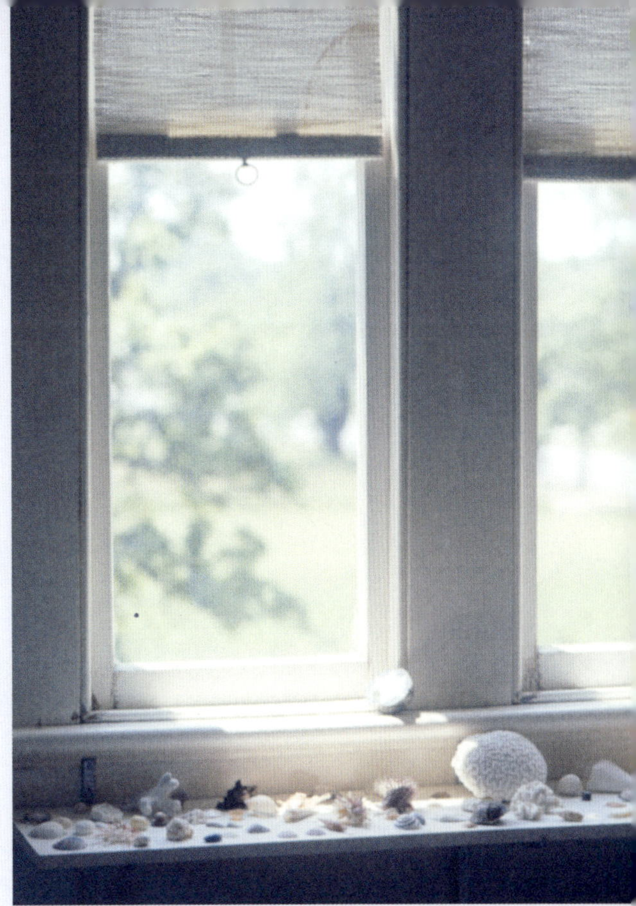

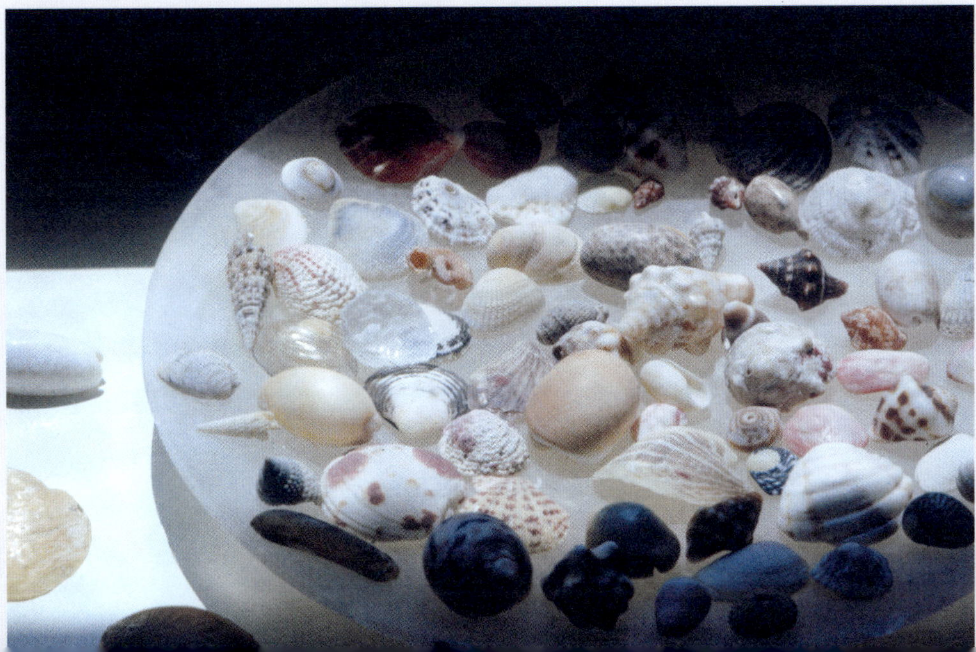

NOTHING OUTSIDE NATURE

When Lee went for a walk she would look at everything and she would remember everything she saw – animals, birds, people, shells, even snakes and fish. And she would bring that back with her.

Richard Howard

The work of Lee Krasner, as many have said (the artist herself most of all), was made in relationship to nature. What that relationship might have been is the question. It encompassed her being a woman, of course – as much of the criticism of the time, as well as revisionist feminist scholarship of the 1970s up to the present, has emphasized. There was also her urban-ness ('urban' in early and mid-twentieth-century America being a code word implying immigrant/Jewish identity). Above all, Krasner's relation to nature took complicated form in her relationship to her own work, to how it was made and to her place in the world. Given all these caveats and complications, Krasner very much takes a place in the universe of modern artists enmeshed in ideas about nature and the natural world.

The European artists of an earlier generation – notably Paul Klee, Wassily Kandinsky, Joan Miró and Jean Arp – branched out beyond their avant-garde ideological roots to contact something larger: the current state of human understanding of the life sciences and the cosmos. These artists turned increasingly to nature as a subject, with the knowledge (in varying degrees of detail) of the newly emerging model in biology of 'organicism'. Obviating the century-long debate between mechanist and vitalist models of life, organicist biologists (in Germany, France, Russia, Britain and the US) promoted thinking about the organism as a whole, driven by complex internal relations; in this conception, 'life' was neither mechanically determined nor obscurely spiritual.[1]

In parallel, artists often saw organicist thinking as a way out of the split between abstraction and representation, between Bauhaus or Cubist methods and Surrealism. The organicist strain in art was sufficiently visible by the mid-1930s for the British critic Geoffrey Grigson and Alfred H. Barr Jr, the first director of the Museum of Modern Art, New York, to essay the term 'biomorphic' to indicate art that was neither solely Surrealist nor solely geometric in style.[2] Naming neither precisely a movement nor a style – in fact, not offering precision at all – the category grew only more apt in the 1930s and 1940s, for a wide range of artists including Agnes Pelton, Isamu Noguchi, Morris Graves, Frederick Kiesler, Barnett Newman, Adolph Gottlieb, Charles Seliger and Kurt Seligmann. They produced objects, reliefs, paintings and diagrams evoking plants, cells and organisms both recognizable and unnamed; seeds, along with eggs and embryos, are often the subjects of these artworks, revealing morphological beginnings, as well as the hidden patterns and rhythms ordering the organic.[3]

Lee Krasner certainly belongs to this context, and throughout her life used the word 'organic' to describe her art. Although her early work was less obviously biomorphic, tending to be heavily outlined and Cubist-related, the organicist orientation provided a way forward, and her own attitudes towards nature shifted

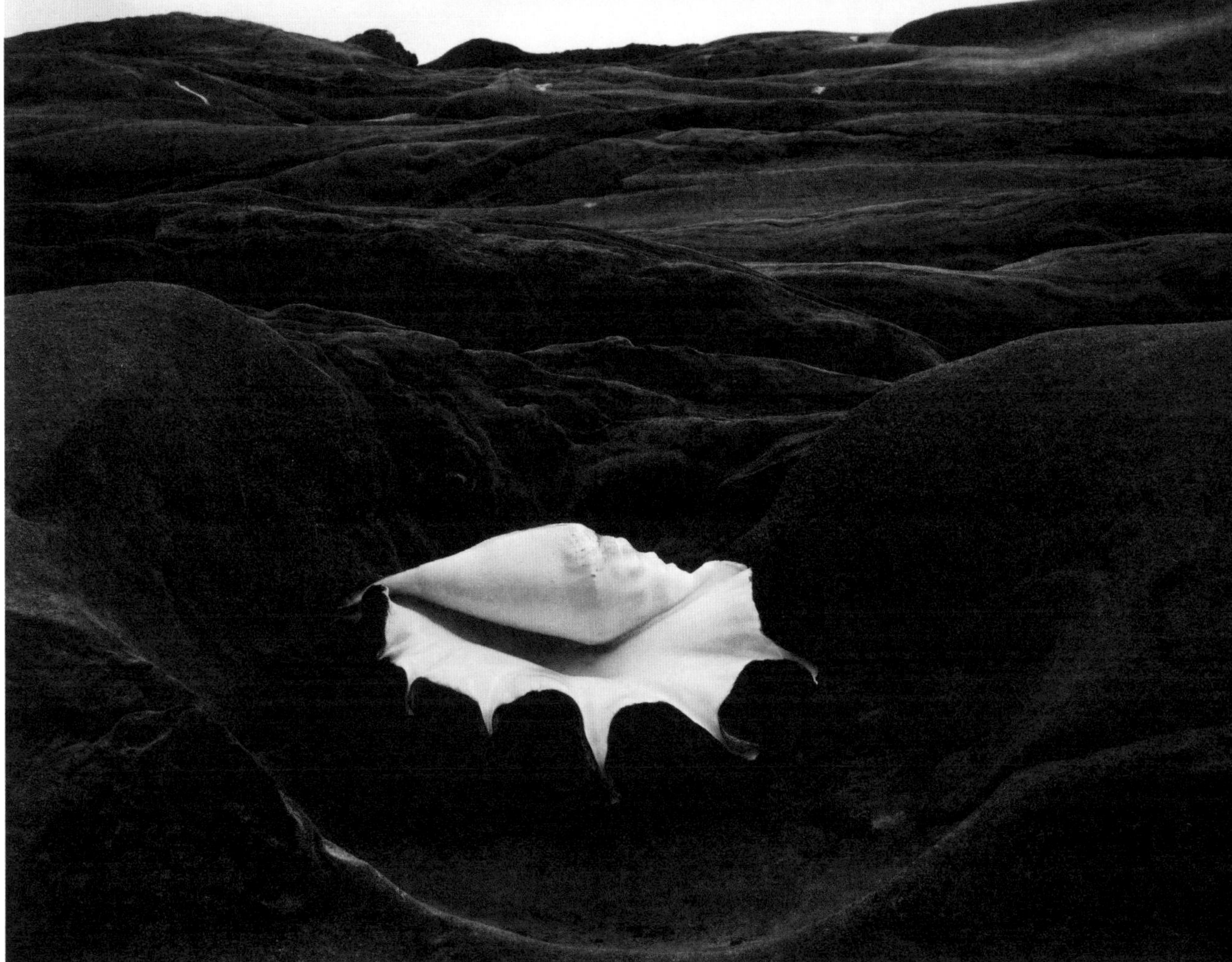

1   Edward Weston, *Shell and Rock Arrangement*, 1931

to something closer to this way of thinking in the early 1940s. Much as Hans Hofmann offered her a way out of the traditionalism of the National Academy, organicist thinking showed her the way out of Hofmann's teaching. Krasner's conversion experience has often been cast as a shift in allegiance from Hofmann to Jackson Pollock, bringing with it (gendered) quarrels and complications over her subordination to or active partnership with Pollock. And indeed, in her often-repeated anecdote, she shorthanded the change in thinking as a move from one man to another.

Instead of focusing on the men, we might look at the *content* of the shift. Hofmann, as Krasner tells the story, warned of the trap set by abstraction without reference to the outside world, which he feared would result in repetition. In 1942 the older painter admonished Pollock to work from nature, to which the younger artist replied, 'I *am* nature.'[4] One can only imagine how Hofmann's kind of instruction sat with Pollock. Krasner, despite her famous will and prickliness, was a compliant student, if out of a voracious wish to learn and succeed, rather than a docile need for approval. Yet within a few months, Krasner had also moved from Hofmann-style still-life painting to the belief that 'I am nature'. The implied 'too' smarts, of course – her move feels secondary, belated.[5] And it can put even more stress on a reading of Pollock's statement that has him casting himself as a god, a force of nature, who can control and take the place of nature.

But – and I'm conscious here of the many, many attempts to read Pollock's statement correctly – the governing idea was not that the artist had supplanted nature, but that he belonged to it, to the larger entity. Hofmann had posed the alternative to depicting nature as painting 'from heart'. He could have meant 'by memory' or 'in an extremely subjective fashion'; for him, painting 'by heart' implied both subjectivity and repetition.[6] In response, Pollock placed his subjectivity and the object of his regard on the same side of the easel, as it were. The artist's subjectivity is scaled down, taking its place as one among many. Putting the artist amid nature at the same time avoids the classic distinction between nature and culture: the human being is an organism like any other, and the things she makes belong equally to the natural world.

Such a view was implicit in the animism (often cast as primitivism) prevalent in the 1940s among artists around the world who sought to restore a vital role for art, with spiritual and social functions. The regard for a larger, natural spirit was widespread; in the United States, it also rhymed easily with the inheritance of American Transcendentalism – as expressed by Walt Whitman and Ralph Waldo Emerson, from whose work Pollock and Krasner took painting titles – with its belief that we are surrounded by previously invisible realities, which the sensitive poet, artist, nature lover need only tune into. The American photographer Edward Weston wrote in his daybook, 'I have come to realize Life as a coherent whole, and myself as a part, with rocks, trees, bones, cabbages, smokestacks, torsos, all interrelated, interdependent – each a symbol of the whole.'[7] Weston's pictorial and verbal observations of the natural world are unusually poetic (fig. 1), but similar sentiments were expressed by artists of Krasner's generation, including Morris Graves and Richard Pousette-Dart.

In an interview with Cindy Nemser, Krasner described her own version of organicism, coming surprisingly close to Grigson and Barr's earlier definition: 'I merge what I call the organic with what I call the abstract, which is what you are calling the geometric. As I see both scales, I need to merge these two into the ever-present. What they symbolized I have never stopped to decide. You might want to read it as matter and spirit and the need to merge as against the need to separate. Or it can be read as male and female.'[8] For Krasner, the split that society had habitually proposed was between living matter, incarnate in gesture, in animals and plants and people, on the one hand, and, on the other, the organizing principles of life, and geometric structural principles in the mode of Piet Mondrian. She sought an art that brought these two halves together. Krasner's later titles evoke biological science, but neither she nor Pollock likely read deeply; her absorption of biomorphic abstraction was visual and experiential, the product of years spent in nature, and the will to rethink her own role as an artist.[9]

Being nature, as Krasner absorbed it and made it her own, was disruptive and transformative. For both her and Pollock, this way of being belonged to a physical shift as much as a change of heart or mind – their move to Springs in 1945, away from Manhattan to a relatively bucolic area of Long Island. Living in Springs was almost immediately productive for Pollock; for Krasner, it began a period of artistic stasis and rethinking as she transformed her artistic identity.[10] Moving to the country, usually for short spans, was not a new phenomenon among artists (who had gone since the nineteenth century to Provence, Tuscany, Maine and Provincetown, among other places), nor was it entirely confined to artists. But each of those modern escapes from the city has its particular character, and taking up life in the South Fork of Long Island in the 1940s was a version specific to its time and place.

Springs was (and still is to some extent) a rural, seaside village, as opposed to the Hamptons, which were already wealthy. Property was cheap and the year-round residents were provincial and working class, which appealed to Pollock more than to Krasner and many of the other artists. Beautiful and not yet crowded, it was a quiet place, where life needed to be made in

2   Lee Krasner on the beach, c.1939.

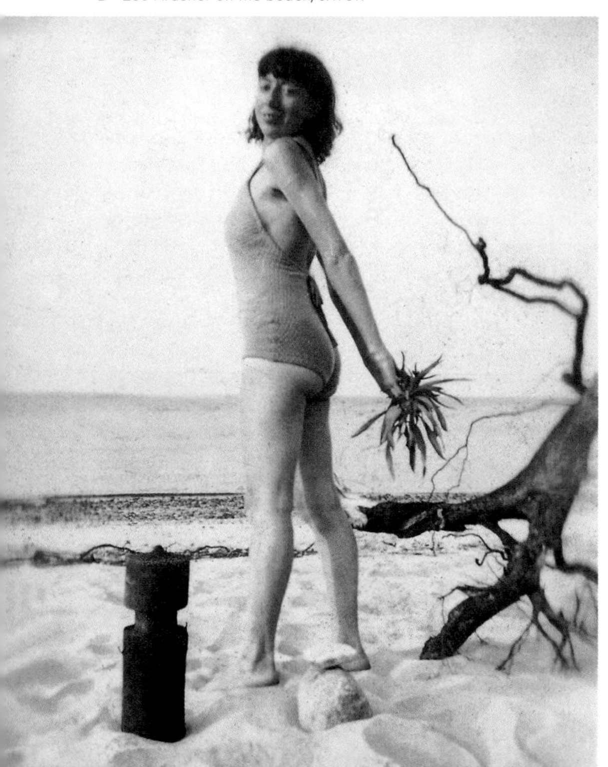

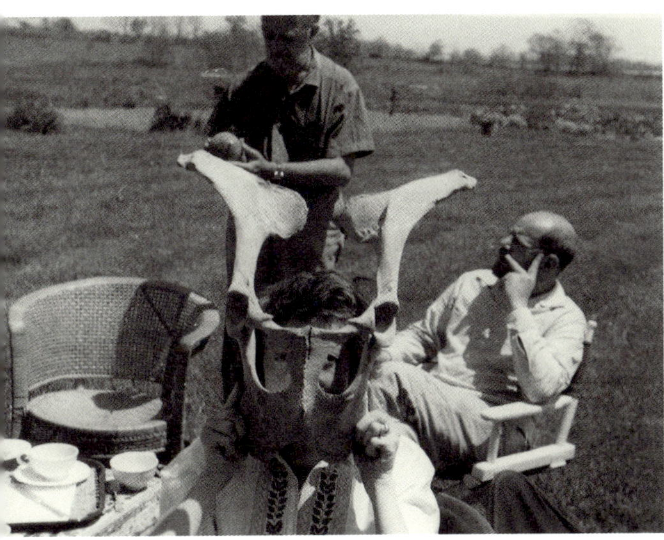

3   Lee Krasner posing with animal bones, c. 1954.

such as the broken anchor he and Krasner found on the beach, seen hanging on their wall in a photograph by Hans Namuth (fig. 4).

Krasner (like Edward Weston, as well as the painters Wols, Theodoros Stamos, Betty Parsons and Morris Graves) was drawn to shells and minerals or rocks, and these things over the years came to take a more prominent place in her and Pollock's – and then later her – home (fig. 5).[12] Large shells sat on tables and smaller ones were grouped together, sometimes with rocks and plants. Her friend Ray Eames photographed these accumulations, clearly empathizing with Krasner's attraction to them. While this mid-century relation to nature and to decorative practice has an element of kitsch, arguably these artists opposed a purism of authenticity and accepted nature and their relation to it as a totality; they took nature as they found it, and found themselves reflected in it. As David Bourdon wrote of a related subject in 1965, 'It is no

a palpable sense; they spent the first year getting the house in some kind of order, knocking down walls, painting, generating heat. It was not entirely unfamiliar: in Krasner's telling, the East New York of her childhood was almost rural, belonging to a Brooklyn filled with dairy cows and buttercups; for his part, of course, Pollock cast himself as a Westerner, a man of the plains.[11] Letters to Pollock's mother and conversations with and observations by friends show the unlikely homesteaders genuinely enjoying working on the house and the barn, gardening and cooking and canning – a life built together, albeit coloured by traditional gender divisions.

Photographs and a film of their time in Springs show Krasner and Pollock in a specifically postwar nature: still rural, but mannered in a decidedly modern appreciation of, and intense play with, the natural world. The hard work of maintaining life with little money, the need to get food from the garden and to keep warm were genuine, but the two artists also revelled consciously in 'nature', as seen in photographs of Krasner and Pollock donning animal bones (fig. 3) or playing with driftwood on a Montauk beach, or an early snapshot of Krasner on a beach, dramatically gesturing with seaweed amid a sculptural setting of driftwood and sand (fig. 2). They walked their land and the beach and brought things home, Krasner especially. Pollock had originally thought he might work with sculpture out on Long Island, and tended to pick up flotsam,

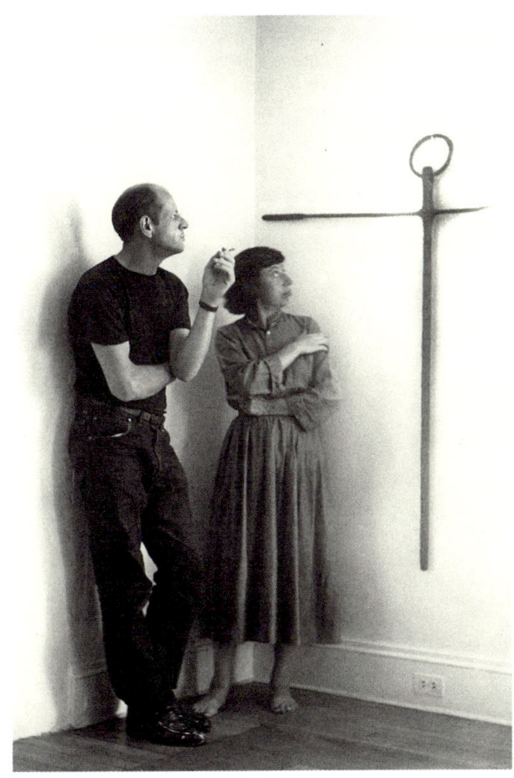

4   Lee Krasner and Jackson Pollock with a broken anchor scavenged from the beach, 1950. Photograph by Hans Namuth.

accident that the driftwood phenomenon coincided with the most fertile period of Abstract Expressionism: the late 'forties and early 'fifties ... Driftwood, like Abstract Expressionism, exhibits an "organic chaos".'[13]

These natural objects and Krasner's playful, decorative use of them showed her a way out of her artistic impasse in the mid-1940s. One winter, when it was too cold to heat the upstairs bedroom she had been using as a studio, Pollock urged her to create furniture, which they needed. Krasner made two gorgeous mosaic tables, using wagon wheels as a base (fig. 6). For the mosaics, she took what was to hand: shells, rocks, glass tiles left over from a mosaic Pollock had made for the Works Progress Administration, costume jewellery hammered flat. The impulse to make the tables is sometimes explained by Krasner scholars as belonging to a Depression-era mentality, and it is certainly true that working-class families with practical skills do often produce artists with this ability.

More generally, and also more specifically, Krasner wanted, *needed* to take from what was around her, the materials and imagery she encountered every day. She worked best *in the midst of*, rather than *standing back from*; when she engaged deeply with her immediate circumstances, with the natural world, she made her most successful work. The tables likely encouraged Pollock to include objects in his own paintings of the time: *Galaxy* and *Sea Change* (both 1947), for example, which include small pieces of gravel. The most intensely aggregated of these paintings, *Full Fathom Five* (1947), is filled with pebbles, nails, tacks, buttons, pennies,

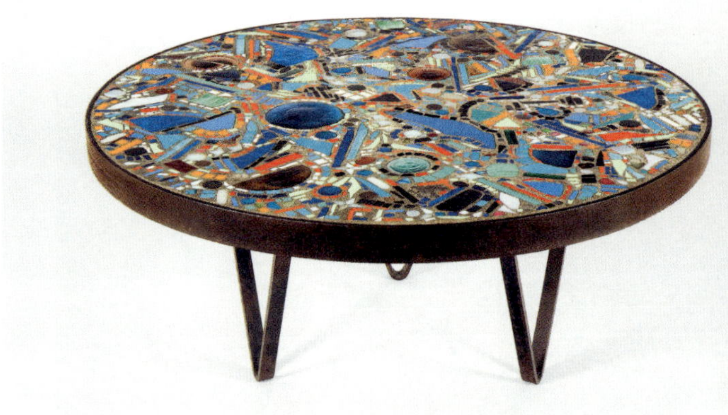
6   *Mosaic Table*, 1947

keys, combs, torn cigarettes, matches and paint-tube tops.[14] Krasner and Pollock's close friend Alfonso Ossorio (fig. 8), whose nearby home, 'The Creeks', the couple had helped find for him, shared the impulse – as did Ossorio's partner, Ted Dragon – to fill both home and studio with finds from local beaches. Inspired by Krasner, Ossorio later built an impressive art practice around paintings and sculptures with mosaic-like surfaces.[15]

The tables took their place in the house as part of everyday life: on the porch or used inside (fig. 7) during an evening of drinking and smoking with friends. The gallerist Bertha Schaefer included one of them in an exhibition on art in the modern home, where it was seen in a more upscale, *moderne* context; another was (reluctantly) given to friends who had supported the couple. Gradually, the tables shifted from being decorative elements in a house filled with natural and useful objects into the realm of art. While Pollock's speculative projects imbricating art and architecture, undertaken most notably with Peter Blake, have drawn considerable attention, it is worth pausing for a moment to consider Krasner's entwining of the natural environment, domestic space, decoration and art.[16]

Albert Gleizes and Jean Metzinger's 1912 Cubist manifesto, *Du 'Cubisme'*, framed the decorative object as merely an organ, incomplete without its context, and contrasted it with the true artwork, cast as an organism independent and self-sustained.[17] Krasner's relationship with the natural world and her environment anticipated the more contemporary biological view of the individual organism as *symbiotic* rather than

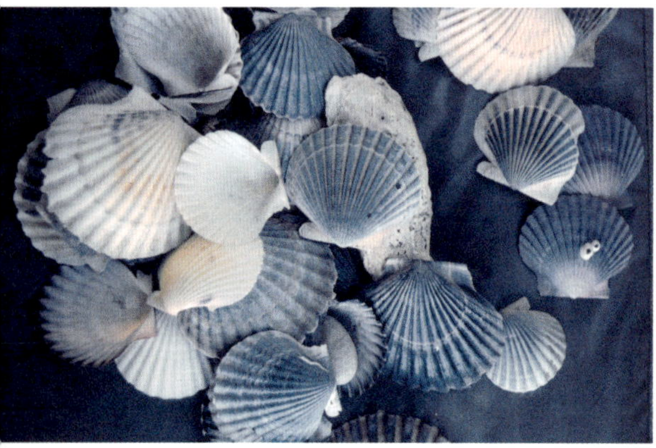
5   Lee Krasner's collection of shells, Springs, 1963. Photograph by Ray Eames.

autonomous, deeply engaged with its environment, taking in elements from and acting on it.[18] Thinking organically about nature and materials to hand changed Krasner's way of approaching painting, despite the fact that she clearly saw her paintings as artworks (and objected when Schaefer turned a proper painting into a tabletop). Such works as *Noon* and *Night Life* (both 1947), while being materialist abstractions, seem to reflect Krasner's interest in natural structure and her collections of natural objects. In her application of paint, each touch is treated like a unit belonging to a moving, organic structure that forms a body or whole of its parts. In an interview, she opposed the way in which her supporters sometimes framed nature – 'what I call the old aspect', which stressed visual resemblance.[19] Invoking the unseen reality of the tree's root systems, as well as the spirit of nature, she insisted, 'I argue or search for the total. The unifying total.'[20]

The art object conceived as part of nature has a life of its own. Artists, in Jean Arp's words, 'do not want to copy nature … We want to produce like a plant that produces a fruit.'[21] Many of the artists who would come to be called Abstract Expressionists, like Arp, emphasized the emergent, creative aspect of organisms in thinking of their artworks as part of a larger, ongoing process. For the New York artists, this was expressed primarily in the wish to keep works 'unfinished' and in this way animate.[22] Krasner did not leave works with an unfinished look in the 1940s or early 1950s – far from it – although her later paintings actively invoke the look of freshness and spontaneity, of an image grown from an impulse. Instead, the organicism of her process has been located, both by herself and by scholars, in its cyclical character.[23] The cycle, as Krasner described it, was a natural one, of impulse or seed and a flowering of intensity, followed by a period

7   Lee Krasner and Jackson Pollock (with backs to camera) with (from left) Vita Peterson, John Little and Gustaf Peterson in the living room in Springs, April 1949. Krasner made the mosaic table and painted the work *White Squares* (1948) hanging on the wall to the right. Photograph by Martha Holmes.

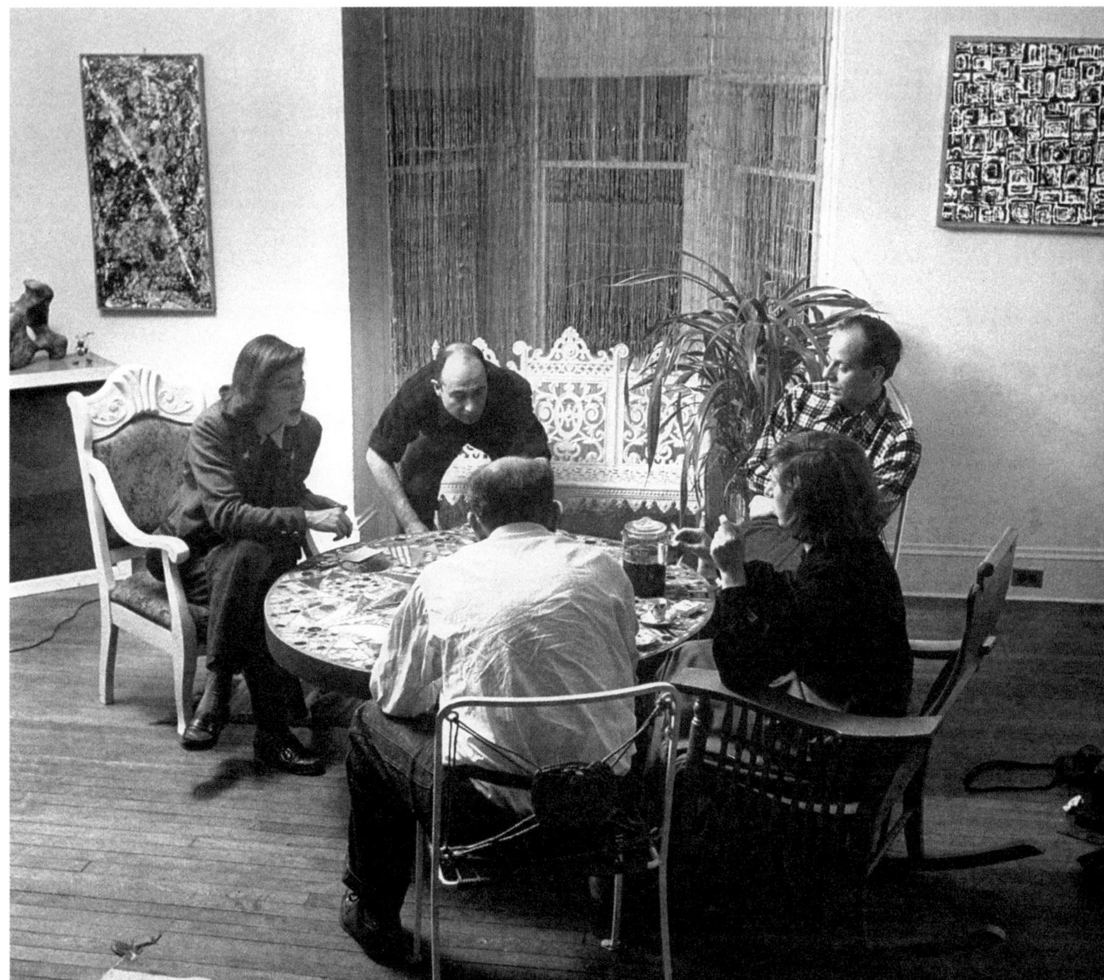

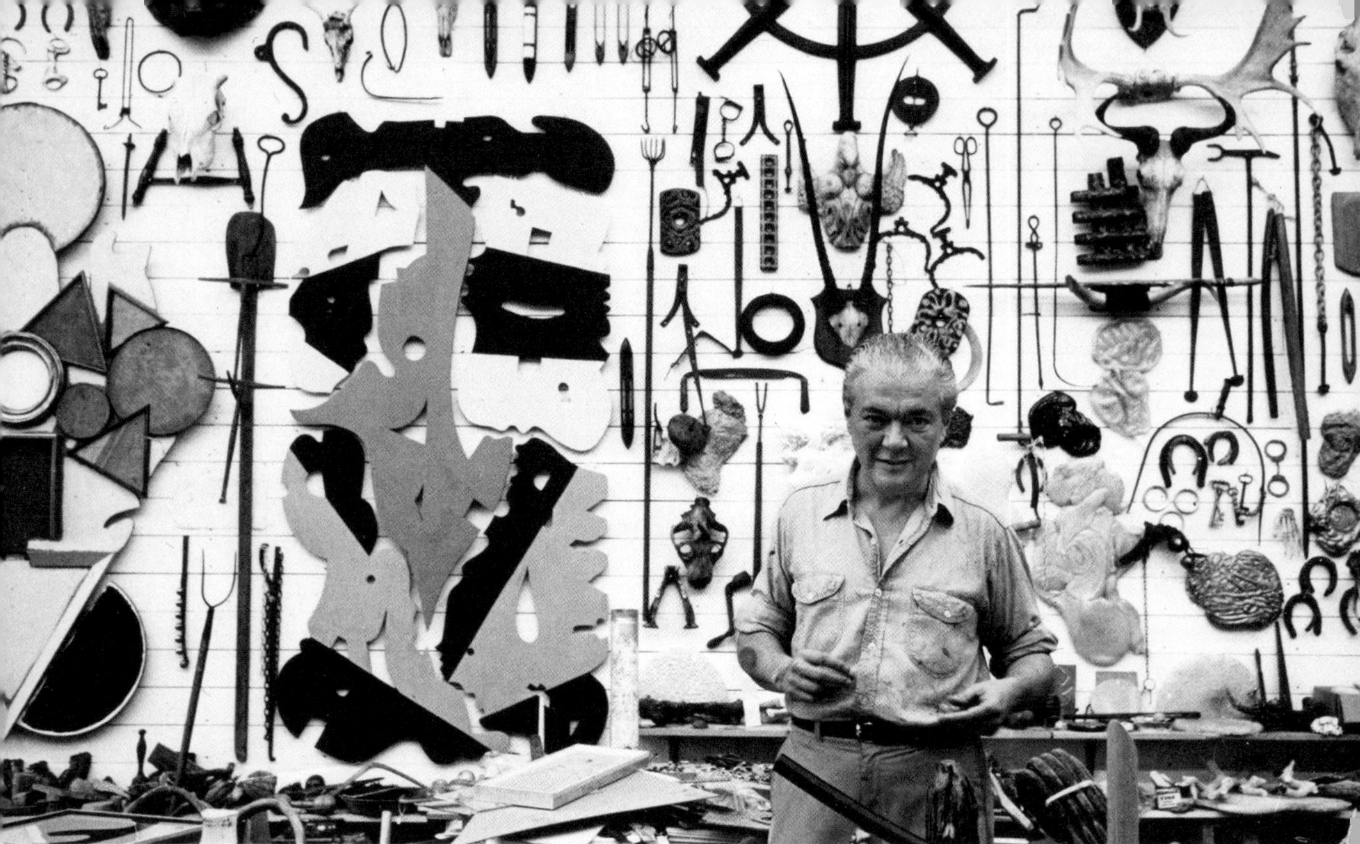

8   Alfonso Ossorio in his studio in East Hampton, c.1962.
    Photograph by Hans Namuth.

of dormancy, quiet, without work, after which the cycle would begin again. To an extent, the period of frustration or fallowness that characterized her move to Springs recurred her whole life, and she was often at pains to give that pattern meaning as a cycle, as natural.

The cycle was also a *recycling*, in which Krasner returned to earlier images and, literally, to earlier work, in order to reuse and revive it. This recycling of her own work first happened in 1953, when, frustrated by a body of drawings, she tore them down, letting them fall on the studio floor, only to notice that something exciting was happening; pursuing the direction, she began actively to cut and collage the drawings on canvas, creating such works as *Burning Candles* (1955; fig. 9). Krasner's move is often connected firmly to the impact of Matisse's paper cut-outs, shown at the Pierre Matisse Gallery in New York in 1949. But in relation to process, they resonate with the *papiers déchirés* of Arp (who also returned to and recycled his own work), who dropped torn papers on to a surface;

for him, the combination of active artistic deliberation and the fact of the pre-existing material embodied 'a passage from art to nature'.[24] For Arp, nature meant the physical laws governing all materiality, as well as the cycle of birth, life, death and decay; Krasner would add rebirth to close the circle. Even the paper that she and Pollock were drawn to (after seeing it in Anne Ryan's collages at the Betty Parsons Gallery in 1951) was born out of recycling, made by the Long Island artist Douglass Morse Howell using household textiles. In such collages as *Forest No. 2* (1954) and *Color Totem* (1955), Krasner repurposed Pollock's discarded drawings as well as her own – cycles on cycles.[25]

Although Krasner made much of not having a signature style, she was always returning to the work of her earlier periods, first in the collages, and later in paintings that revived her own or Pollock's past imagery. Krasner used her self as a resource, and that self was exterior, a matter of fact, as much as interior. She struggled to locate the push and pull of inspiration and expression that supposedly drove New York painting of the 1940s and 1950s; time spent without producing, seemingly in the shadow of Pollock, was in fact fundamental to the rhythm of the way Krasner worked – and didn't. Facing the 'void' of the blank canvas, she could be at a loss, and yet she was often truly great when there was material to move around. That material was various: it is a cliché that, early on, Krasner quickly passed through the influence and lessons of most major European and American modern artists; in the 1940s, 1950s and beyond, she drew from her environment in Springs; and in her collages and later paintings she repurposed her own art, cutting up older works and returning to previous themes and images as reference points.[26]

In all these guises, exteriority and relatedness have often been gendered as a lack. This is true as well of the personal descriptions that haunt the artist's reputation: Krasner's concern with her own role and status in the art world, as well as that of Pollock. This

putative careerism and her performance as 'art widow' have been seen as a betrayal of the autonomy demanded by modern art and also by feminism. We might choose to reject these complaints as sexist or as gossip; we might also choose to reconsider our demand for autonomy. We might appreciate Krasner's alertness to the world and to her place in it as the embodiment of an intense relatedness to environment, the organism as an open system, as it increasingly came to be defined in the middle of the twentieth century.

We might also conceive of nature broadly: as Richard Howard says, Krasner walked in the city, alert to people and buildings, in the same way she walked in the countryside; and she brought back as images the things she could not bring back physically to her studio, and used them in her work. Her earlier natural habitats included art school, the New York scene and museums, and she developed her 'inner aspect' with materials taken from these environments. She was sensitive also to the social world and its pecking orders and opportunities. Altogether, as Howard observes, 'She was interested in the world, and she was interested in how she was doing in the world. She was alert to the world, and to how she was seen in the world.'[27] In an interview with Krasner – one that is both posthumous and semi-fictional – John Bernard Myers voices both parts, based on years of recalled conversations with the artist, repeating her favourite themes (which she herself repeated). S/he says 'my "subject matter" would be myself … an organism as much a part of nature and reality' as any other element in the environment.[28]

Here, Krasner draws close to the mathematician and philosopher Alfred North Whitehead's idea that the perceiving subject is part of what is being sensed; as part of a whole, she is both seeing and herself apprehended in that whole. Trying to understand Lee Krasner can push us to think harder about the nature of nature. According to Whitehead, arguing against 'the vicious bifurcation' of nature into subject and object, 'Nature is nothing else than the deliverance of sense-awareness.'[29] Krasner seems to have grasped this in a very early self-portrait, in which she painted herself painting in the woods, a mirror nailed to the trunk of a tree. The perceiving self is here emphatically located in its environment, seeing and seen, on both sides of the easel, the self reflected in nature and vice versa. Krasner herself said it best, with a directness that hints at an ontological enormity: 'I cannot conceive anything outside nature.'[30]

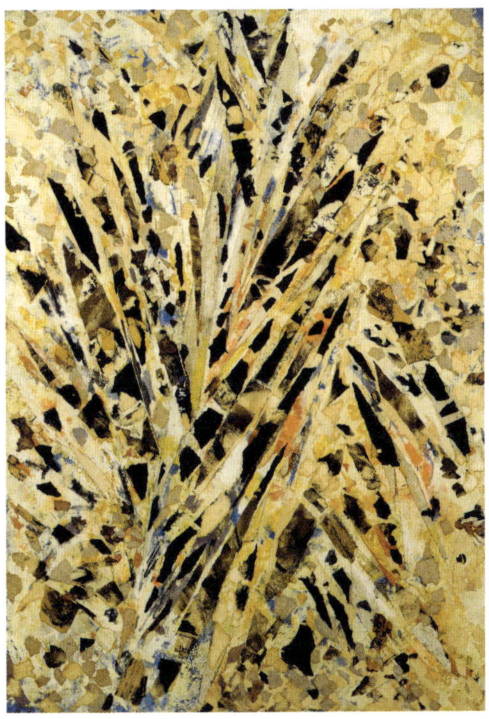

9 *Burning Candles*, 1955

Katy Siegel

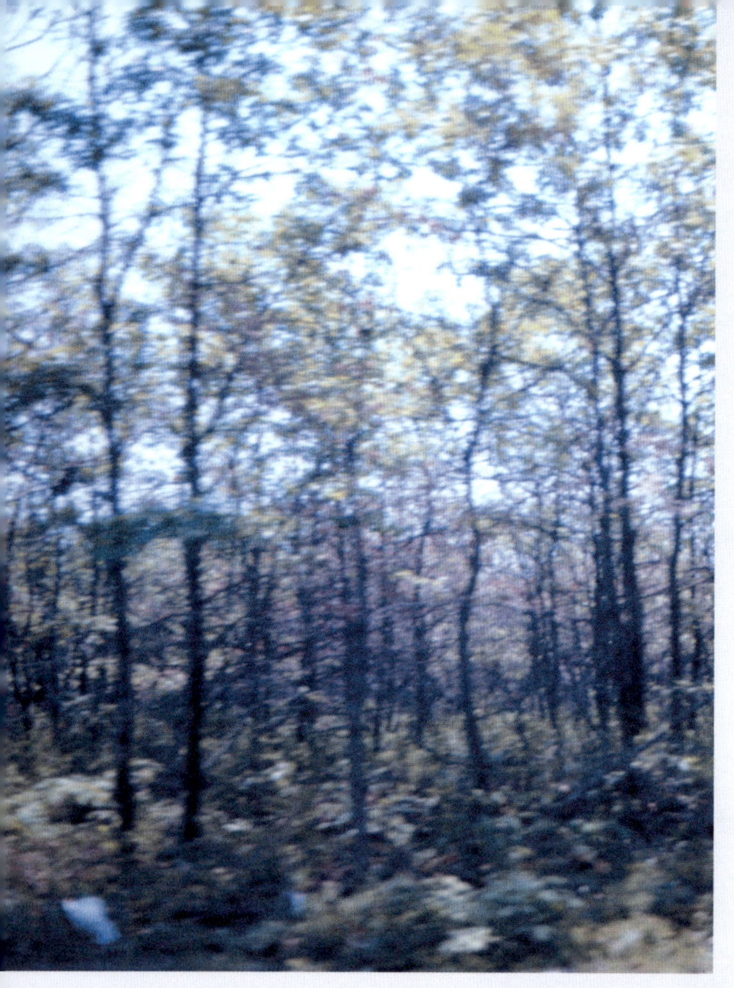
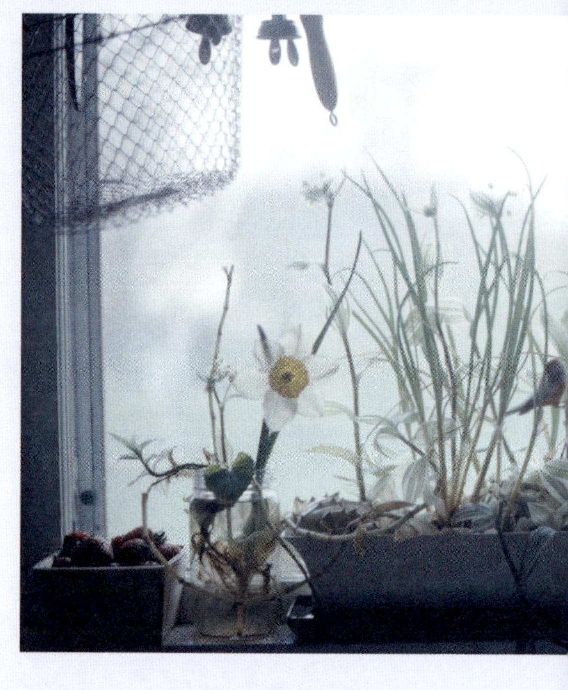
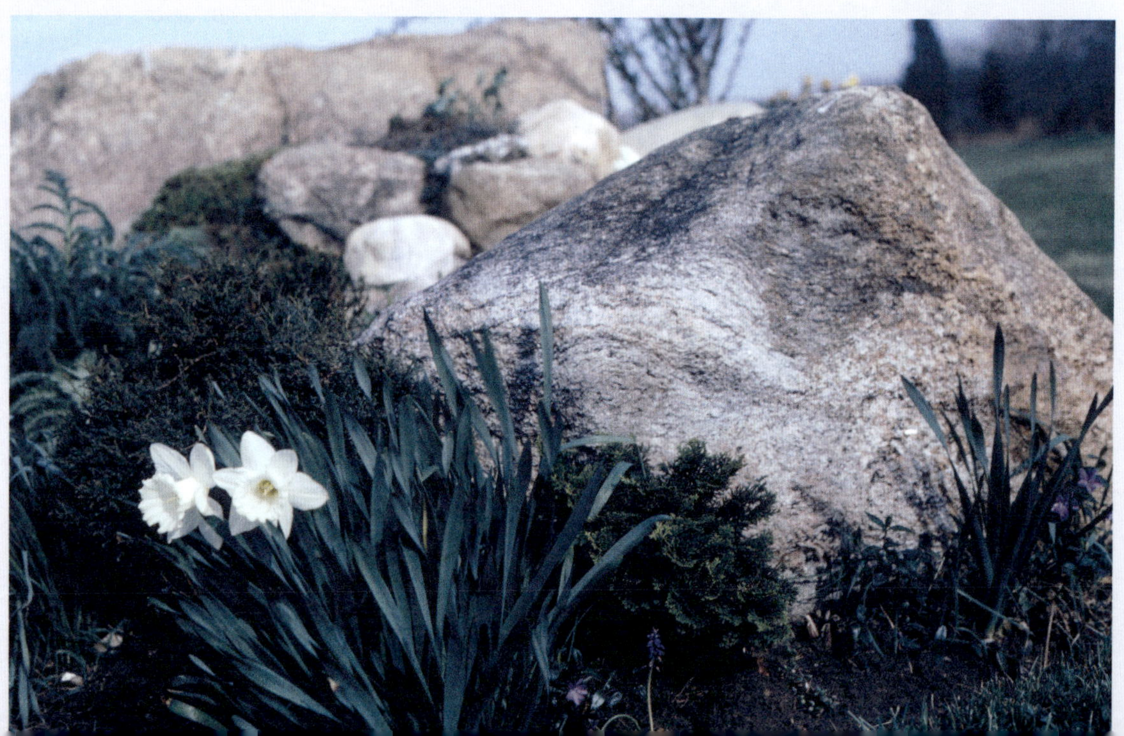

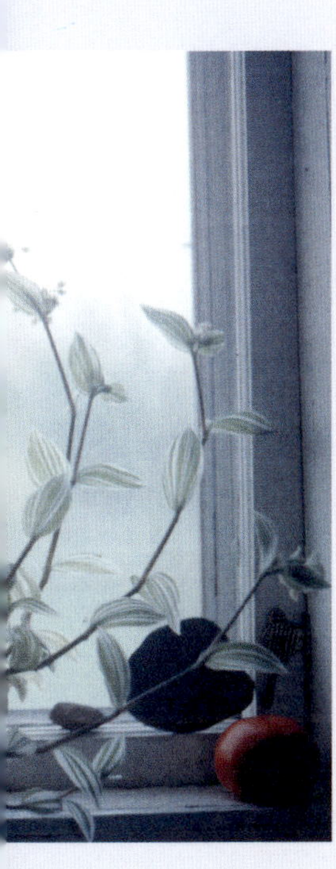
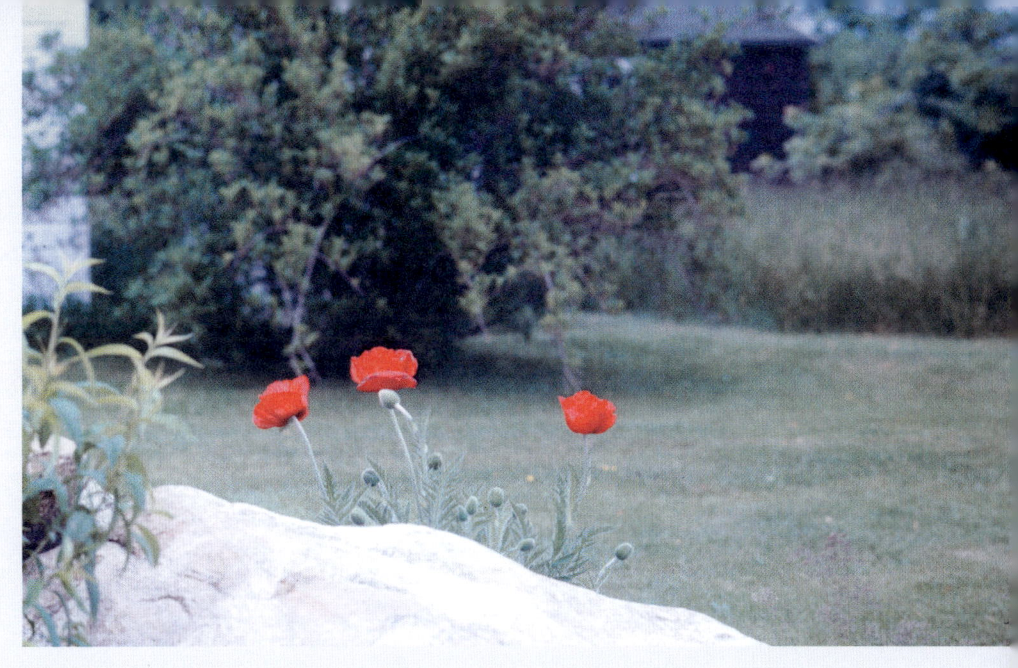
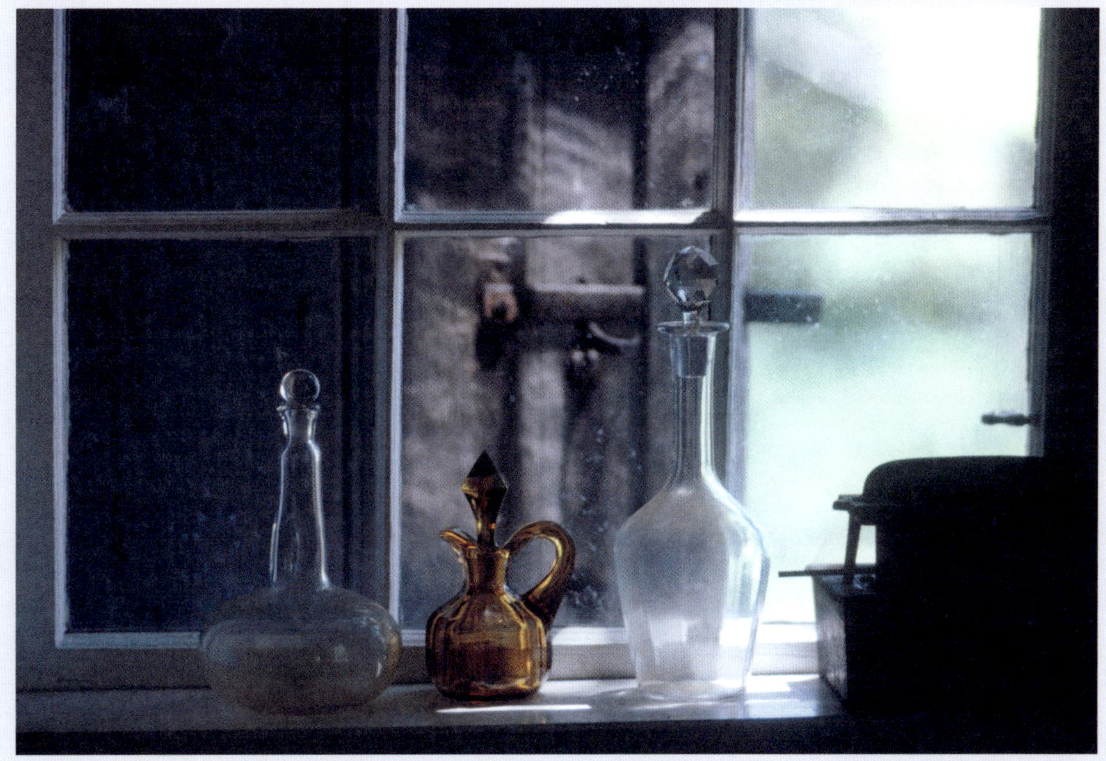

WRITING RIMBAUD ON THE WALL

There is a widely held view that, for more than a third of her life, Lee Krasner was at least two people: the painter Lee Krasner, and the widow Mrs Jackson Pollock, who managed her husband's estate. If we dig deeper, however, we learn that she was already more than one person long before she met Pollock, whom she married on 25 October 1945 (fig. 1).

Krasner was born Lena Krassner in Brooklyn, New York, on 27 October 1908. When she was a teenager she began calling herself 'Lenore', which was most likely derived from her reading of the American writer and poet Edgar Allan Poe, whose stories and poems had 'an enormous effect' on her during her adolescence.[1] By the time she was in her twenties, she identified herself as 'Lee'. In 1936, when she was arrested during a protest against the Works Progress Administration's decision to lay off 500 artists, she told the police officer that her name was 'Mary Cassatt', the great, American-born Impressionist painter. From the late 1930s, she signed some of her works with the more elliptical 'LK'.

Another writer who excited the artist during her teenage years was Maurice Maeterlinck. His book *On Emerson and Other Essays* (which also contains pieces on Jan van Ruysbroeck and Novalis, the pseudonym of the German Romantic writer Georg Philipp Friedrich Freiherr von Hardenberg) was published in English in New York in 1912. Reading this translation, Krasner would have learned of Ralph Waldo Emerson's belief that the individual must shun conformity and consistency.

In his foreword to the English edition of Maeterlinck's book, the translator, Montrose J. Moses, explains why Maeterlinck's texts on Emerson, Ruysbroeck and Novalis were gathered into a single volume:

> [Maeterlinck] deals in all three essays with men to whom the external event was nought beside the inner life. Save in the instance of the pathetic love tragedy of Novalis, he does not relish the fact as much as he does the discovery of the soul's expression. He hastens over the few events in Ruysbroeck's sainted life, relieved that he can pass quickly to the core of his philosophy. And as for Emerson, he altogether ignores locality and time.[2]

The opening paragraph of the essay on Emerson begins with the following lines:

> 'Only one thing matters,' says Novalis, 'and that is the search for our transcendental self.' This self we discern at moments in the words of God, of poets, and of sages; in the depths of certain joys and sorrows; in sleep, in love and sickness, and in

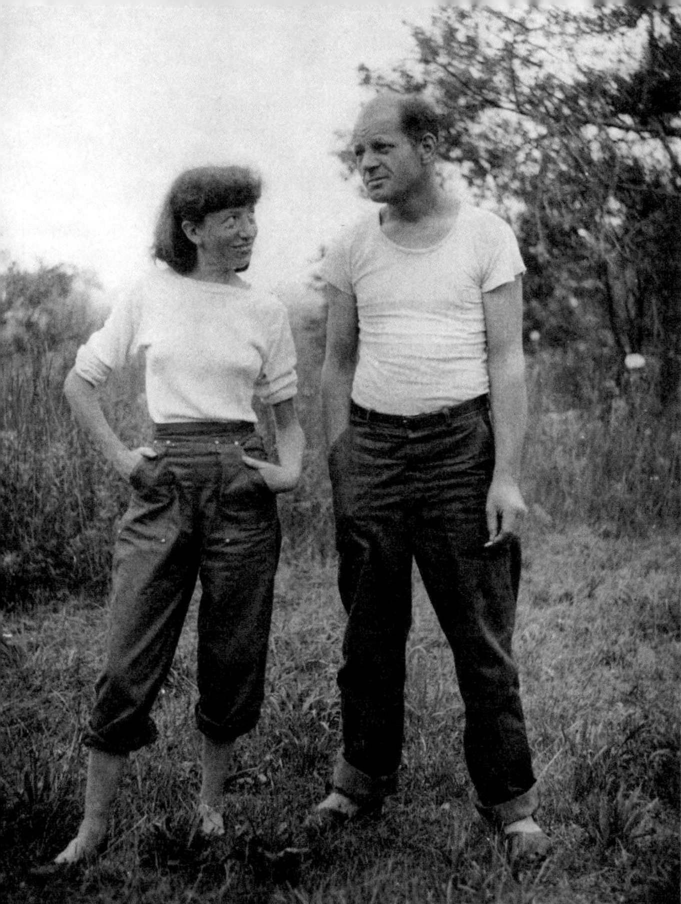

1 Lee Krasner and Jackson Pollock, Springs, 1946.
Photograph by Ronald Stein.

unforeseen crises where it signals us from afar, and points out our relations with the universe. Some philosophers devote themselves solely to this investigation, and they write those books in which only the extraordinary prevails. 'What is there of value in books,' says our author, 'if it be not the transcendental and the extraordinary?' These philosophers are as painters striving to seize a likeness in the dark.[3]

I believe that Krasner's early experience of Poe's poems and stories, Maeterlinck's essays (particularly on Emerson) and, later on, her reading of Arthur Rimbaud helped her to attain the unique position that she occupies in postwar American art. According to the American poet Allen Tate, 'Poe is the transitional figure in modern literature, because he discovered our great subject, the disintegration of personality.'[4] Shunning realism and the realm of appearances, Maeterlinck and Rimbaud shared Poe's interest in the inner world of the individual and in heightened states of receptive consciousness. Together, these writers helped to lay the groundwork for Krasner's interest in abstraction as a 'transcendental and extraordinary' opening to an enhanced sensitivity, while shaping her ideal of the artist as a self-sufficient individual in touch with her multiple, inner selves.

In his essay 'Self-Reliance' (1841), Emerson describes the individual's relationship to society:

> These are the voices which we hear in solitude, but they grow faint and inaudible as we enter the world. Society everywhere is in conspiracy against the manhood of every one of its members. Society is a joint-stock company, in which the members agree, for the better securing of his bread to each share-holder, to surrender the liberty and culture of the eater. [...] Self-reliance is its aversion. It loves not realities and creators but names and customs.[5]

While Emerson's celebration of nonconformity must have appealed to Krasner, it seems likely that she also understood that its intended audience was male society.

Krasner's isolation from this society was twofold: she would have to forge her own path as a woman in the art world, but, once she had found it, there was little likelihood that the art world would take her seriously, simply because she was a woman. She enrolled at the Hans Hofmann School of Fine Arts in 1937 and stayed until the early 1940s, even after Hofmann paid her work what Krasner called a 'double-edged compliment': 'This is so good you would not know it was by a woman.'[6] He might respect her, but never as much as he would a male artist.

It is clear from the interviews that Krasner gave after Pollock's death in 1956 that she was highly conscious of how sharply the art world (like much of society) diminished the role of women, expecting them to be subservient rather than independent. She was also aware that the multiple roles she inhabited – artist, wife, widow, estate executor – were only the more obvious ones. By the time Krasner had read the writer and poet Delmore Schwartz's 1939 translation of Arthur Rimbaud's *Une saison en enfer* (*A Season in Hell*), in her early thirties, she already believed in the existence of a fragmented inner self (or selves). In Rimbaud's long poem in prose, she discovered some of the many voices animating her interior life.

2   Barnett Newman, *Onement VI*, 1953

Lee Krasner (1908–1984) was born amid the first generation of Abstract Expressionists: Willem de Kooning (1904–1997), Barnett Newman (1905–1970; fig. 2), Jackson Pollock (1912–1956) and Ad Reinhardt (1913–1967). Living and working in New York City and its environs between the mid-1930s and the late 1960s, this generation of artists can be roughly divided into three stylistic groups: the gestural Abstract Expressionists (de Kooning and Franz Kline (1910–1962; fig. 3)); those who favoured strict geometries (Newman, Reinhardt and Agnes Martin (1912–2004)); and a third, seldom talked-about group, which was relentless in its pursuit of pure, rounded forms, with a focus on shapes, lines and edges. In this latter, still unheralded category, I would include Paul Feeley (1910–1966; fig. 4) and Myron Stout (1908–1987).

Krasner, who explored all of these styles, does not fit comfortably into any of the groups that practised them or the narratives in which they have been embedded. Despite her unique position in the middle of it all, she must be considered an outlier. This is because – in contrast to the artists I have cited – Krasner adamantly refused to develop a signature image or method. This is how the art critic Emily Wasserman characterized Krasner when the artist was in her mid-sixties: 'Unlike so many who painted in the Abstract Expressionist vein, she has not allowed a resolved style to degenerate into a mannerism.'[7]

Krasner may have painted expressionistically at points in her career, as in her 'Umber' paintings (1959–62; fig. 5), but she cannot be pegged as a gestural expressionist disposed to slathering thick brushstrokes on to a canvas; she may have divided her surfaces into rectangles, as in *Untitled* (1950; fig. 6), but she would not become known for stringent geometry; and she may have developed rounded forms in such paintings as *Portrait in Green* (1969; fig. 7), but she never pursued the distillation of these forms or the evocation of a classical order. In contrast to her peers, many of whom were jolted by Pollock's breakthrough 'drip paintings', which he perfected around 1947, Krasner never simplified her imagery or eliminated detail.

Krasner's resistance to categorization is one of her enduring strengths. The fact that her work stands outside of the tendencies that we now recognize as constituting the central thrust of postwar American painting is a remarkable achievement, as well as a testament to her independence. I believe that Krasner's resistance is inextricably bound up with her determination to achieve autonomy, which at the time was impossible to attain if you were a woman without the imprimatur of a male art critic. She had to believe in her work strongly enough to pursue it with the certainty that almost no one would publicly support her. Most of the 'Little Image' paintings (1946–50), for example, were not exhibited until several years after they were made. Krasner was mostly neglected or dismissed while Pollock was alive, and was marginalized for nearly a decade after his death.

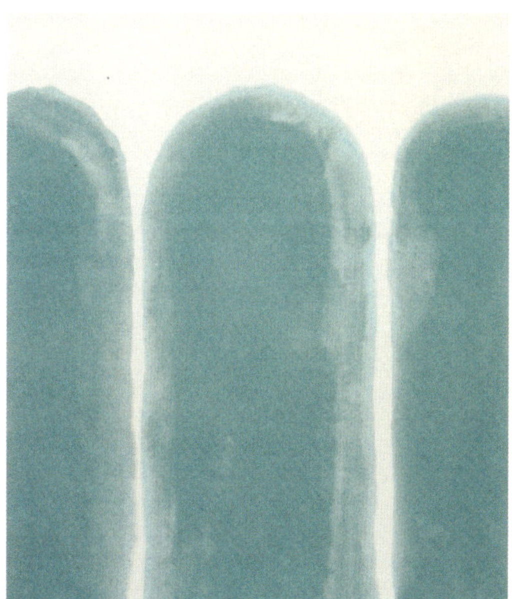
3 Franz Kline, *August Day*, 1957

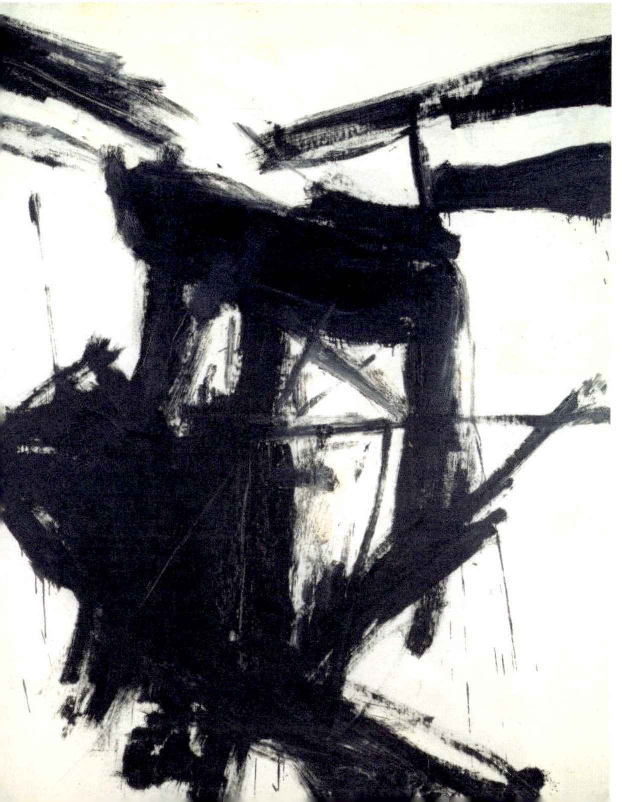

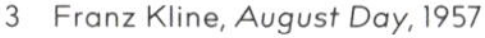
4 Paul Feeley, *Melos*, 1958

It is important to remember that Krasner did not come into her own only after Pollock died, but while they were living together on Fireplace Road in Springs, Long Island. More importantly, she did so by following her own trajectory, which involved an original use of collage. In the first significant group of collage works that Krasner made (1953–55), she incorporated fragments of her own cut-up paintings and, in some cases, cut-ups of Pollock's rejected drawings.

Given that Krasner lived through the Great Depression, her use of discarded materials could be seen as thriftiness, but I believe that there is more to it than that. Her use of such materials provides evidence of her desire to gain parity, to be seen as the equal of her husband, rather than the dutiful wife living in his shadow. If she had to tear up her art and combine it with her celebrated husband's discarded drawings – especially those associated with his groundbreaking drip technique – in order to gain some measure of equality, then Krasner was up to the task. Her collage paintings speak to her powerful, no-holds-barred drive for artistic freedom.

I wish to consider Krasner's use of discards, both her own and Pollock's, in light of the poetry that Krasner had written on the wall of her studio at 51 East Ninth Street in Manhattan's East Village, where she worked from 1939–42, before she and Pollock started living together. The lines come from Rimbaud's *A Season in Hell*, specifically the 1939 translation by Delmore Schwartz. Krasner had asked Byron Browne, a painter and friend whose handwriting she admired, to transcribe the text on to her studio wall:

> To whom shall I hire myself out? What beast must one adore? What holy image attack? What hearts shall I break? What lie must I maintain? In what blood must I walk?[8]

According to Krasner's biographer, Gail Levin, 'The words were entirely in black paint except for "What lie must I maintain?" in blue.'[9] While Levin suggests that Krasner may have chosen this quote as a reaction to the sudden departure of her then lover, Igor Pantuhoff, I think that such a reading is too narrow.[10]

Rimbaud's compact cluster of accusatory questions seems to cast a light on Krasner's approach to making art: she cared less about being original than being authentic. In order to be genuine, Krasner recognized that she had to acknowledge her destructive side and her rage. Making genuine art required these aspects of the inner self to be faced, as well as a recognition that any work she made would embody her fury only temporarily.

The translator Wyatt Mason, in the introduction to his masterful *Rimbaud Complete*, describes *A Season in Hell* as 'a complex, polyphonic, highly compressed collection of dramatic monologues'.[11] Mason goes on to say: 'No matter how one elects to read *A Season in Hell*, it presents a struggle in both its content and its form. The poem is as articulate a document of existential ambivalence as we have, and its method, for better and worse, is expressive of that very ambivalence.'[12] Mason also describes the poem's many parts as 'vessels of indeterminacy, ambiguity and frequently strange beauty'.[13] It seems to me that in trying to fit Krasner into one of the stylistic categories associated with Abstract Expressionism – to pin her down, so to speak – we fail to see these qualities in her work.

I believe that the questions posed by Rimbaud in *A Season in Hell* spoke to Krasner's inner voices and to the inescapable contradictions and conflicts that, for her, were central to making art. Krasner identified with the contentious, polyphonic voices arguing throughout many of the poem's monologues, particularly in the way in which they embody the individual's multiple selves. She would have found a mirror of her own struggles in their frantic disagreement over how to move forward after uniformly rejecting beauty, justice and hope as false ideals. In an interview with Gaby Rodgers, Krasner stated: 'The one constant in life is change. I have regards for the inner voice.'[14]

Two of the questions posed by Rimbaud, 'What holy image attack?' and 'What hearts shall I break?', come to mind when thinking about the way in which Krasner would cut up her own works, especially pieces on which she had dripped paint. Viewed in the context of her work and life, Rimbaud's questions – which focus on compromise, power relationships, betrayal and the killing of sacred cows – articulate some of the obstacles Krasner had to face consciously in order to gain agency.

Krasner must have recognized that the struggle to attain personal and artistic liberation was likely to be – metaphorically speaking – violent and crucial ('In what blood must I walk?'). At times, she must have

5 *Assault on the Solar Plexus*, 1961

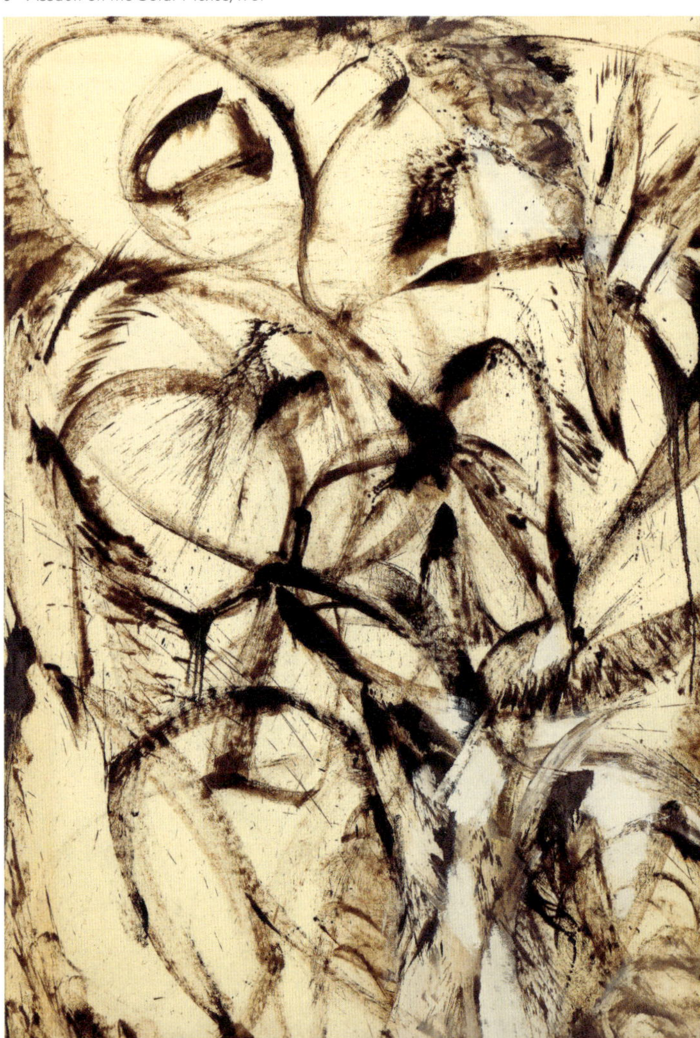

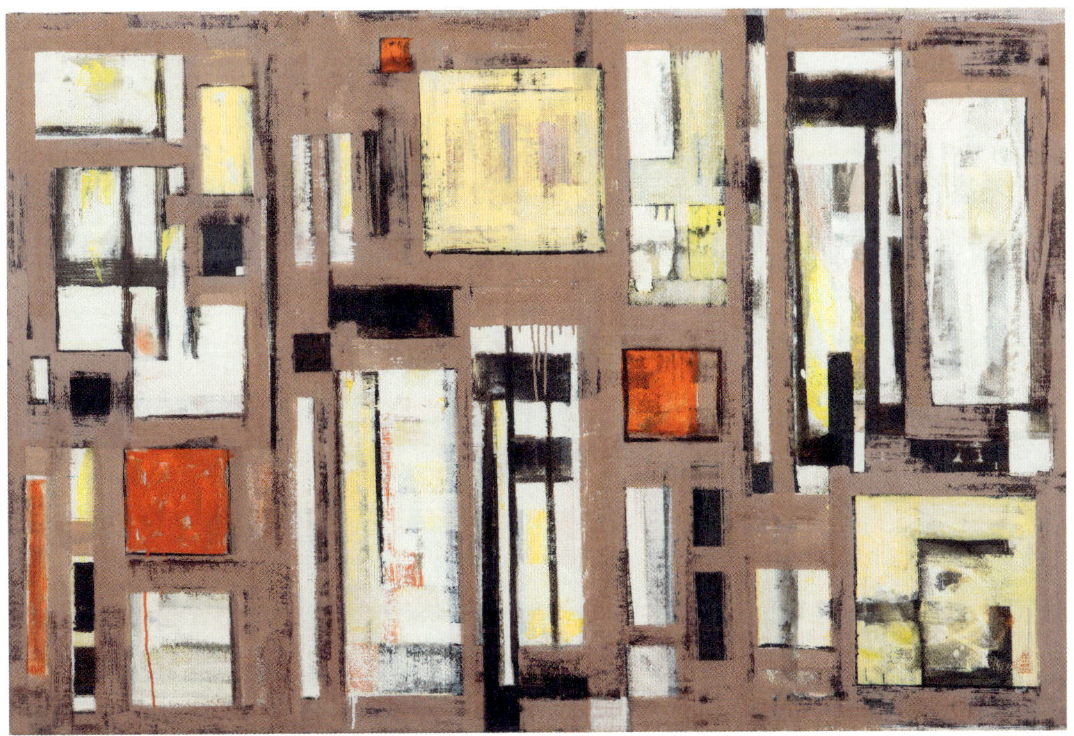

6 *Untitled*, 1950

wondered whether any single voice or self would triumph. Would any victory not be contingent and partial at best? Is volatility not the best that one can hope for, rather than complacency?

Writing Rimbaud on the wall, Krasner recognized that the struggle for artistic freedom was a complicated, arduous and ceaseless undertaking. Since individuals cannot escape reality and the limits it imposes on their lives, before they can act they must first recognize the nature of their circumstances. For Krasner, the circumstances were a male-dominated society harbouring numerous myths and prejudices about a woman's capacity to be creative. Given her own nature as a fiercely ambitious artist, she understood that conflict of some kind was unavoidable.

There are two other statements of Rimbaud's that I am sure Krasner was familiar with. The first is that the poet must initiate the 'rational derangement of all the senses',[15] the other that the 'I is someone else'.[16]

By advancing that the self is other, Rimbaud proposes that the 'I' is something constructed by the individual out of the multiple facets of consciousness. Rimbaud's notion of the 'I' as a fictive construct helps to explain Krasner's resistance to adopting a signature style. As she told the art historian Barbara Novak, 'I've never understood the fixed image. I've never experienced this state of being where you fix an image and this becomes your identification … It's rigid. Its purity is alarming, so to speak. It terrifies me in a sense.'[17]

In a conversation with her then studio assistant, John Post Lee, Krasner rejected the view that she clarified nature in her paintings, maintaining instead that '*It* filters through.'[18] Krasner's statement conveys her belief in being receptive to circumstances, whatever they may be. After destroying some of her drawings in 1953, she had to be open to what she could make of them. Krasner's focus on being open departs completely from the famous declaration Pollock made to Hans Hofmann: 'I *am* nature.'[19]

The whirling unrest of conflicting selves in *A Season in Hell*, in tandem with the unpredictable, often jolting emotional shifts (which are faithfully echoed in Schwartz's translation), must have appealed to Krasner on multiple levels, from the personal to the artistic. Take a look at *The City* (1953; fig. 8) and you will get a sense of what I mean. In this hybrid work, made from torn pieces of painted paper and cut-up fragments of one of her dripped oil paintings, which she mounted on a panel measuring 122 × 91.5 centimetres (48 × 36 in.), Krasner assembled a tumultuous, disrupted surface, a rhythmic staccato. In contrast to many of her contemporaries who, in the wake of Pollock's poured paintings, pared down and harmonized their elements in the service of an all-over composition, Krasner does something very nearly the opposite: she calls attention to details and ruptures. If we continue to look at Krasner's work through the lens of Pollock's paintings, we will fail to understand this crucial distinction. Moreover, hunting for signs of influence in either direction seems beside the point. While there are unquestionably times when Krasner borrowed from Pollock, and vice versa, my interest is in what distinguishes her work from that of her contemporaries, its 'strange beauty'.

The violent tearing and cutting that rip through *The City* (and other collages from 1953–55) are inseparable from its content; the internal, disjointed rhythms are at once destructive and methodical, dispassionate and brimming with rage. Rising from the bottom of the painting, long black strips fan out across the surface, as red-spattered fragments emerge in the recesses. The forces of destruction and creation are one and the same.

Echoing Rimbaud, Krasner has rationally deranged her forms. She has done this, first of all, by using cut and torn fragments, as in *Bald Eagle* (1955), which includes pieces of Pollock's work. Secondly, she has knowingly arranged the torn and cut sections into an unsettled composition in which the destructive violence of her actions is self-evident. Rather than use a brush (or sticks, as Pollock did) to draw in paint, Krasner wielded scissors and a knife. Finally, by using discards from her own, unknown paintings in combination with drawings branded in Pollock's world-famous style, she is both attacking the failed works and transforming them into something fresh and new – simultaneously mocking and superseding the male power structure.

According to Gail Levin, Krasner began making these works after 'she finally got her own separate studio, after they bought an acre adjoining their house on the north side and moved onto it a little shack, which had once been a smokehouse, for her to work in'.[20] As Krasner told Phyllis Braff, a critic and curator writing for the *East Hampton Star*: '[The works] were inspired by earlier drawings that I had torn, feeling somewhat depressed. The studio was hung solidly with drawings I couldn't stand. 1953 was the deluge in this spurt of collage. It led to the exhibit at the Stable Gallery in 1955.'[21]

7   *Portrait in Green*, 1969

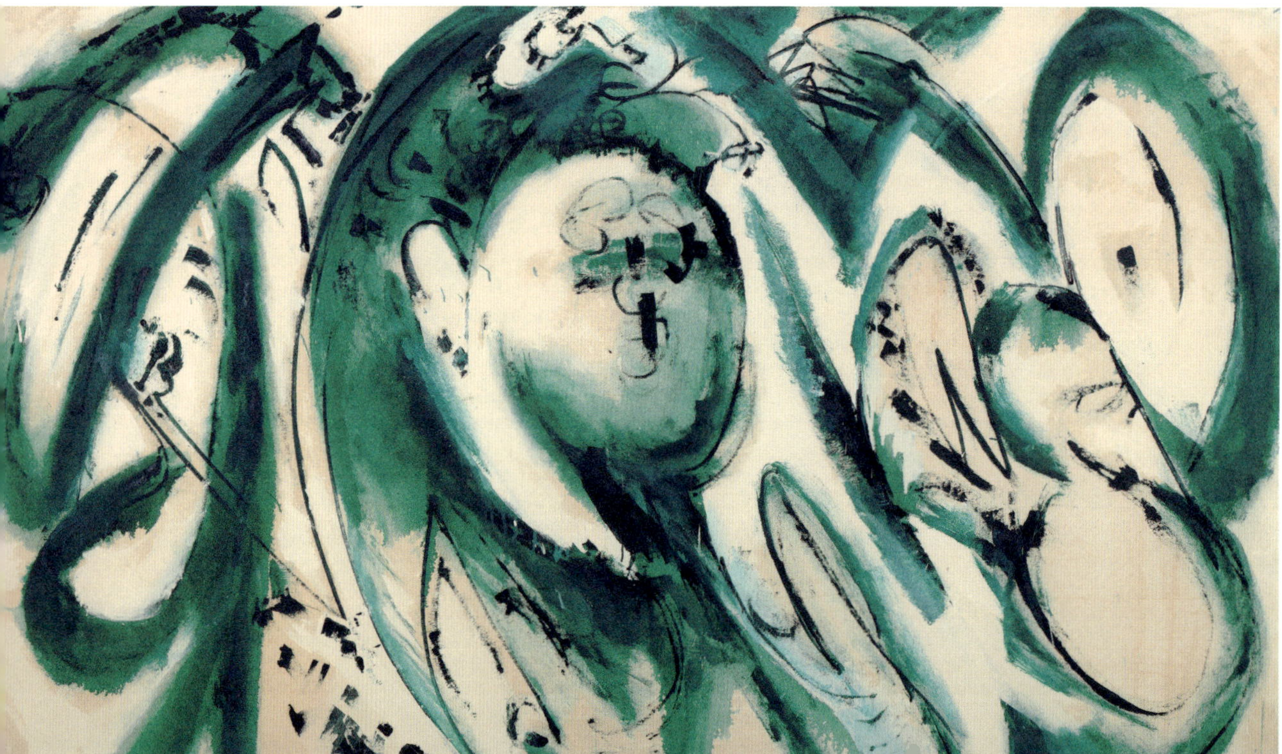

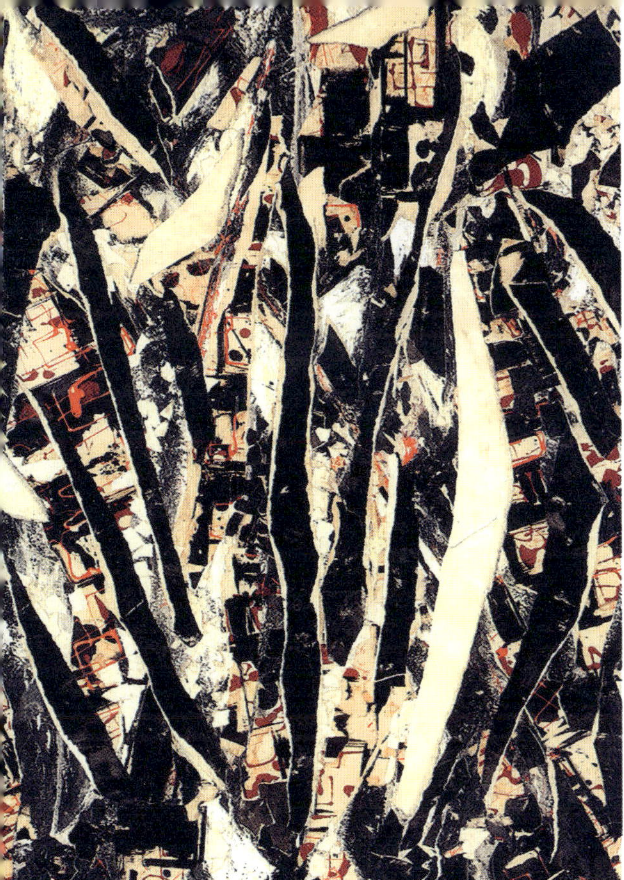

8 *The City*, 1953

During these years, Pollock was drinking heavily and his and Krasner's marriage was falling apart. It is impossible not to feel Krasner's rage in these works. And yet, I would suggest that we should avoid being reductive and reading them purely in light of her relationship with Pollock. These are not works made by an unhappy wife; rather, they are works made by a resolute artist determined to attain parity with her more celebrated male peers, as well as to make something that felt her own. What Krasner got from Rimbaud, I believe, was the sense that art is made within a milieu that makes betrayals inevitable.

True to her inner voices and her resistance to repeating herself, Krasner moved on to other bodies of work.

Nearly twenty-five years after she had cut up her paintings and drawings, she returned to this approach in the mid-1970s, with a group of works collectively titled 'Eleven Ways to Use the Words to See', which were shown at Pace Gallery, New York, in 1977. In these works, Krasner did something radically different from her previous explorations: she cut up charcoal drawings that she had made as a student in Hofmann's school, drawings that had been stored for decades in the barn in Springs until their discovery by a friend, the curator Bryan Robertson.

It is hard to know what to think of these deeply unsettling works, which is one reason why I believe they must be counted among Krasner's greatest achievements. Surgically precise and visually dissonant, they resist definition. By cutting up her early drawings, often in sharply angled sections (echoing their Cubist armature) on a collision course with one another, Krasner destroys her historical past (as a student of Hofmann), even as she changes, builds on and reuses it. In these works, Krasner exposes three irreconcilable actions: destruction, revision and creation. The means by which she makes these works have again become a central part of their content.

According to the writer and art dealer John Bernard Myers, Krasner said that she felt almost commanded to create them, which is why she titled the first piece in the group *Imperative* (1976).[22] Who or what had commanded her? Which of her inner voices was she listening to? Certainly it seems as though she was listening to more than one. In these works – as in her earlier collaged hybrids – Krasner's overwhelming desire to break the constrictions and circumstances that limited her art engendered an entirely new way of looking at form.

From 1945 to 1956, Krasner was seen as Pollock's wife; in the nearly thirty years that she lived after his death, she was seen as his widow and the caretaker of his estate. Rather than simplifying or jettisoning the past, Krasner brought it back, systematically destroyed it with scissors or a knife, and reconfigured it. She literally and metaphorically authored her own history. I think this is what Krasner wanted to achieve more than anything else.

John Yau

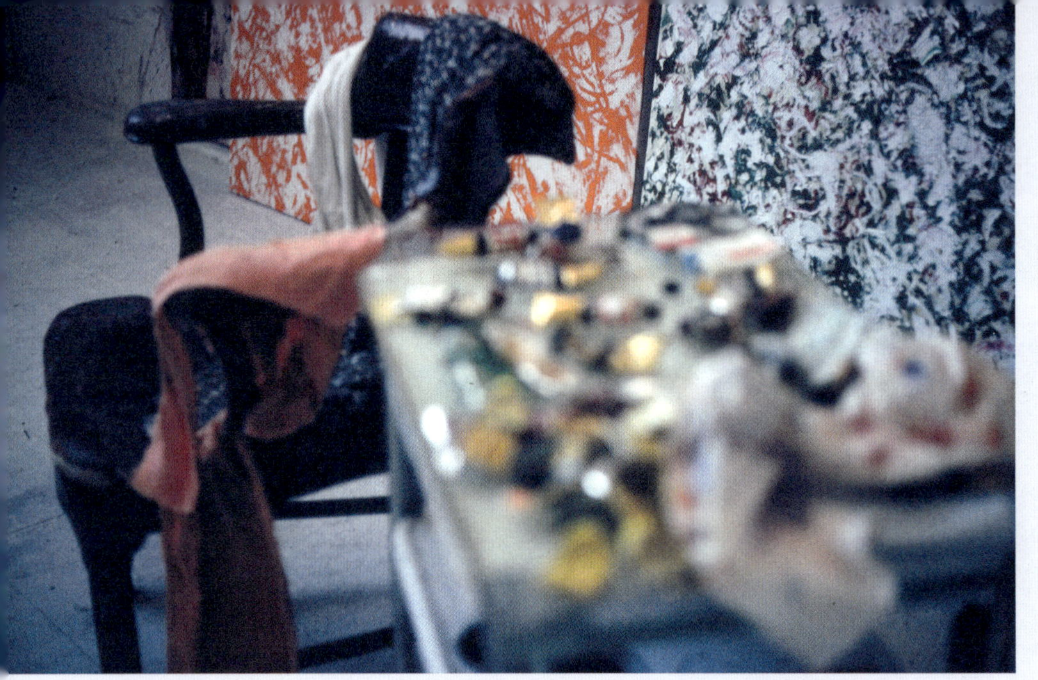

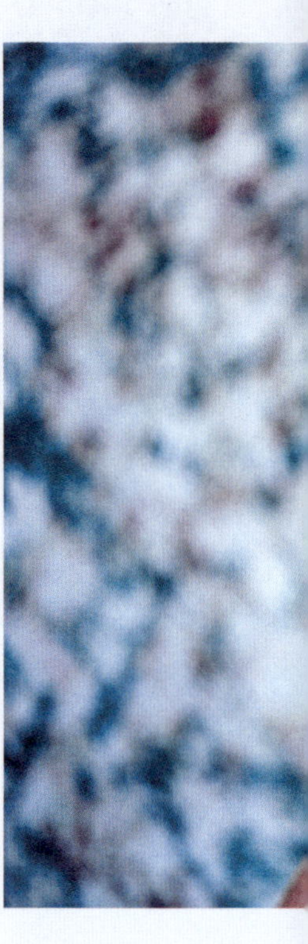

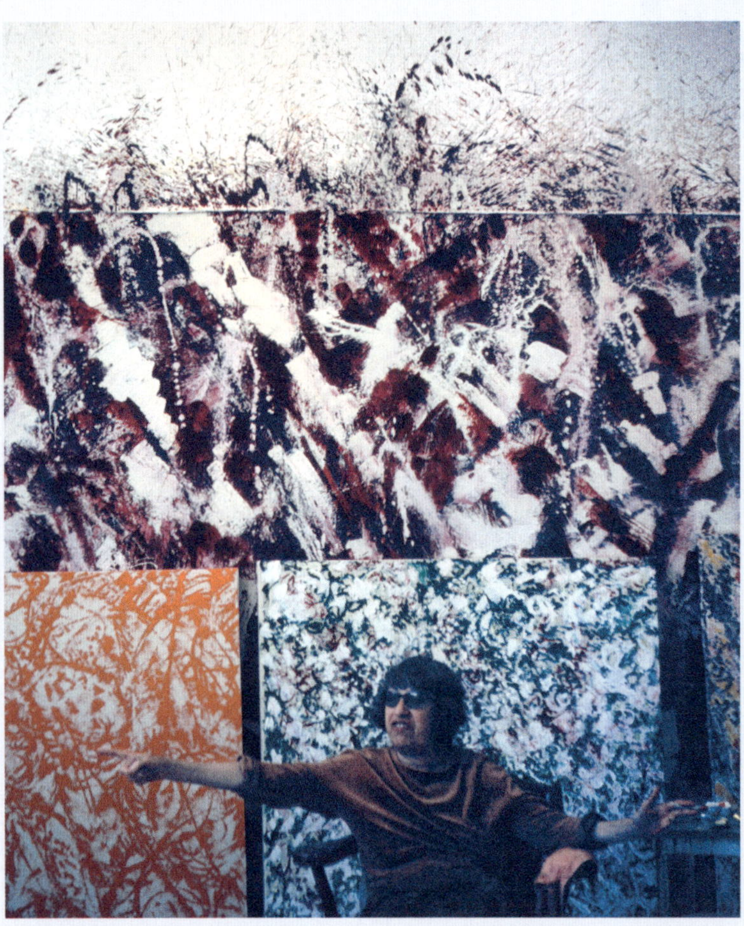

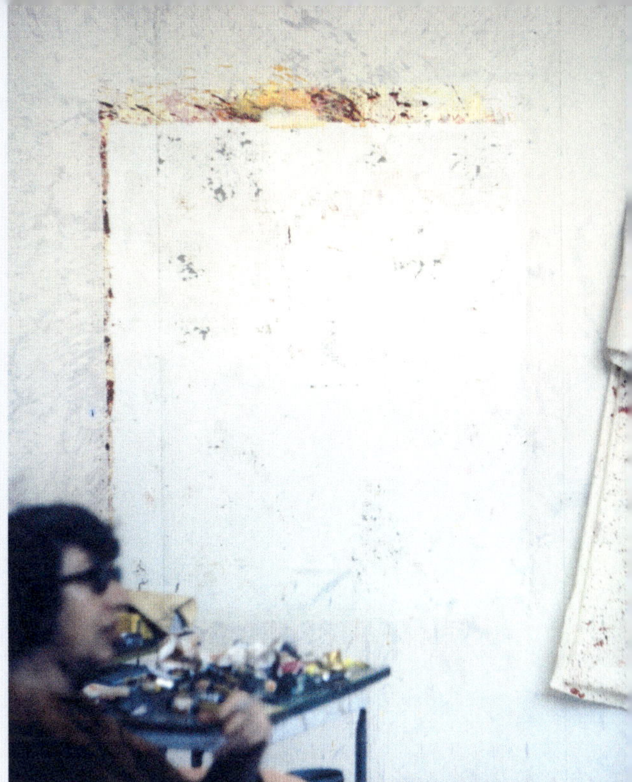

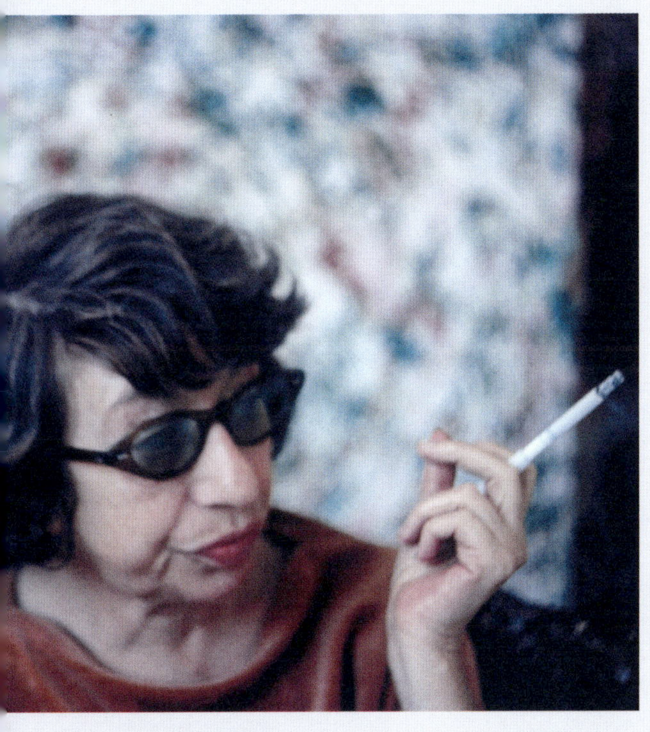

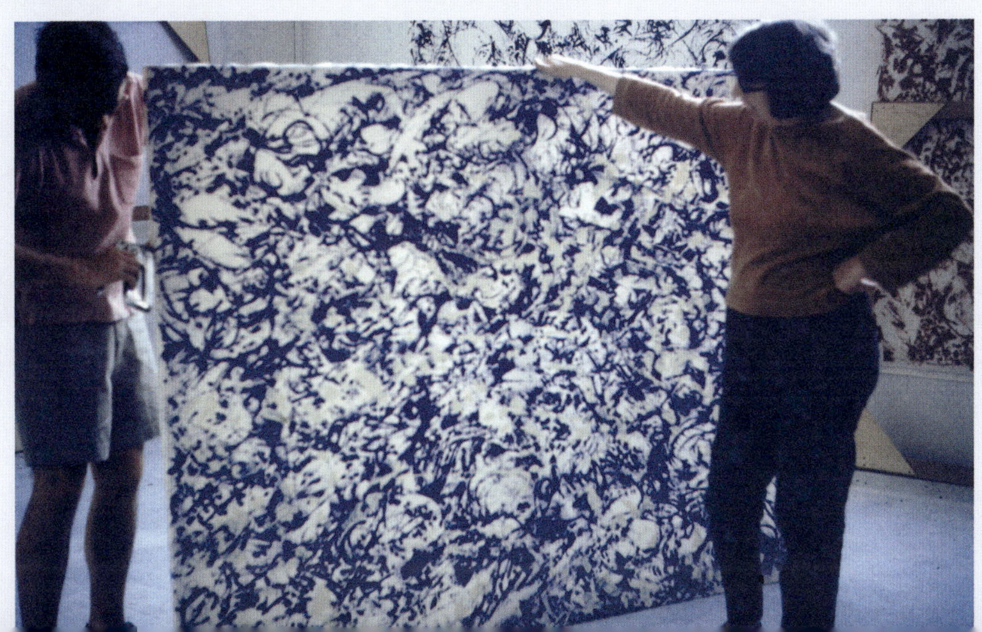

PRESENT CONDITIONAL

Coming some hundred and fifty pages into a tightly researched text, the epilogue of Barbara Rose's catalogue for the Lee Krasner touring retrospective of 1983–85 labours especially hard to secure the apotheosis of its subject. For Rose, attempts at canonization in the previous decade came under the sign of a feminism that arrived too late to have ameliorated, much less obviated, the compromising conditions in which Lena Krassner passed through 'Lenore' and 'Lee' to become the artist 'LK'. (In a 1972 *Vogue* article titled 'American Great', Krasner is quoted as saying, 'I'm an artist – not a "woman artist".')[1] In what is a gesture of solidarity, Rose claims for Krasner the privileged function of the critic whose 'insights shaped the taste of both [Clement] Greenberg and [Jackson] Pollock at a crucial time'.[2] Authorship granted retroactively nevertheless would seem a tacit acknowledgement of the fact that this evaluative job was for so long performed by others, Greenberg and Harold Rosenberg chief among them. And it also unwittingly suggests that this right to assessment once taken by Krasner was directed elsewhere, most obviously at Pollock, and away from her own work.

In the ensuing account, in which Rose visits Krasner on the South Fork of Long Island, the reader encounters the artist readying herself to return to Manhattan at the end of the summer; she prepares paintings for transport and surveys what could be changed in others. Rose describes Krasner's tendencies for 'revision and auto-criticism': 'She makes up her mind whether to sign a work, which means she accepts it as finished, to cut it up into pieces to re-use as painted textures in future collage paintings, or, as she puts it, to "re-enter" [to correct or revise] the work.'[3] Amid these routines – which punctuate the seasons and give measure to a life, as well as closure to Rose's book – Rose has Krasner remembering an incident that proved irrevocable, a sort of Rubicon crossed. In a 1959 visit to Krasner's studio, Greenberg balked at the change in her work, which seemed to be ossifying into Krasner's *style*; and on the basis of his displeasure in her new paintings, he revoked the solo show that he was

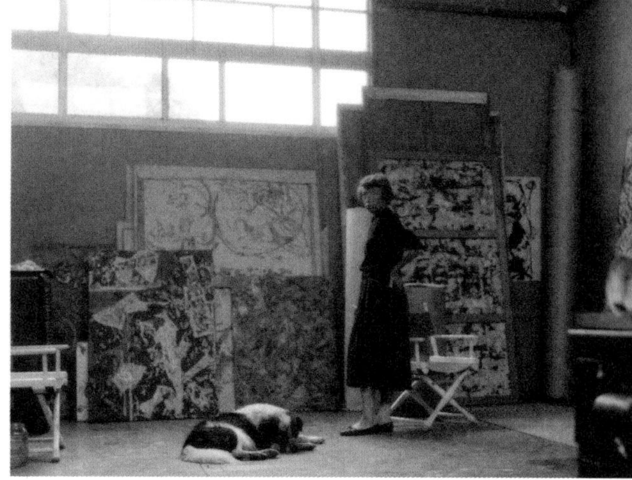

1   Lee Krasner with her dog Gyp in Jackson Pollock's studio, Springs, August 1956. Photograph by Maurice Berezov.

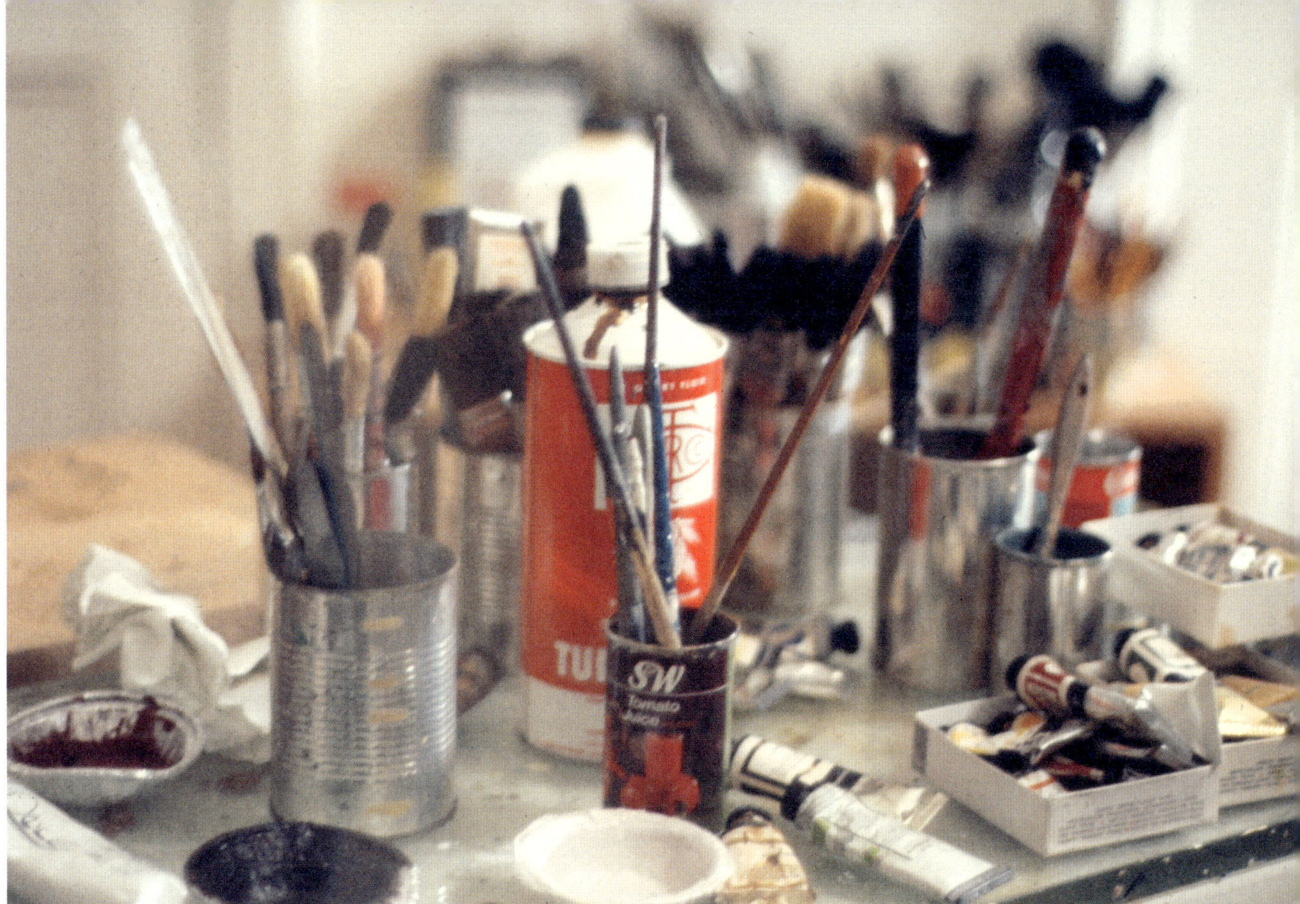

2 Lee Krasner's painting materials in her studio
   in Springs, 1964. Photograph by Ray Eames.

planning at the gallery French & Company.[4] Elsewhere described as a 'big blow up', Krasner here recalled a somewhat more measured exchange: 'We had words … and he exited.'[5] This, Rose triumphantly writes in the culminating paragraphs of her book, was the precondition for Krasner's arrival: her becoming a critic of and for her own work.

An ending that is also a beginning is perhaps a structural ploy, effectively creating a scene of origin for Krasner's emergence as an artist on her own terms. Rose acknowledges that the public reckoning of this emergence was not exactly coincident with the 1959 Greenberg showdown; nor was it, at that juncture in 1983, anywhere near accomplished. Indeed, Rose's work – alongside that of Gail Levin, Ellen G. Landau and Cindy Nemser, among others – underscored the persistent need for narrative possession, a goal they worked mightily for. As Anne Wagner glossed in 1989, when the paintings – to say nothing of their legacy – had settled, '[Krasner's] rehabilitation, interestingly enough, was solidified by media attention as symptomatic of its day and age, as were the first journalistic responses to Pollock of theirs. In 1949 *Life* asked the question, "Jackson Pollock: Is He the Greatest Living Painter in the United States?" In 1973, *Time* declared unequivocally that Krasner was "Out of the Shade".'[6] Before and after, Krasner operated in a self-directed mode that was ultimately dialogic – since it was always already imbricated within relations between people and histories far beyond herself, as well as inescapably close.

Krasner's critical stance was material more than discursive, or such is the argument developed in this essay in relation to her various engagements with collage. In these works, she incorporated surplus materials from completed projects; would-be remnants sourced from Pollock with his apparent consent (such as in *Forest No. 2* (1954), *Color Totem* (1955; fig. 3) and *Bald Eagle* (1955)); and ready-mades from her own prior but, ultimately, only penultimate achievements. To be clear, this interrogatory perspective informs Krasner's identity as much as her art (although it is the latter that this essay addresses, if hardly in imagined isolation). 'LK' admits the impossibility of this segregation,[7] while Ellen G. Landau further avows her relationality: 'One very conspicuous way Krasner chose to distance herself from others' expectations was to periodically re-create her identity by revising her name.'[8]

The self-portraits Krasner made between 1928 and 1931 likewise attest to her questioning of subjectivity as beholden to social and aesthetic conditions. Working in 1928 at her parents' house on a portrait to gain admission to the life-drawing class at the National Academy of Design, where she was already enrolled, Krasner matter-of-factly nailed a mirror to a tree and painted a version of herself planted in a dense thicket with light-flecked hair and strawberry-coated lips, brushes and rag in hand. Pictured in the act of making the image, the tautology of *Self-Portrait* (c. 1928) embodies totalizing self-reflexivity. In fact, a reading

of Krasner's accomplishments might well unfurl from this point: one that sees not an absence of self-regard but a surfeit. Another might take this as the ground from which Krasner began to mark her place, syntactically, in relation to extant pedagogical conventions.

It is worth recalling that it was in the context of her subsequent studies with Hans Hofmann that Krasner watched the master rip one of her sketches to pieces. In a kind of deflection of this unwelcome intervention into the sanctity of her creation, she structured a response. *Mosaic Collage* (c. 1942; fig. 4) is a game perversion of Hofmann's 'push-pull' technique, in which life teems from the boxes of a partial grid, the expressive colour inherent in (instead of applied on) the materials-become-surface. By 1942 Krasner was using collage in a rather different way. At the time, she was employed by the War Services Project (previously the Works Progress Administration, or WPA) to design a series of twenty department-store window displays for the Higher Education Division of the City of New York Board of Education, advertising local courses significant to the war effort. Krasner made tableaux – using enlarged photographs that she took, cut out and montaged, in accordance with other contemporary WPA photomural projects (such as those on view at the 1939 New York World's Fair; fig. 5)[9] – selling the value of cryptography or chemistry across the contiguous spaces of dynamic fractured planes. The window displays recuperate Hofmann's affront as a visual and conceptual strategy capable of effecting didactic and clearly legible communication for passers-by.

But like the mirror tacked to the tree for Krasner's early self-portrait, collage was also a pragmatic recycling out of thrift.[10] She took what she could and made do. In one important instance, she extended the combinatory logic into three dimensions, fashioning two round tables. Salvaging iron wagon wheels as her armatures, she mosaiced tesserae left over from a WPA project of Pollock's on to the surface, together with other things at hand (including coloured glass, coins, shells, keys and broken bits of her own costume jewellery). She likewise reused the so-called 'Gray Slab' paintings of 1943–46 to recover canvases for herself and Pollock. The 'Little Images', with their dense surface aggregations – so many layers of painted signs – seem to harbour this sensible record. More explicitly, in 1953 Krasner returned to collage. This time, she decided to tear recent drawings into slivers, an enactment of mastery that she considered a 'recycling of the self in some form',[11] especially as many of this group used unsold paintings from her 1951 show at the Betty Parsons Gallery as supports.

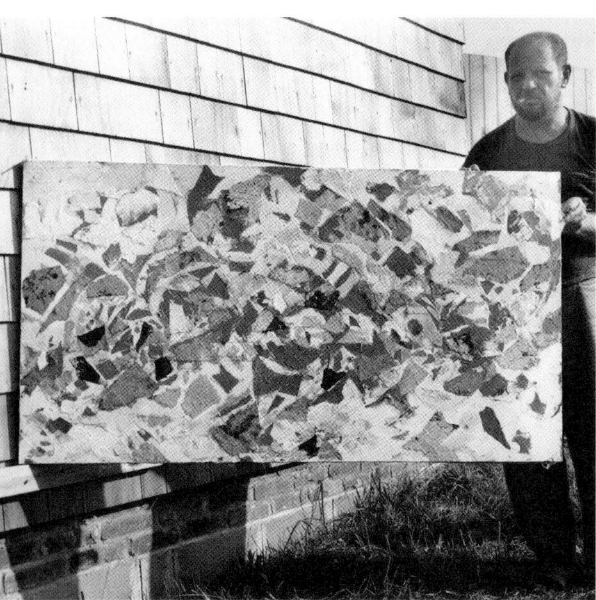

3   Jackson Pollock holding Lee Krasner's vertical painting *Color Totem* (1955) horizontally, Springs, 1955. Photograph by Hans Namuth.

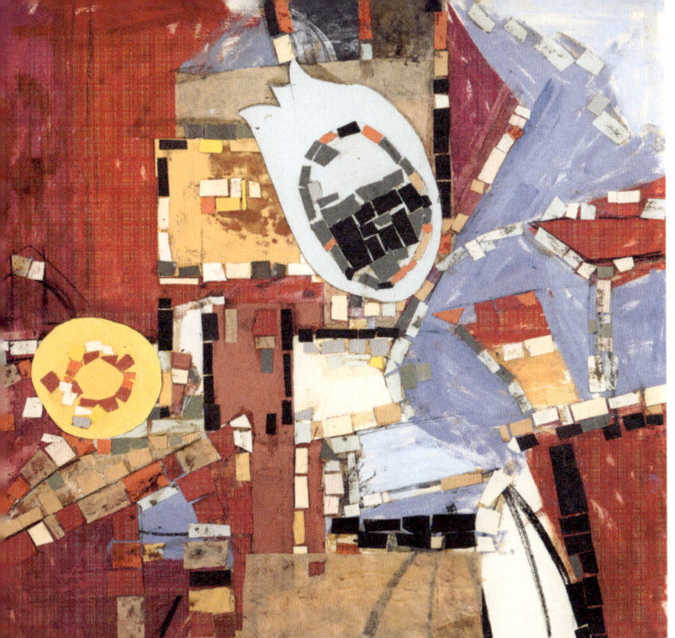

4   *Mosaic Collage, c.1942*

As Krasner told it, in one among so many similar versions of this story:

> It started in 1953 – I had the studio hung solidly with drawings, you know, floor to ceiling all around. Walked in one day, hated it all, took it down, tore everything and threw it on the floor, and when I went back – it was a couple weeks before I opened that door again – it was seemingly a very destructive act. I don't know why I did it, except I certainly did it. When I opened the door and walked in, the floor was solidly covered with these torn drawings that I had left and they began to interest me and I started collaging. Well, it started with drawings. Then I took my canvases and cut and began doing the same thing, and that ended in my collage show [at the Stable Gallery] in 1955.[12]

These collages included fibrous paper and cloth, unravelling at the ragged edges, attached to painted, pressed-wood supports or stretched textiles (linen or cotton duck) – the latter salvaged from Krasner's Betty Parsons show, which for all intents and purposes was a commercial failure that would prove her last outing at Parsons' gallery. These 1950s collages grow progressively large in both scale and ambition (this despite the fact that Krasner was working in the small barn that she and Pollock had converted into a studio, while Pollock occupied the large barn, suggesting that the Little Images

were comparatively diminutive not just because of the cramped bedroom where they were made).[13]

Barbara Rose explains that Krasner would 'step back and evaluate the overall effect of a collage painting while the material was still pinned to the surface, modifying the work over a period of time as it stood on the easel or against the wall. Once satisfied, she would put down the canvas on a table and glue the pieces down. She might then add color with a brush to further unify the elements and imbed the pieces between the brushed surface and the support in a process resembling lamination.'[14] *Desert Moon* (1955), like *Milkweed*, *Blue Level* and *Stretched Yellow* of the same year, is finally exultant, the result of carefully arranged snippets of painting cut into shapes that are also physical seams – lines with volume. It is exemplary in its paradoxical twinning of insistent biomorphism and pronounced verticality, and its perfectly lurid palette: tangerine and lavender, flecked with red paper almost clean enough for Piet Mondrian, and sections of perfect pitch black. The flat, overlapping forms in *Desert Moon* interpenetrate, freely evoking a range of interlocutors from the Italian Futurists to Willem de Kooning.

Shortly after Pollock's death, Krasner would go outside to his studio and rotate panels in a horizontal orientation. And she would spread out her opus-like mural, *The Seasons* (1957), asserting the passage of time that is,

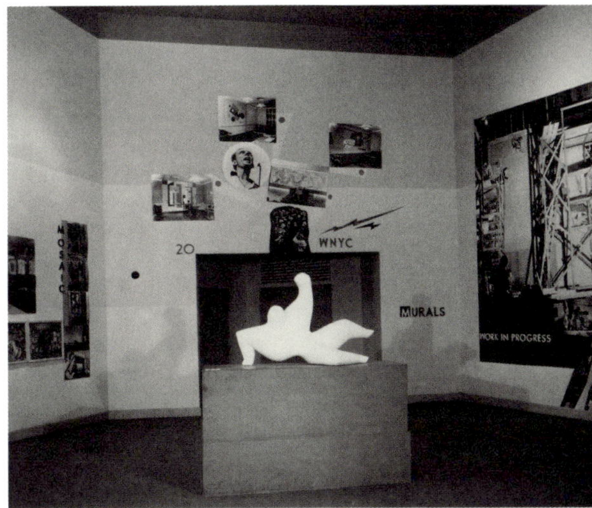

5   Installation view of WPA photomural projects at the 1939 New York World's Fair.

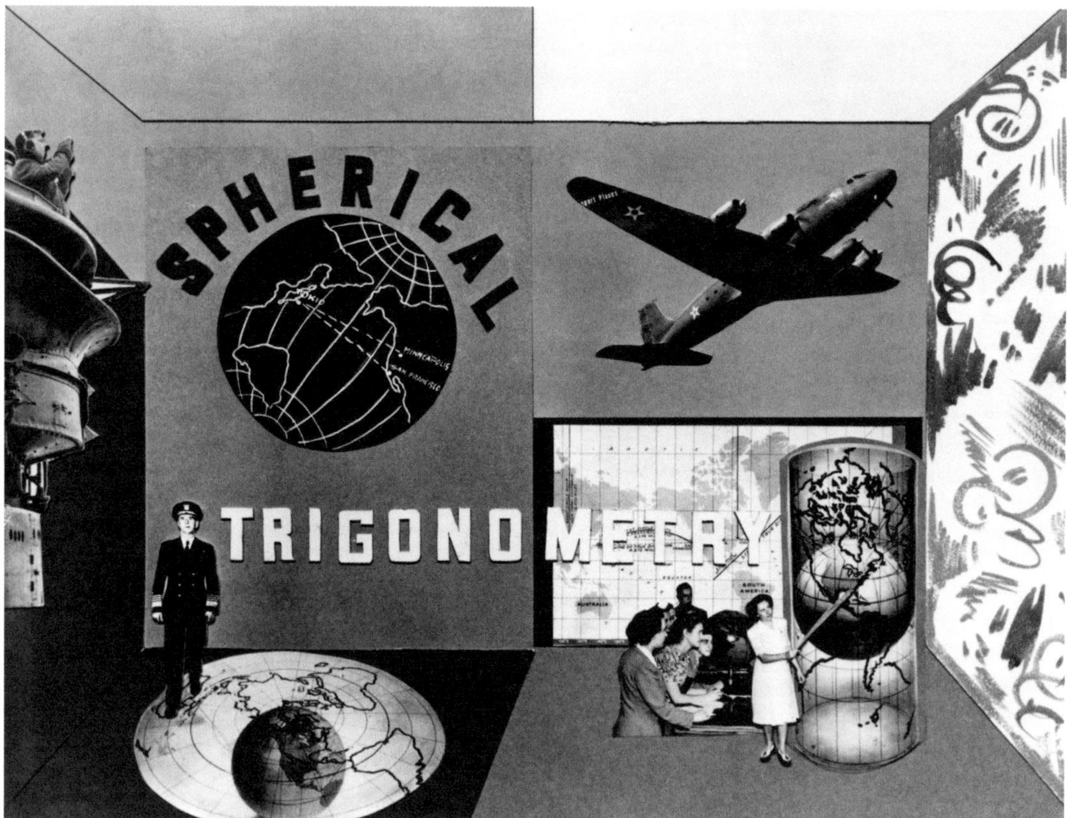

6   Design for War Service Window Display, 1942

too, a taking up of space in which to consider it. In 1975, in an interview with Cindy Nemser in the *Feminist Art Journal*, when asked why she did not 'fight to have her achievement … acknowledged along with Pollock's', she answered: 'I couldn't run out and do a one-woman job on the sexist aspects of the art world, continue my painting and stay in the role I was in as Mrs. Pollock … What I considered important was that I was able to work and other things would take their turn. Now rightly or wrongly, I made my decisions.'[15]

This emphasis on making decisions by making work found a profound outlet the following year, when Krasner took up collage by returning to a number of the charcoal life drawings that she had produced under Hofmann's tutelage, and which she had found when rummaging through her storage racks with Bryan Robertson. Rather than having become too precious to alter, the drawings compelled her to act on them; she recognized that these compositions harboured still other possibilities when incorporated whole or disposed on bare canvas as fragments. She titled the first one *Imperative* (1976; fig. 8), by which she meant that she 'experienced the need not just to examine these drawings but a peremptory desire to change them; a command, as it were, to make them new'.[16] Robert Hobbs adds that 'in 1975 the art critic Gene Baro organized the circulating exhibition *Lee Krasner: Collages and Works on Paper, 1933–1974*. That same year Marlborough Prints and Drawings Gallery featured a solo exhibition of her early modernist pieces entitled *Works on Paper: 1937–1939*. During the preparations for both exhibitions, Krasner had ample opportunity to reexamine her early works, to study her collages, and to see potential relationships between the two.'[17] The chasm of nearly half a century provided the distance for Krasner to objectify her work fully. Where Barbara Rose would describe this as her signal accomplishment, Hilton Kramer cast it darkly as 'a cold-blooded act of self-criticism that is also a bizarre form of artistic self-cannibalization' (fig. 7).[18]

The action of collaging past bits – used paper, as it were, covered with work – is portrayed by Kramer as something like an appetite, a consumption of the found, appropriated object that is also a production of what will yet become another. Paul Brach put it in differently sanguine language in 2001: 'These painting-collages are perfect examples of the theory that artists in their youth feed on the history of art, later on their own ideas and feelings and, in the end, on their own work.'[19] One might extend Brach's implication and specify the Ouroboros eating its own tail, which Carl Jung understood as archetypal, its ring-like picturing of an endless cycle of birth and death. Taken as another kind of self-portrait, the collages conjure a ceaseless and necessarily unfinished process that is also – and no doubt this would have appealed to Krasner – symbolic of immortality, if not actually an instantiation of its achievement.

Krasner's 1976 collages are especially acute in this regard. Like *Imperative*, *Past Continuous*, *Present Conditional* and *Future Indicative* all shunt fantasies of integration – its realization tenuous, possibly in the end for the good. Krasner exhibited the collages in 1977 at Pace Gallery, New York, calling the group 'Eleven Ways to Use the Words to See', and keeping a list of the meanings for each form of the verb. When asked a question about not knowing what would happen when she carved up her work, she replied: 'How could I help thinking it might be a mistake to slice them up? Why destroy perfectly good drawings? But the next title gives you a clue. I make the decision to go ahead.

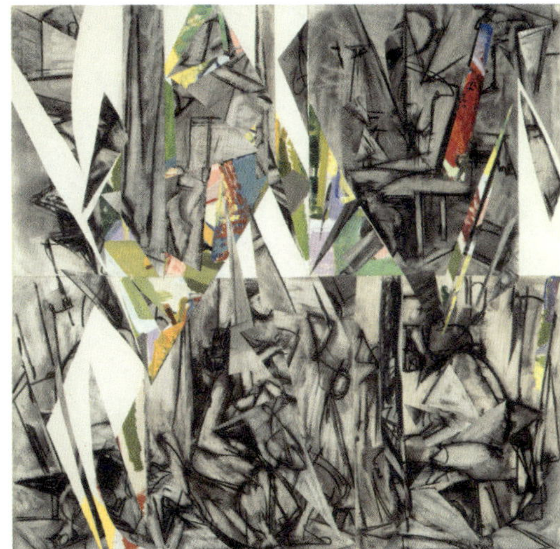

8 *Imperative*, 1976

Present Conditional, a big one, 72 by 108 inches, with lots of white, near-white, blurred over layers of white, is a signal that the action has occurred, but it is still conditional. *Imperfect Indicative* is replete with the past; you can see quite clearly much of how I worked in the early days, as it really looked then.'[20]

In remarks relating to *Present Conditional*, Krasner gave the verb form for the title as 'I would be seeing'. Are these visions of the past or the future, of how things might have transpired or still might? A modal verb, *would* – like *could* – behaves irregularly in English usage. While discussing a hypothetical scenario in the present tense (after such phrases as *what if*, *in case* and *suppose*, to talk about the future if it is thought likely to happen), the verb remains in the present, yet it switches to a past tense when talking about an unlikely future scenario. Modals – *would* and *could* – are used for imagined futures (with the past in a subordinate clause, e.g. 'I would give her money if she really needed it') and impossible pasts (e.g. 'I would have told you the answer if you had asked'). Krasner's twinning of these temporalities, what could have been and what might still come, was her way of asserting that she was still there.

Suzanne Hudson

7 Lee Krasner cutting up some of her old Hofmann School drawings to incorporate into one of the collages for the 'Eleven Ways to Use the Words to See' series, 1976. Photograph by Ray Eames.

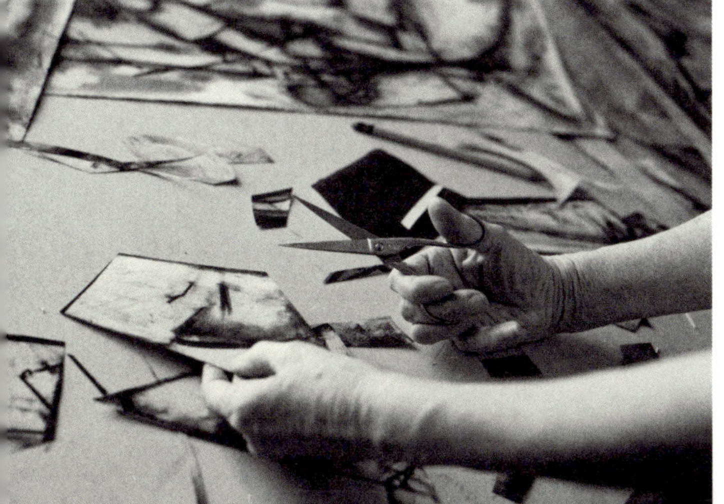

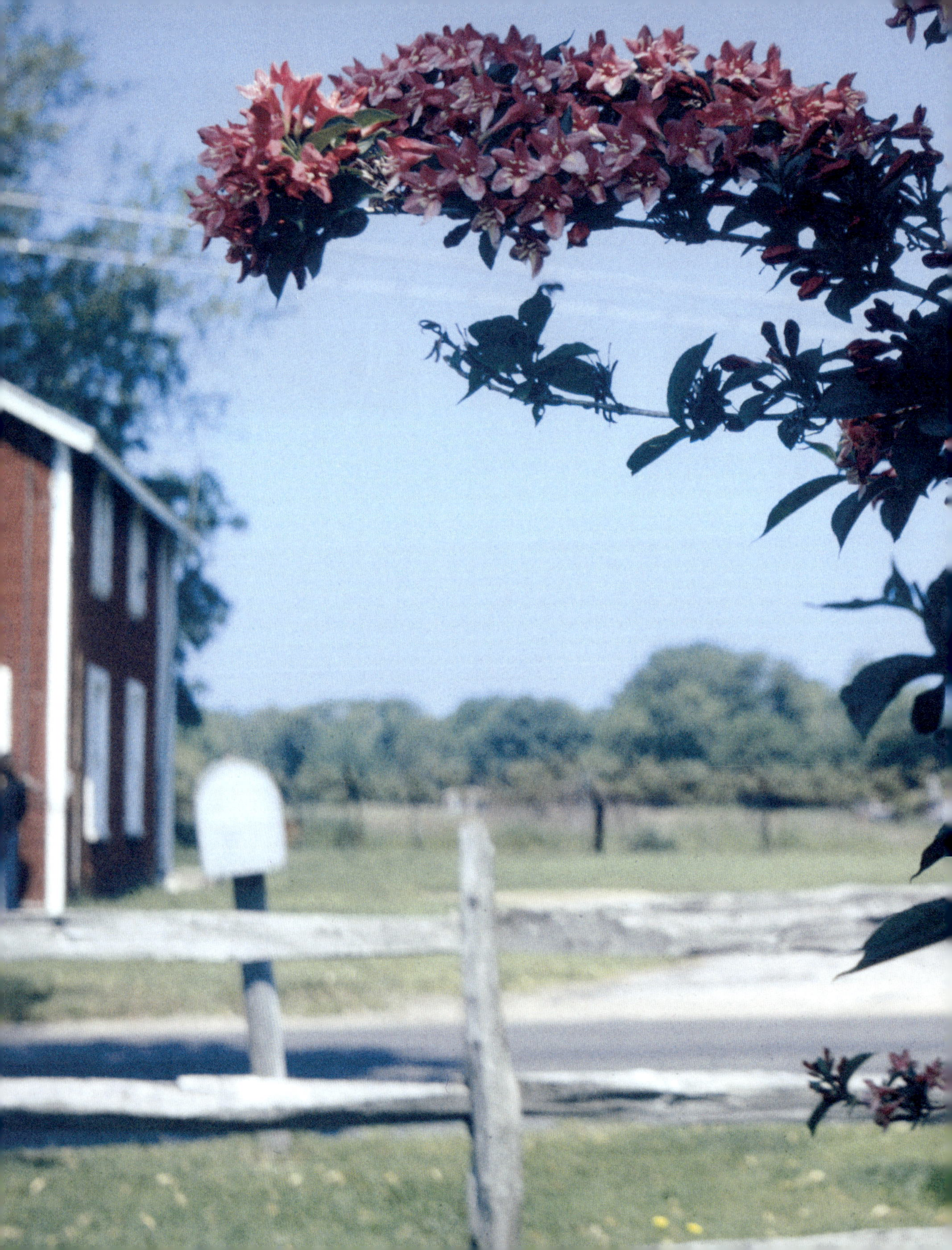

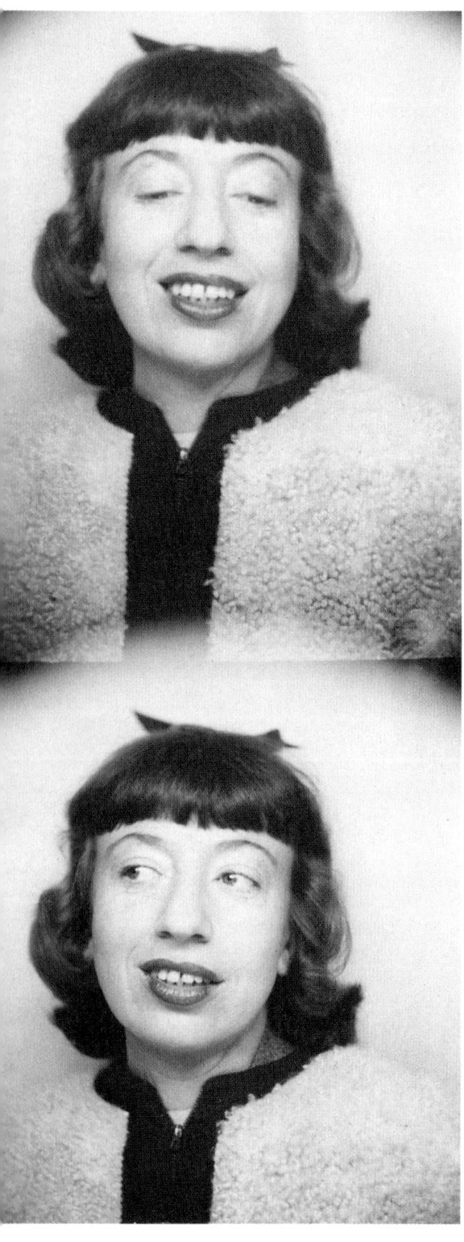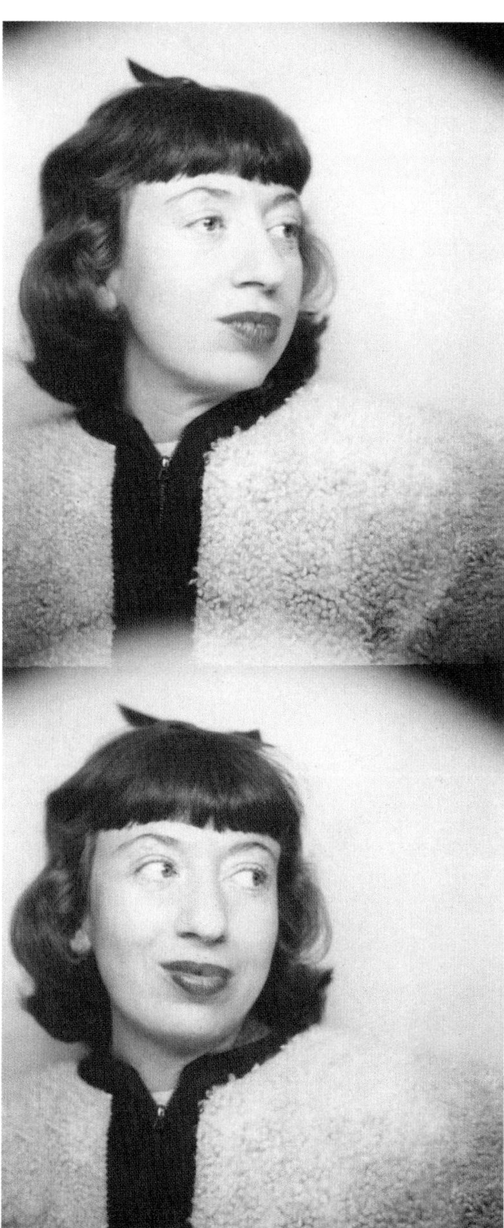

Lee Krasner, *c.*1938–40

BECOMING LEE

In the summer of 1928, Lee Krasner began work on an ambitious self-portrait. Now nineteen years old, she had graduated from the Women's Art School at Cooper Union, and (following a brief spell at the Art Students League) was due in the autumn to begin studying at the prestigious National Academy of Design in Manhattan, where she hoped her self-portrait in oil would gain her promotion to the life-drawing class. For now, the trees were still in leaf in the garden of her parents' home in Greenlawn, Long Island; she nailed a mirror to a tree and set about capturing herself against this woodland backdrop.

Wearing an artist's apron and clutching a rag and brushes in her hand, she is the poster image for a young painter at work, whose forceful gaze suggests the strength of her intent. During interviews, Krasner loved to recount how the National Academy had refused to believe that she had actually painted her self-portrait *en plein air*: they 'took one look at my painting and said, "That's a dirty trick you played – don't ever pretend that you painted outdoors"'.[1] Krasner protested and was reluctantly promoted, but she continued to struggle with the traditionalism of the Academy, which she would later condemn as a 'completely sterile atmosphere of permanently congealed mediocrity'.[2]

The small number of early self-portraits that Krasner made around this time offer a rare insight into the ways in which she was shaping her artistic identity. She was the first child in her Orthodox Jewish, Russian émigré family to be born in the United States, and as a teenager she had changed her birth name 'Lena' first to 'Lenore' and then to the more androgynous 'Lee'. American women had gained the right to vote in 1920, and a spirit of emancipation was in the air, which is felt in the defiance of Krasner's expression in each of these works. A fire at her parents' home destroyed most of her student work, making the few self-portraits that survive particularly precious.

Self-Portrait, 1929–30

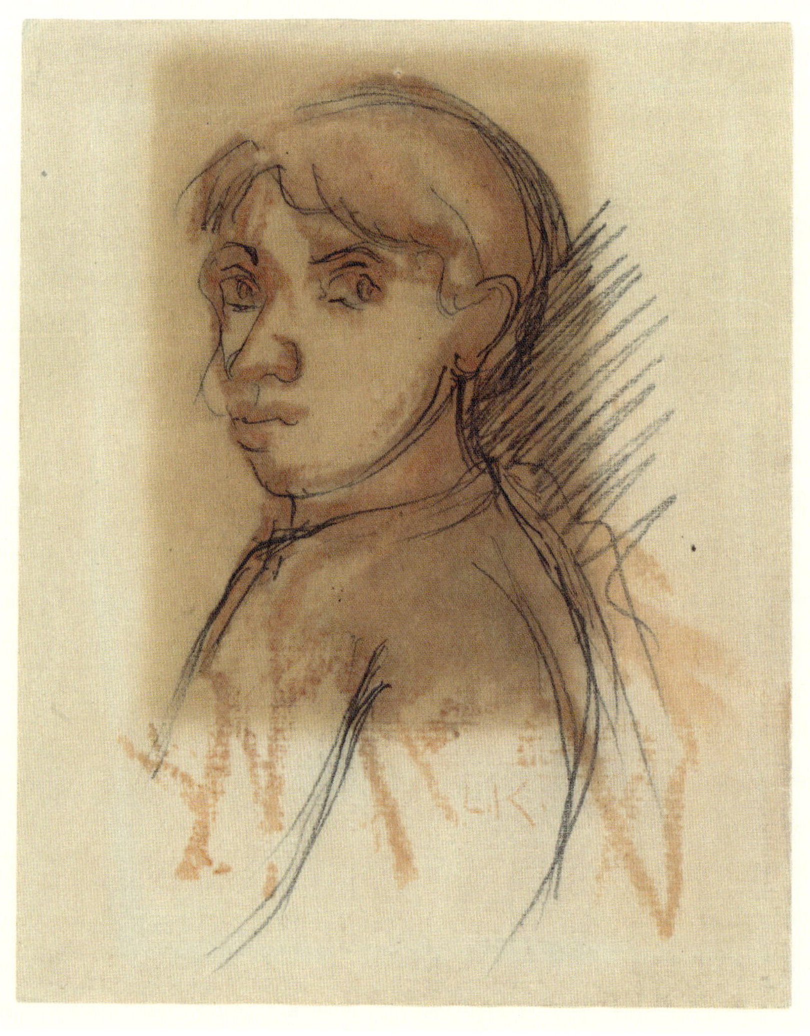

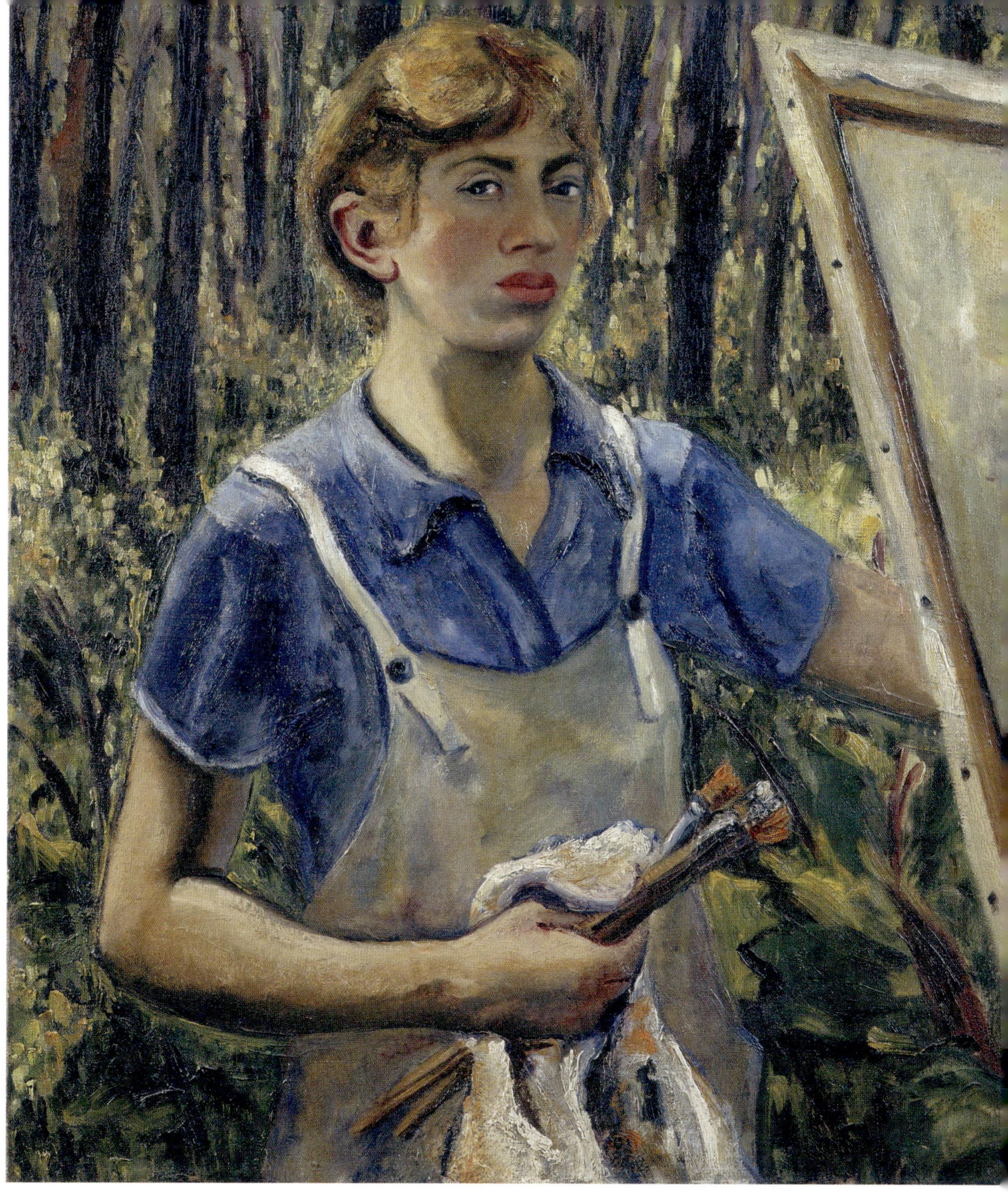

Self-Portrait, c.1928

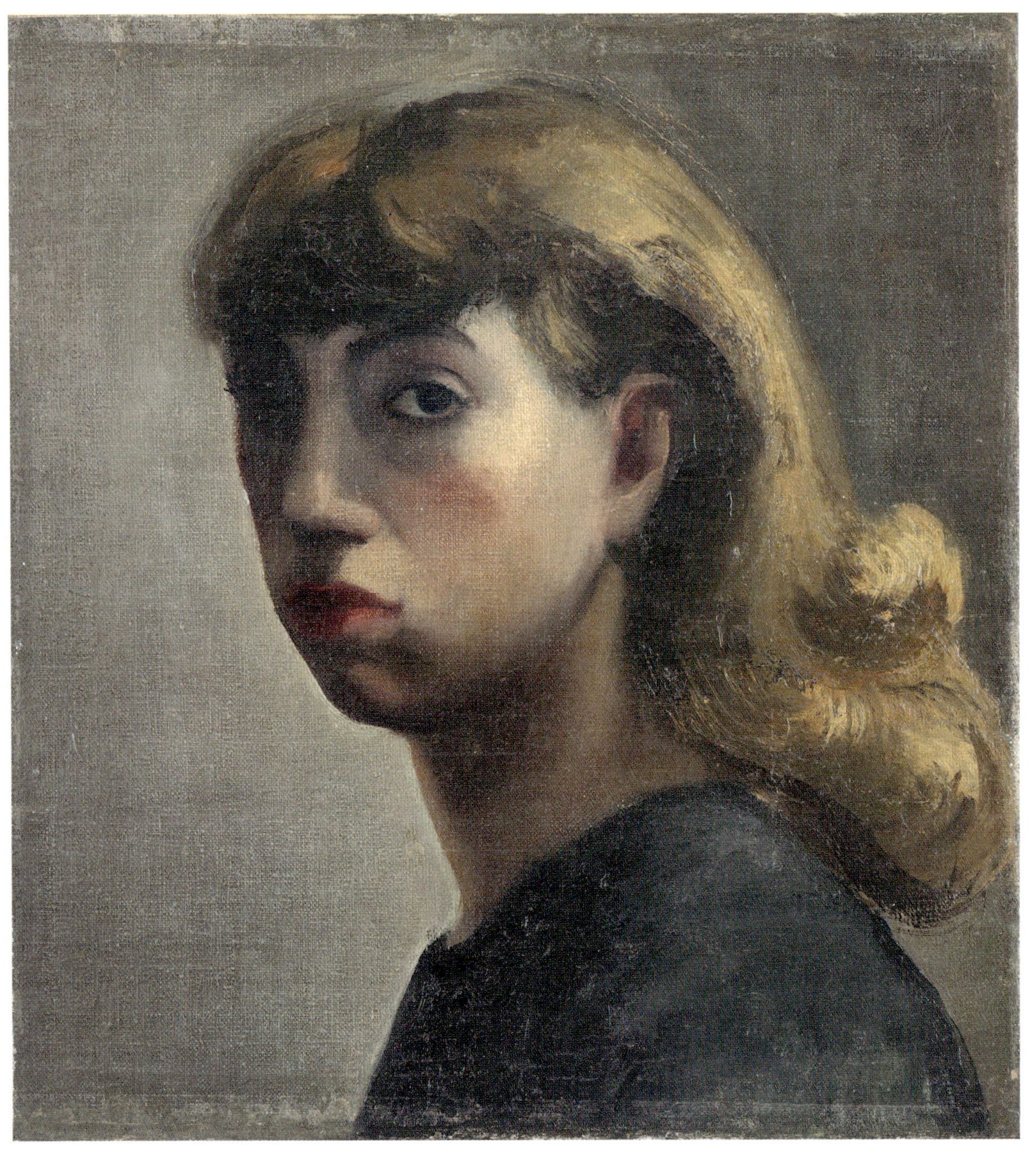

Self-Portrait, c. 1931–33

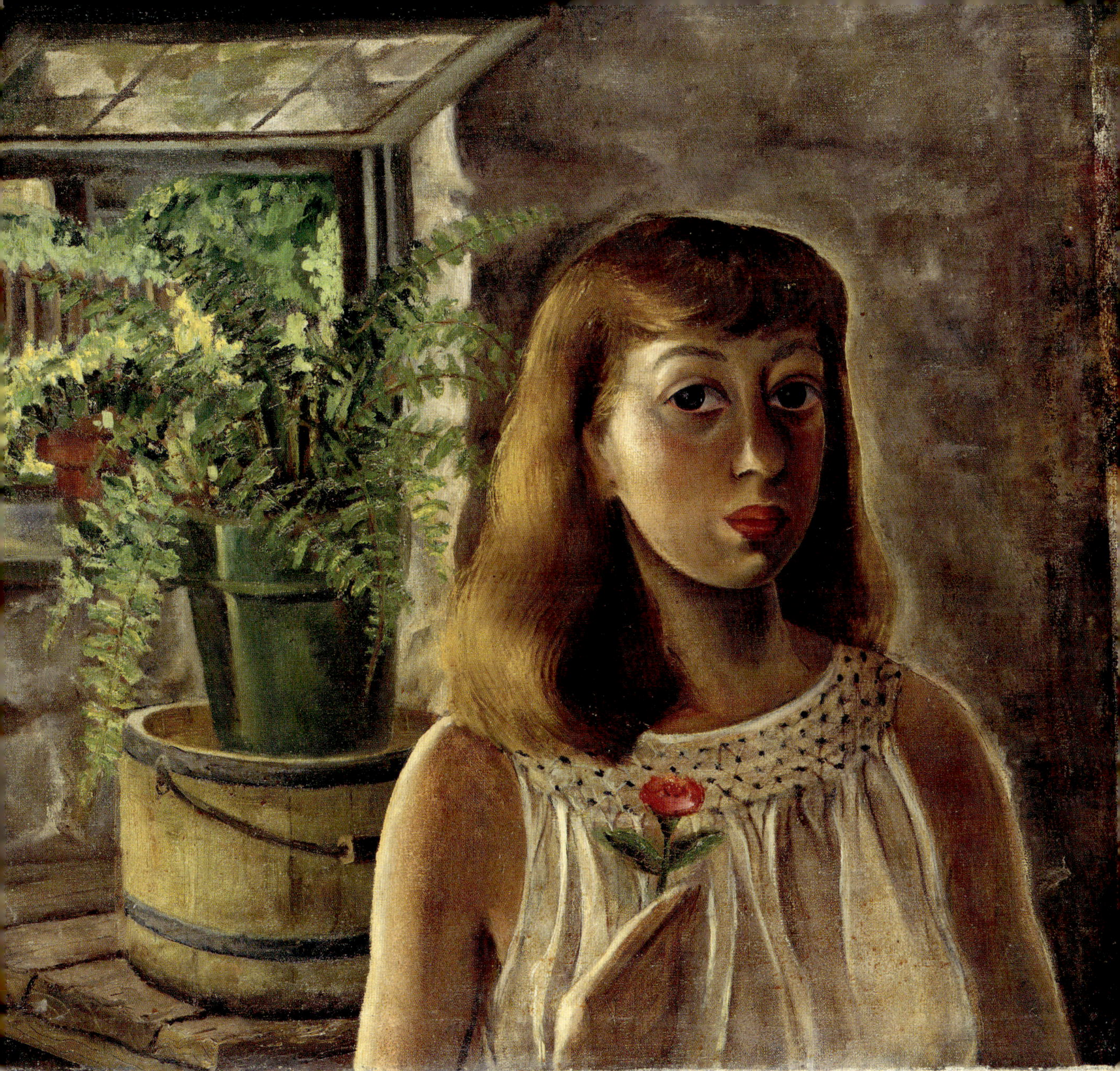

Self-Portrait, c.1929

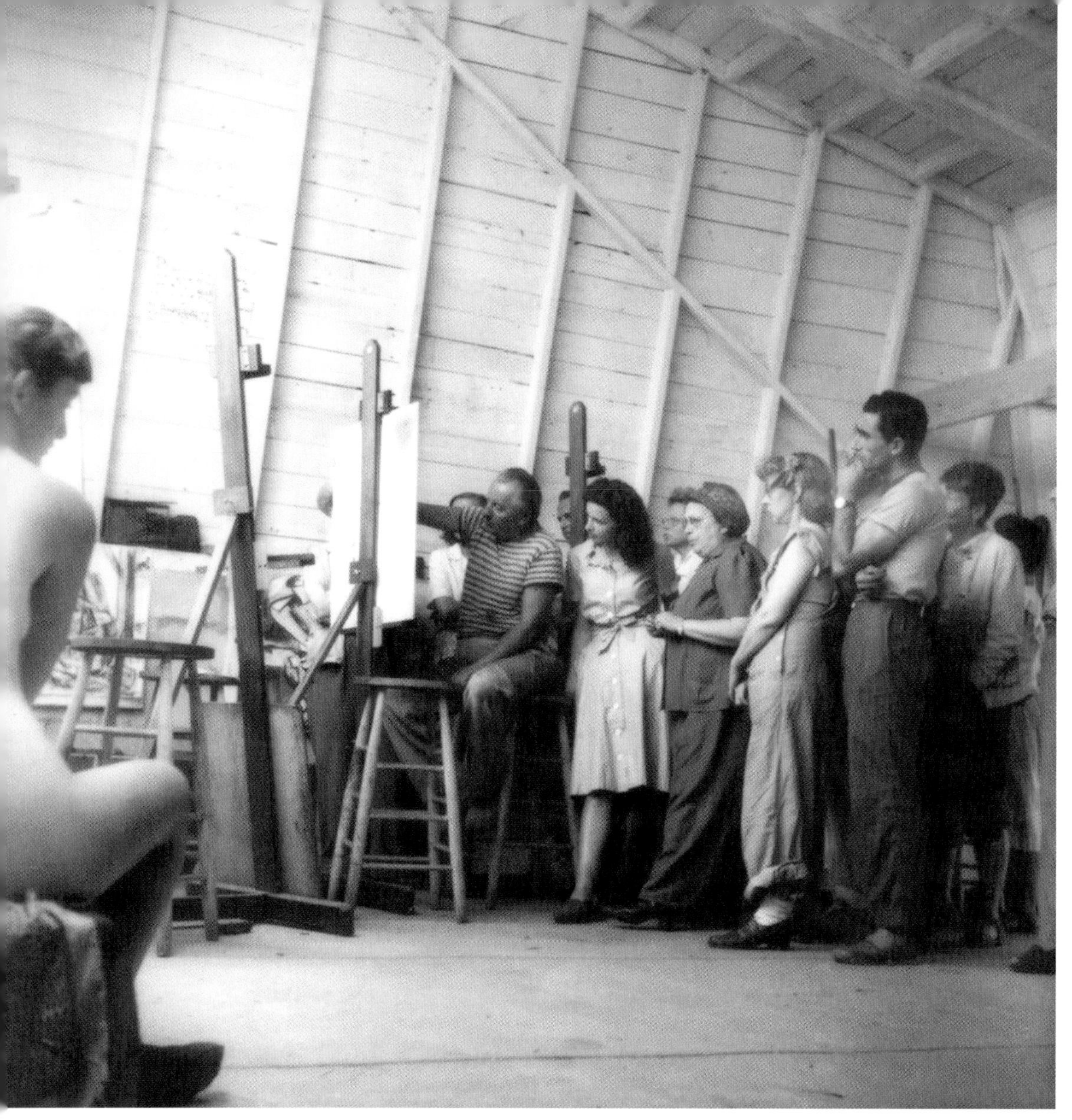

Hans Hofmann teaching a life-drawing class, 1945.
Photograph by Maurice Berezov.

LIFE DRAWING

'TO MOVE FROM THE
ACADEMY INTO CUBISM
WAS A VIOLENT SITUATION'

In 1932 the American economy was in crisis. Three years earlier the Wall Street Crash had triggered the Great Depression, leading to widespread unemployment. The worsening economic climate forced Krasner to leave the National Academy of Design and enrol on a teacher's course at the City College of New York, where tuition was free. Working as a waitress at Sam Johnson's, a Greenwich Village nightclub and café, Krasner was able to support herself financially and become familiar with local artists and intellectuals, including the writer Harold Rosenberg.

While studying for her teaching certificate, Krasner began taking life-drawing classes at Greenwich House – a community centre in Manhattan – with the painter Job Goodman, a Russian-born Jewish émigré. Goodman was a former student of the Regionalist artist Thomas Hart Benton (who would later become a mentor to Jackson Pollock), and his classes advocated a classical method of drawing from life, taking inspiration from such Renaissance masters as Michelangelo. Working mainly in oil or Conté crayon on paper, Krasner produced drawings that achieved a keen anatomical likeness while emphasizing muscularity through tonal shading.

In 1937 Krasner was awarded a scholarship to attend classes at the Hans Hofmann School of Fine Arts at 52 West Ninth Street.[1] Hofmann was a German modernist who had lived and worked in Paris alongside Picasso and Matisse – two of Krasner's self-proclaimed 'gods'.[2] A dynamic teacher, Hofmann was prone to very involved criticism, often drawing corrections directly on to a student's work. Hofmann taught a version of analytical Cubism and was primarily concerned with the tension between flatness and three-dimensionality, which he called the 'push-pull' of a work.[3] His approach to the nude was a radical departure from Krasner's previous training: instead of focusing on parts of the body, Hofmann would arrange objects around the model, setting up dramatic lighting to emphasize the relationship of the figure to space. Krasner admired Hofmann for his 'terrific enthusiasm for painting', while he later described her as one of his finest students.[4]

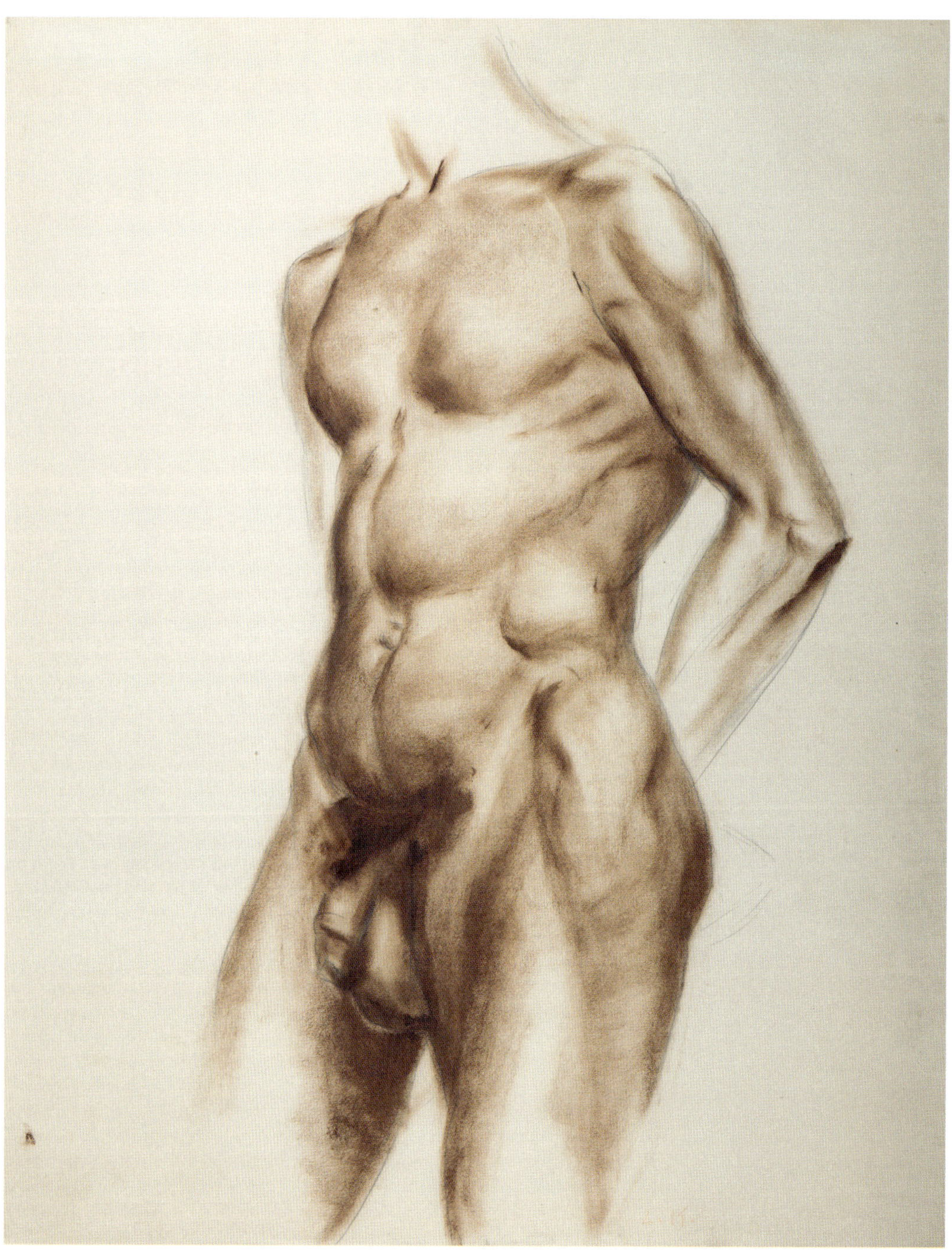

Study from the Nude, 1933

Study from the Nude, 1933

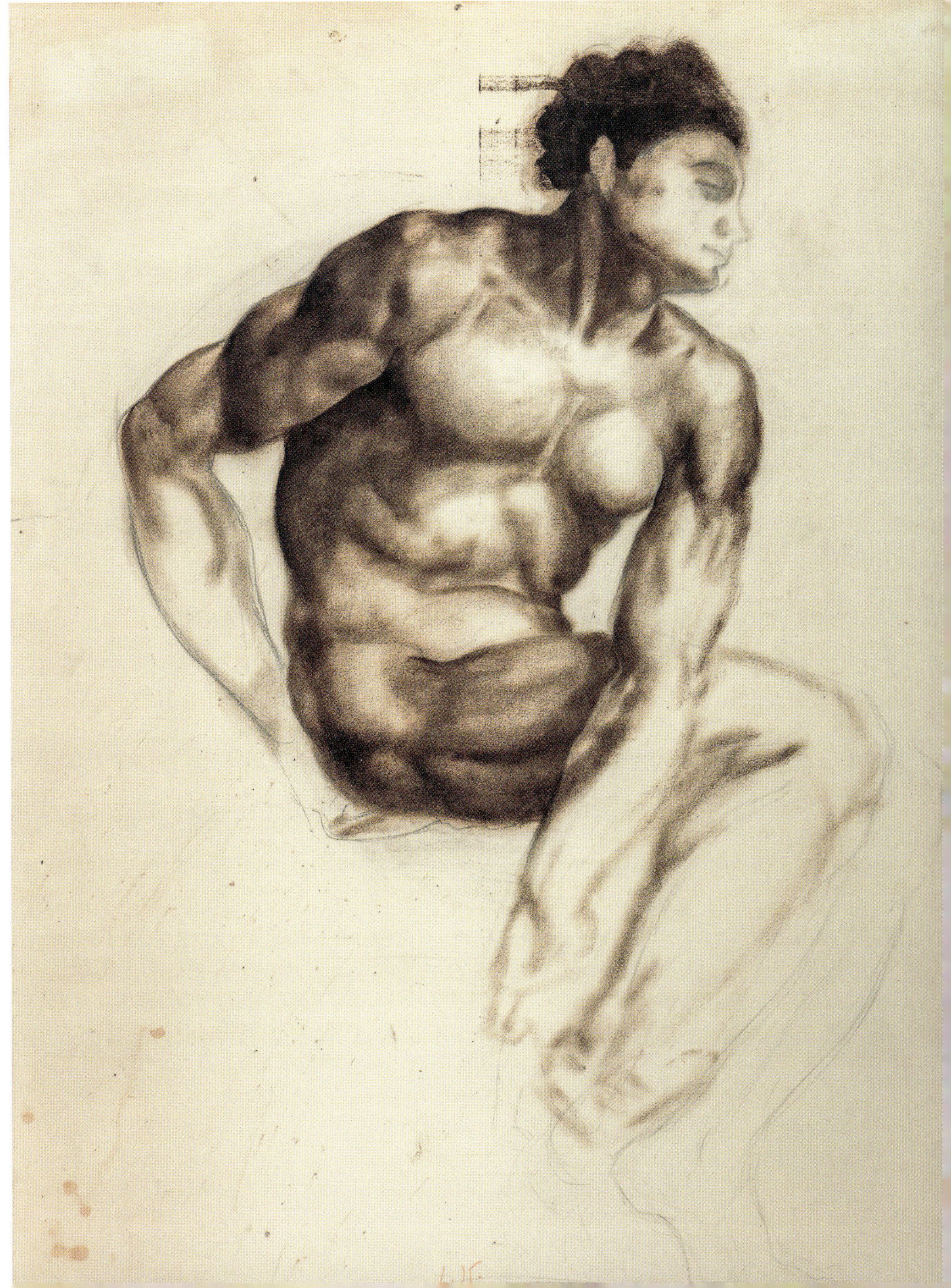

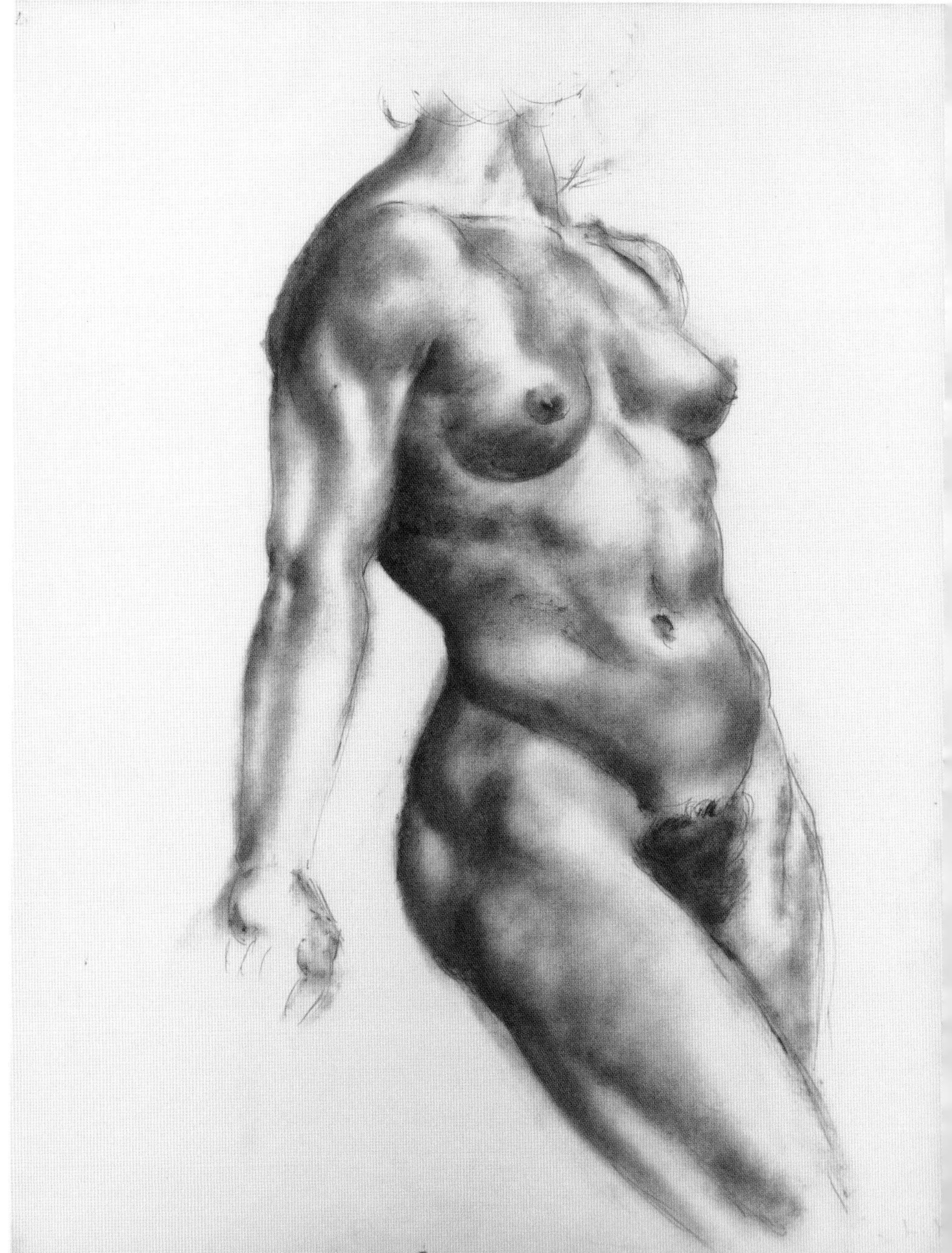

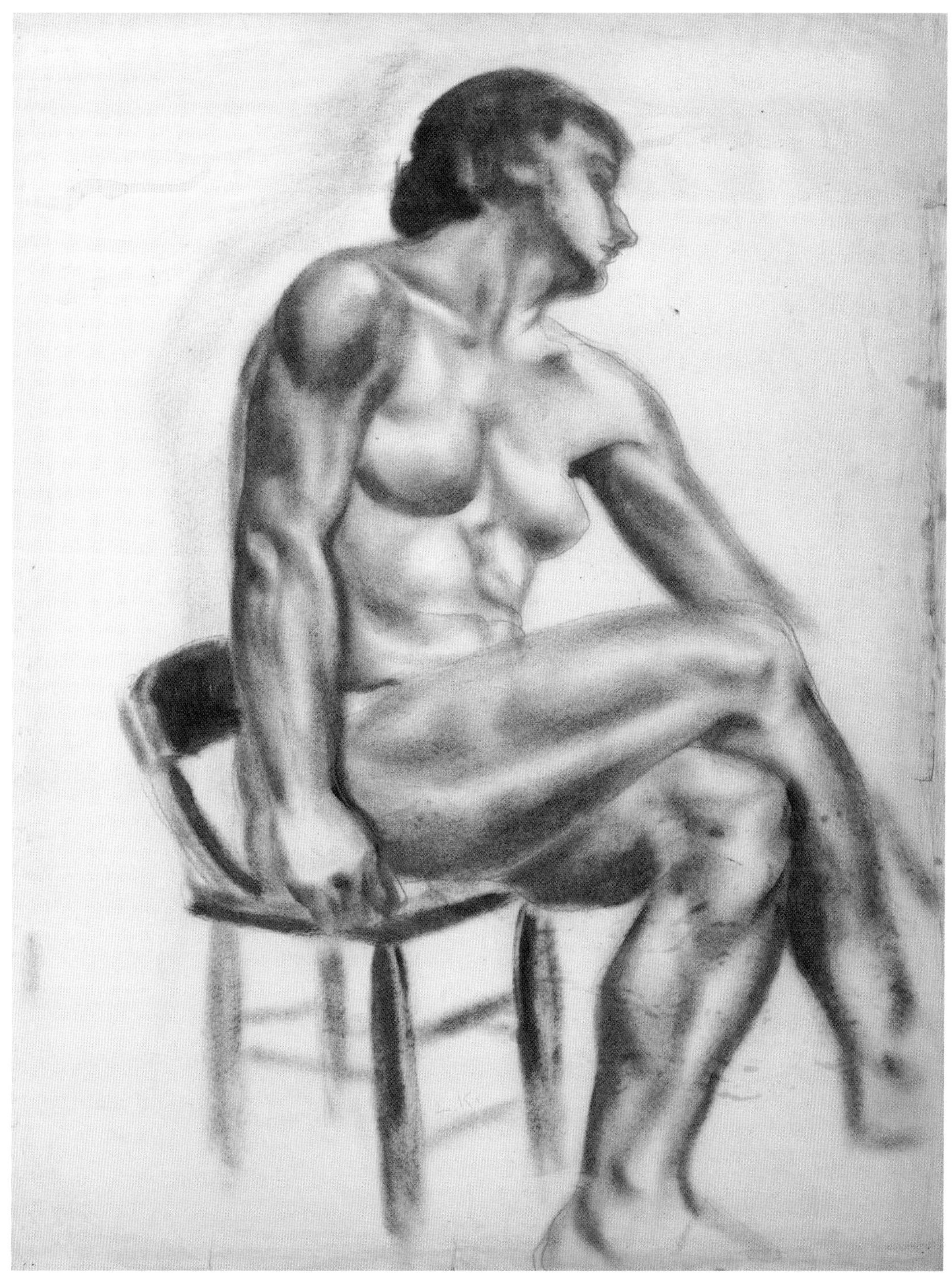

Study from the Nude, 1933

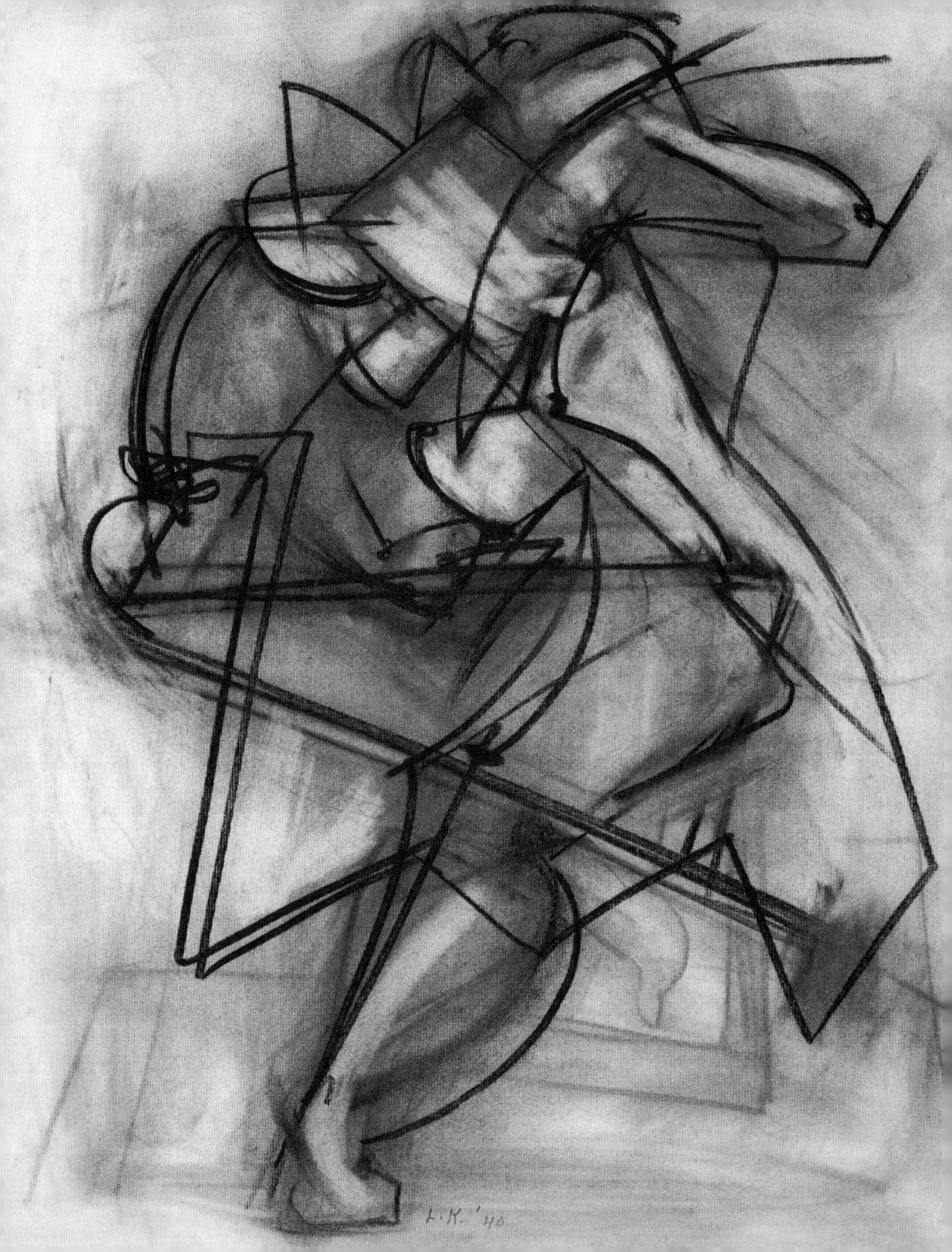
L. K. '40

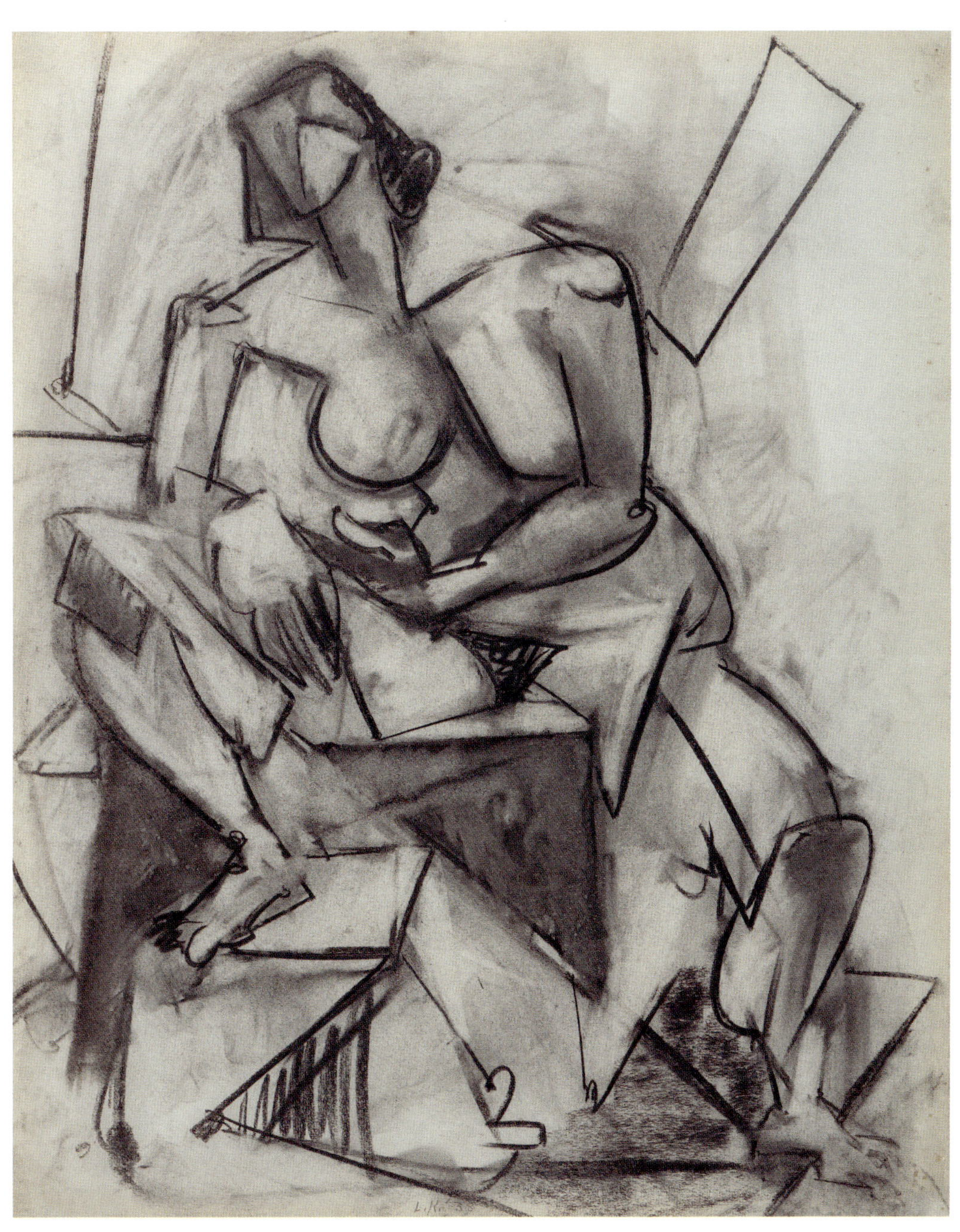

Above: *Nude Study from Life*, 1938
Opposite: *Untitled*, 1940

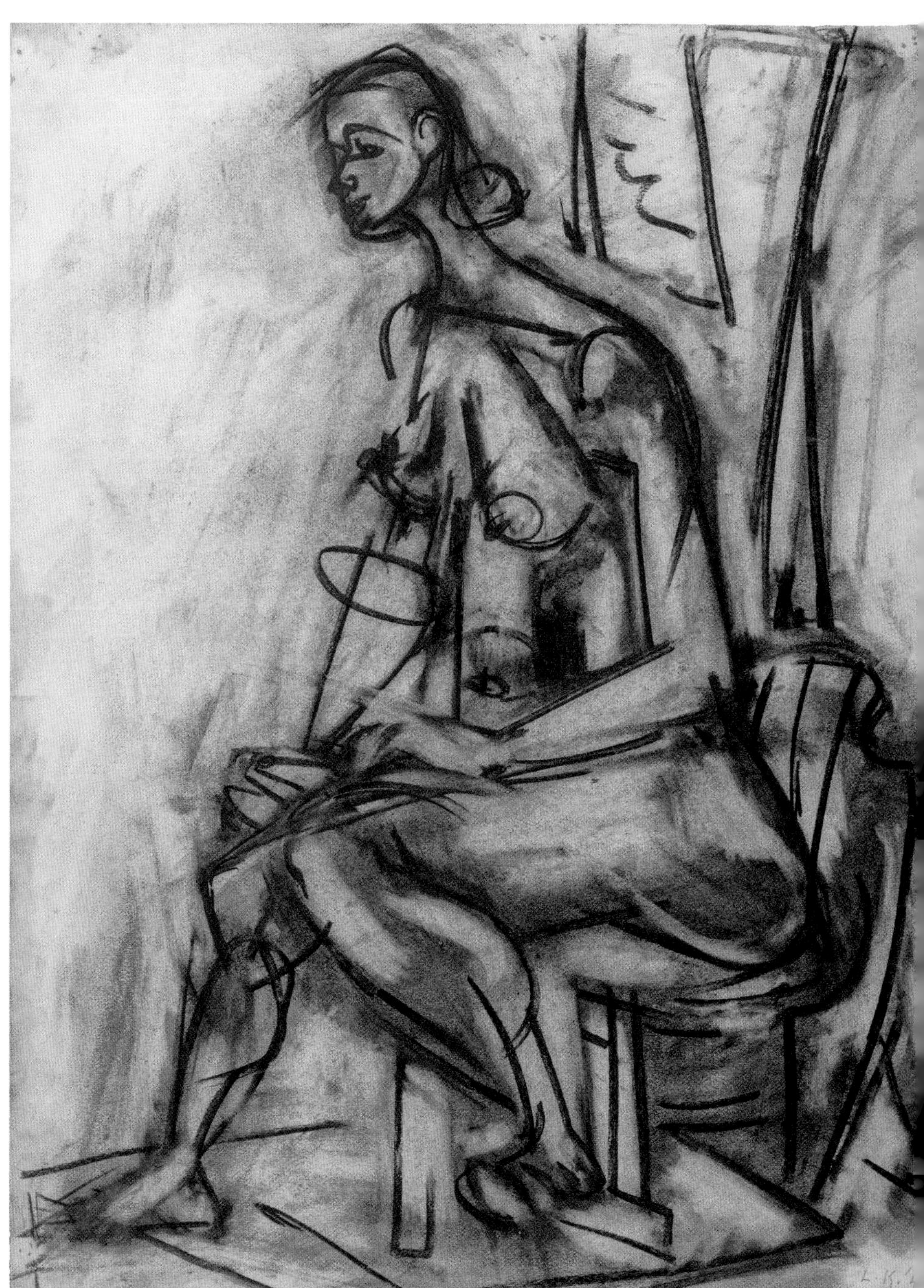

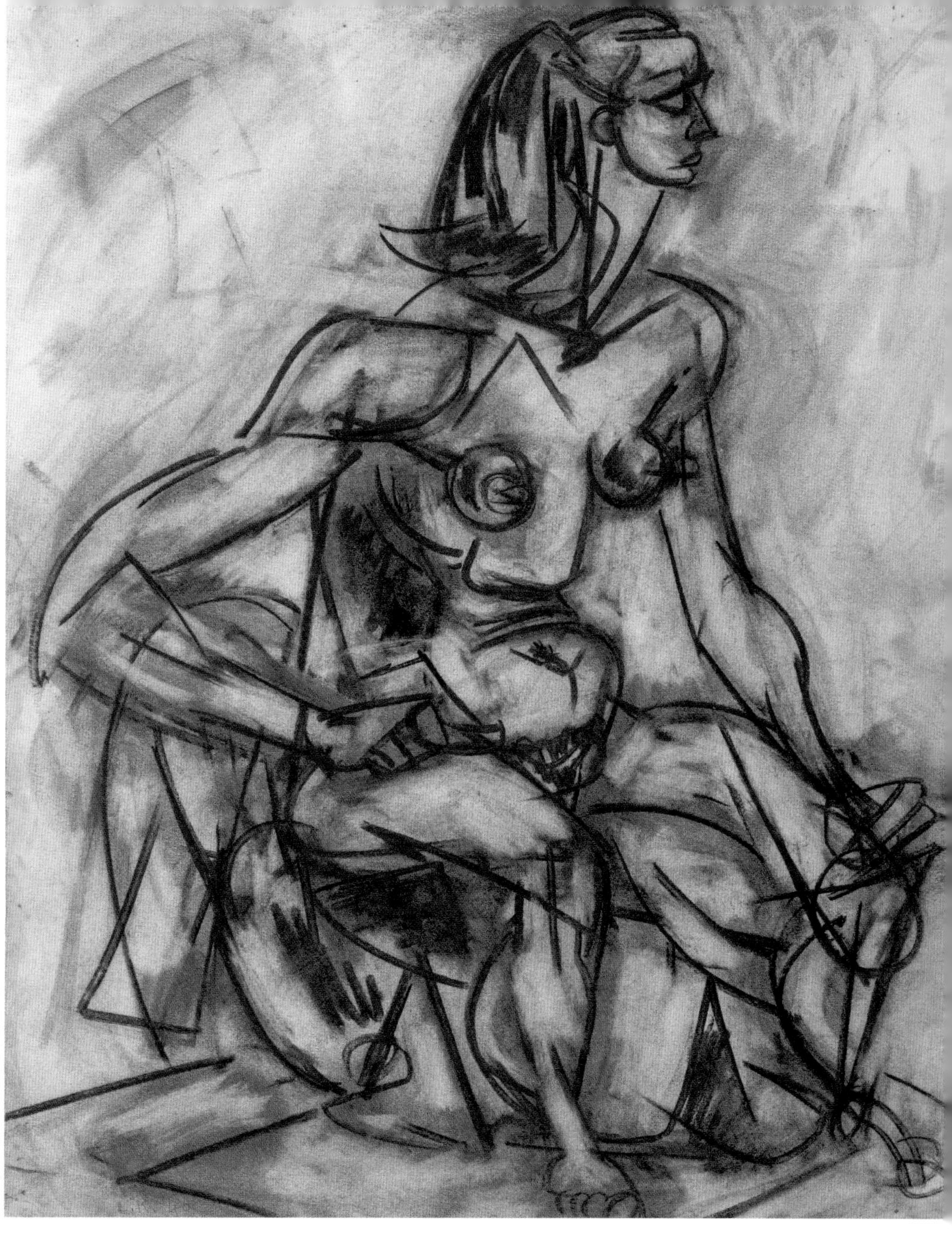

Nude Study from Life, 1940

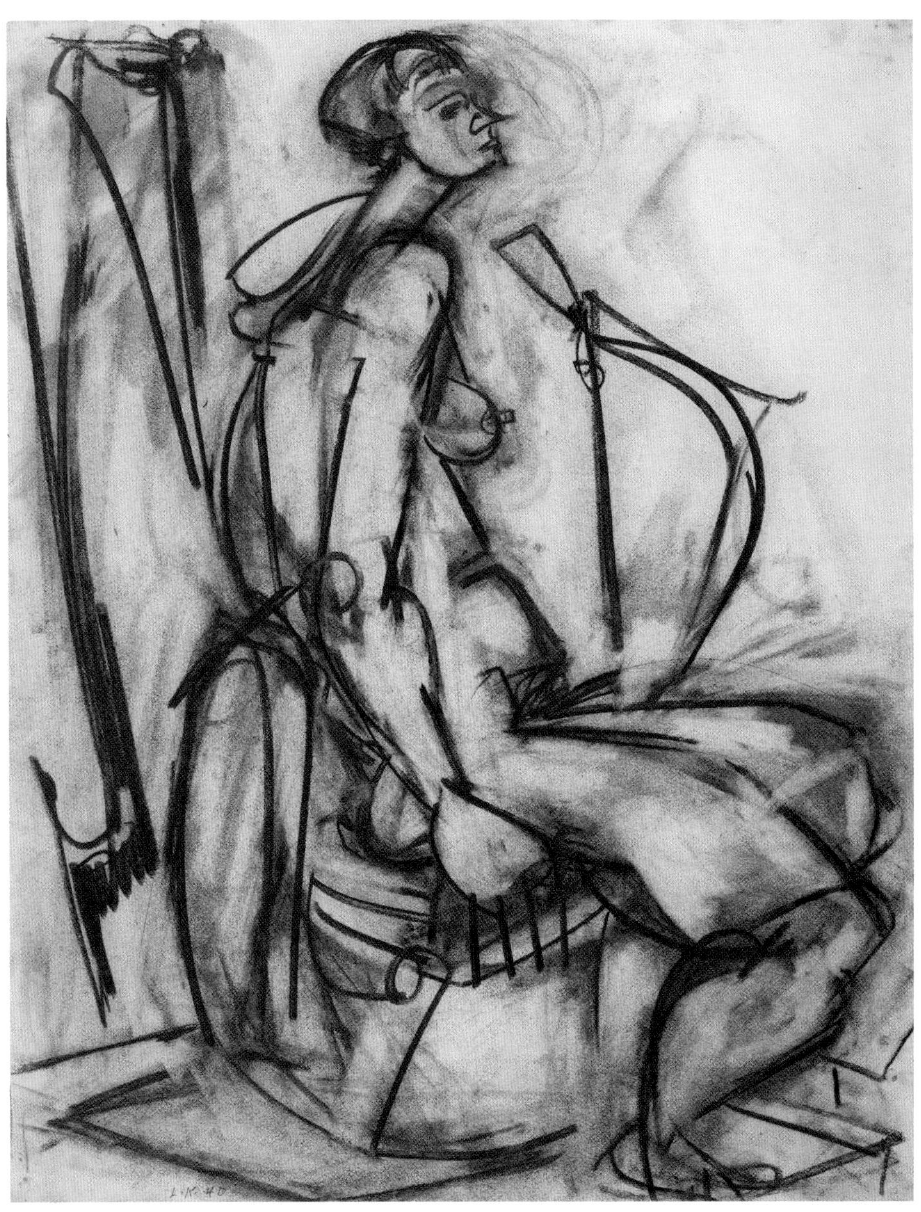

Above: *Nude Study from Life*, 1940
Opposite: *Nude Study from Life*, 1940

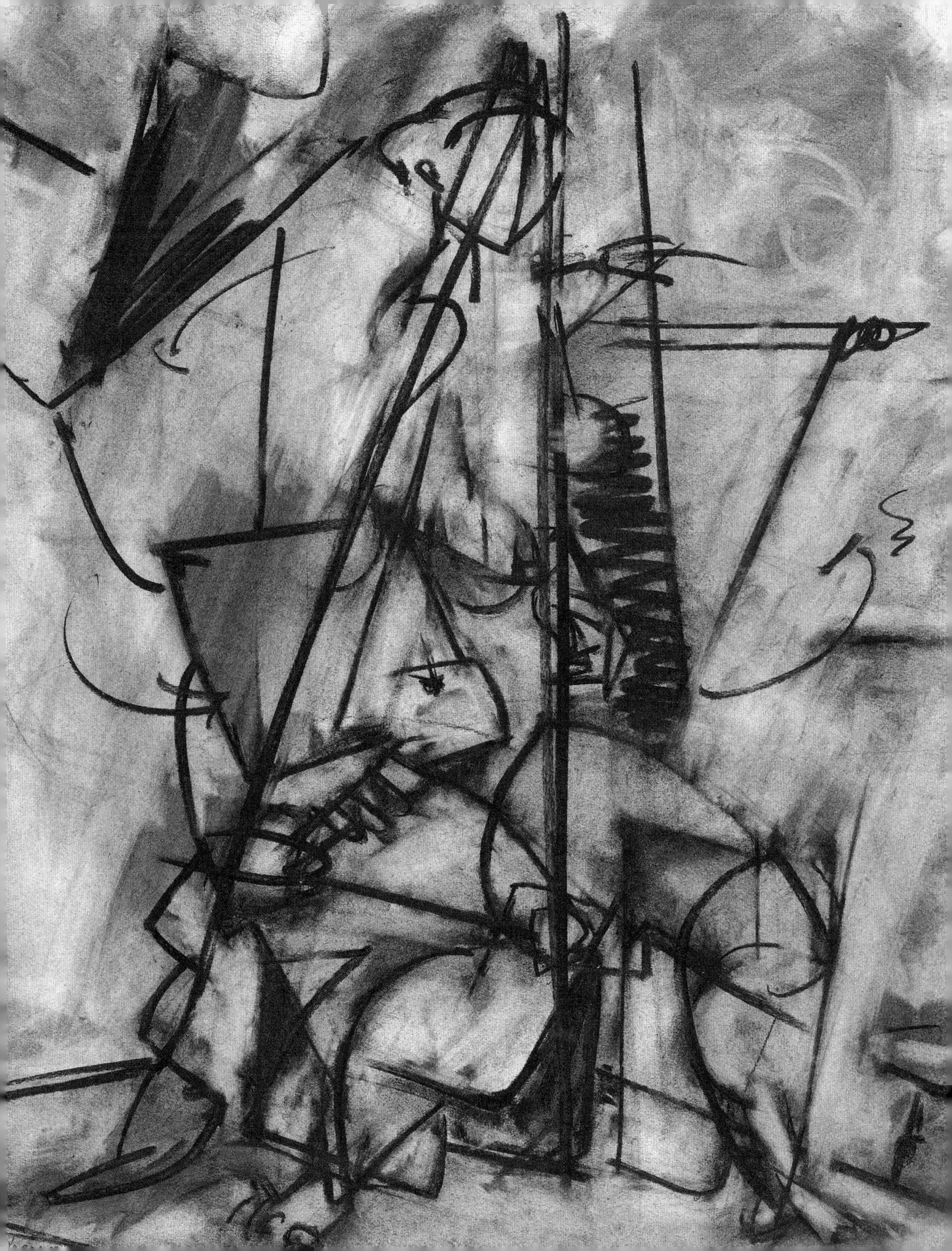

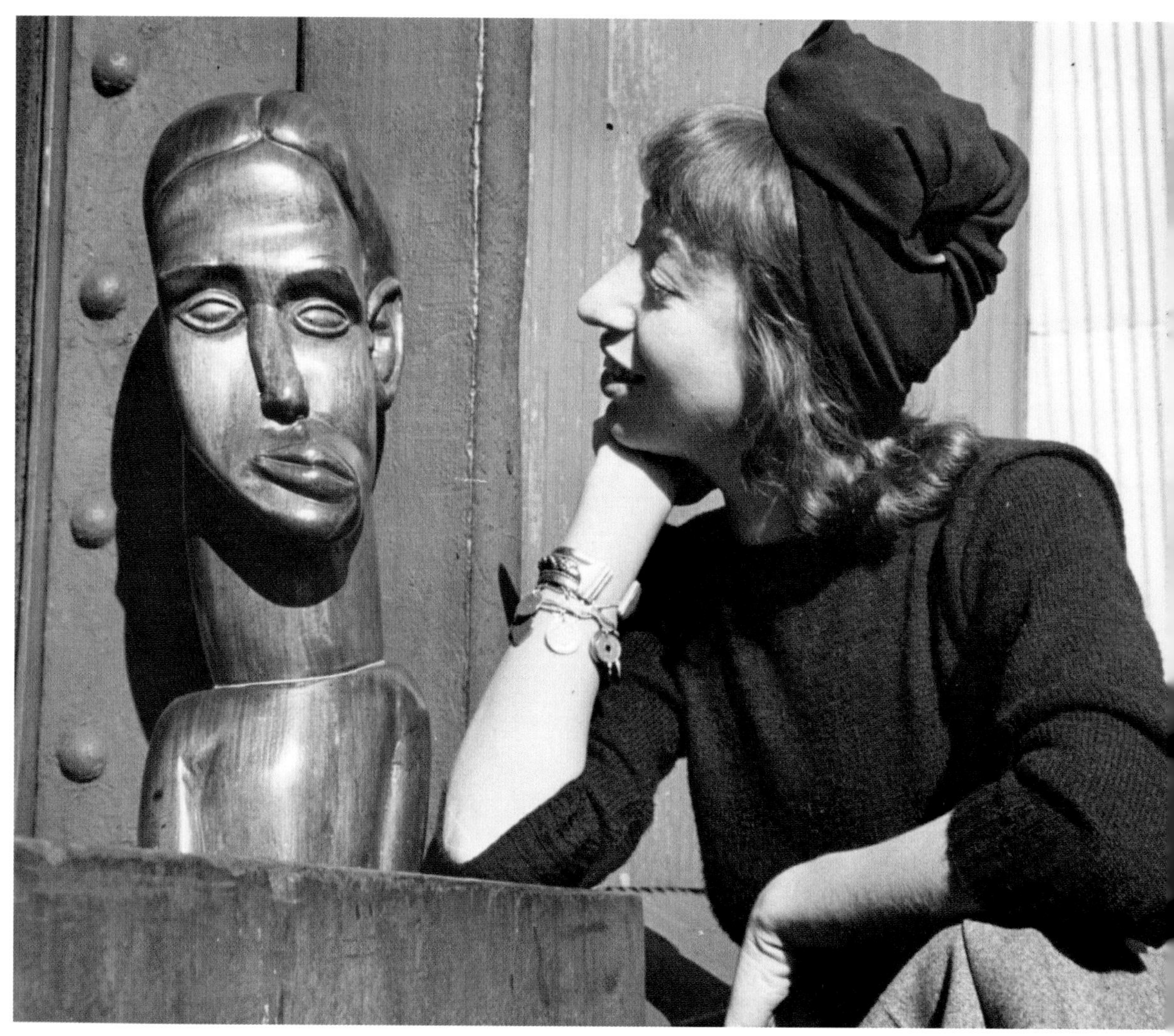

Lee Krasner at the WPA Pier, New York City,
where she was working on a WPA commission,
c.1940. Photograph by Fred Prater.

WAR SERVICE WINDOWS

'I WOULD SAY IT WAS A SMALL LITTLE BOHEMIAN WORLD'

On 6 March 1932 a group of artists affiliated with the Unemployed Councils protested in Union Square, New York, against the widespread hardship they were experiencing because of the Great Depression. Four months later, Franklin D. Roosevelt made a speech pledging his assistance to the suffering American population and launched the New Deal programme to counter widespread poverty. The Public Works of Art Project (PWAP) was born, a scheme that would employ more than 3,700 artists to decorate public buildings. Following on from the PWAP, Roosevelt's government created the Works Progress Administration (WPA), which included the Federal Art Project (FAP).

Krasner, who had recently exhibited work in several important exhibitions and was widely respected by her peers, was approached in 1942 to supervise a new commission for the War Services Project (the final iteration of the WPA), which was focused on the war effort.[1] The job was to oversee the design and execution of twenty department-store window displays in Manhattan and Brooklyn, advertising war training courses being made available to the public in colleges.[2] Krasner accepted the commission, later recalling: 'I was given this group of artists – "misfits", they called them – to work with: [William] Baziotes, [Willem] De Kooning, [Jackson] Pollock among others.'[3]

After attending a number of the courses herself – including one on the chemistry of explosives, which she described as an 'alchemist's dream' – Krasner decided to use photography to document the courses and integrate the images into her designs. The resulting photomontages, which incorporate photography, drawing and typography in a Russian Constructivist vein, were described by the art historian Francis O'Connor as 'extremely advanced stylistically, in terms of techniques of montage and assemblage'.[4] Although the original designs no longer exist, a number of documentary photographs of the finished collages were made, offering us an insight into this lost body of work.

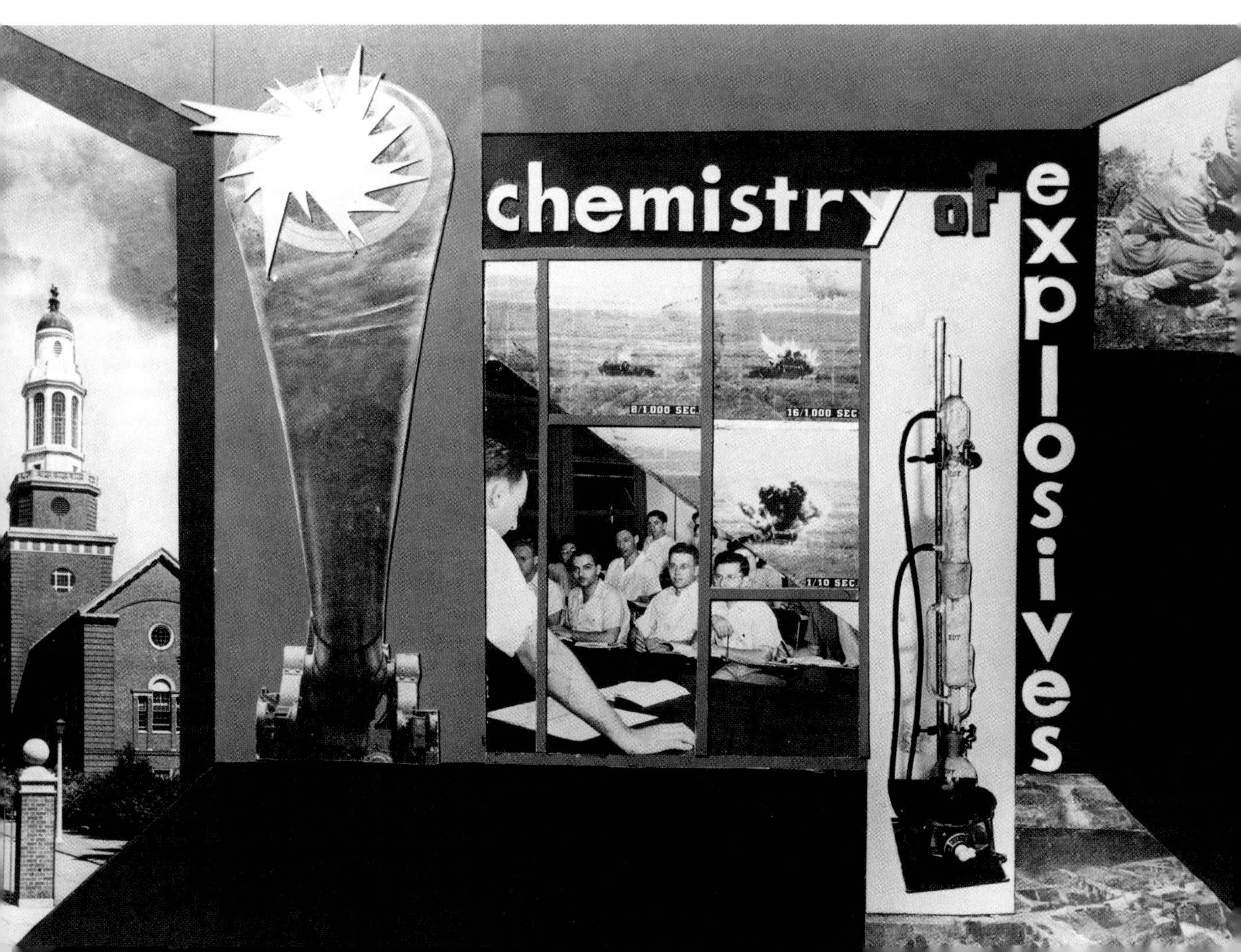

Photographs of designs for War Service Window Displays (original collages lost), 1942

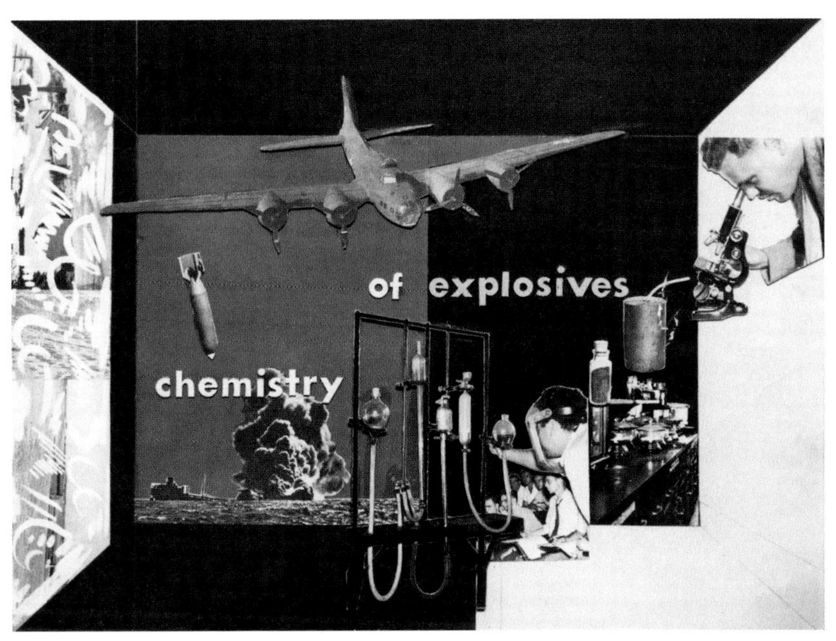

of explosives
chemistry

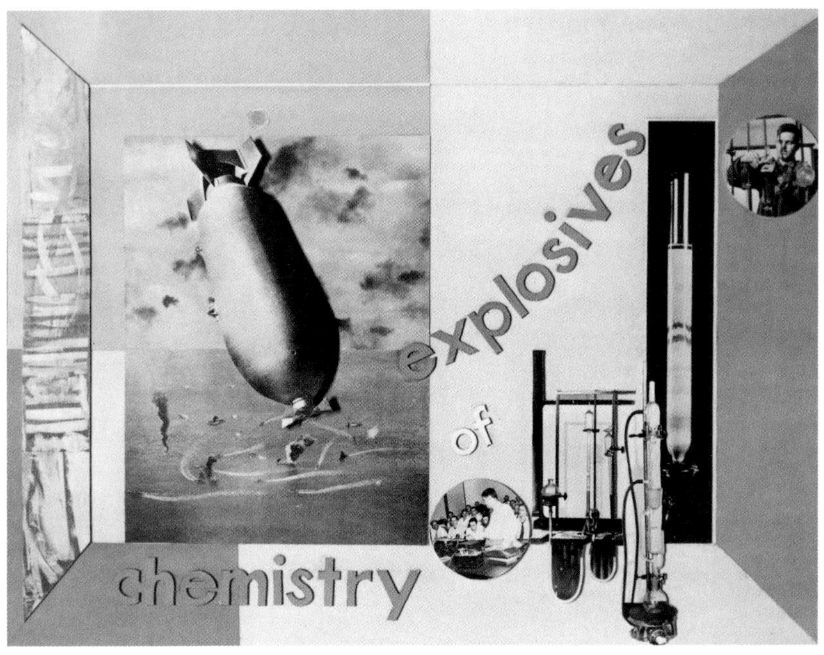

explosives
of
chemistry

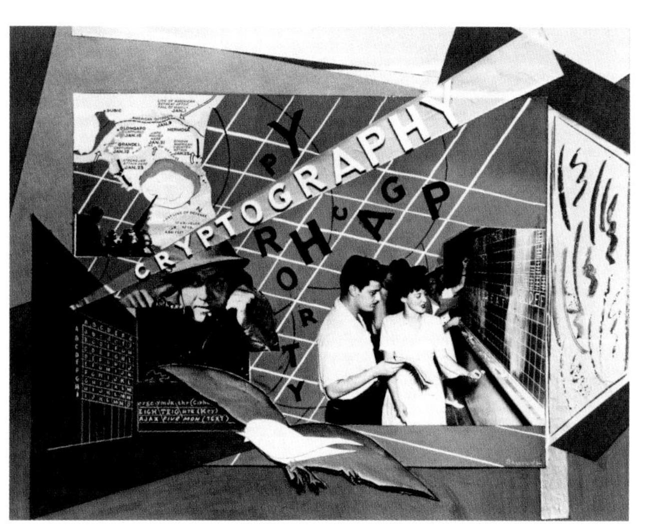

CRYPTOGRAPHY
PY
RH GP
Y

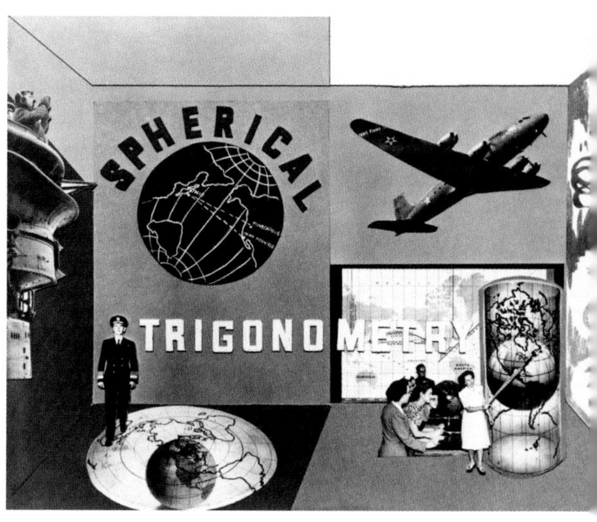

SPHERICAL
TRIGONOMETRY

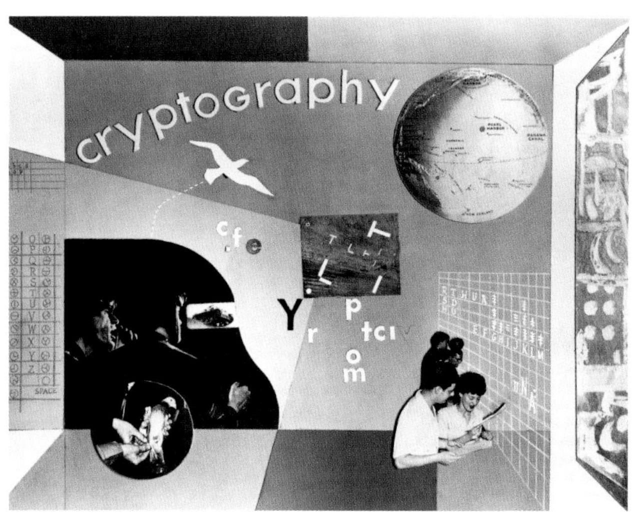

cryptography

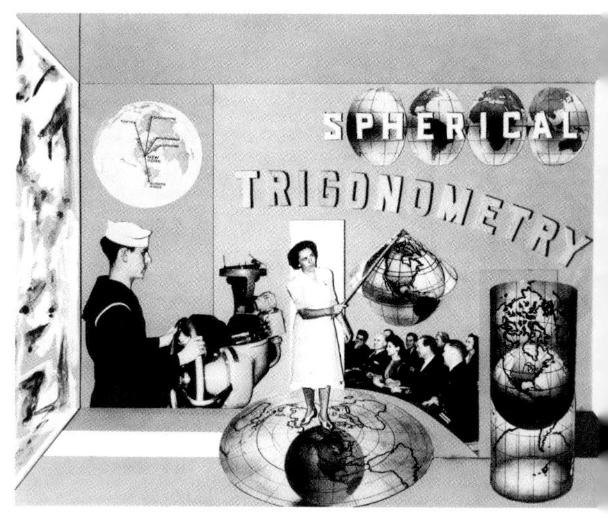

SPHERICAL
TRIGONOMETRY

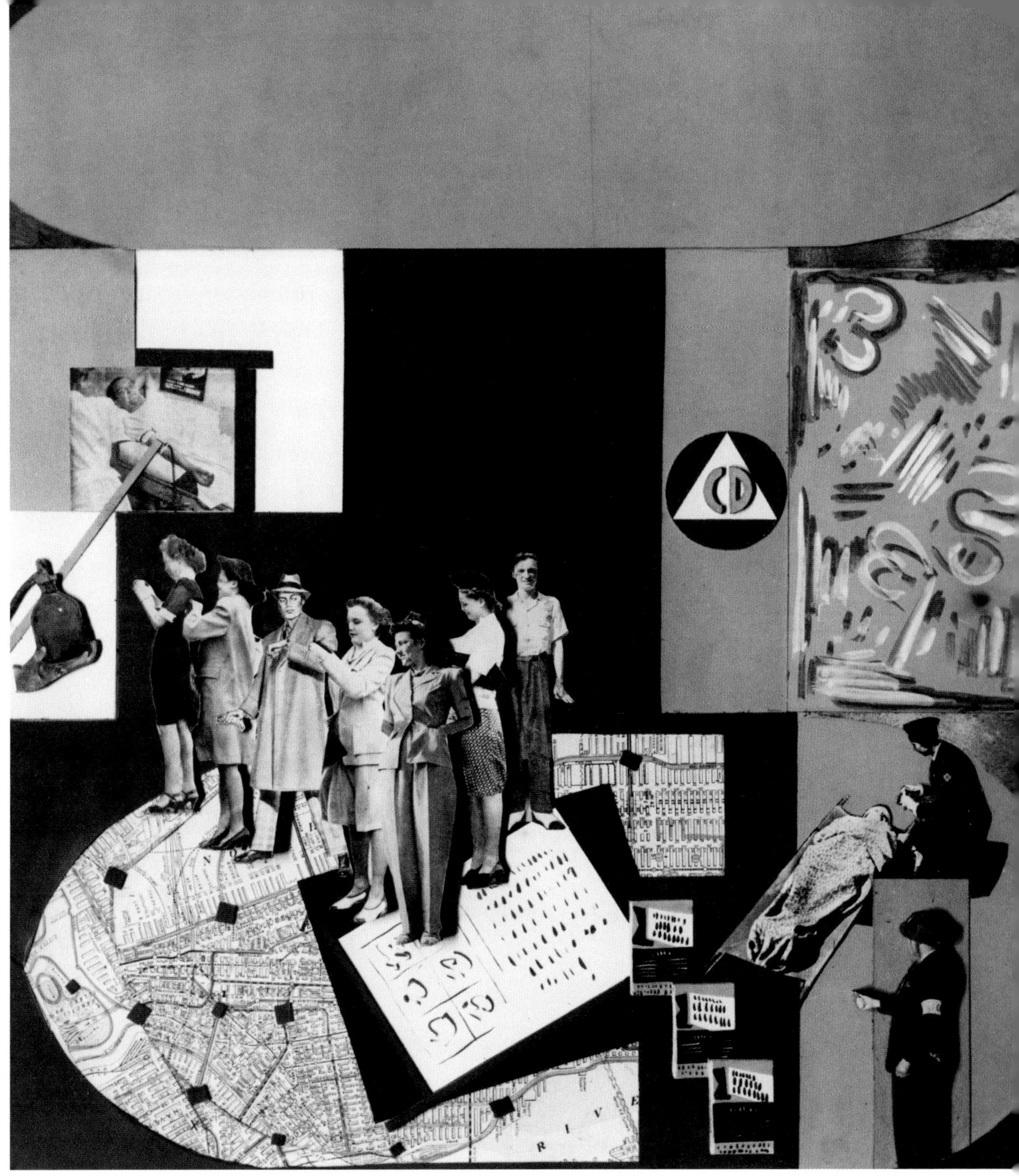

CD
RIVE

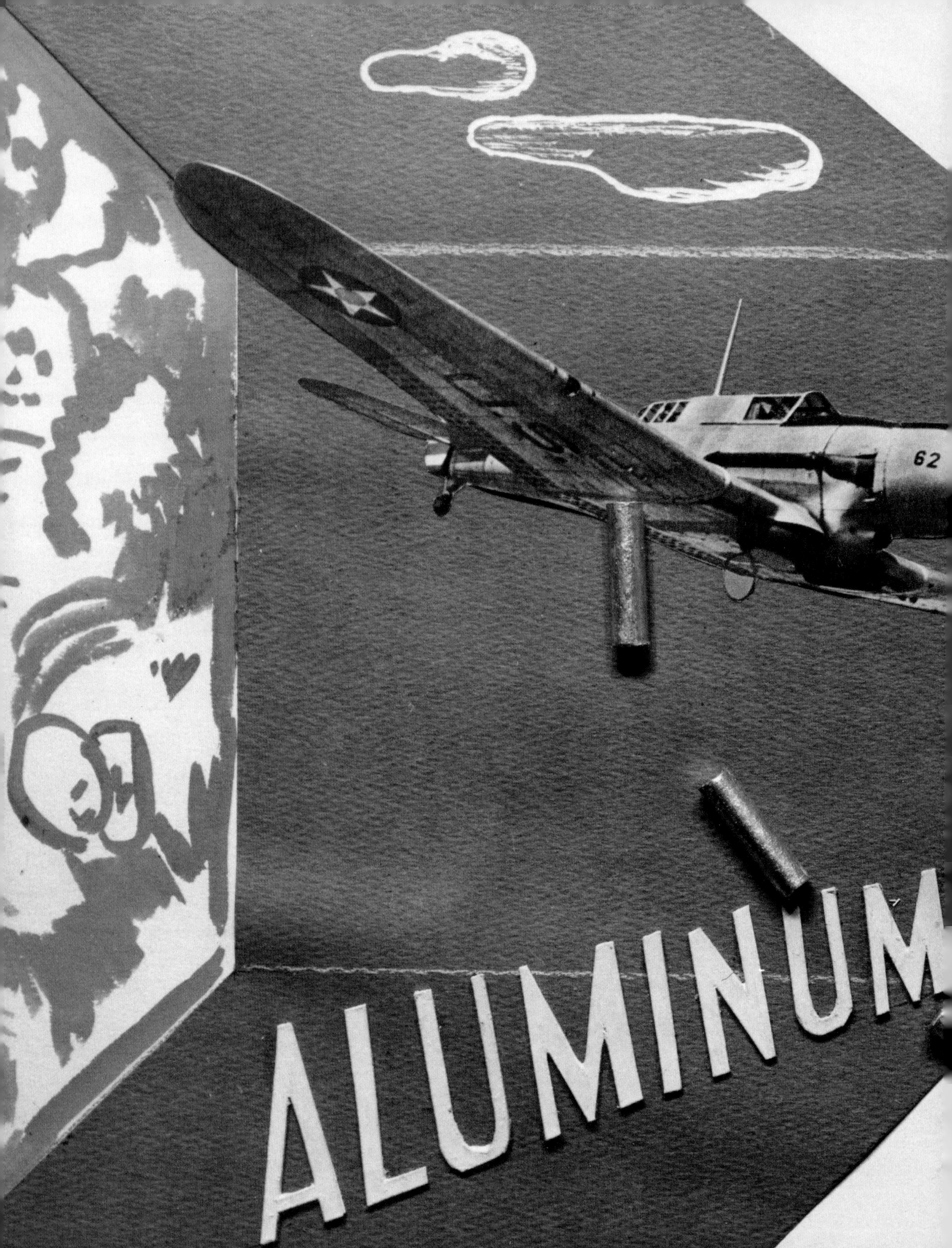
62
ALUMINUM

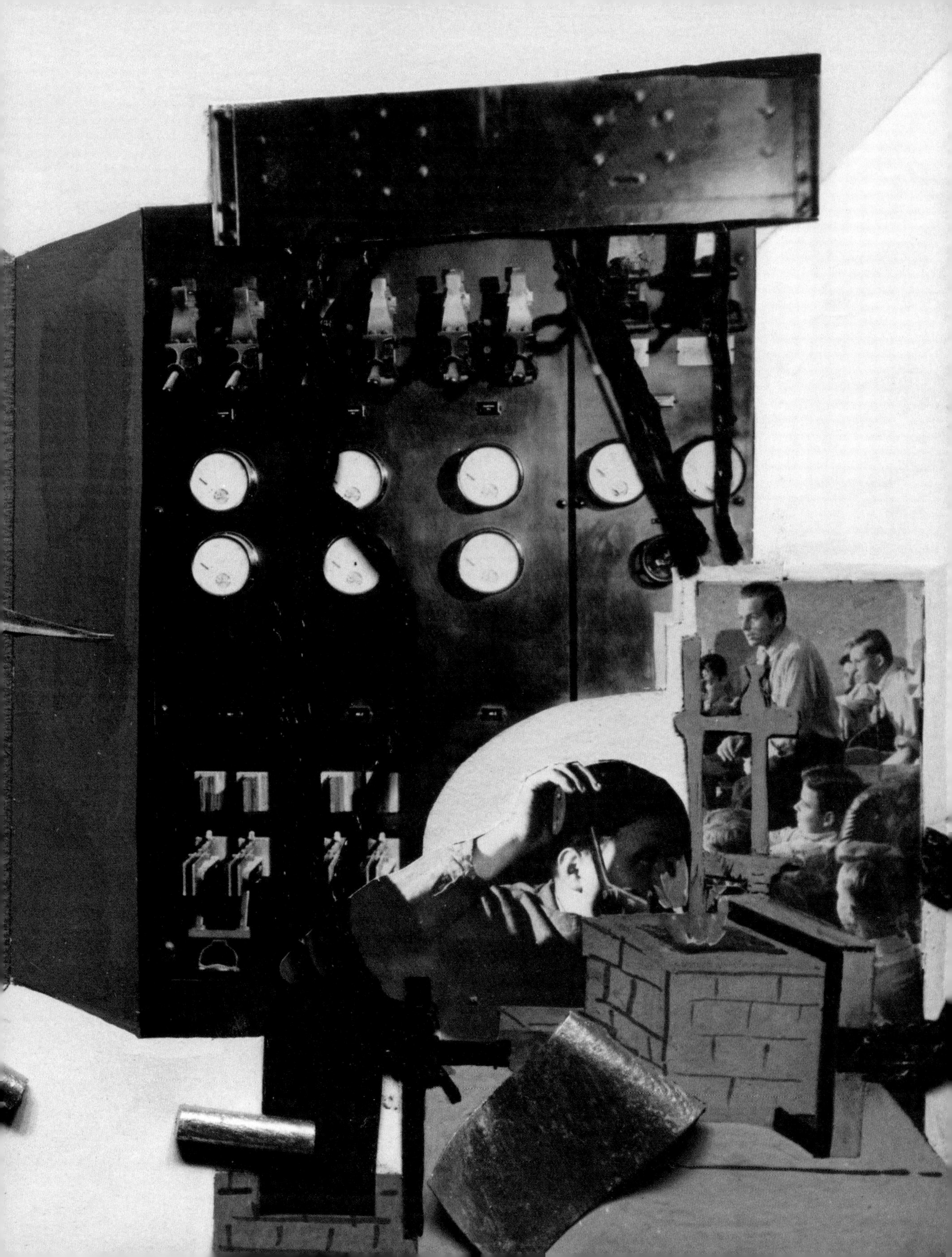

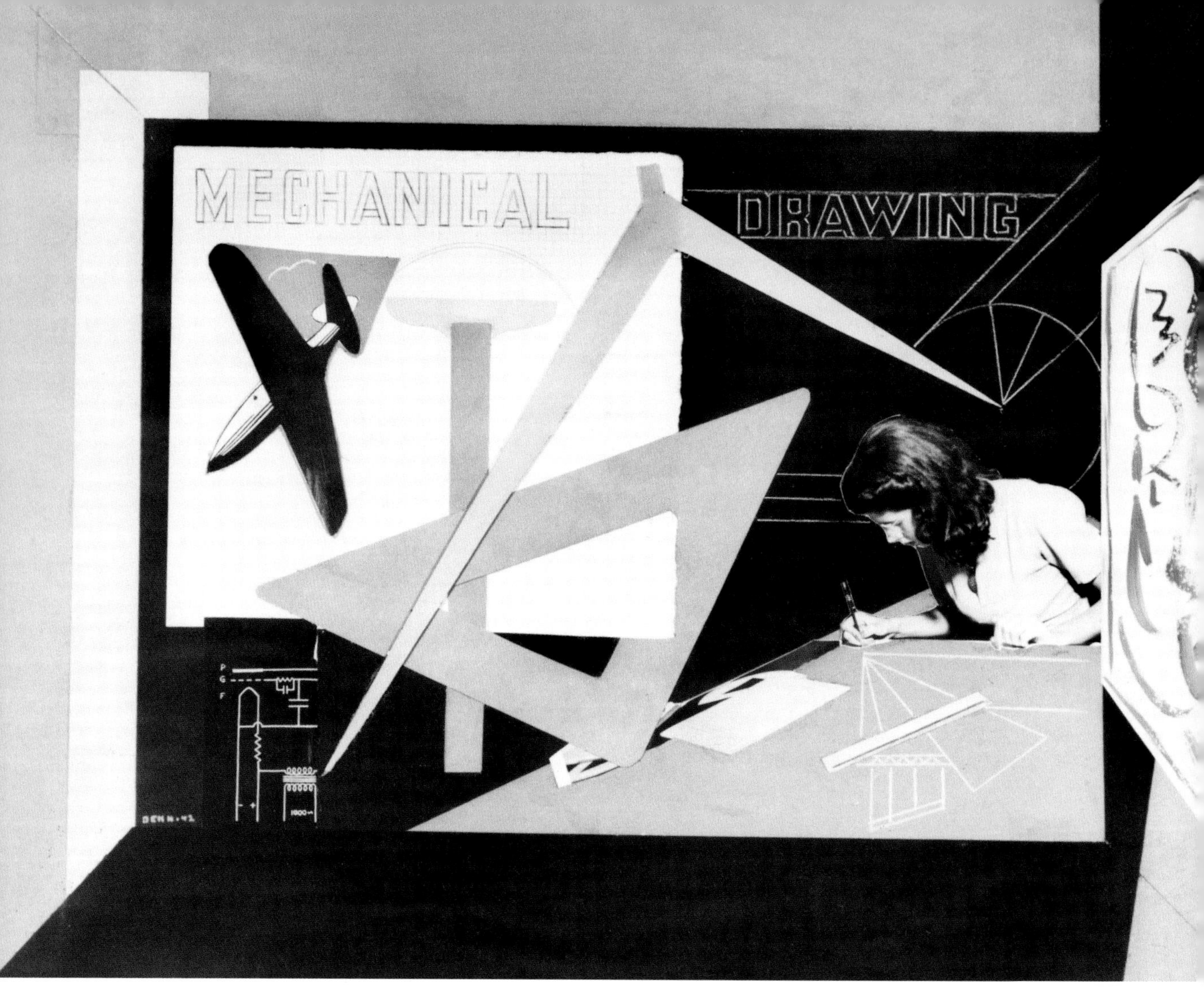

MECHANICAL
DRAWING

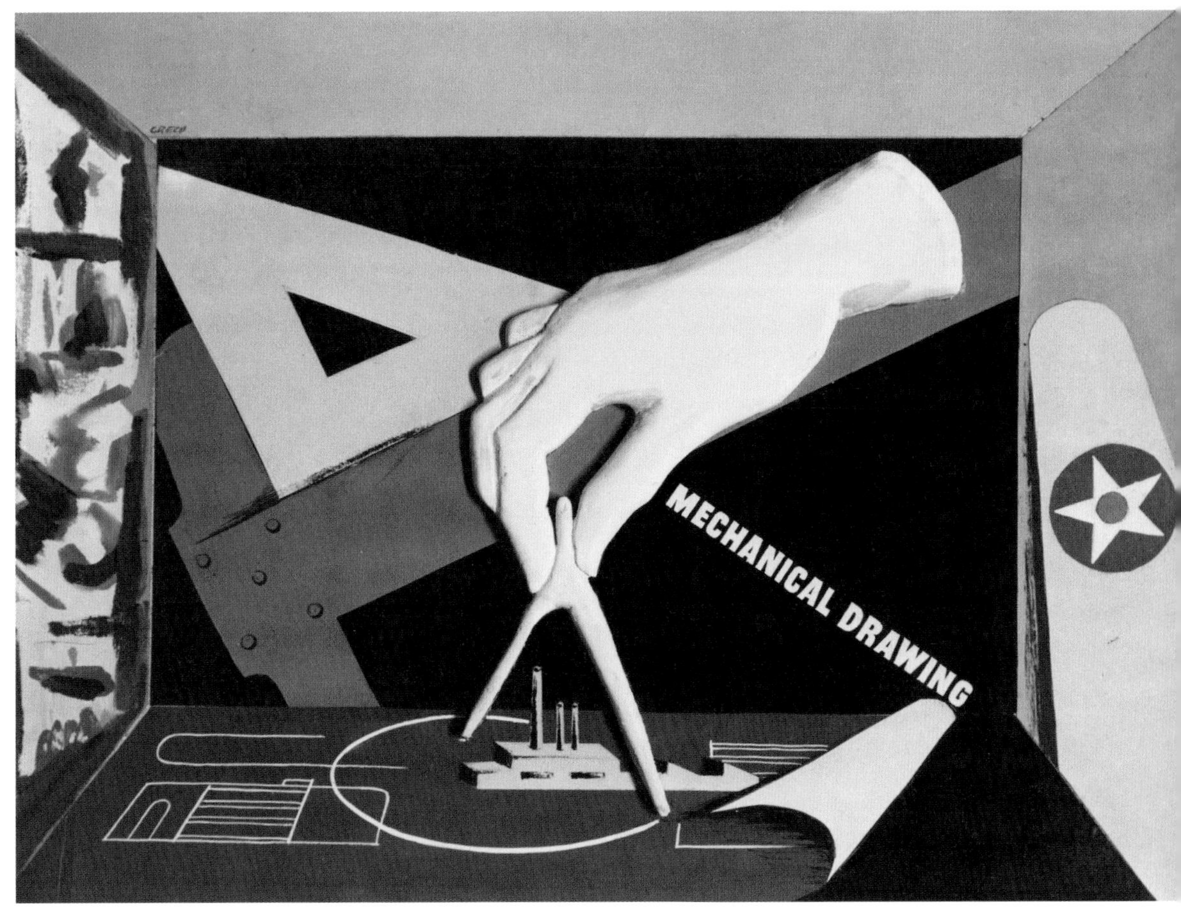
MECHANICAL DRAWING

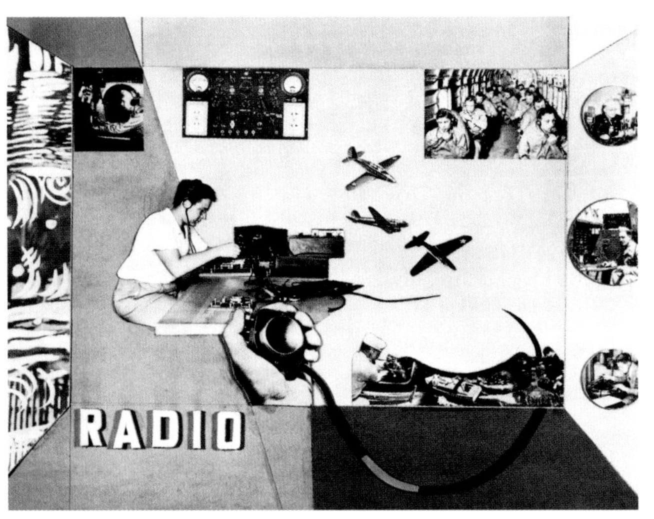
RADIO

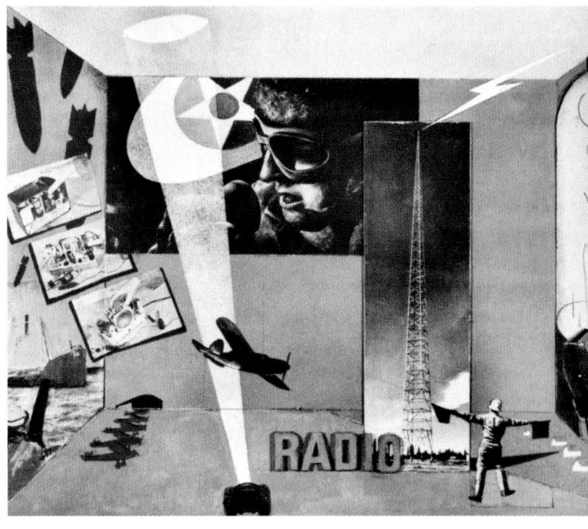
RADIO

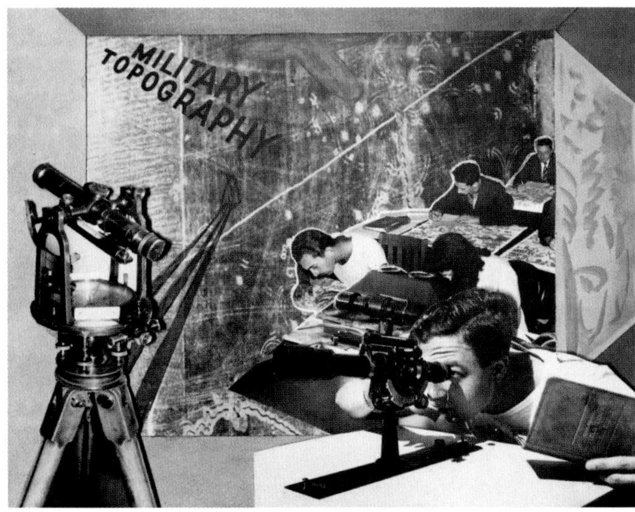
MILITARY
TOPOGRAPHY

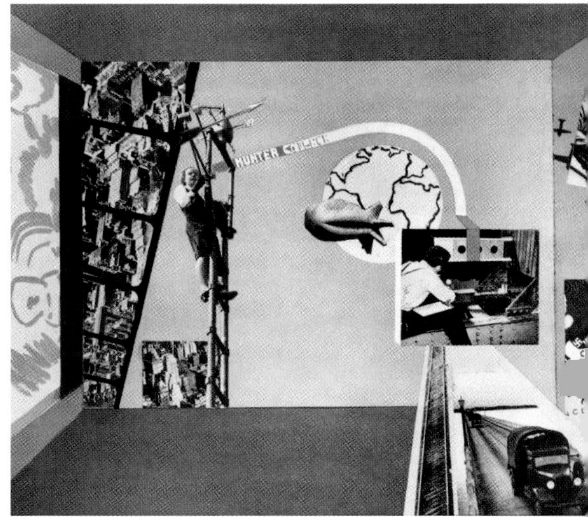

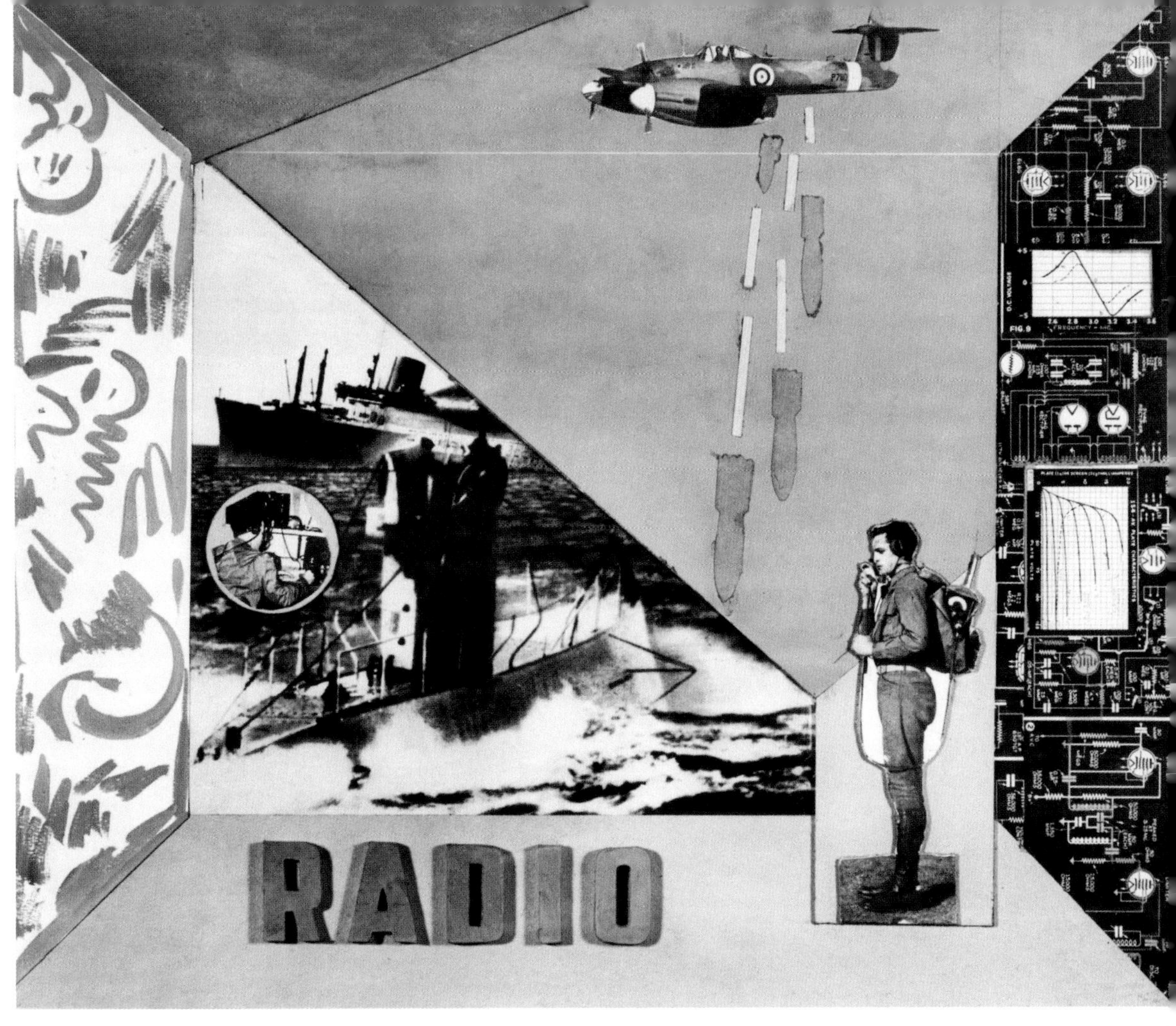
RADIO

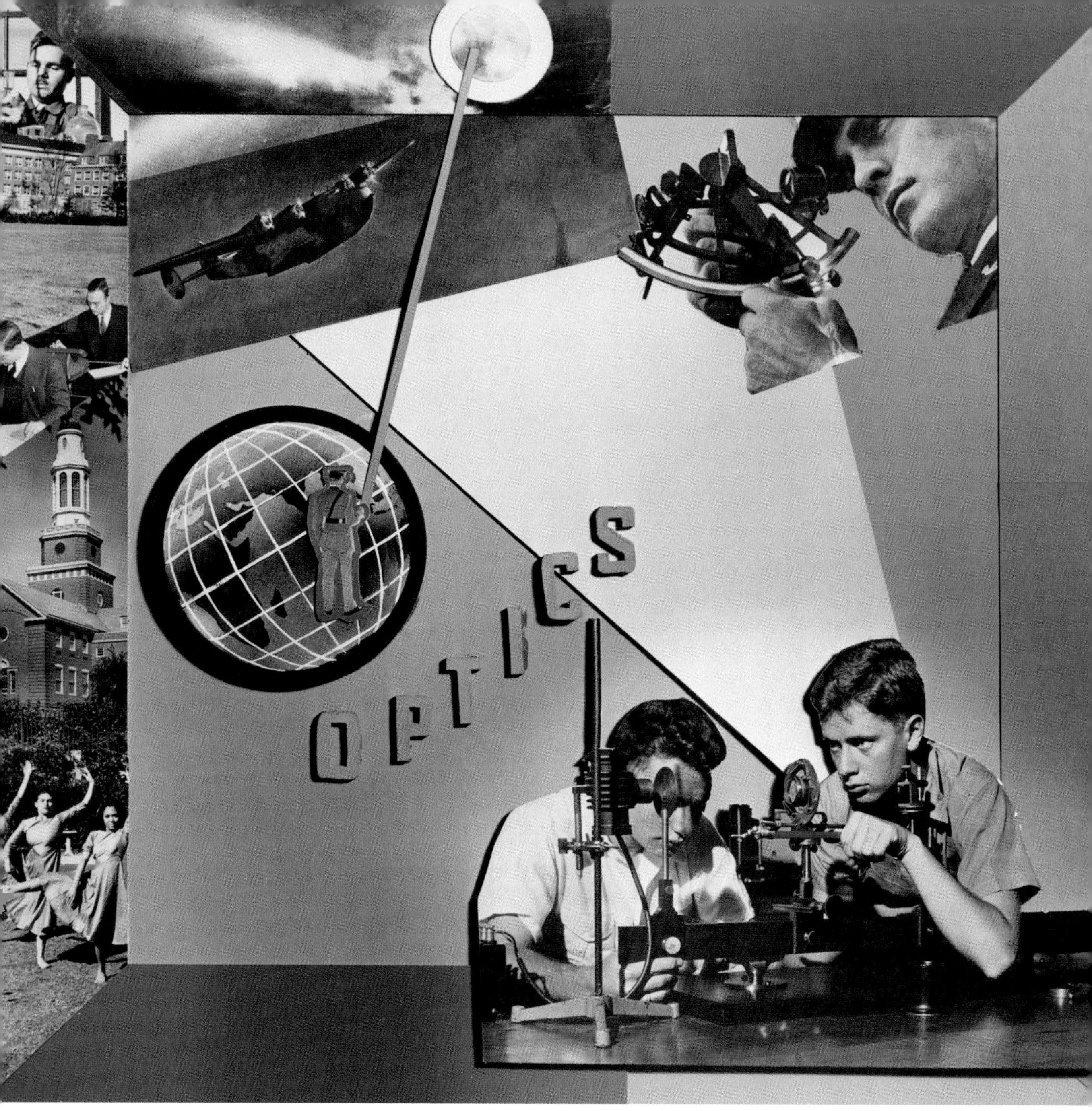

OPTICS

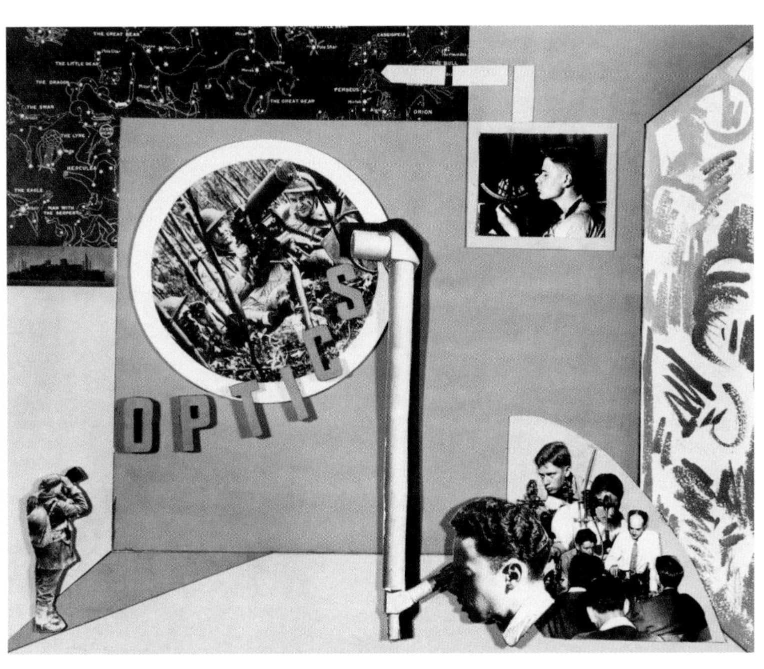
OPTICS

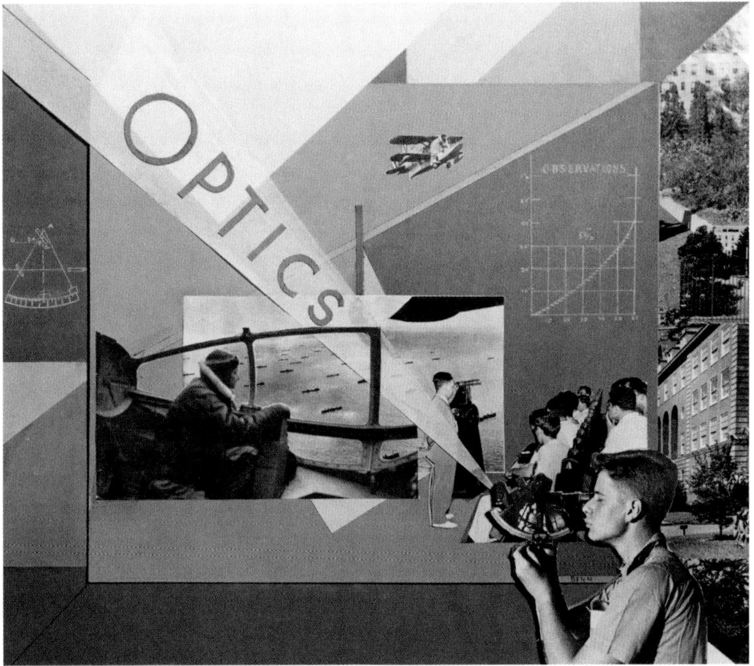
OPTICS
OBSERVATIONS

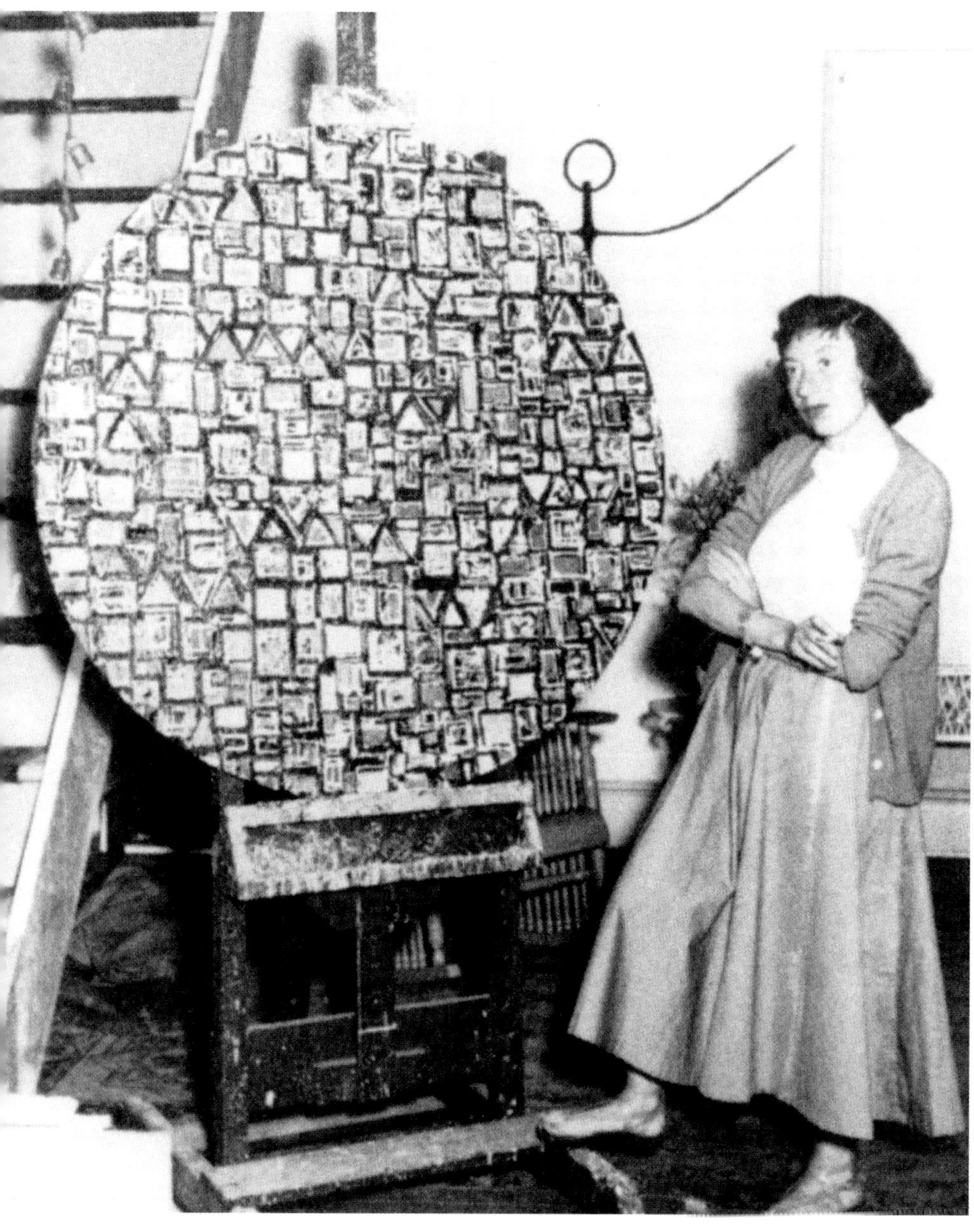

Lee Krasner with *Stop and Go* (1949–50), c.1949

LITTLE IMAGES

In the autumn of 1945, Krasner and Pollock moved permanently to Springs, Long Island, where – with the help of a loan from Pollock's patron and dealer Peggy Guggenheim – they bought a nineteenth-century farmhouse, with a view across the salt marshes to Accabonac Creek. Krasner had been suffering from a creative block, making nothing but what she called her 'gray slabs'; now, suddenly surrounded by nature, she found that a new imagery was beginning to blossom. Turning the upstairs bedroom into a makeshift studio, she began work on her 'Little Image' paintings.

Positioning the canvas flat on a table or the floor, Krasner created vibrant, jewel-like abstractions that pulsed with an even rhythm across the surface. For some, she would layer the paint thickly with a palette knife and then work into it with a stiff paintbrush; for others, she covered her canvas with a lace overlay of paint that she had thinned down with turpentine in a can. She always worked in oil, explaining in an interview that 'I tried a few things in acrylic ... [but] I find it opaque, dense, dead as a doornail.'[1]

In 1947 the cold winter forced Krasner to work downstairs by the stove, where she made two mosaic tables using old wagon wheels she had found in the barn. One of the tables was exhibited at Bertha Schaefer Gallery in September 1948 (accompanied by a few of Krasner's new 'hieroglyphic' Little Images), where it prompted the *New York Herald Tribune*'s critic to state that 'the total effect [is] to come right out with it, magnificent'.[2] Krasner hung several of her Little Images in the guest room at Springs, where such visitors as the critic Clement Greenberg and the artist Bradley Walker Tomlin would admire their delicate intensity.

Untitled, 1946

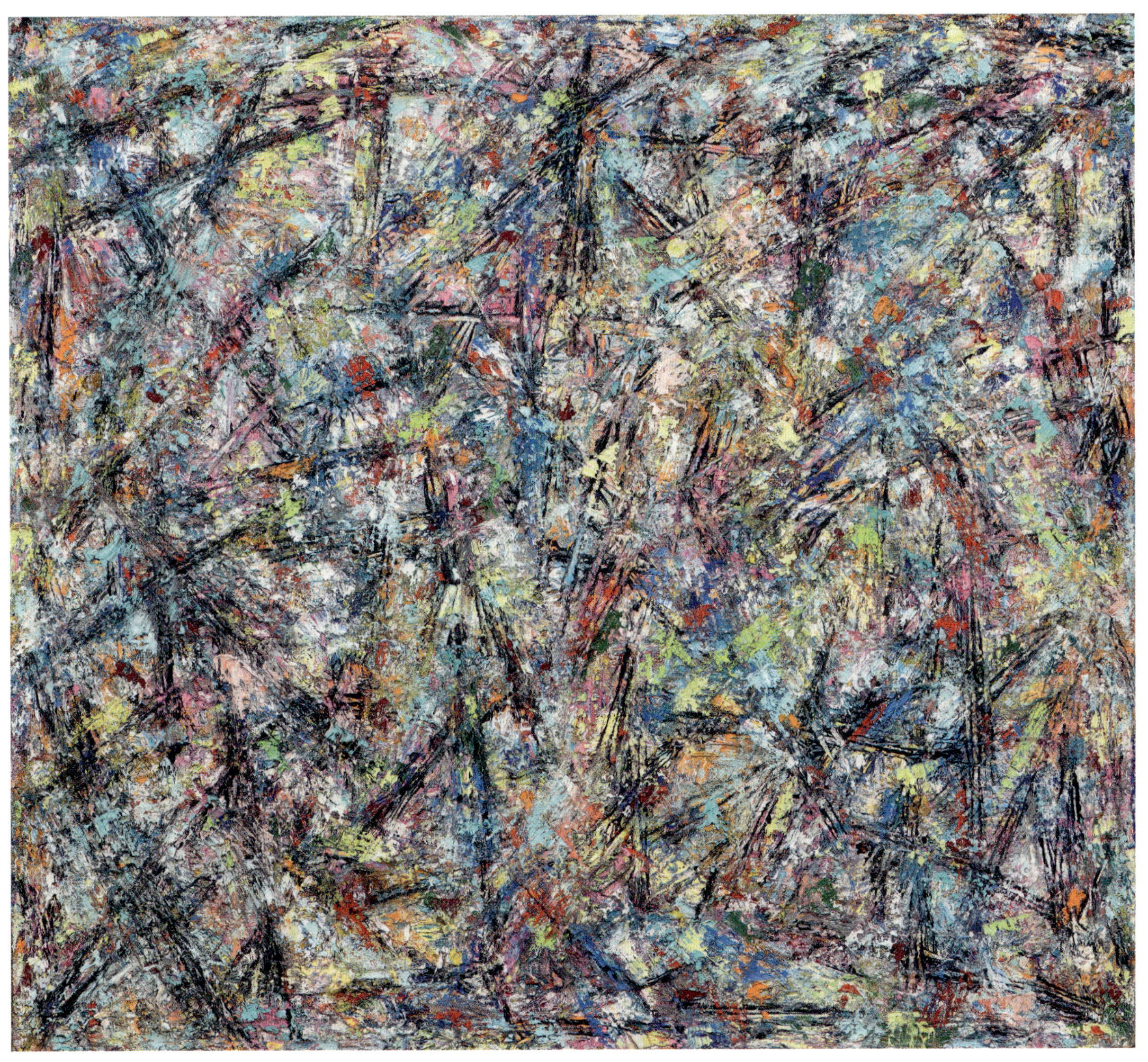

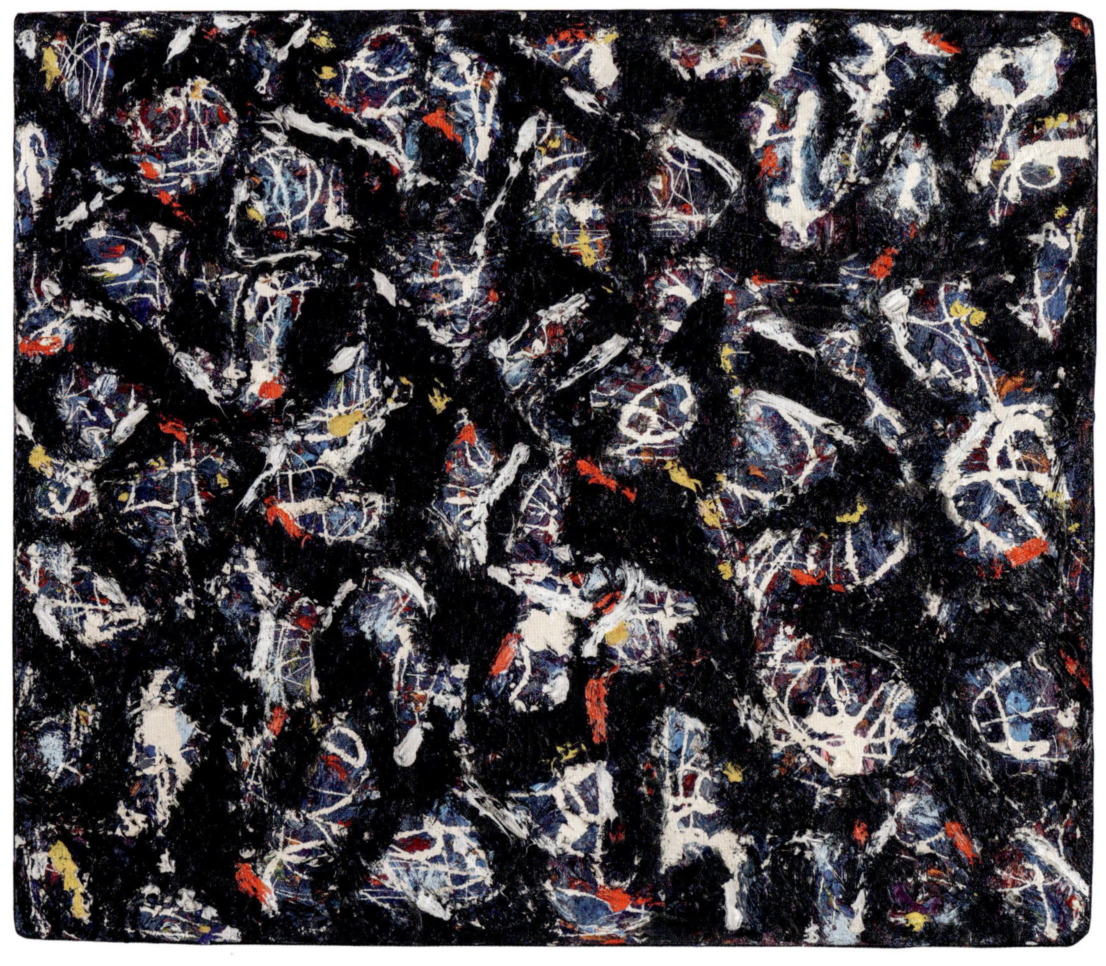

Abstract No. 2, 1946–48

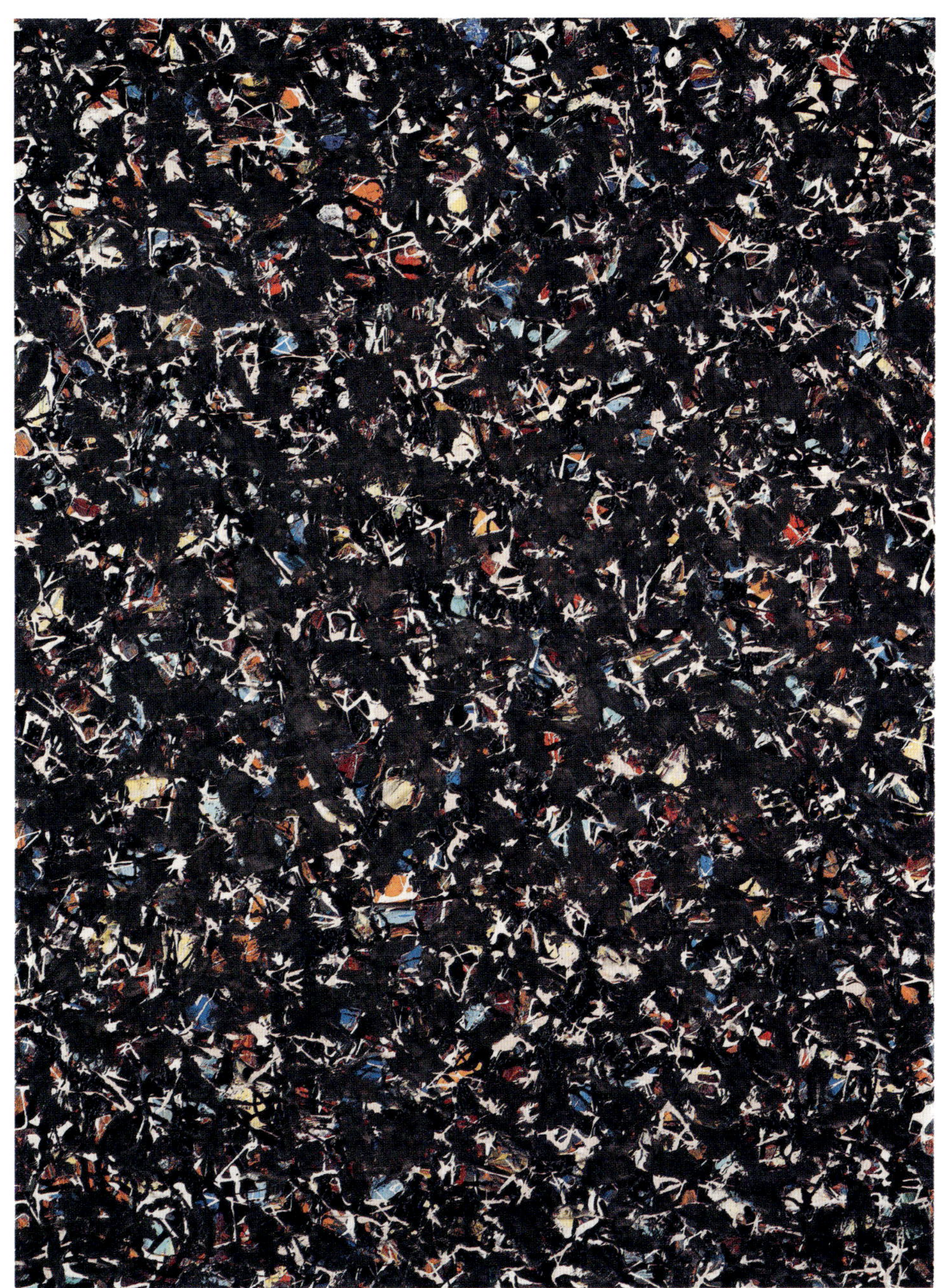

Untitled, 1947

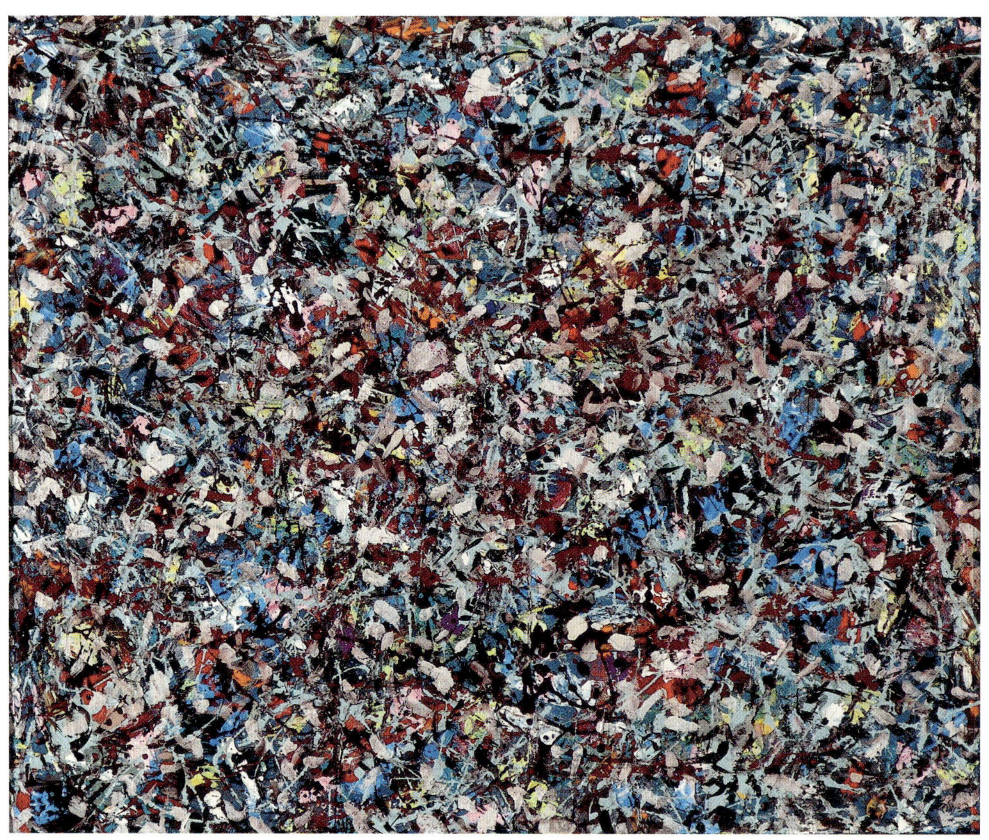

88

Shattered Color, 1947

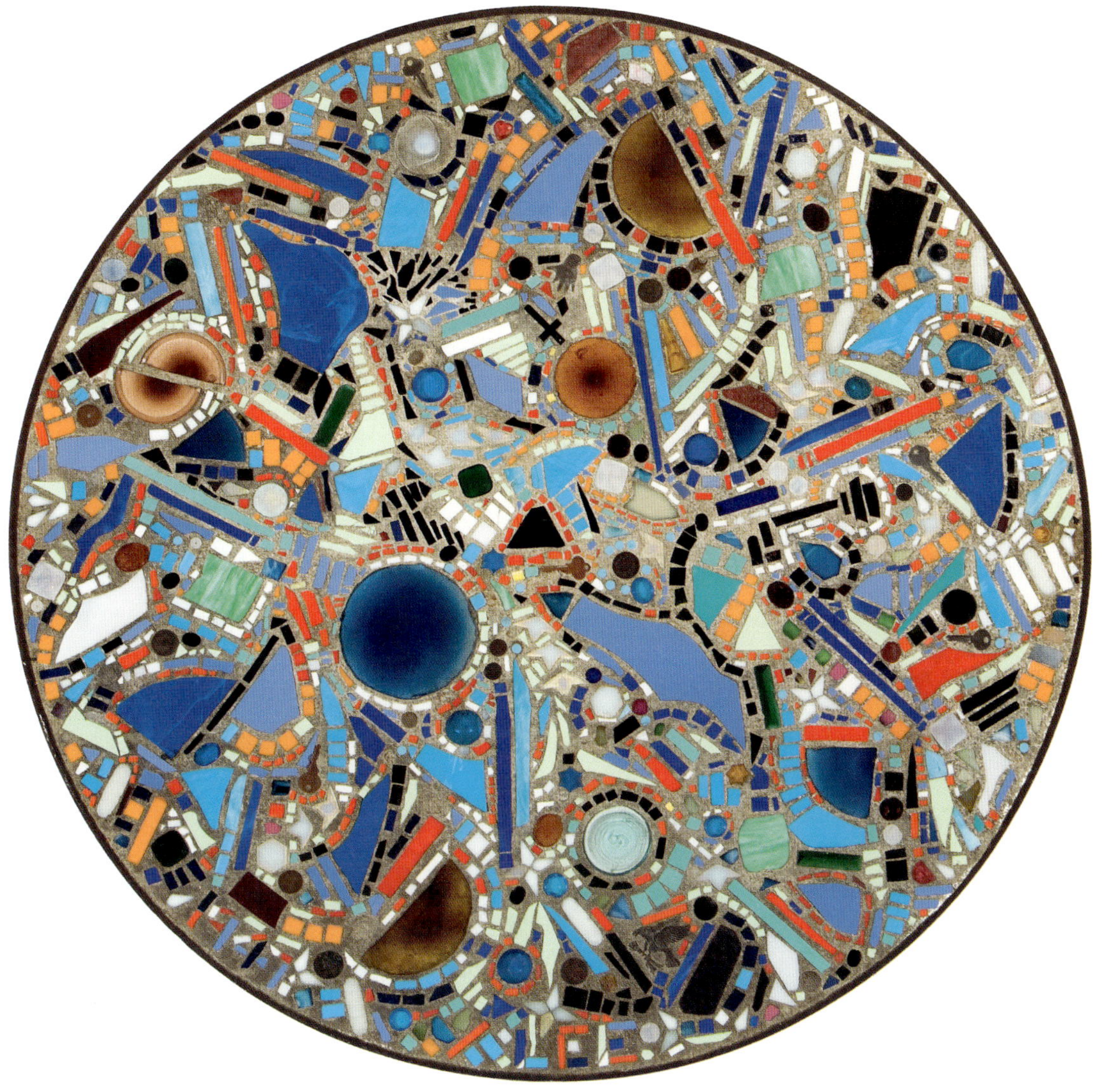

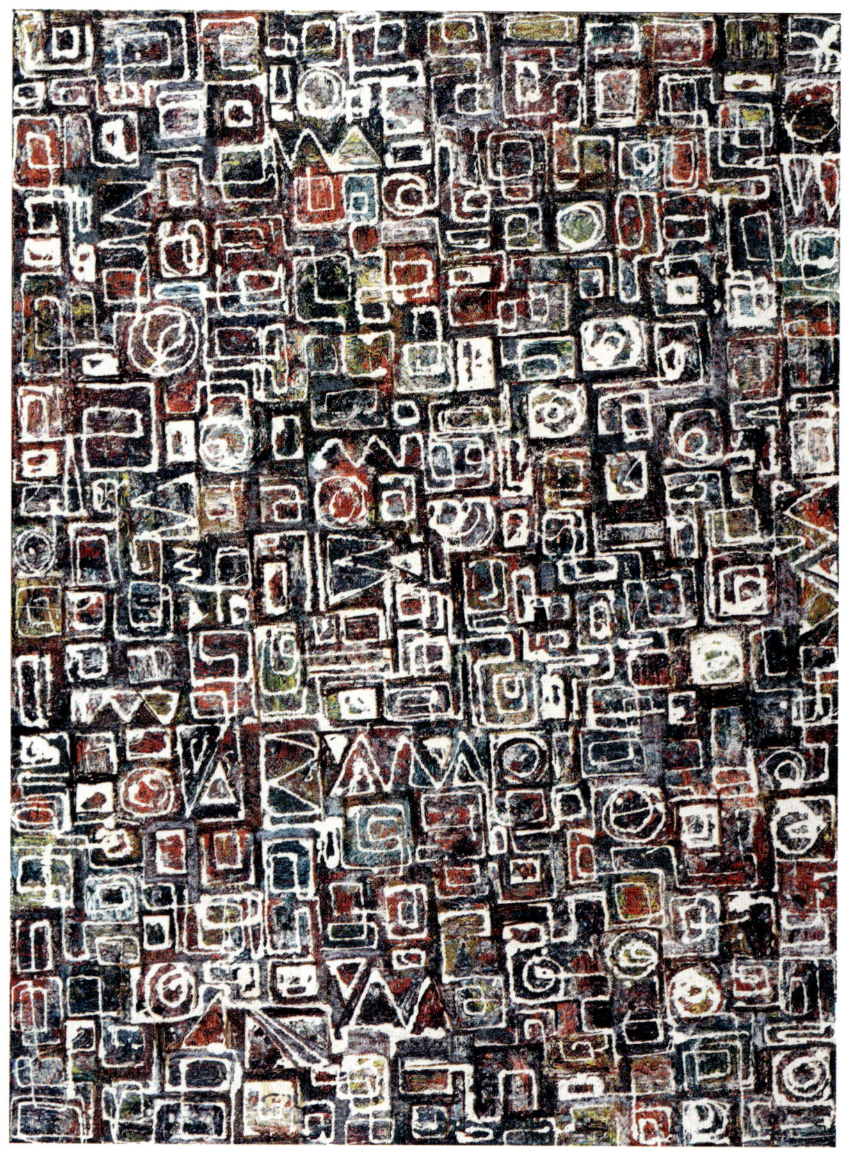

Composition, 1949

Stop and Go, 1949–50

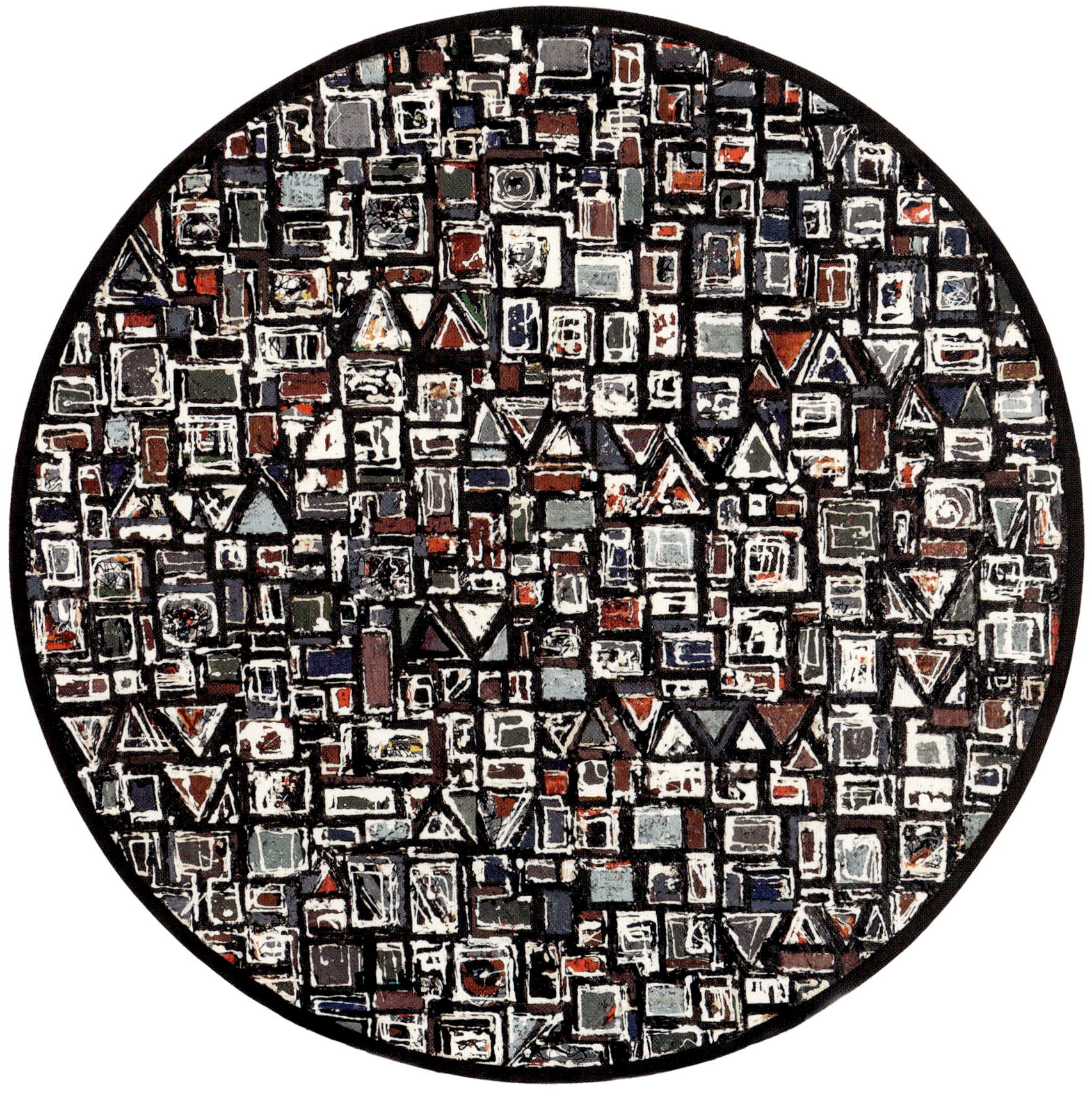

Black and White Squares No. 1, 1948

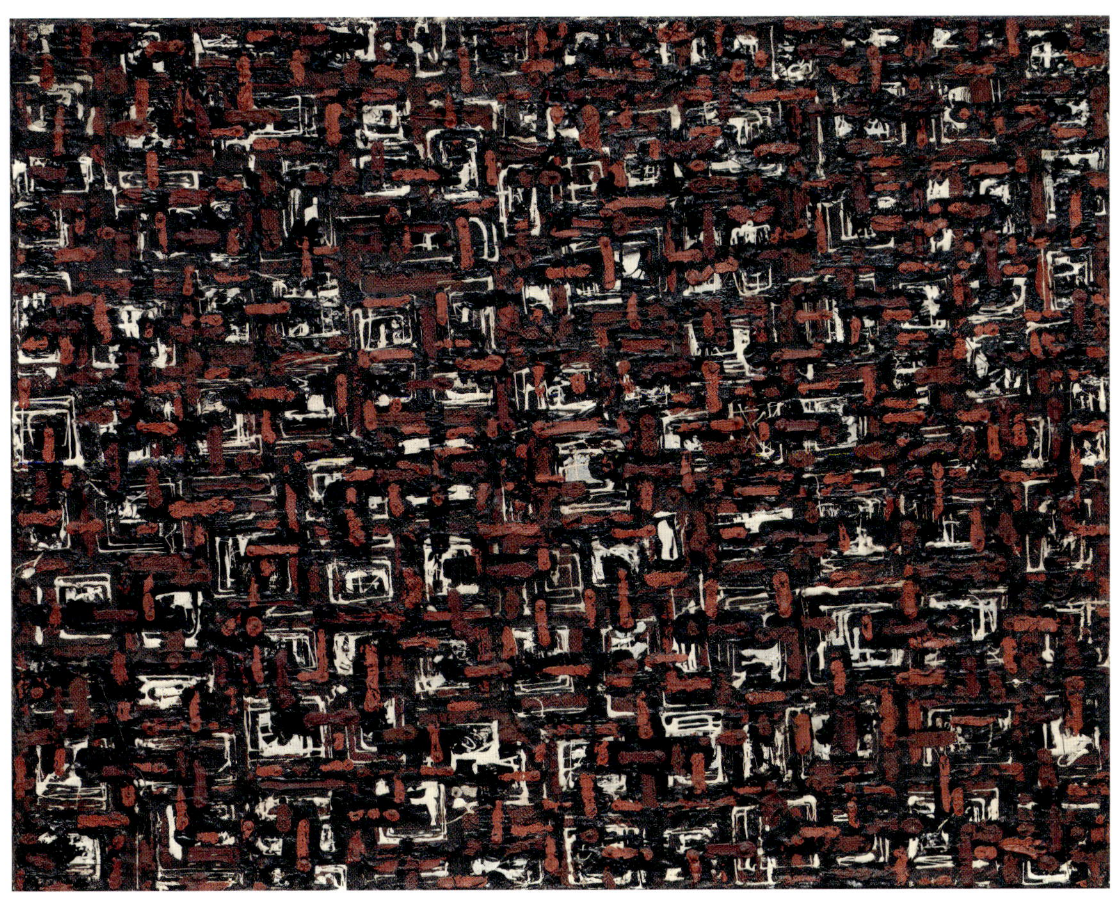

Untitled, c. 1948–49

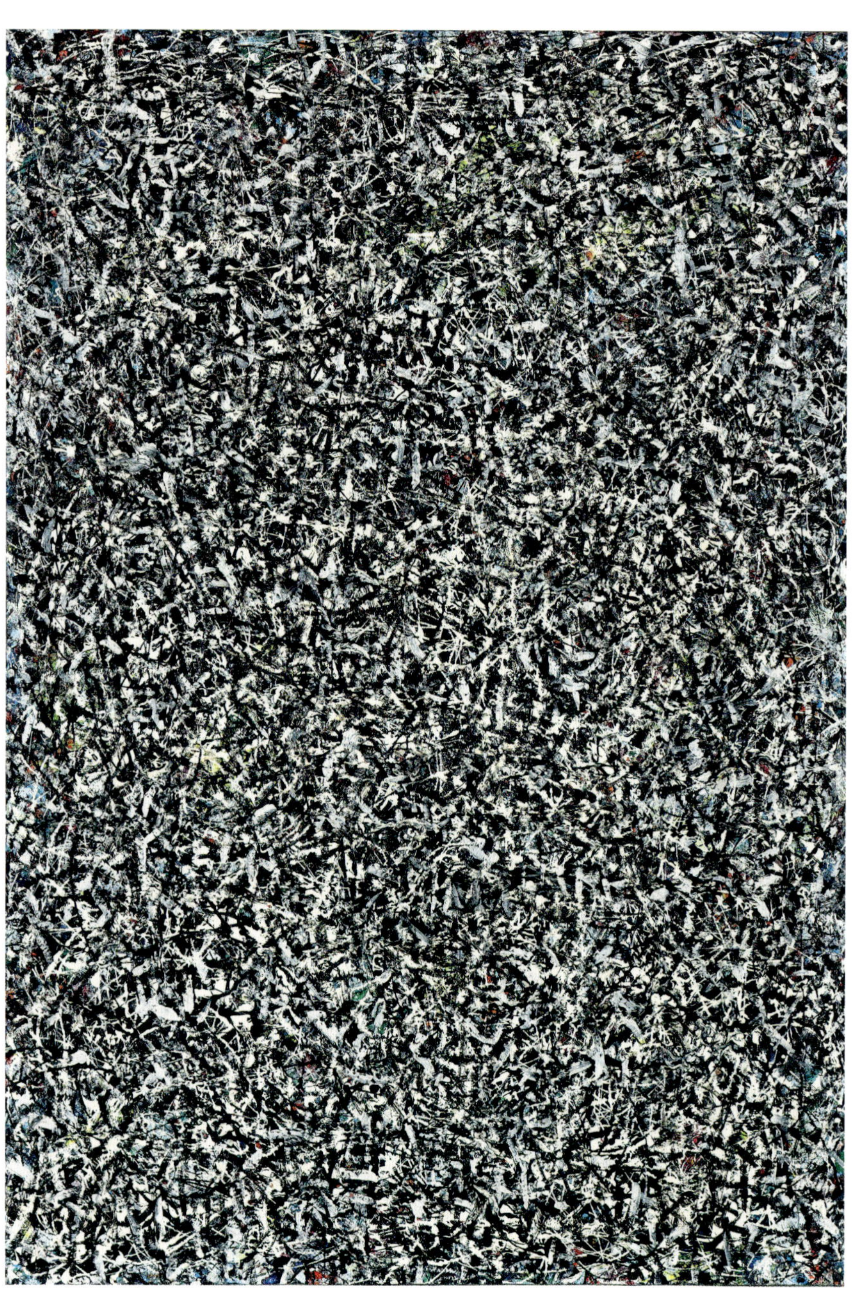

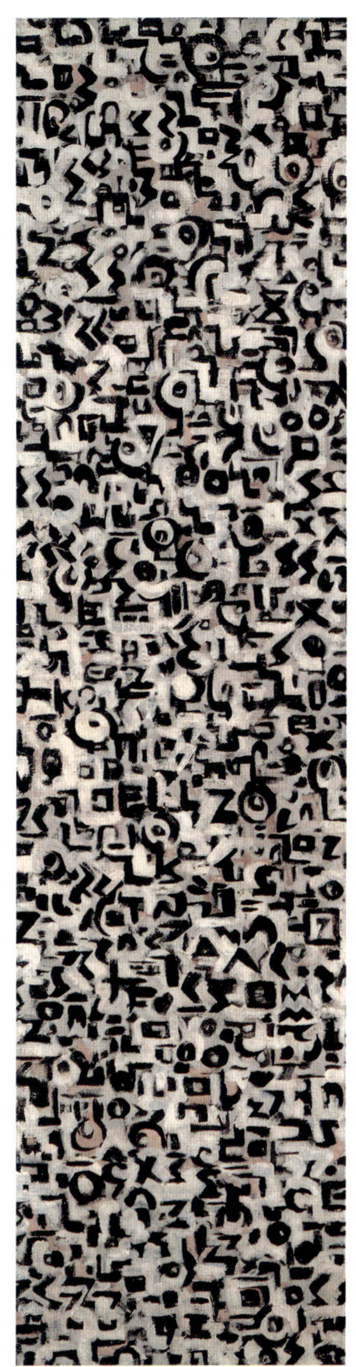

Right: *Untitled (Little Image)*, 1950
Opposite: *Night Light*, 1949

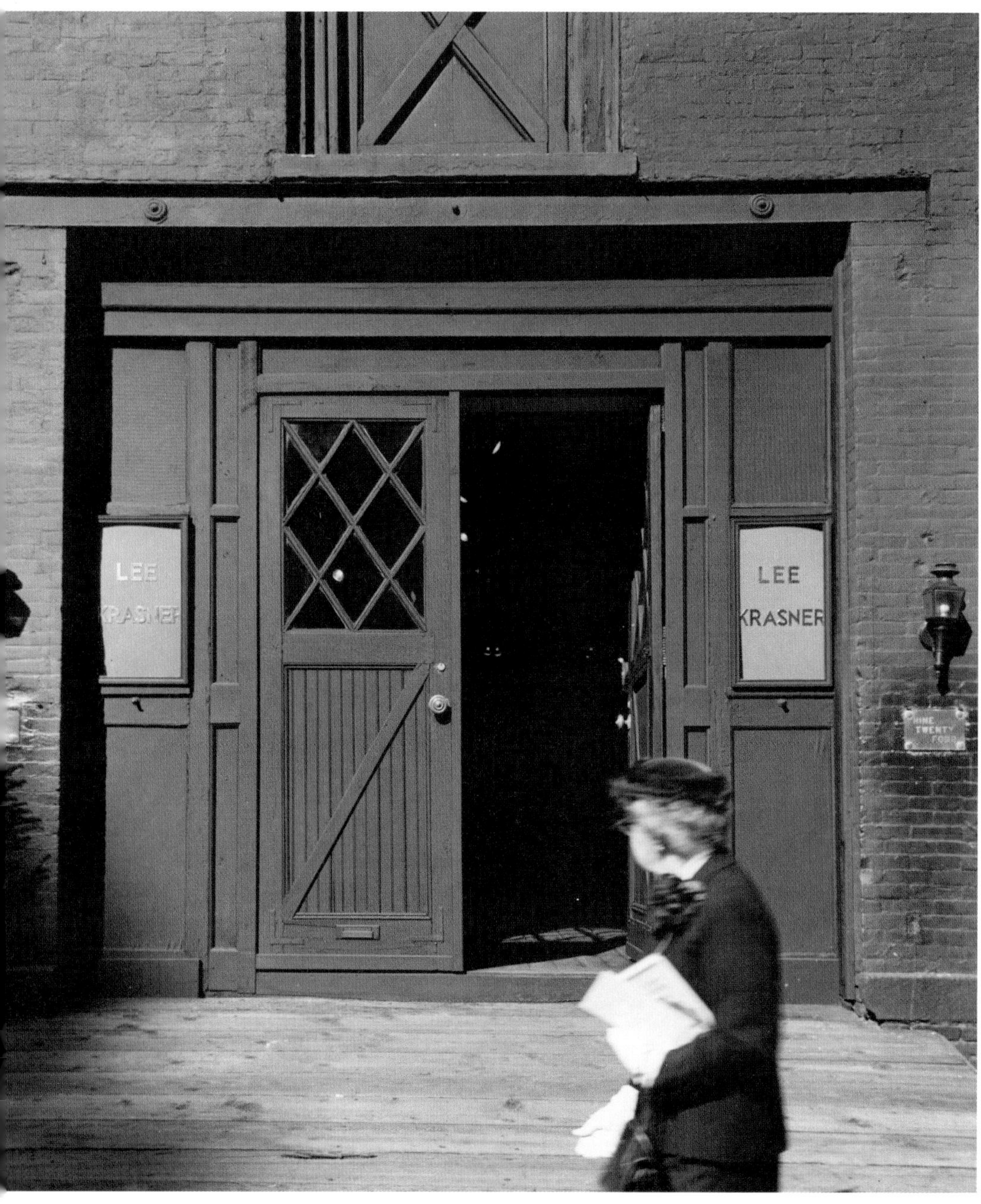

The Stable Gallery, New York, 1955

STABLE GALLERY

In 1951 Krasner presented fourteen abstract paintings at her first solo exhibition, held at Betty Parsons Gallery, New York. Although generally well-received by the critics, Krasner's new body of work did not find any buyers, which prompted a period of considerable self-doubt. An artist who always worked in cycles, Krasner began making a series of black-and-white drawings in the hope that they would ease her into a new phase. These were pinned from floor to ceiling on to her studio walls. Krasner walked in one day and felt that she despised everything she saw. Tearing the drawings from the walls and ripping them into shreds, she left them strewn on the floor.

Krasner was unable to return to the studio for a number of weeks. She recalls eventually re-opening the door and being surprised to see 'a lot of things there that began to interest me. I began picking up torn pieces of my own drawings and re-gluing them. Then I start cutting up some of my oil paintings. I've got something going here and I start pulling out a lot of raw canvases and slashing [them] as well.'[1] The Betty Parsons works became supports for many of these new collages, as Krasner began layering a combination of her own discards with pieces of burlap, newspaper and heavy black photographic paper, sometimes interspersed with discards of Pollock's drawings. These radical new 'collage paintings' were presented in an exhibition at the Stable Gallery, New York, in 1955.

The show was a success, with Clement Greenberg later heralding it as 'a major addition to the American art scene of that era'.[2] Stuart Preston, a critic from the *New York Times*, described the exhibition as a 'dense jungle of exotic shape and color', referring to the raucous fuchsia, blue and orange hues and the blooming biomorphic shapes that jostled for the viewer's attention.[3] 'The vitality [the work] possesses, when it does, comes from within', concluded Preston,[4] reflecting Krasner's insistence on drawing inspiration from her inner self: 'I never violate an inner rhythm. I loathe to force anything. I do not force myself, ever ... I have regard for the inner voice.'[5]

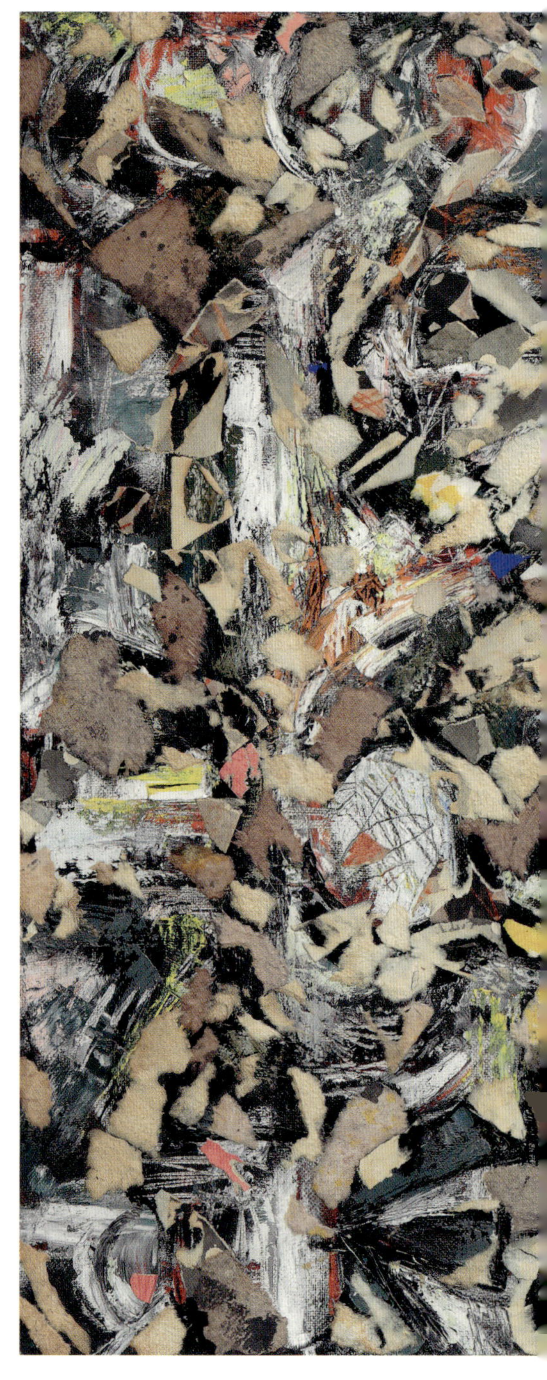

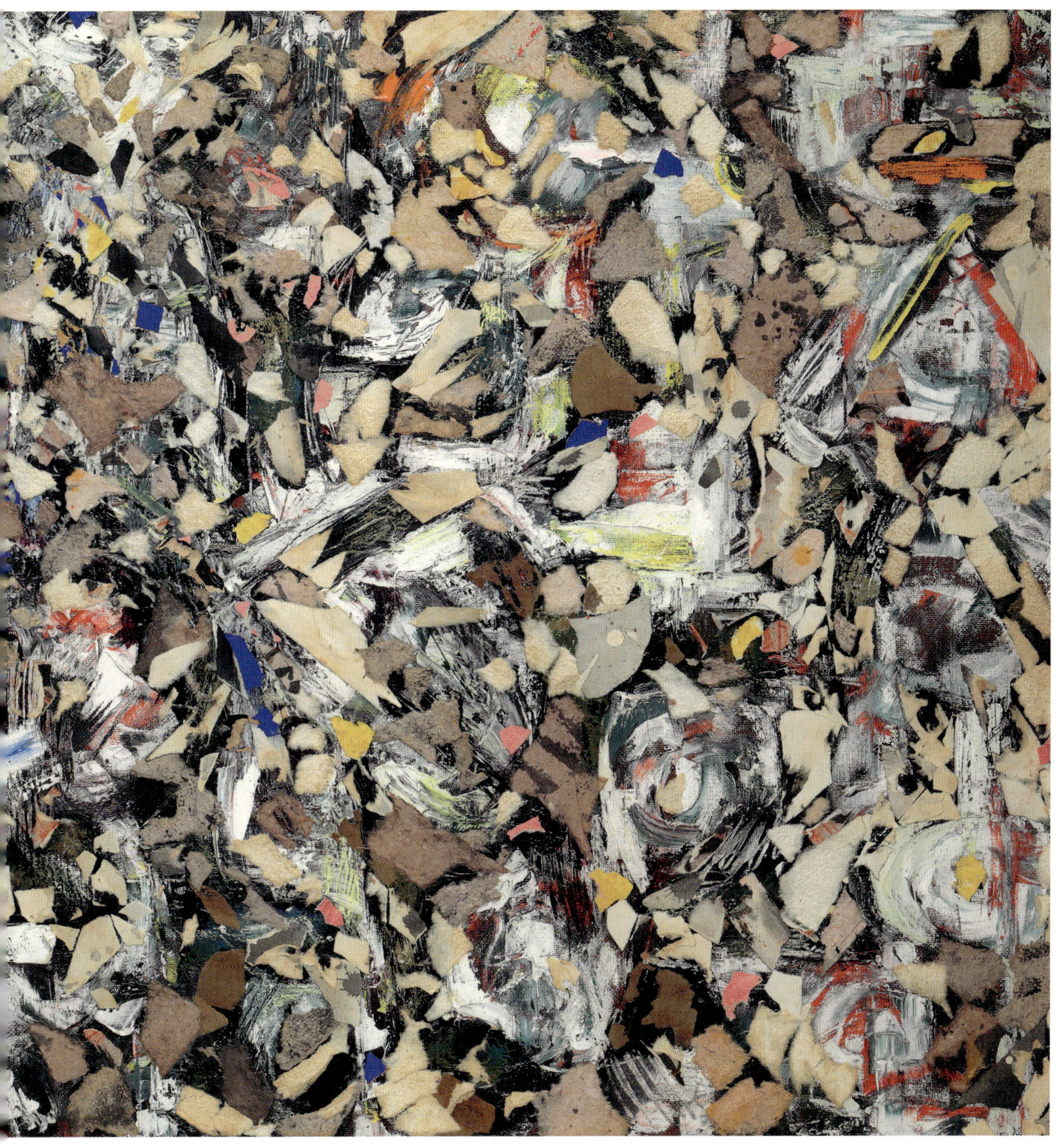

Shattered Light, 1954

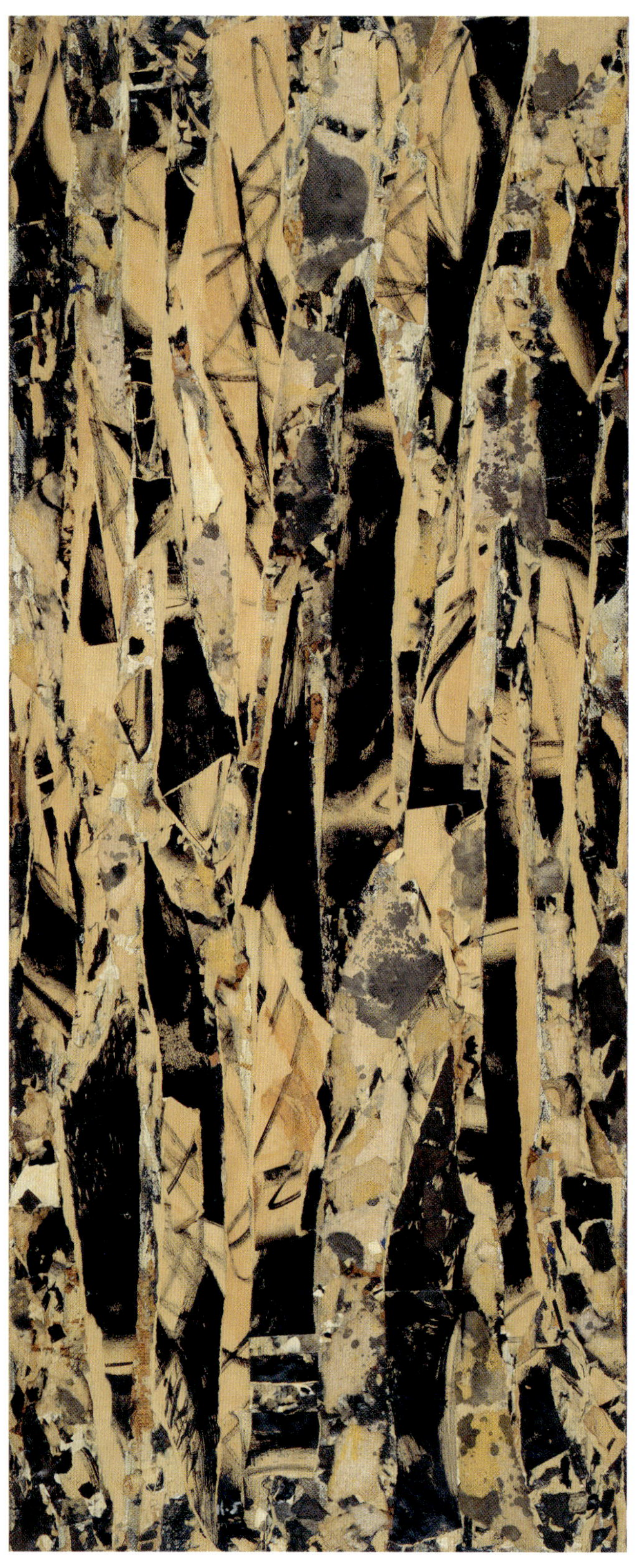

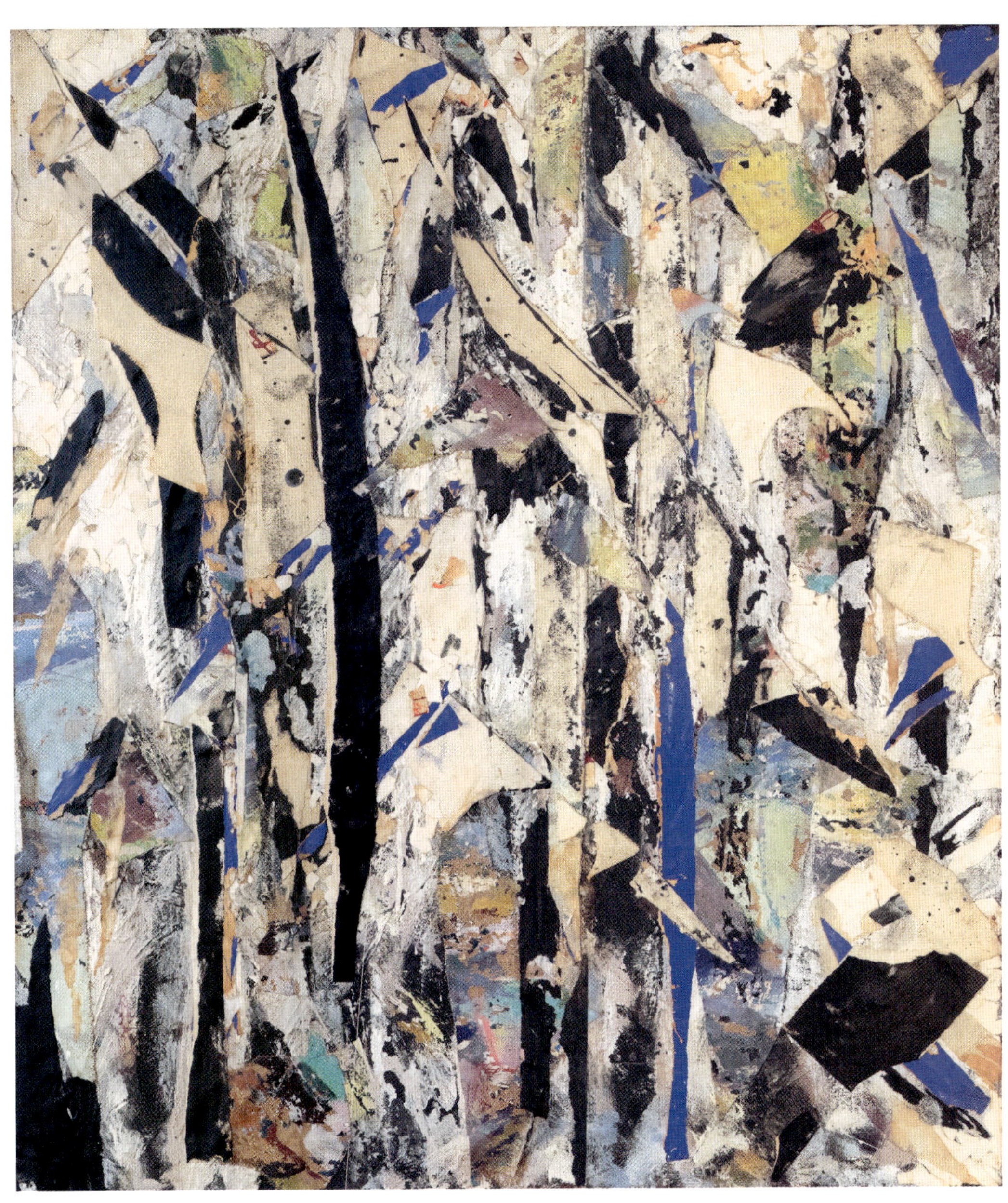

Above: *Untitled*, 1954
Opposite: *Forest No. 2*, 1954

Burning Candles, 1955

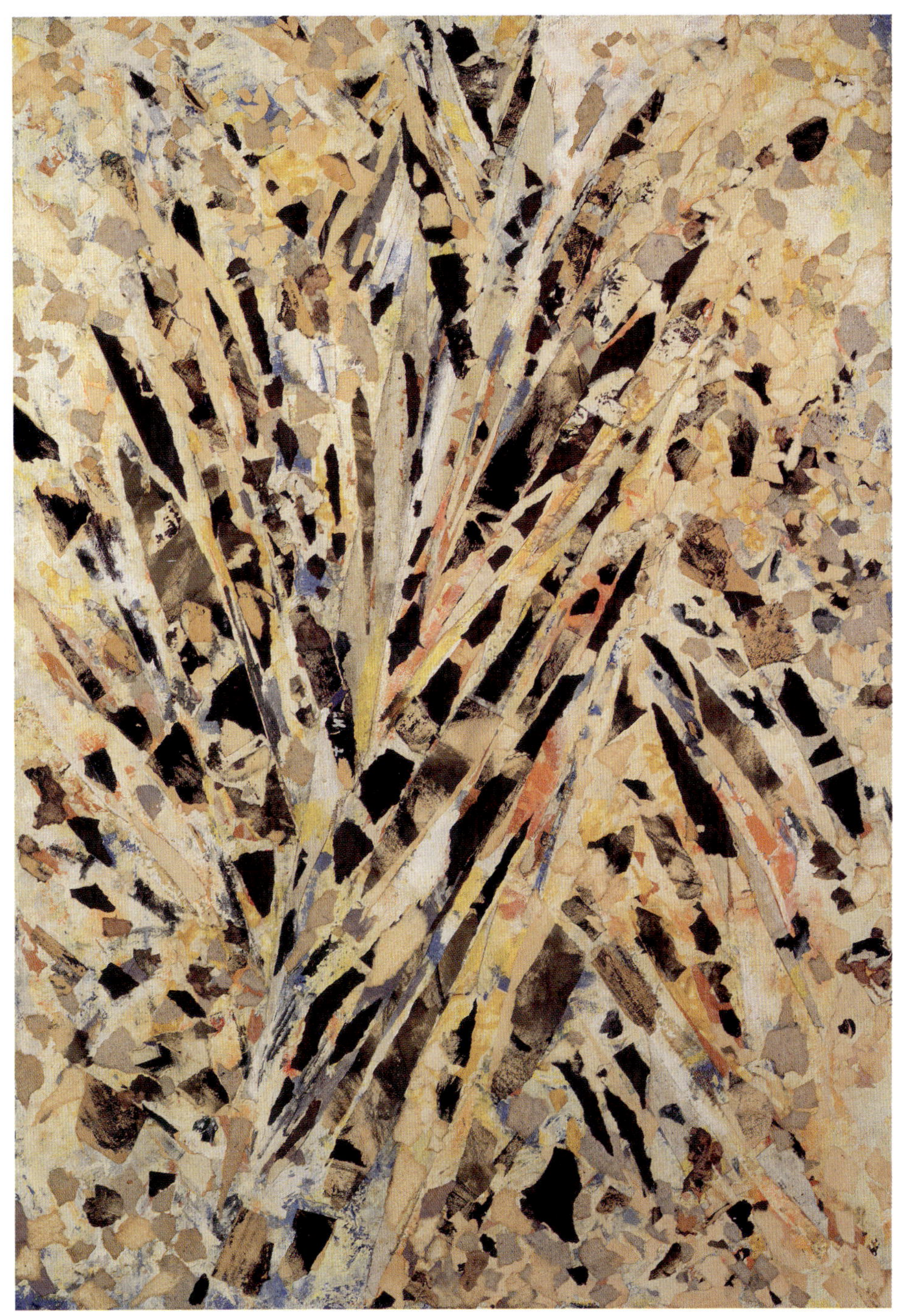

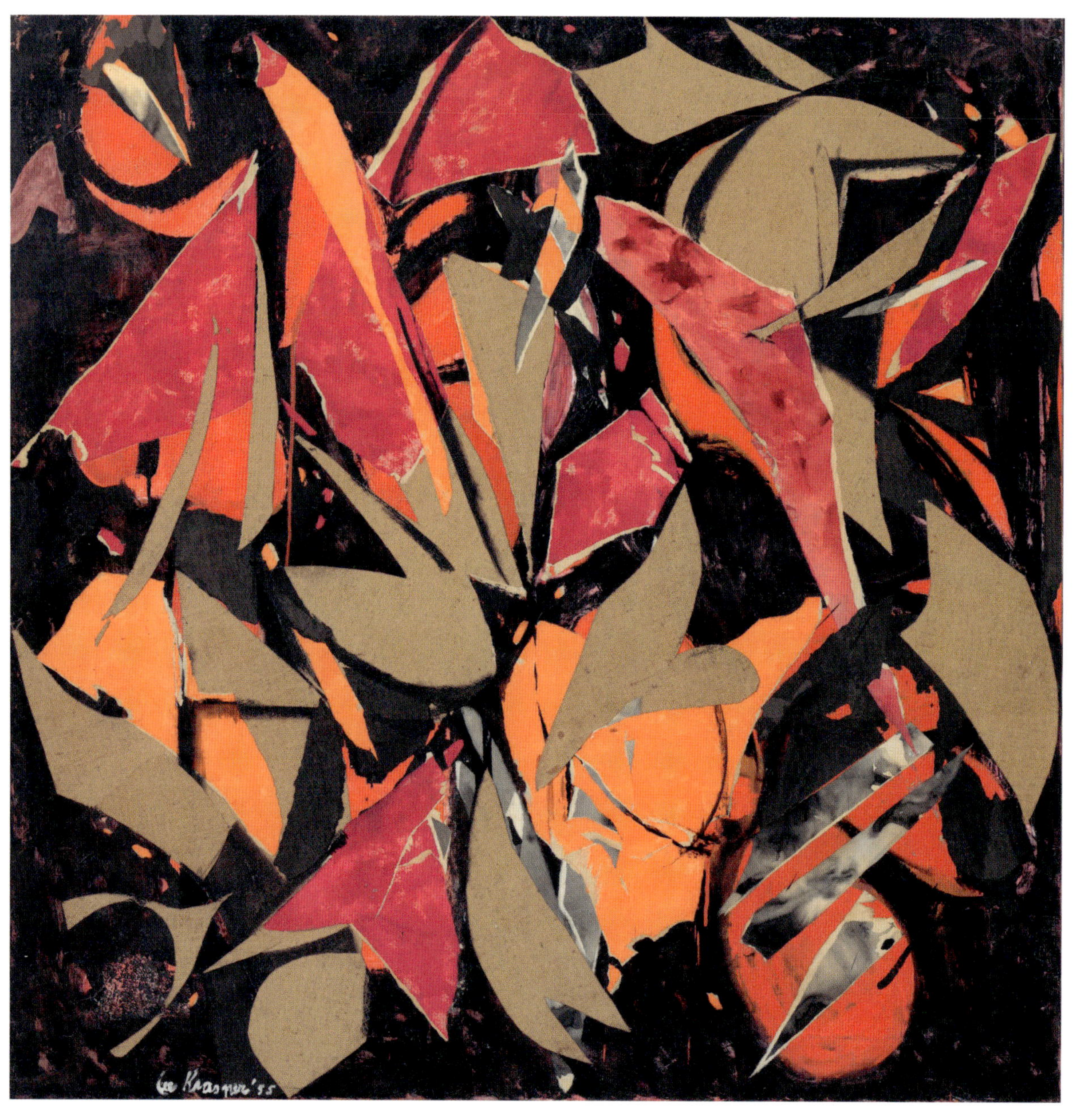

Above: *Bird Talk*, 1955
Opposite: *Bald Eagle*, 1955

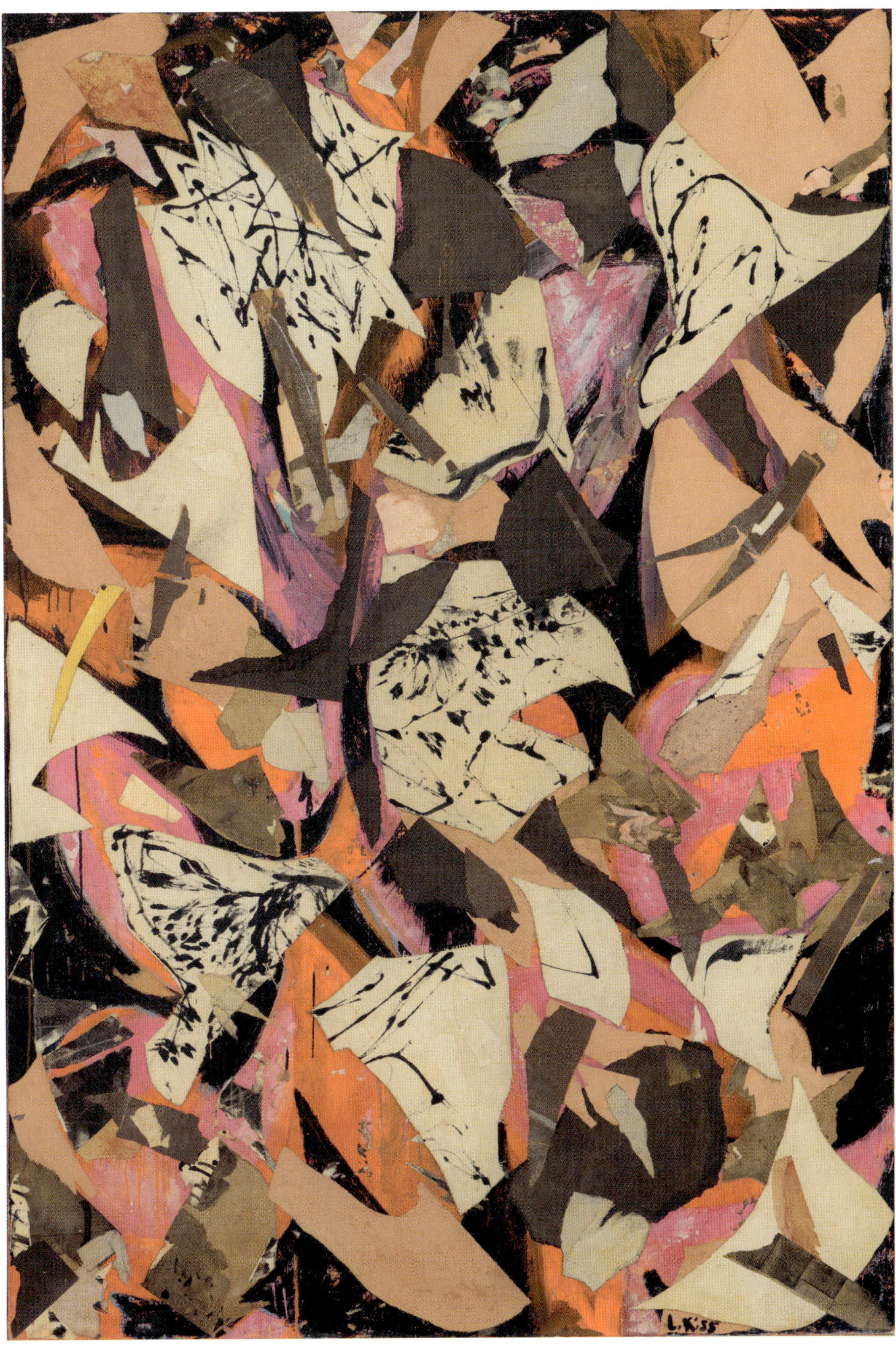

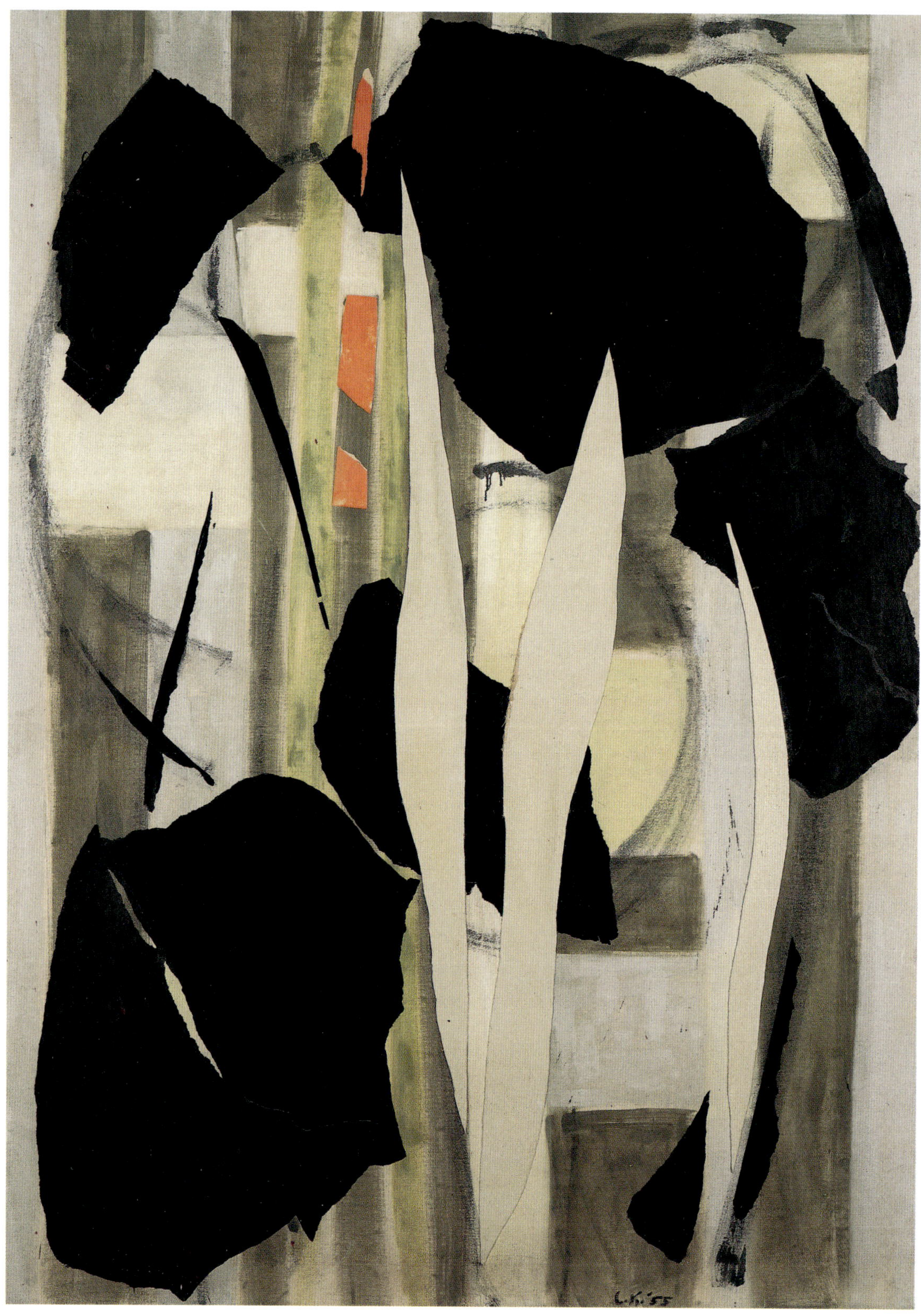

Opposite: *Milkweed*, 1955
Below: *Desert Moon*, 1955

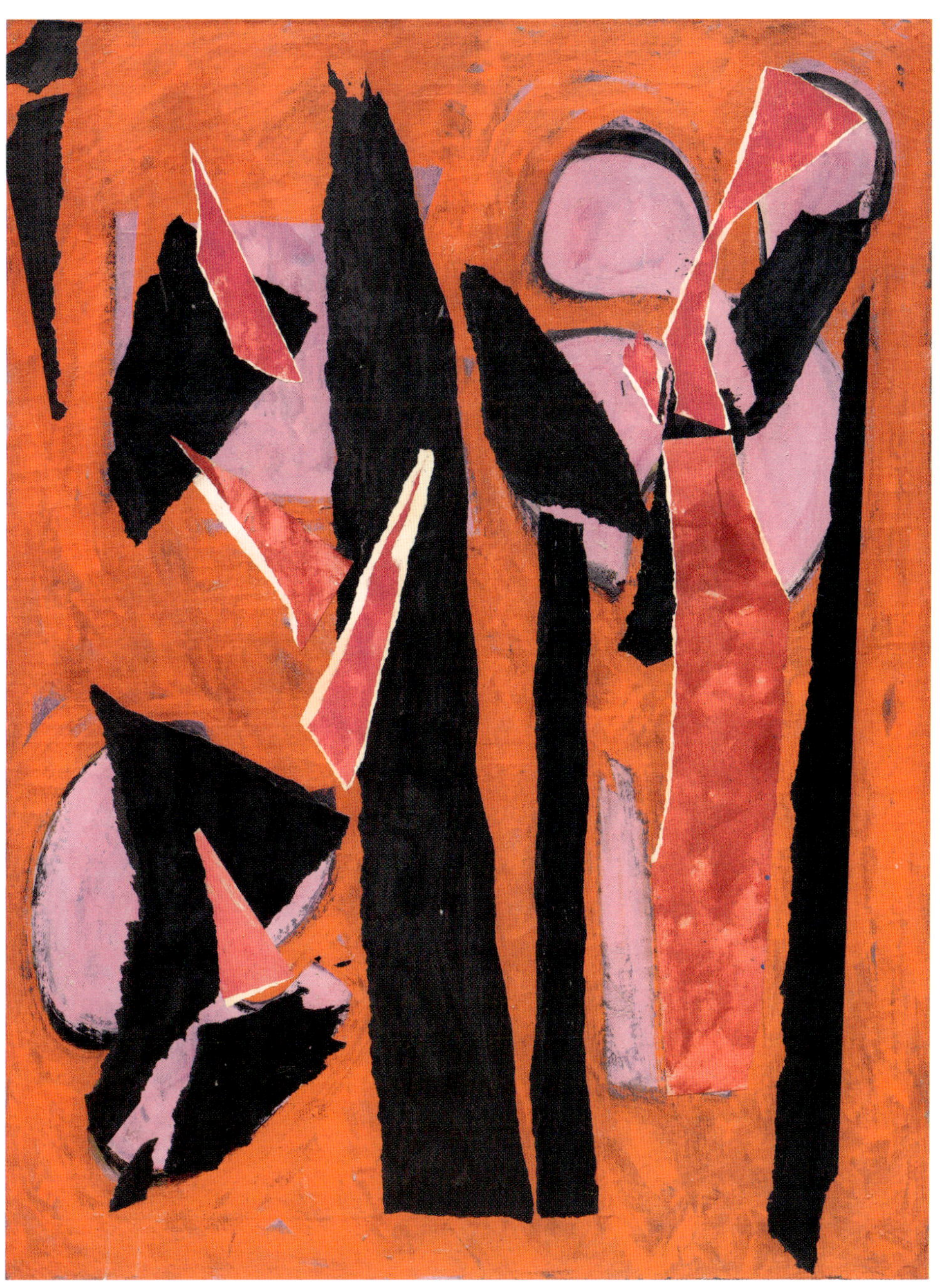

Blue Level, 1955

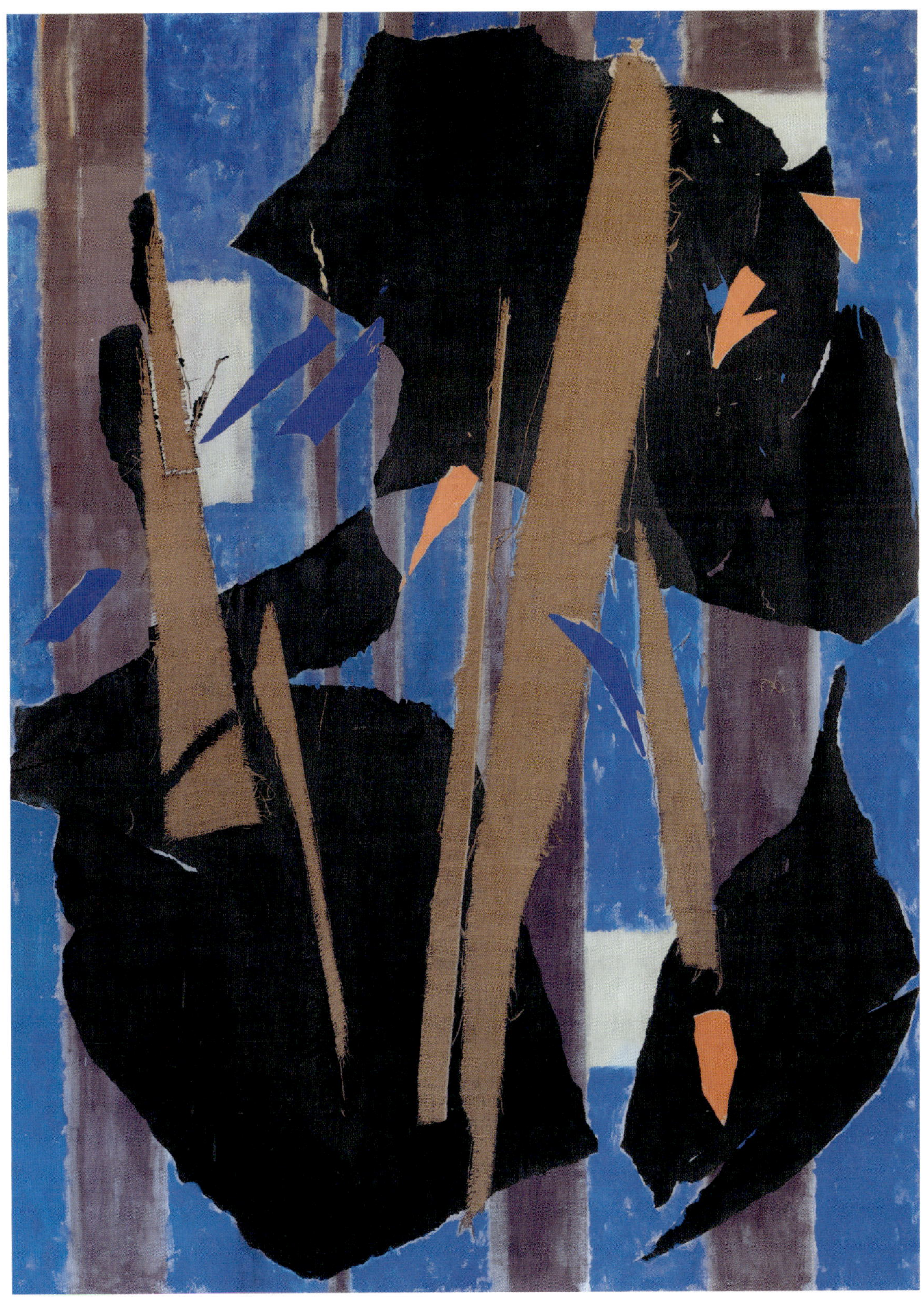

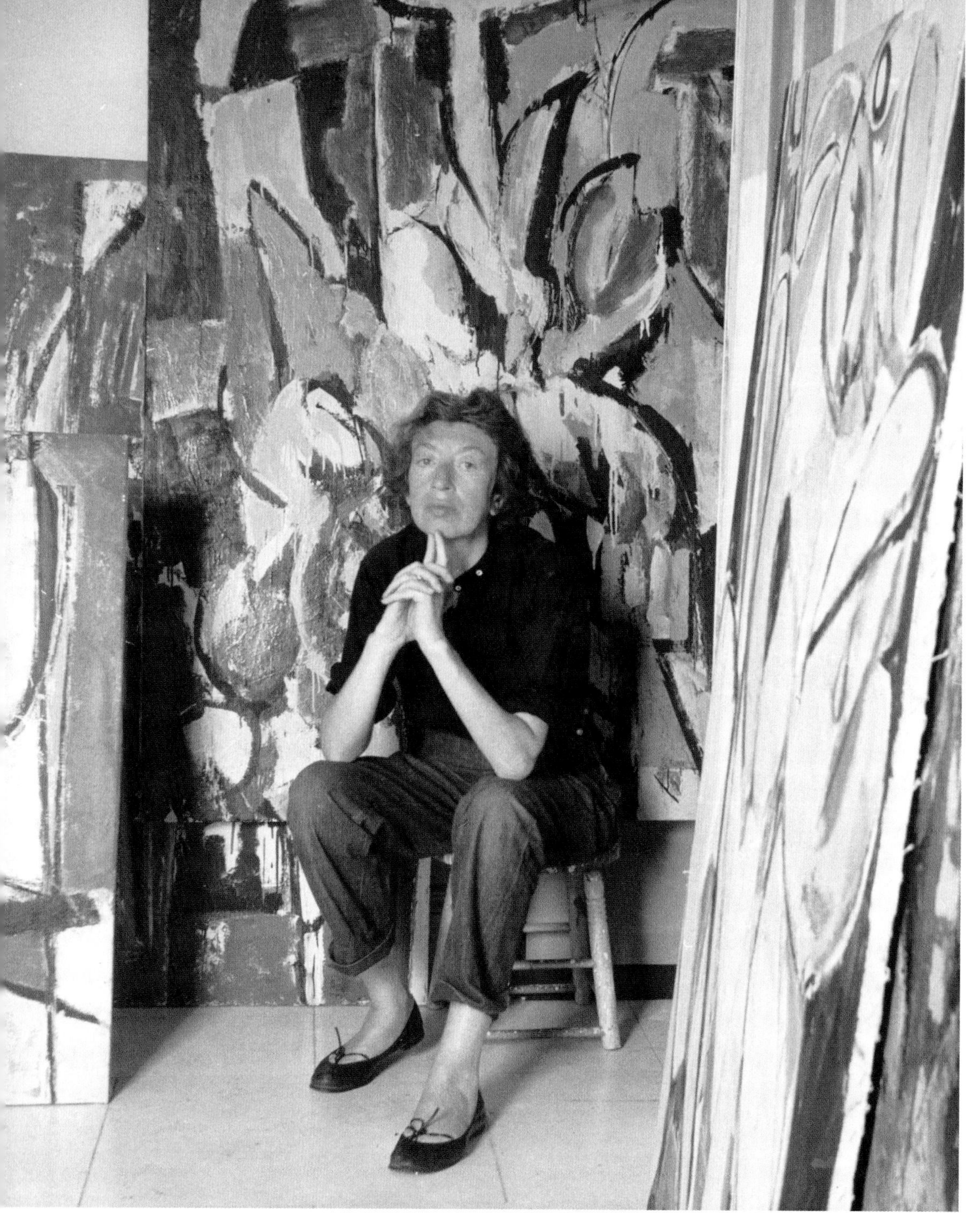

Lee Krasner in her studio in Springs, 30 August 1956, two weeks after Jackson Pollock's death. *Prophecy* (1956) is positioned to the right. Photograph by Waintrob-Budd.

PROPHECY

'PROPHECY WAS FRAUGHT WITH
FOREBODING. WHEN I SAW IT, I WAS
AWARE IT WAS A FRIGHTENING IMAGE,
BUT I HAD TO LET IT COME THROUGH'

In the summer of 1956, Krasner painted a work unlike any other she had made to date. The canvas is dominated by looping, fleshy forms, which are lined with black and accented with touches of pinky-red, amplifying the bodily imagery. *Prophecy* was painted at a moment when Pollock's alcoholism was worsening and their relationship felt under considerable strain. Krasner recalled that her new work 'disturbed me enormously', although Pollock reassured her that 'it was a good painting, and said not to think about it, just continue'.[1] It remained on her easel when she left for France in July for some respite.

In a letter to Pollock dated 21 July, Krasner described how 'the Louvre … is overwhelming – beyond belief. I miss you and wish you were sharing this with me … The painting here is unbelievably bad. (How are you Jackson?)'[2] An answer came on 12 August, when Clement Greenberg telephoned with the news that Pollock had crashed his car the night before, killing himself and Edith Metzger, a friend of Pollock's lover, Ruth Kligman, who had survived. At the age of just forty-seven, Krasner found herself a widow. She flew back to New York that same evening.

Just weeks after Pollock's funeral, Krasner returned to painting, making three works that continued the series she had begun with *Prophecy*: *Birth*, *Embrace* and *Three in Two*. Evoking Picasso and *Les Demoiselles d'Avignon* (1907), Krasner created seething landscapes in which disembodied eyes seem to stare out between contorted limbs. The black was thicker and the red was now richer, making these corporeal scenes feel both violent and erotic. When asked how she managed to paint in the midst of such profound grief, Krasner replied: 'Painting is not separate from life. It is one. It is like asking – do I want to live? My answer is yes – and I paint.'[3]

Prophecy, 1956

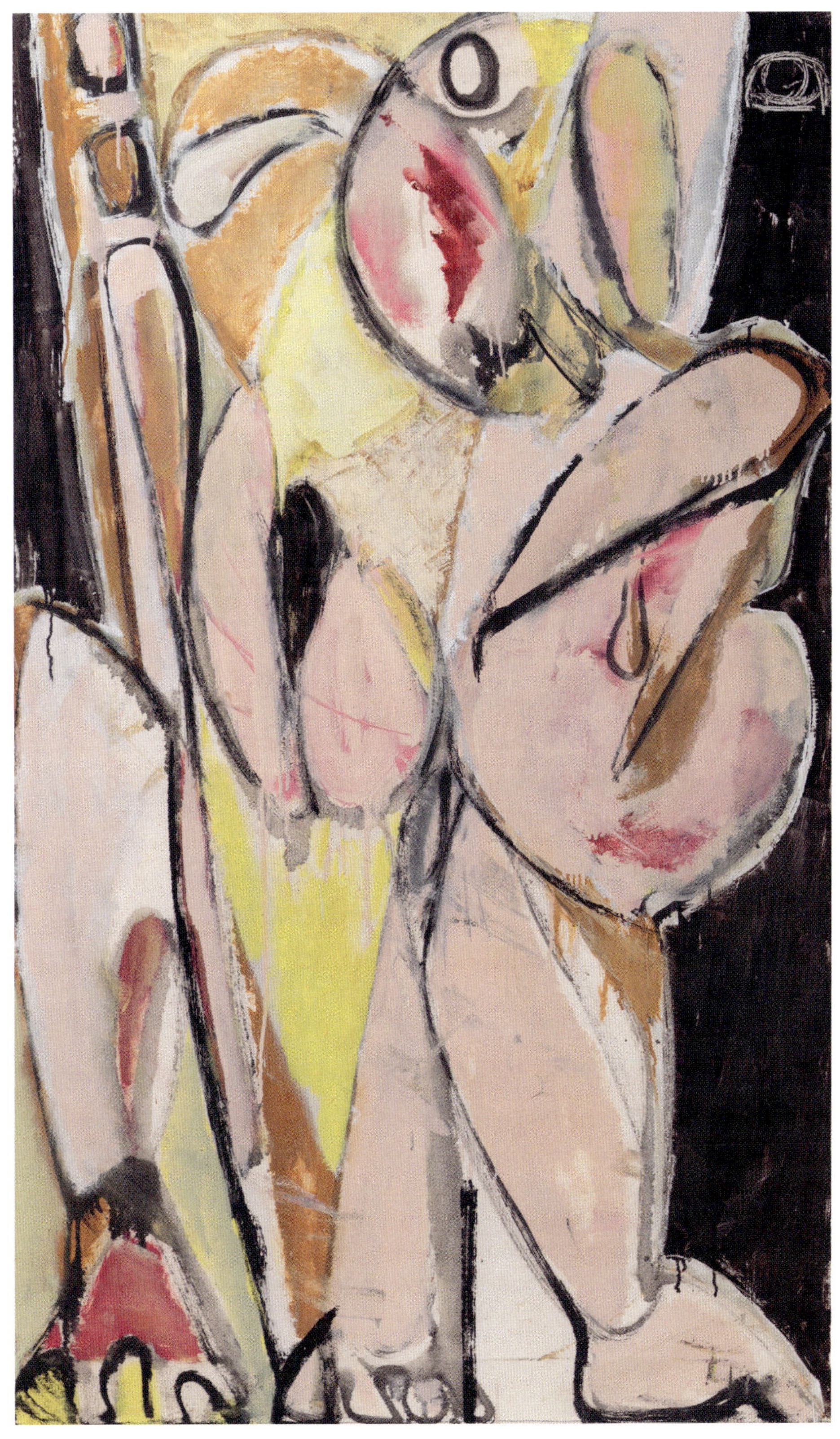

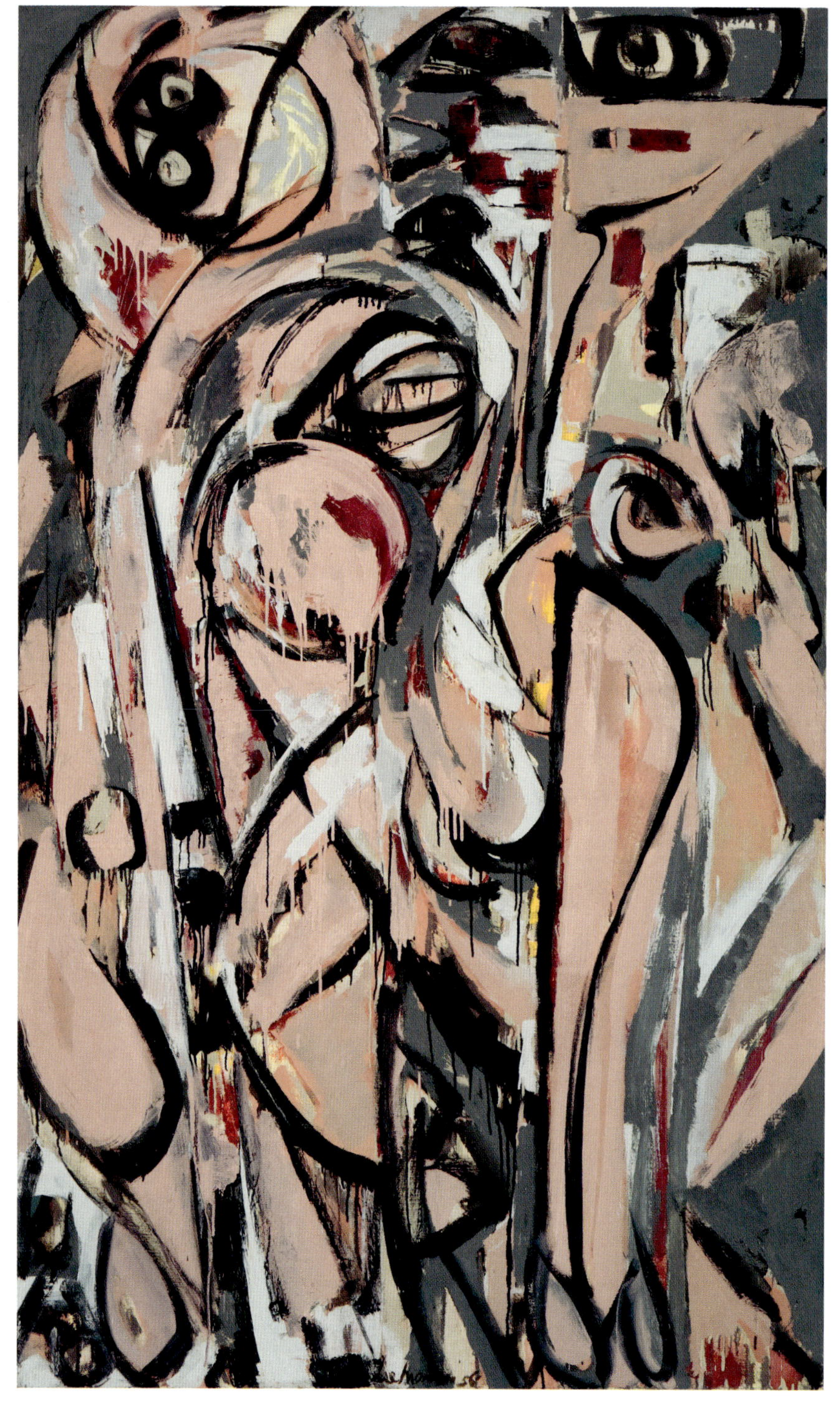

Birth, 1956

Embrace, 1956

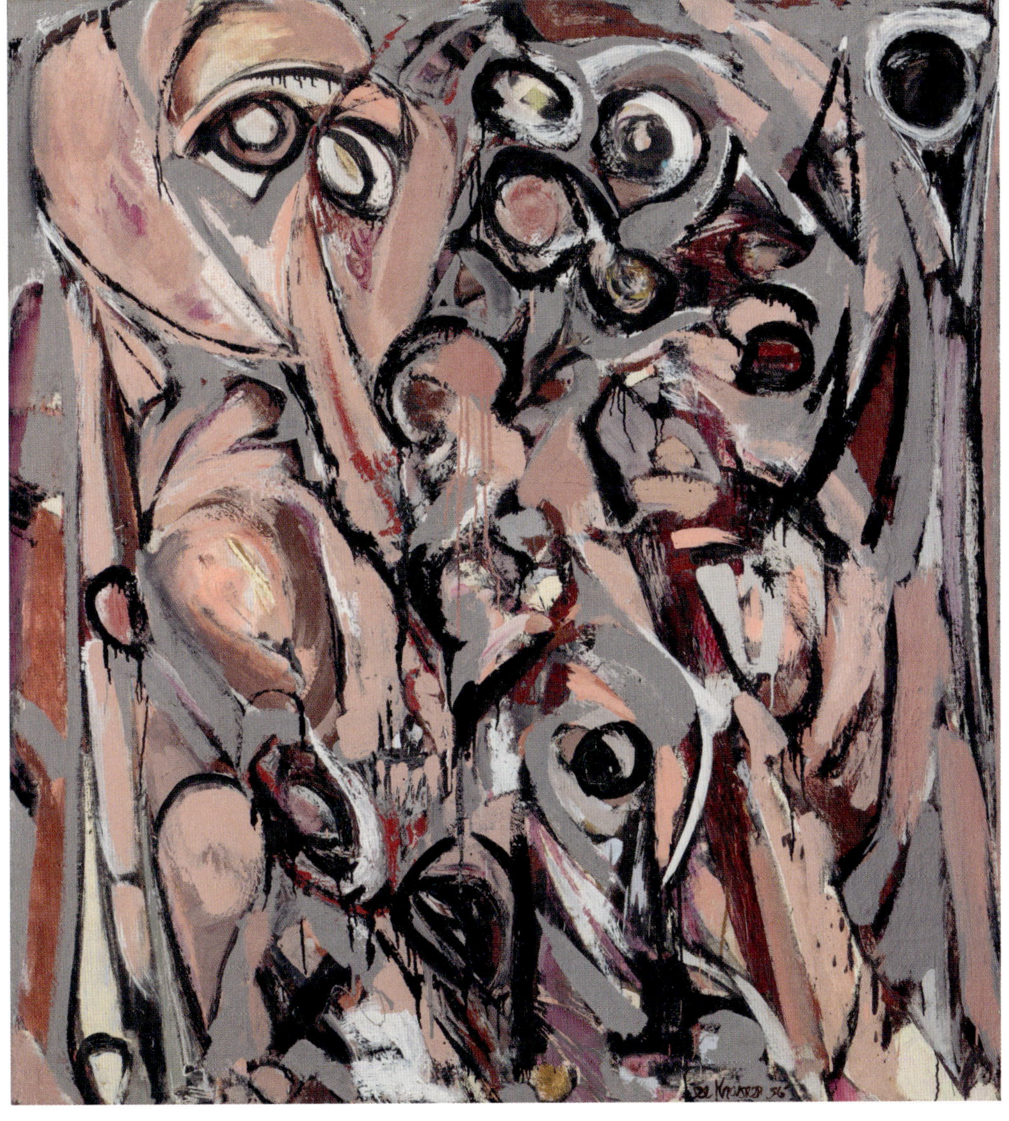

Three in Two, 1956

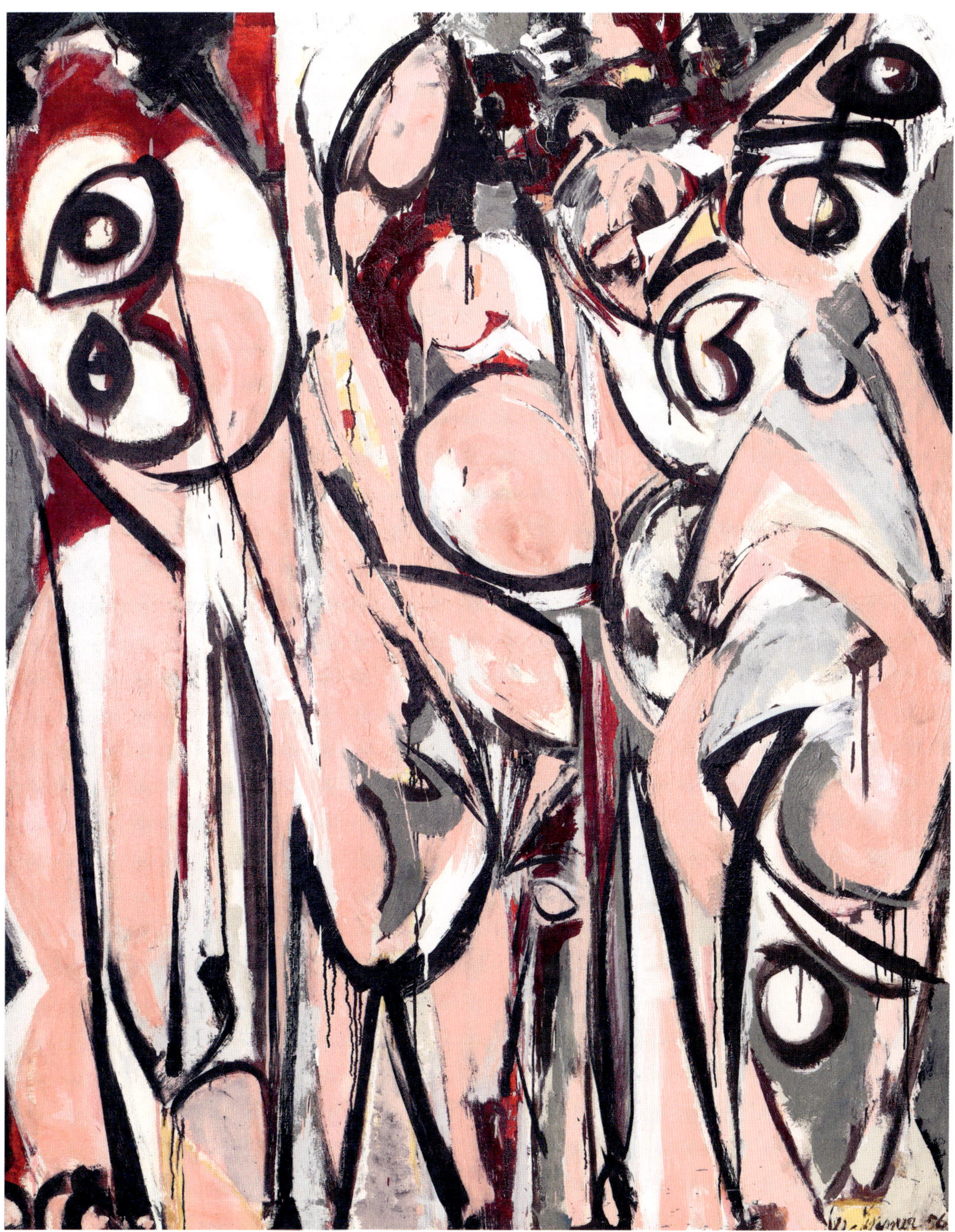

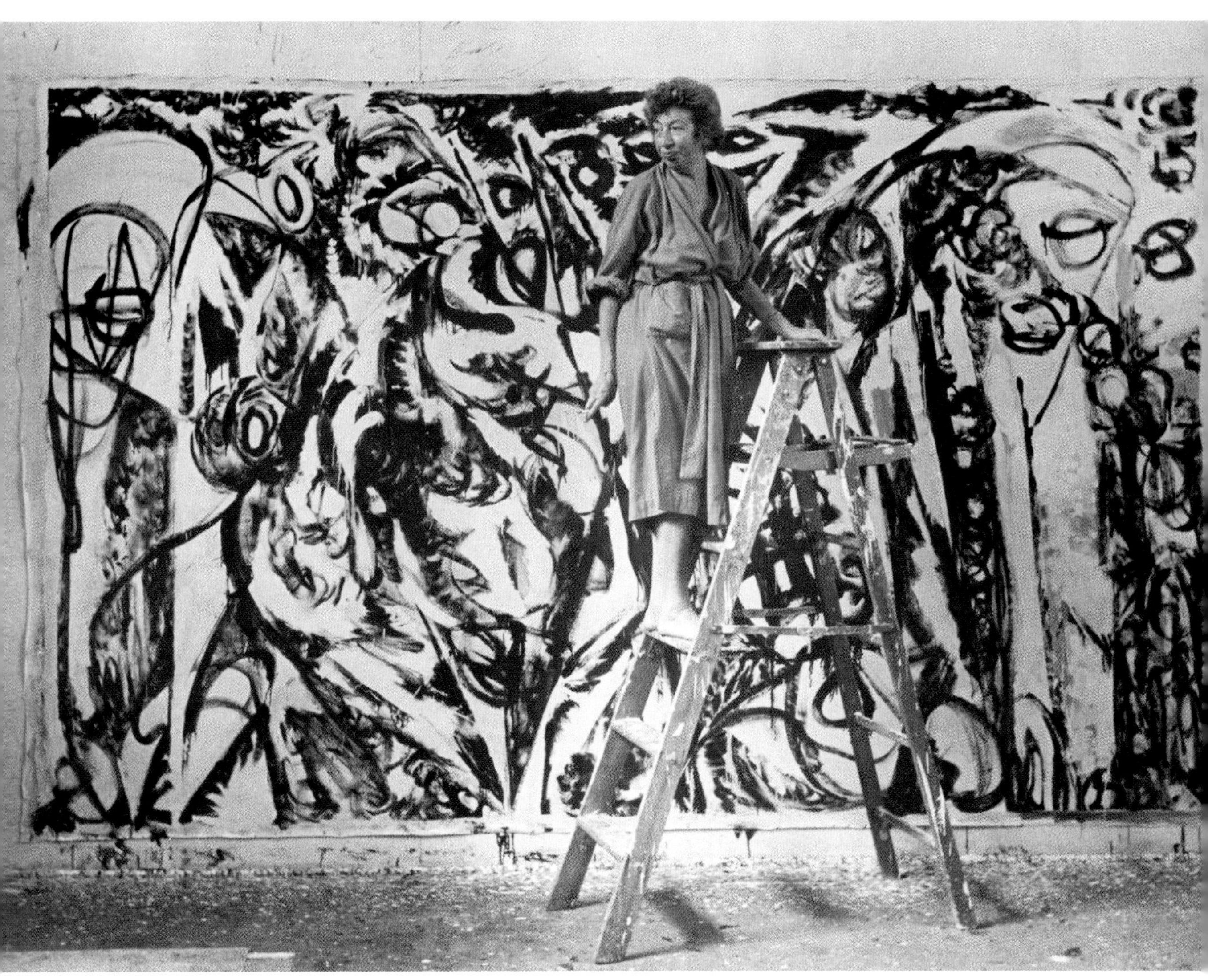

Lee Krasner standing on a ladder in front of *The Gate* (1959) before it was completed, Springs, July or August 1959. Photograph by Halley Erskine.

NIGHT JOURNEYS

Sometime in 1957, Krasner decided that she would take over Pollock's barn. Although it must have been a space loaded with painful memories, it was also the largest working area with the best natural light. Ever practical, Krasner explained in an interview that 'there was no point in letting it stand empty'.[1] Suddenly, she found she could work on an unprecedented scale, tacking lengths of unstretched canvas directly to the wall. She was suffering from chronic insomnia at the time and so worked at night – a practice that led her to restrict her palette to white and umber (both raw and burnt), since she hated working with colour under artificial light.

The result was an explosive series of paintings, which her friend the poet Richard Howard called her 'Night Journeys'. The choice of umber instead of black gives the frenzied scenes an organic quality, like churned-up muddy water or a wild desert storm. The titles of the works, such as *Polar Stampede*, accentuate the impression of natural drama; as Krasner wryly commented, 'a stampede is something that you don't watch casually'.[2] In the same interview, she went on to explain that the titling of *Assault on the Solar Plexus* was 'embarrassingly realistic … I had had the blow-up with Greenberg, my mother died shortly before … I didn't know how to deal with Pollock. It was a rough life.'[3]

The 'blow-up' Krasner refers to came when Clement Greenberg decided to cancel the exhibition he had offered her at the gallery French & Company because he did not like the direction her new work was taking. Rather than abandon the series, however, Krasner threw herself into its midst. These were demanding works to create: *Polar Stampede* is 2.4 metres (8 ft) in height and 4.1 metres (13½ ft) wide, while Krasner was 1.6 metres (5¼ ft) tall. They forced her to use her entire body, sometimes leaping from the floor with a long-handled brush to reach the furthest corners. She called them 'physical paintings', in which a staccato rhythm is built out of a repeated 'gesture [of] thrust'.[4]

Triple Goddess, 1960

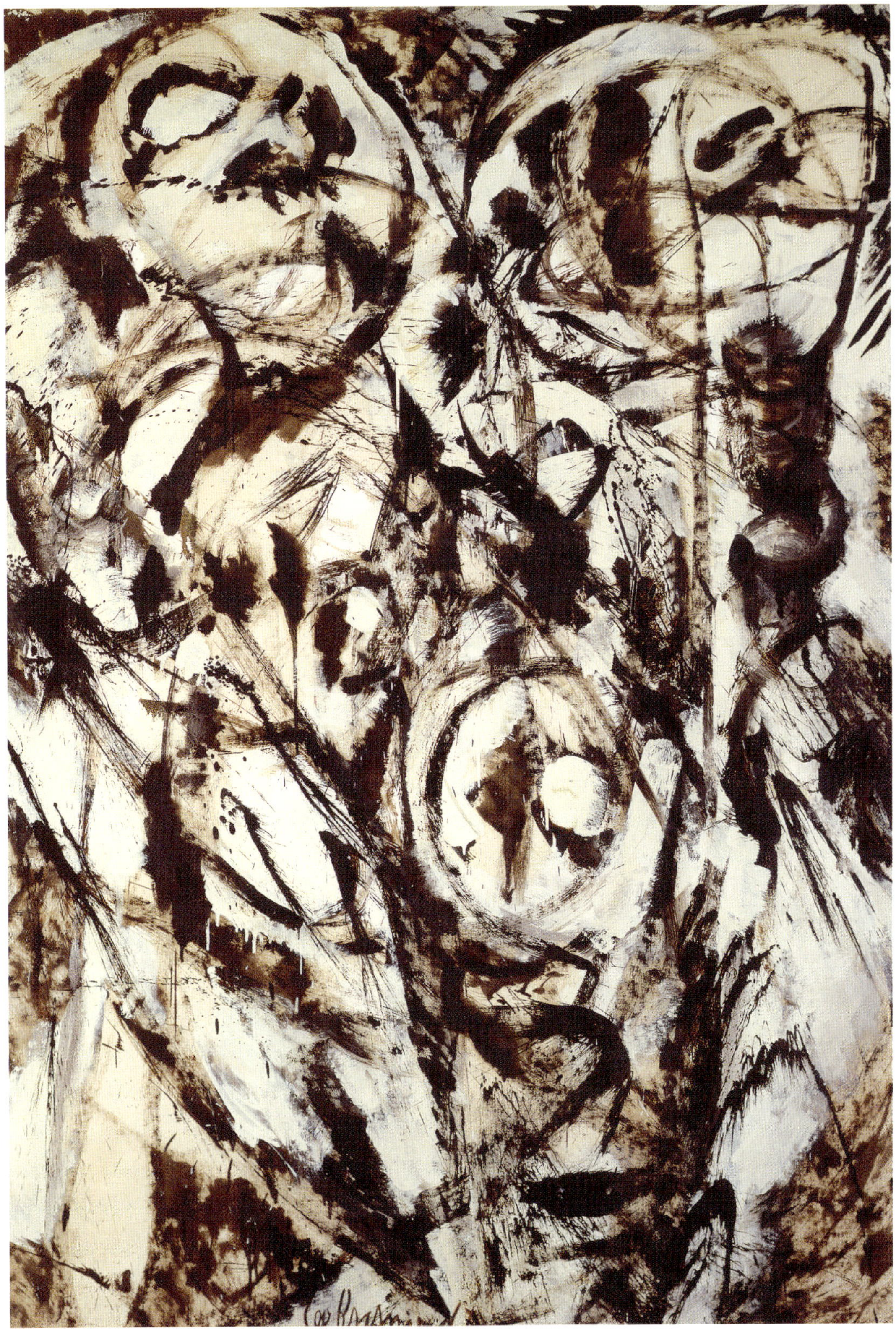

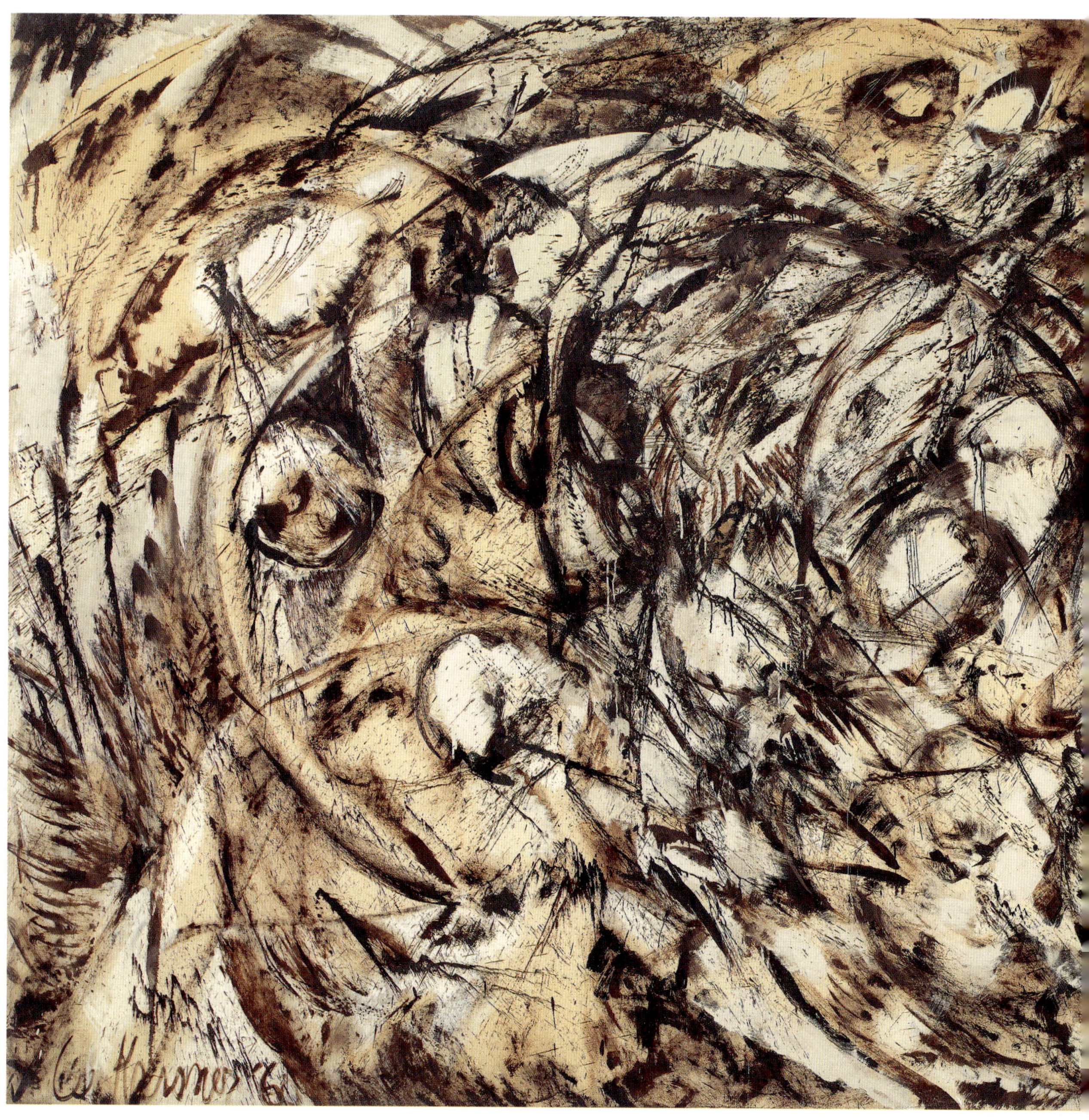

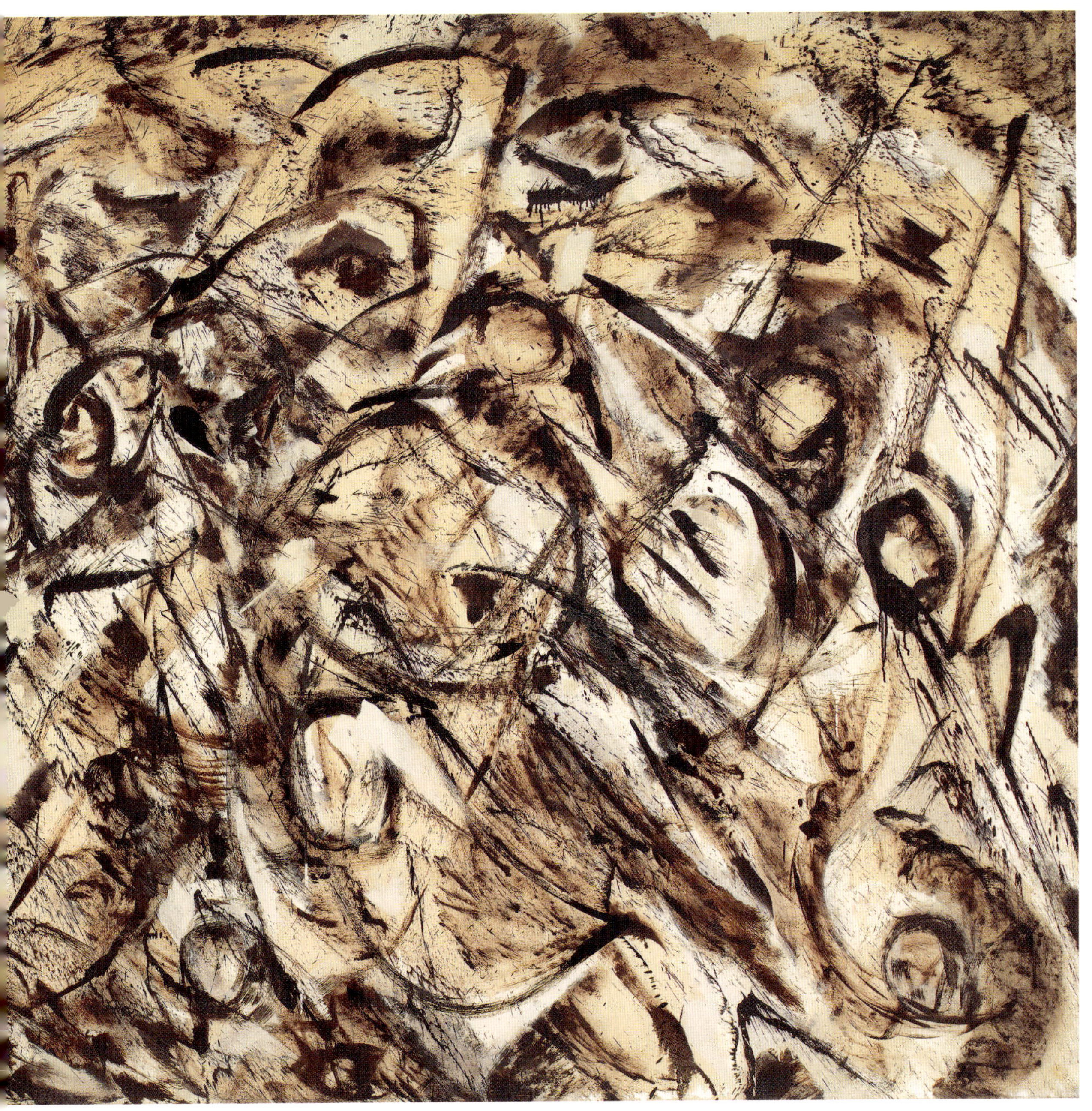

The Eye is the First Circle, 1960

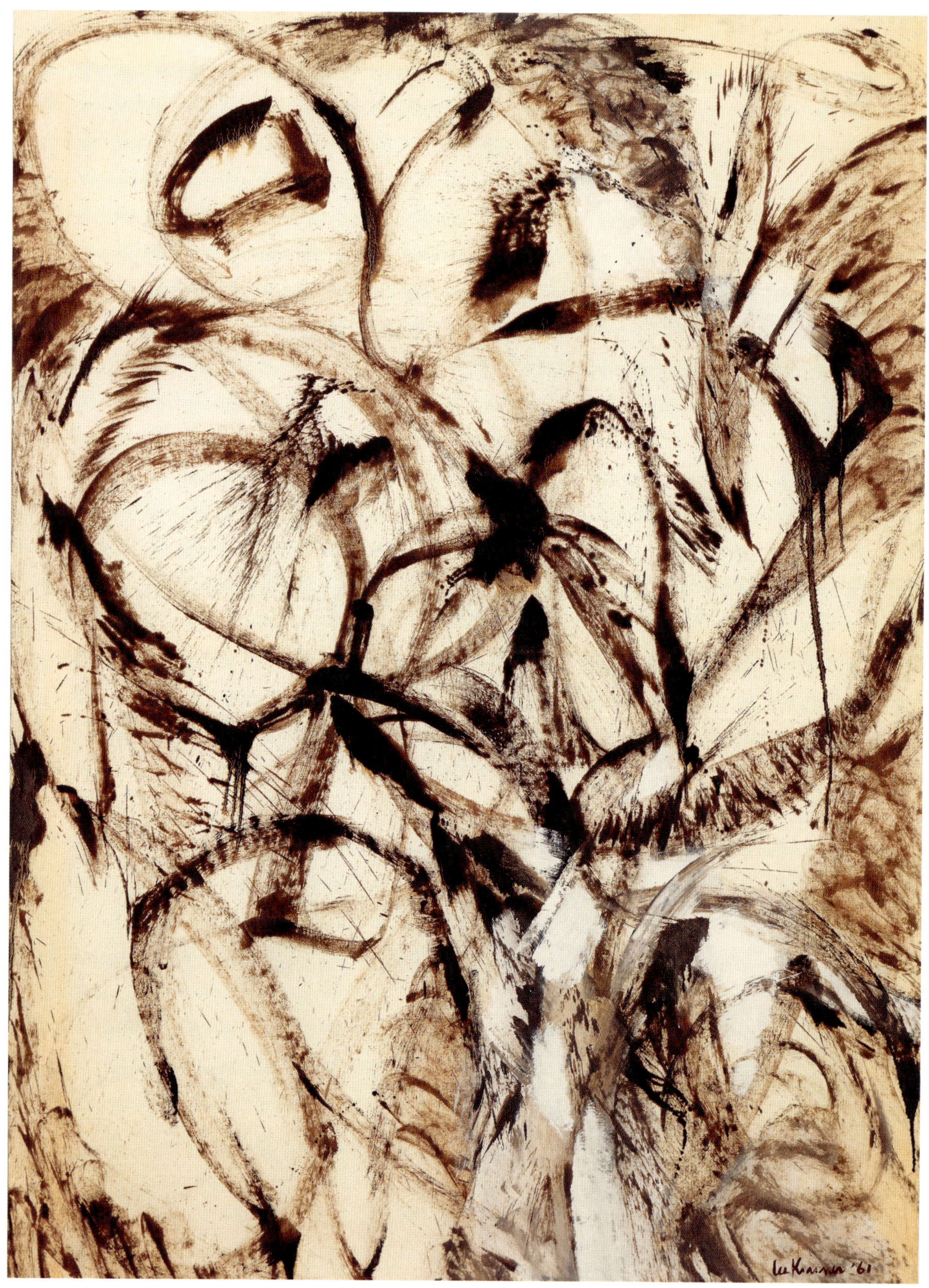

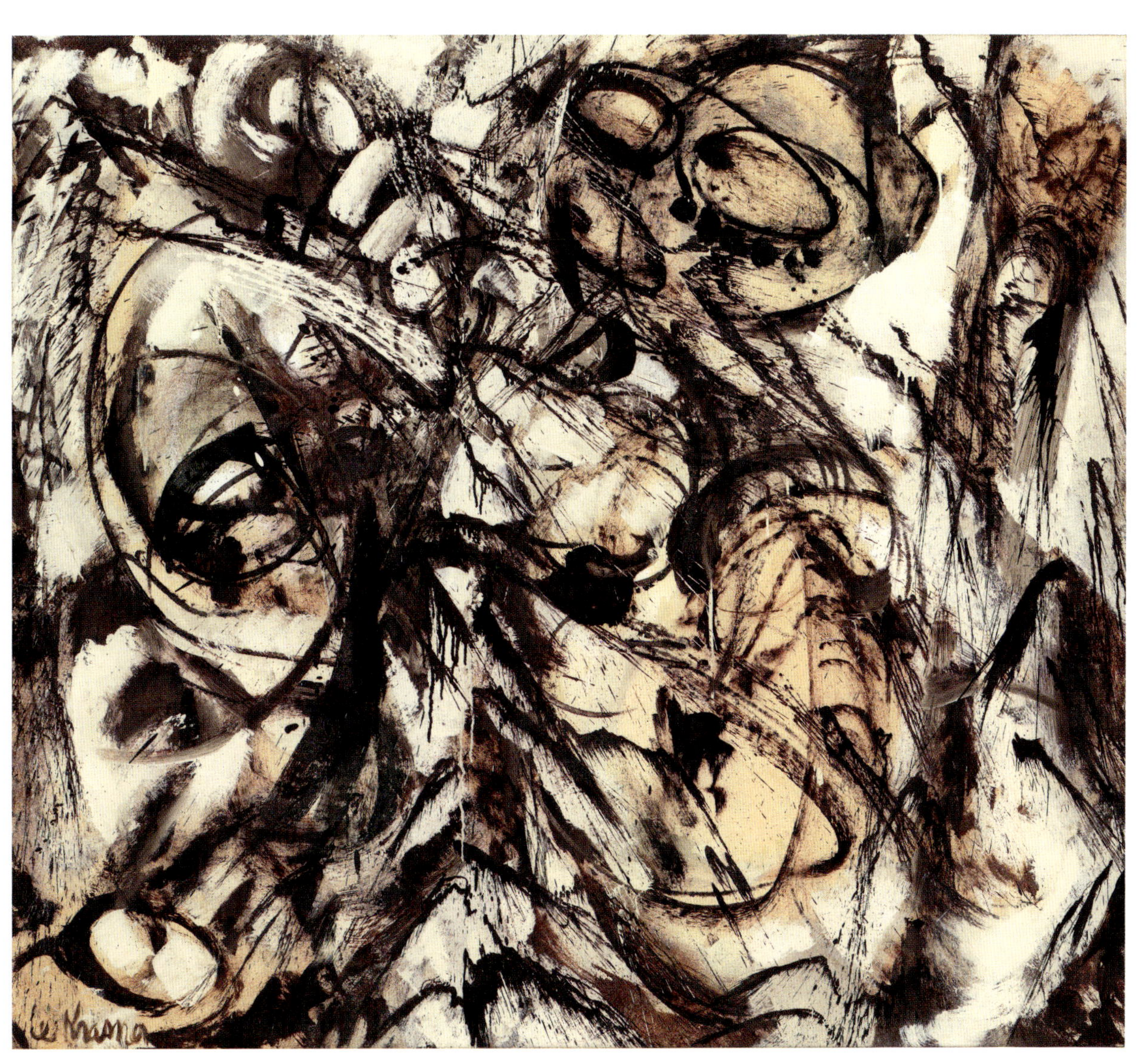

Above: *The Guardian*, 1960
Opposite: *Assault on the Solar Plexus*, 1961

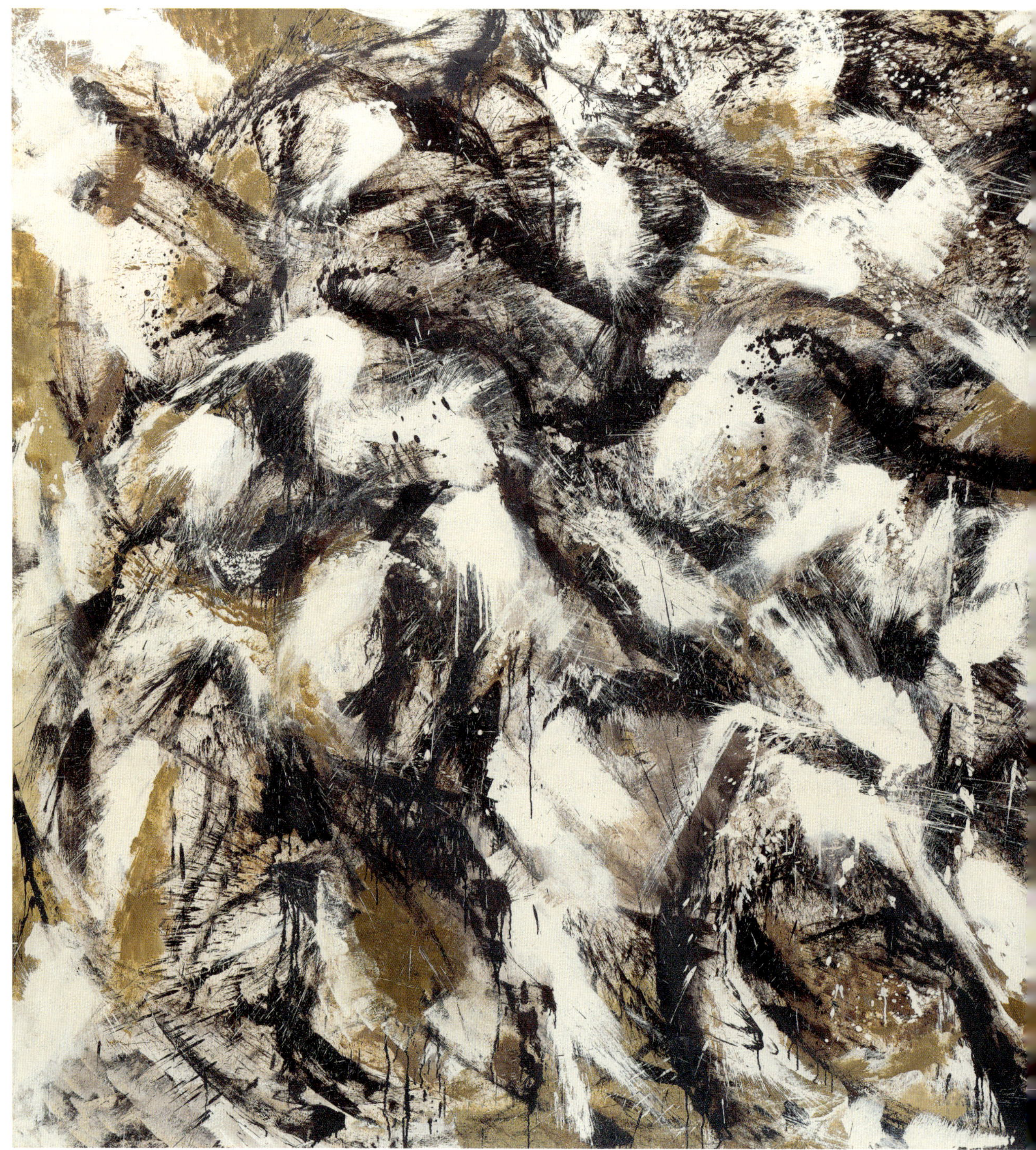

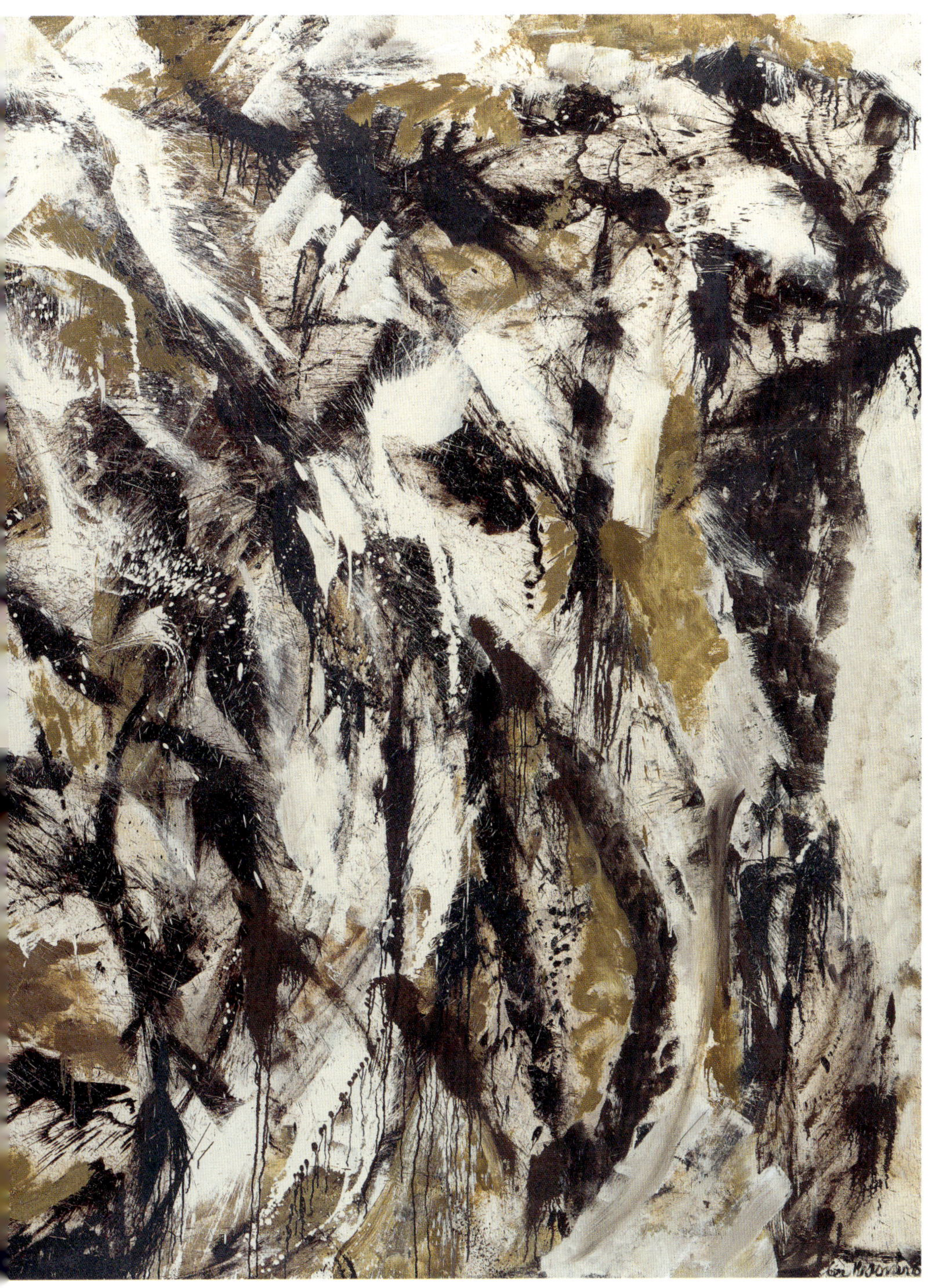

Polar Stampede, 1960

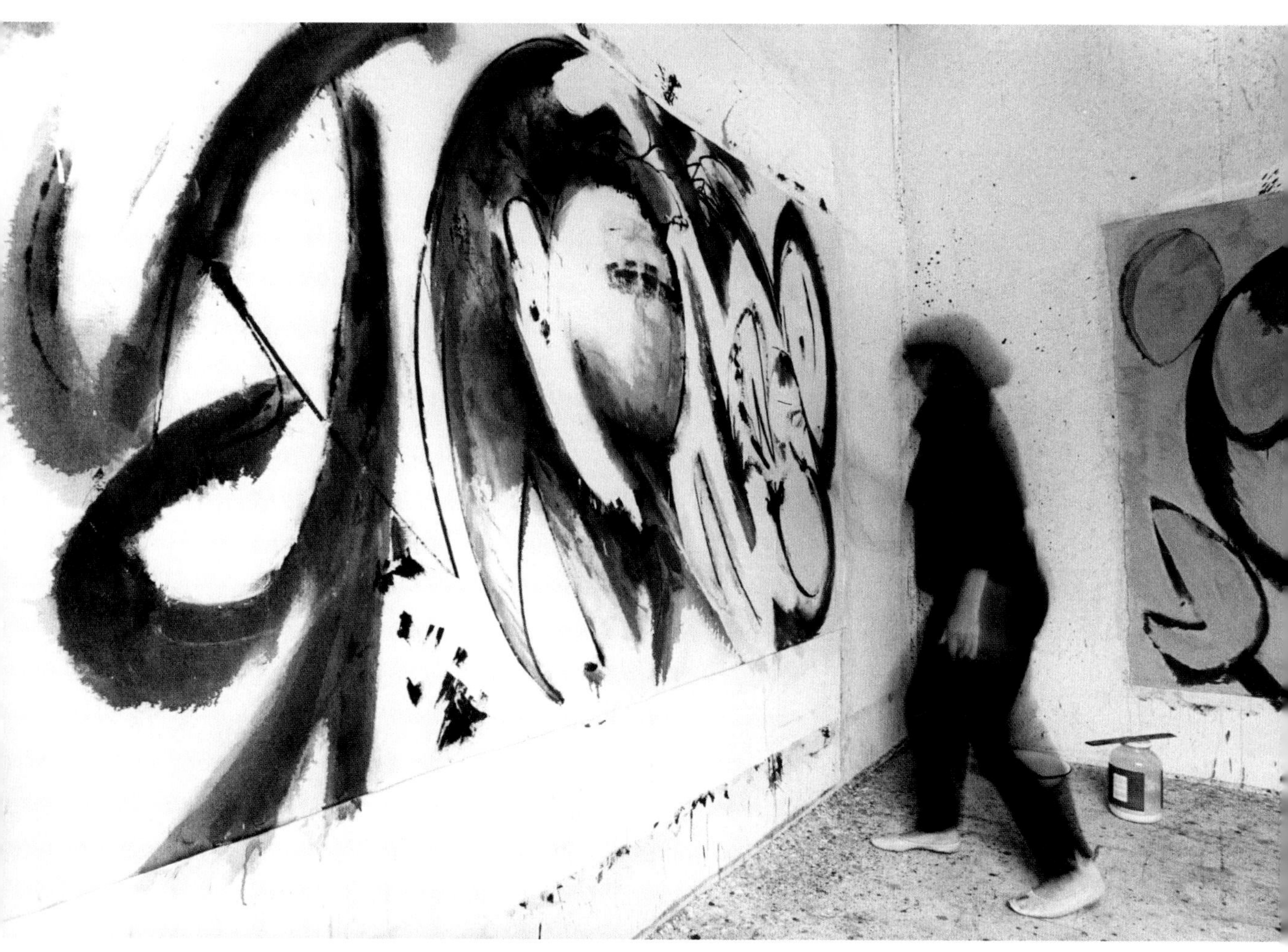

Lee Krasner painting *Portrait in Green* in her studio,
Springs, 1969. Photograph by Mark Patiky.

PRIMARY SERIES

In the early 1960s, Krasner allowed colour to burst back into her painting. *Another Storm* (1963) retains the reduced palette of her 'Night Journeys' but replaces the subdued umber with a blazing alizarin crimson, punctuated with strokes of white that resemble froth on fast-flowing water. When Krasner fell in East Hampton and broke her dominant right arm, she simply taught herself to work with her left, squirting paint directly from the tube and using the fingertips of her right hand to guide the movements. This resulted in more tactile works, such as *Through Blue* (1963) and *Icarus* (1964).

In the years that followed, Krasner's gestures would become looser, more calligraphic, with bold forms tumbling and somersaulting across the canvas in dissonant hues. *Combat* (1965) could well be titled after the clash between fuchsia pink and hot orange that plays out across its 4-metre (13-ft) width. Krasner's colours, in what she called her 'Primary Series', feel floral, exuberant, even decadent at times, much like those of her artistic hero Matisse, who declared that 'with colour one obtains an energy that seems to stem from witchcraft'.[1] Krasner's confidence might have come from the survey of her work that was organized by Bryan Robertson at the Whitechapel Gallery in London in 1965 – the first institutional exhibition of Krasner's art – which was met with very positive reviews.

For Krasner, each work had to emerge authentically from within, so she never made sketches or preparatory studies in advance of a painting; as she herself explained, 'there's a … blank, and something begins to happen, and the hope is … that it comes through.'[2] In 1968, however, Krasner came across a stash of handmade paper that she had collected over the years, made locally in Long Island by the artist Douglass Morse Howell, and decided to use them for a new body of work. She experimented with the simplicity of just one or two gouache colours and the reaction of the pigment with the textured supports: 'I was just mad for doing them and they went at quite a clip.'[3]

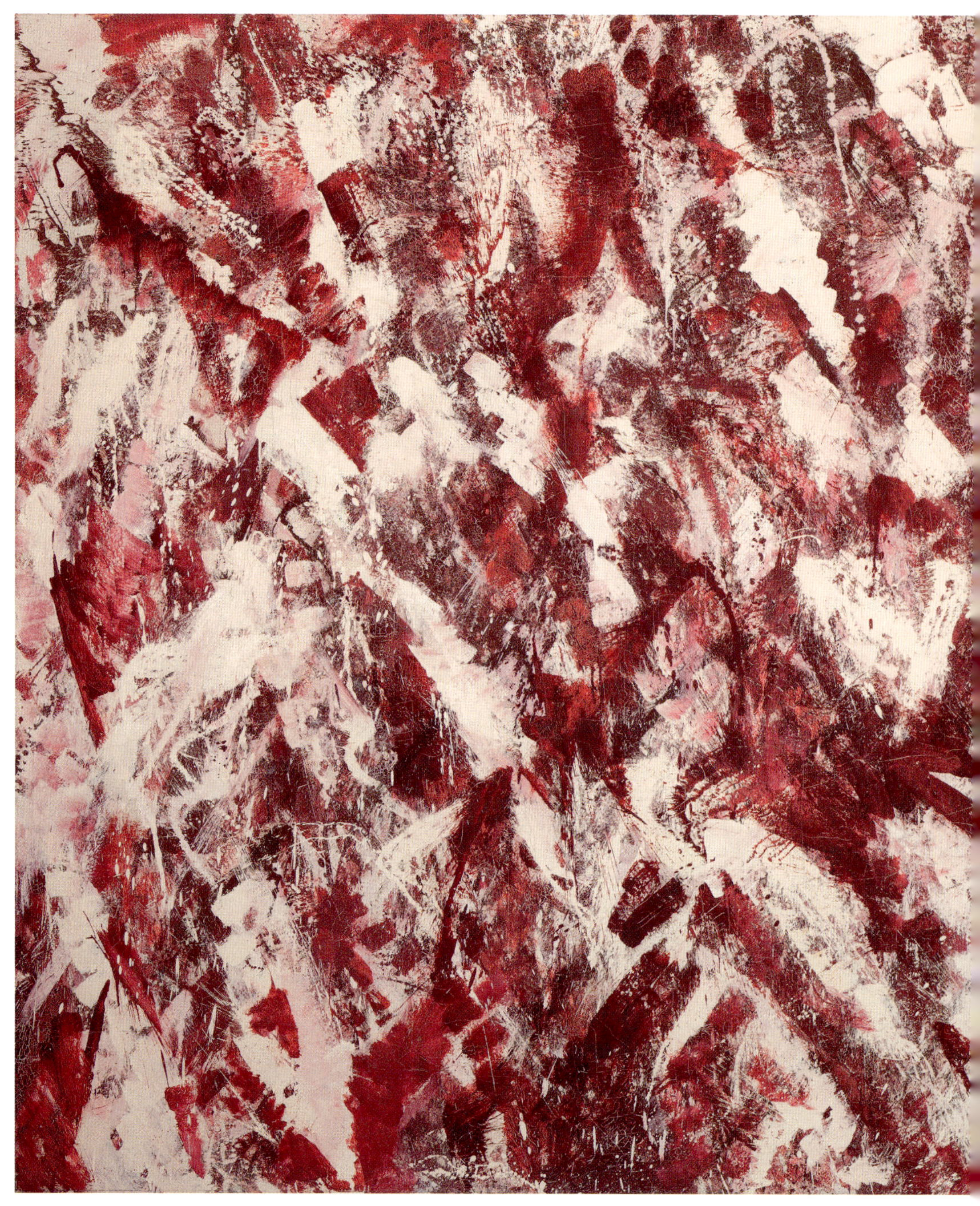

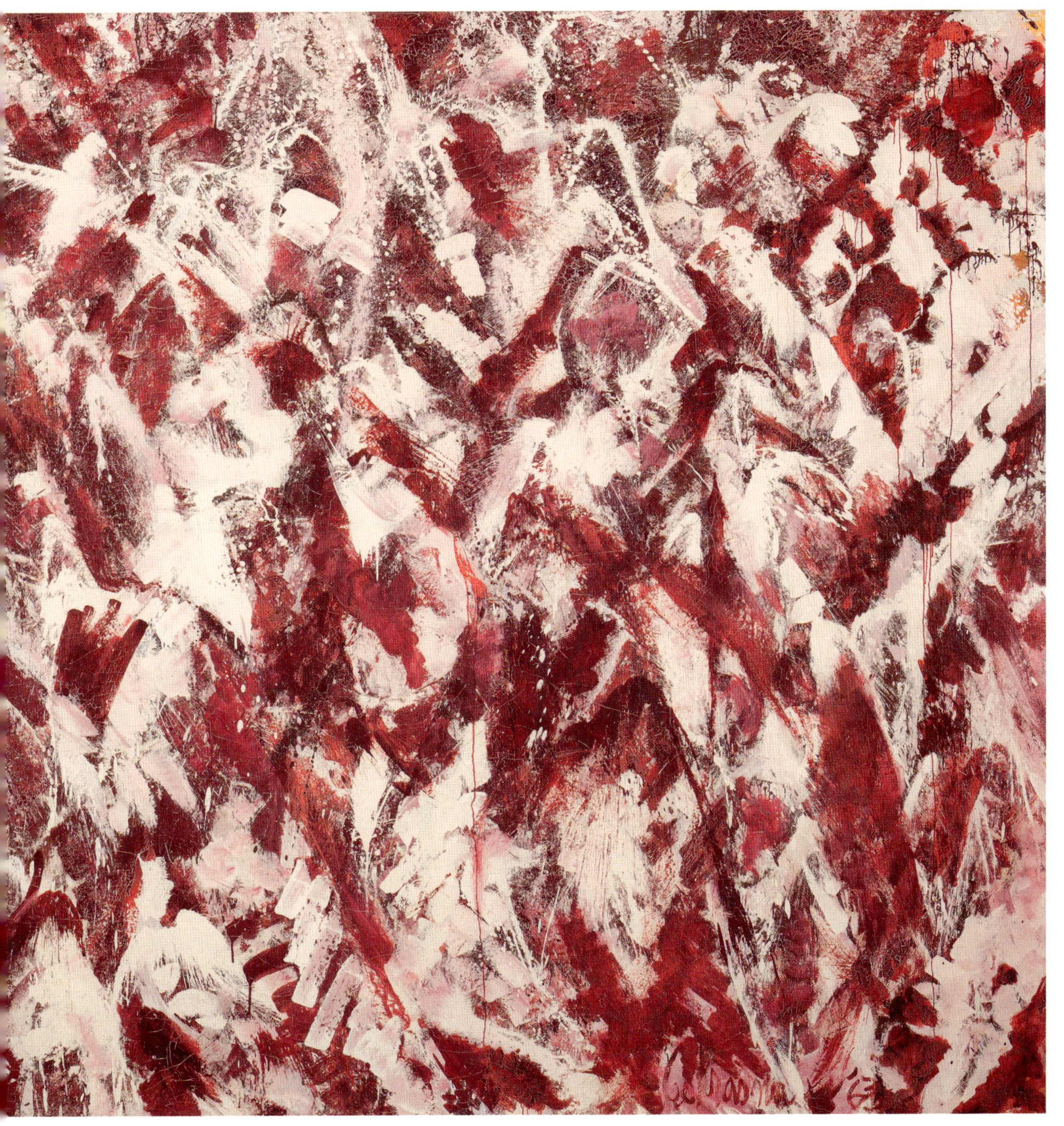

Another Storm, 1963

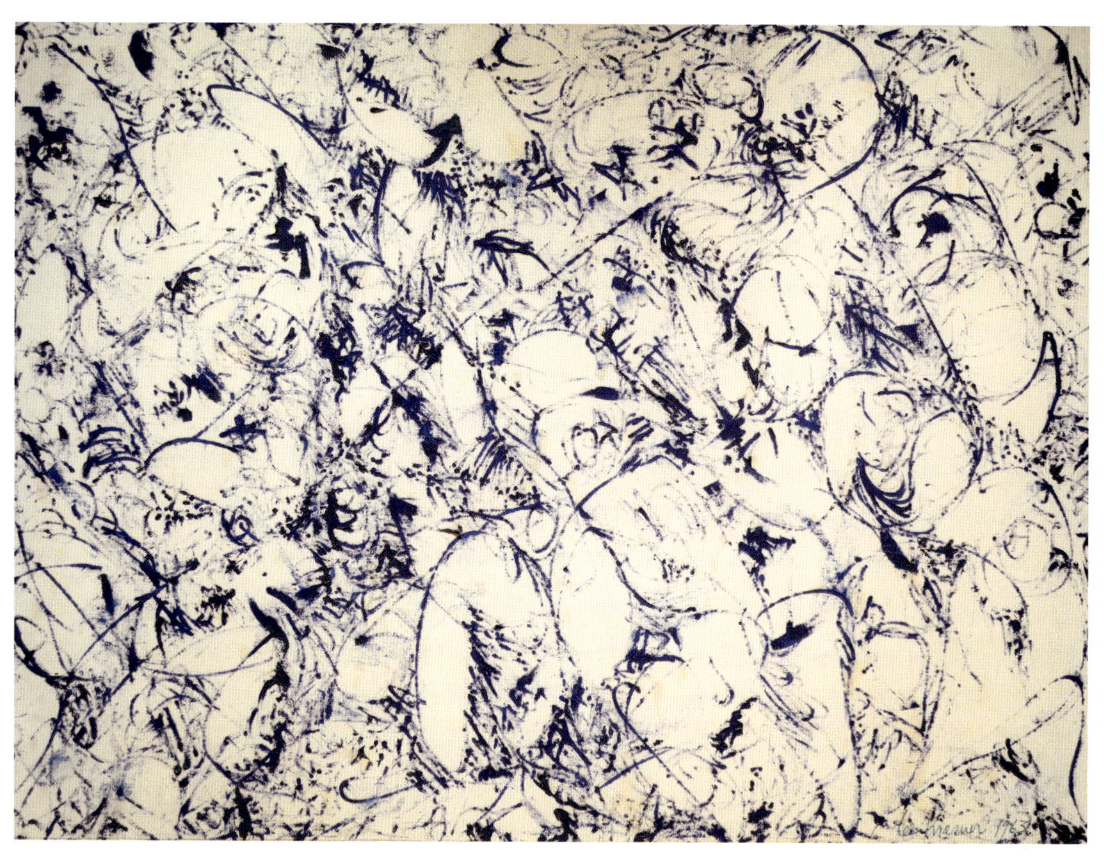

Happy Lady, 1963

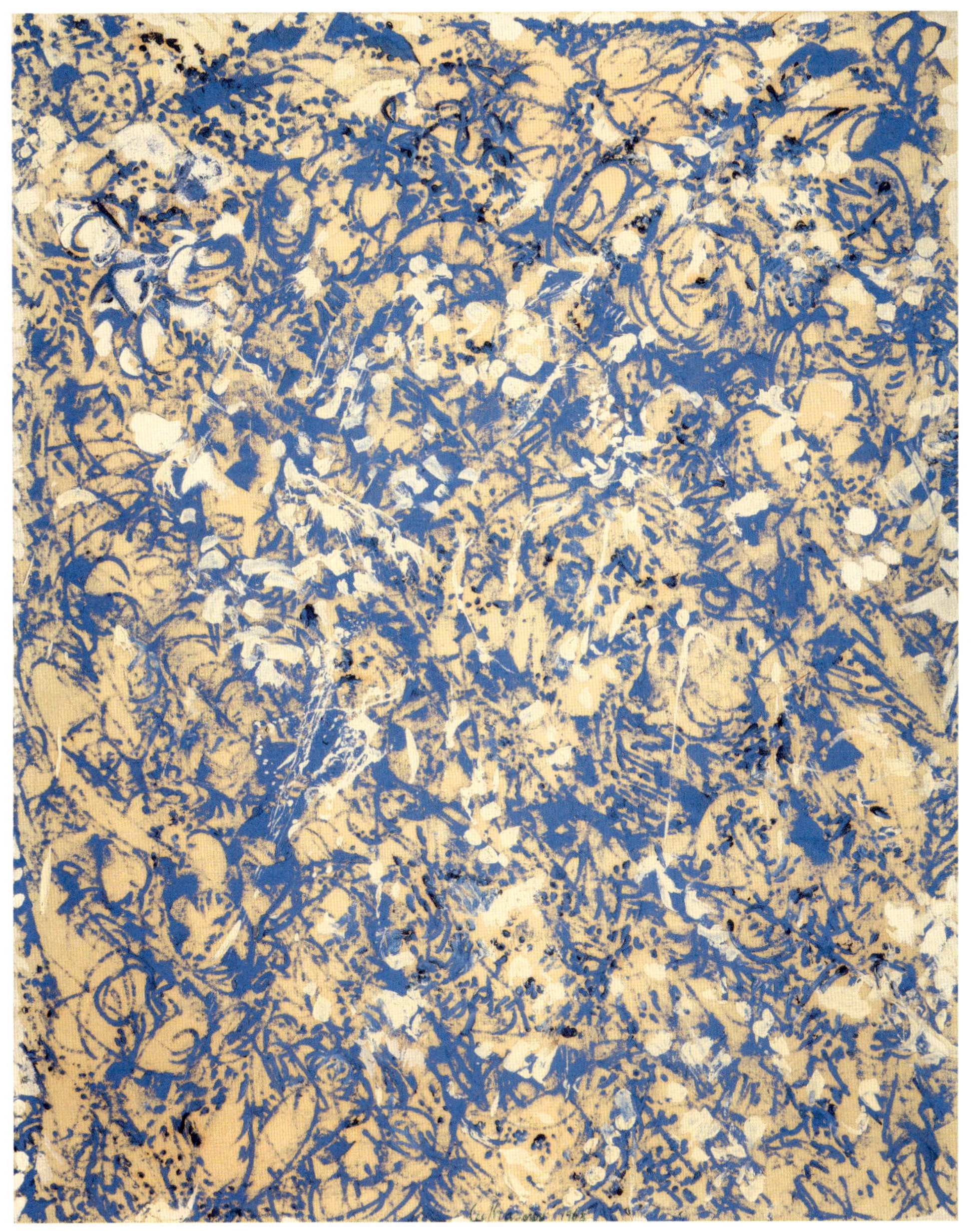

Through Blue, 1963

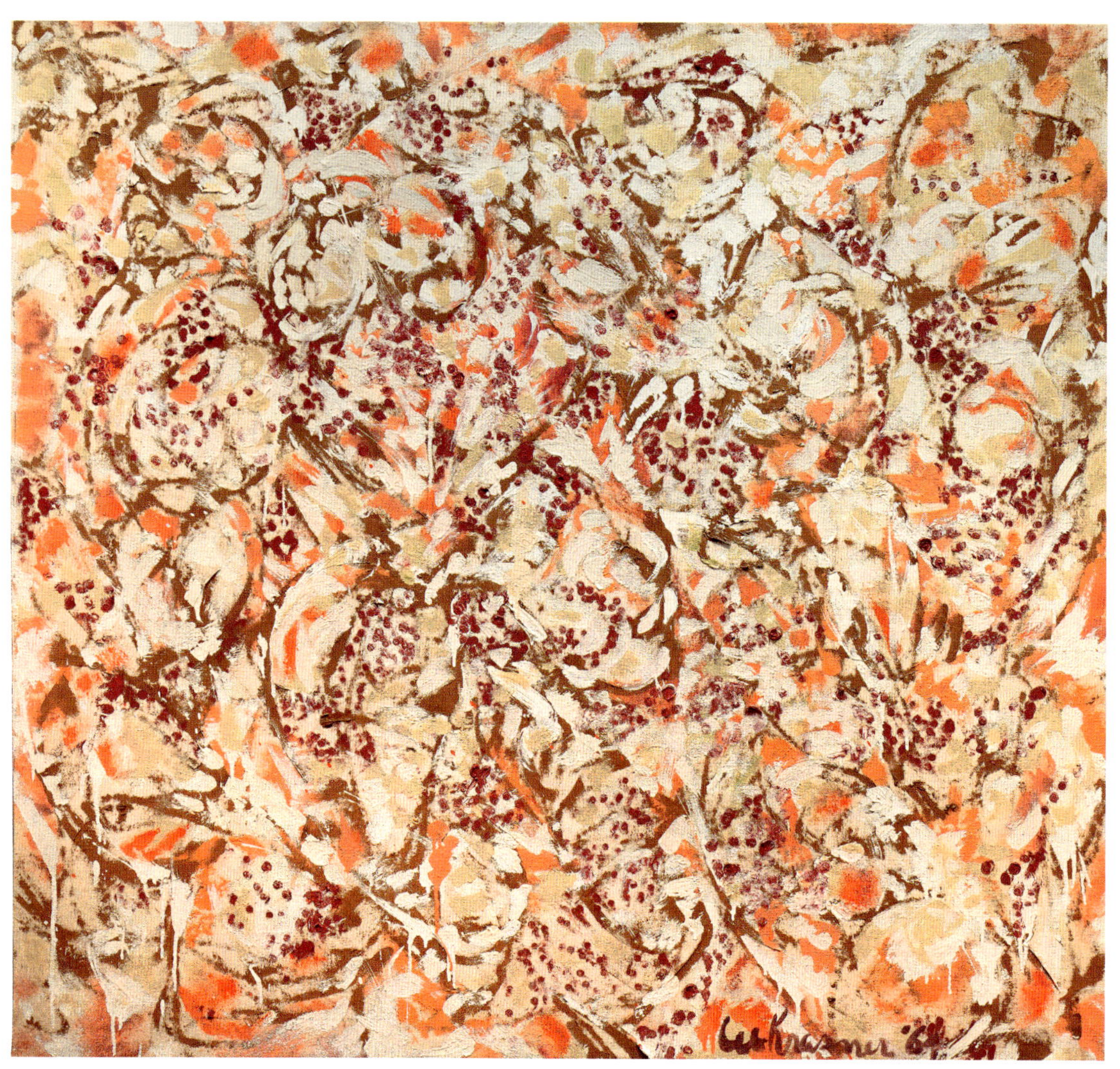

Chrysalis, 1964

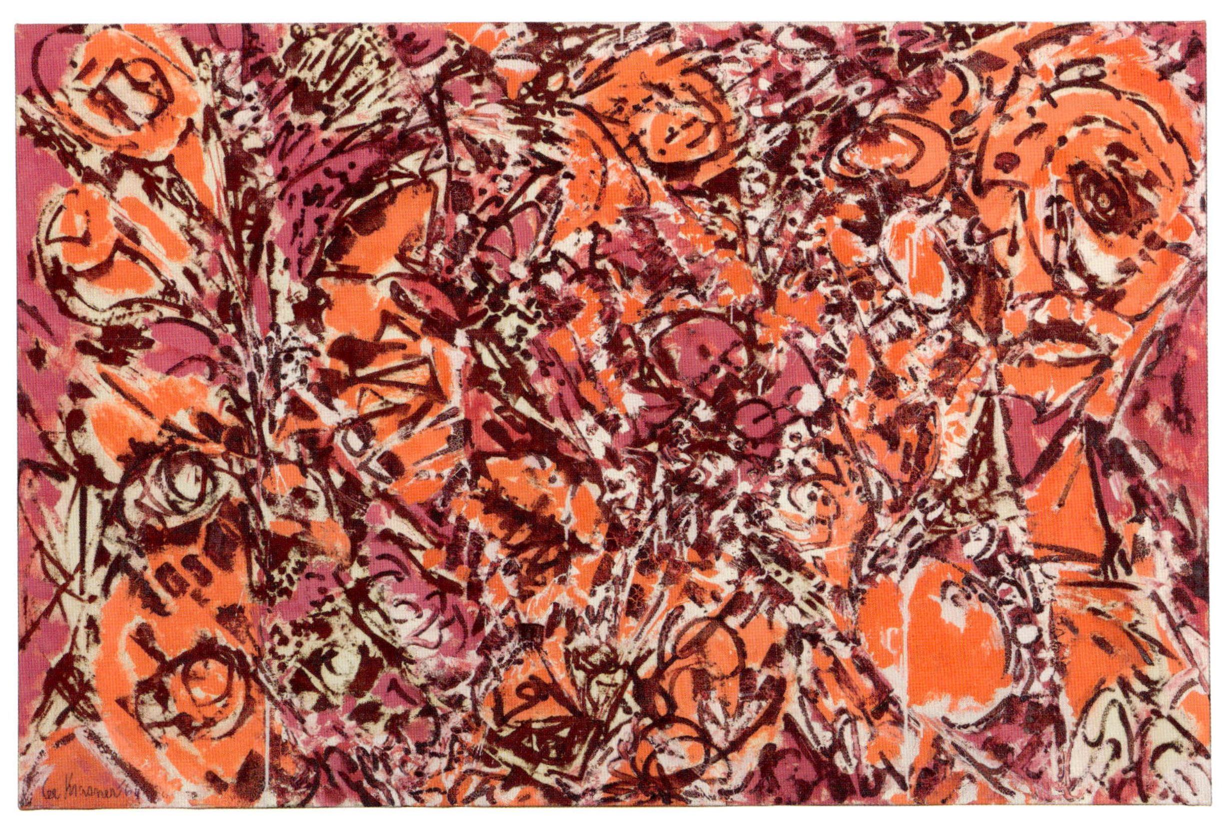

Icarus, 1964

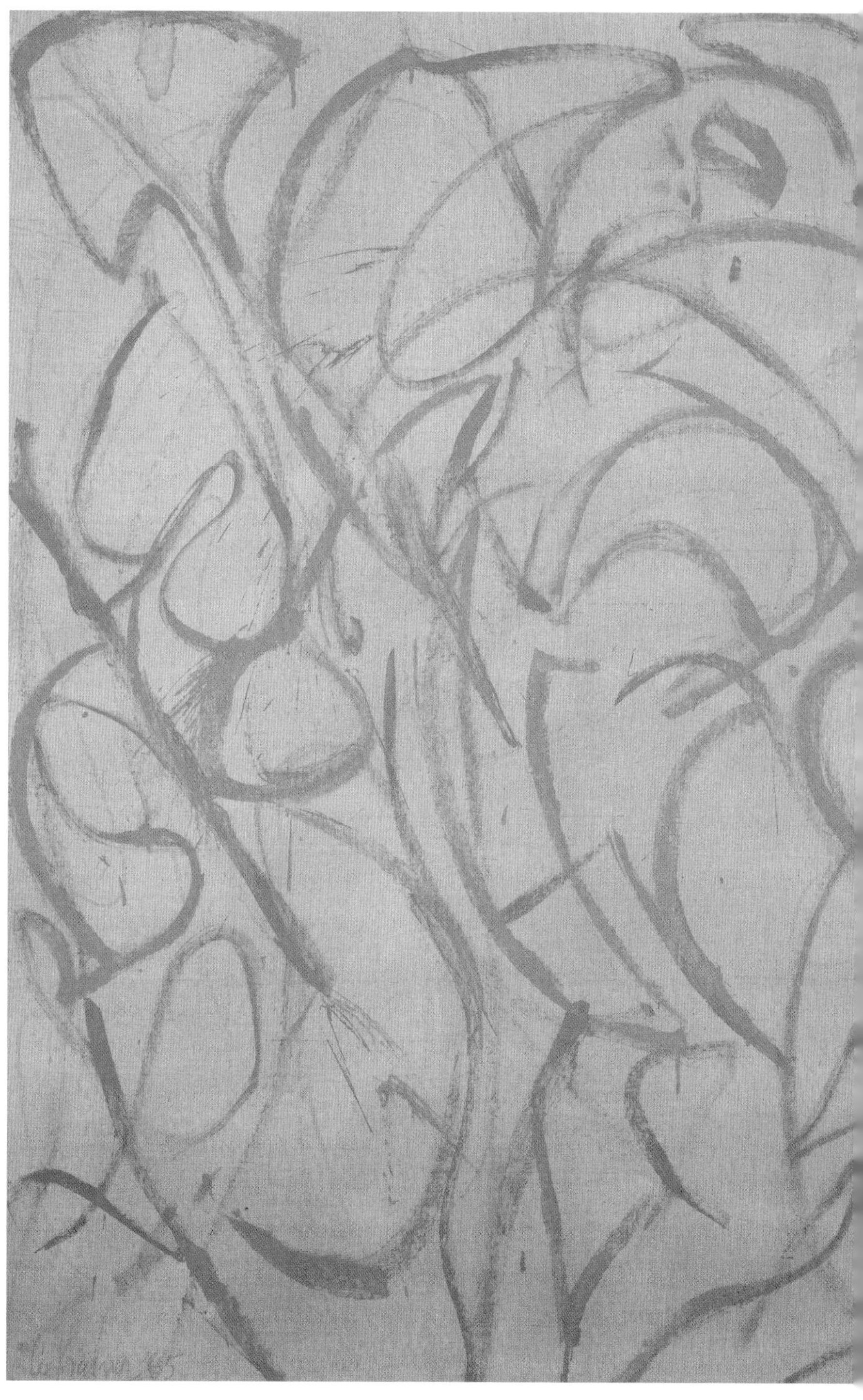

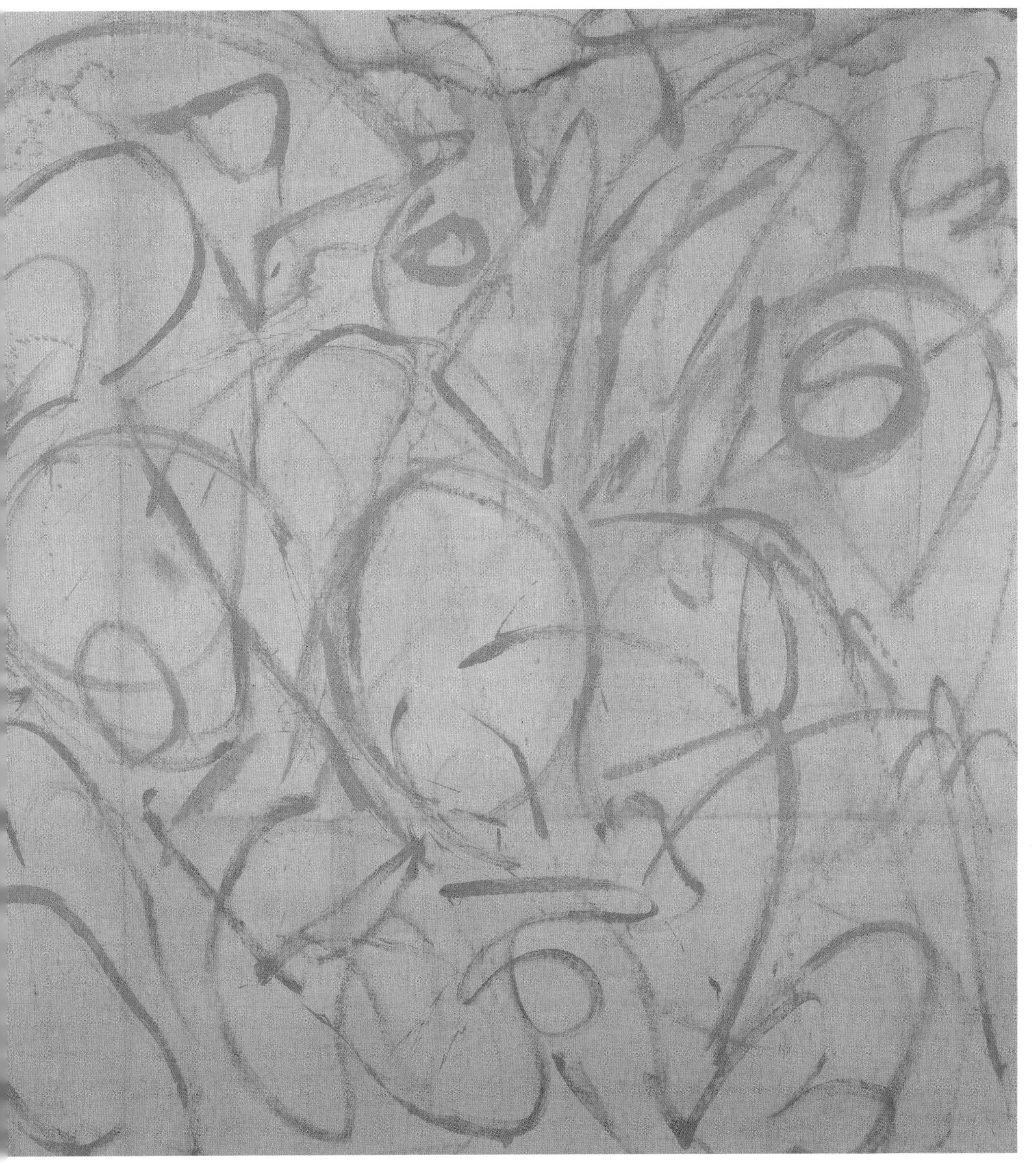

Kufic, 1965

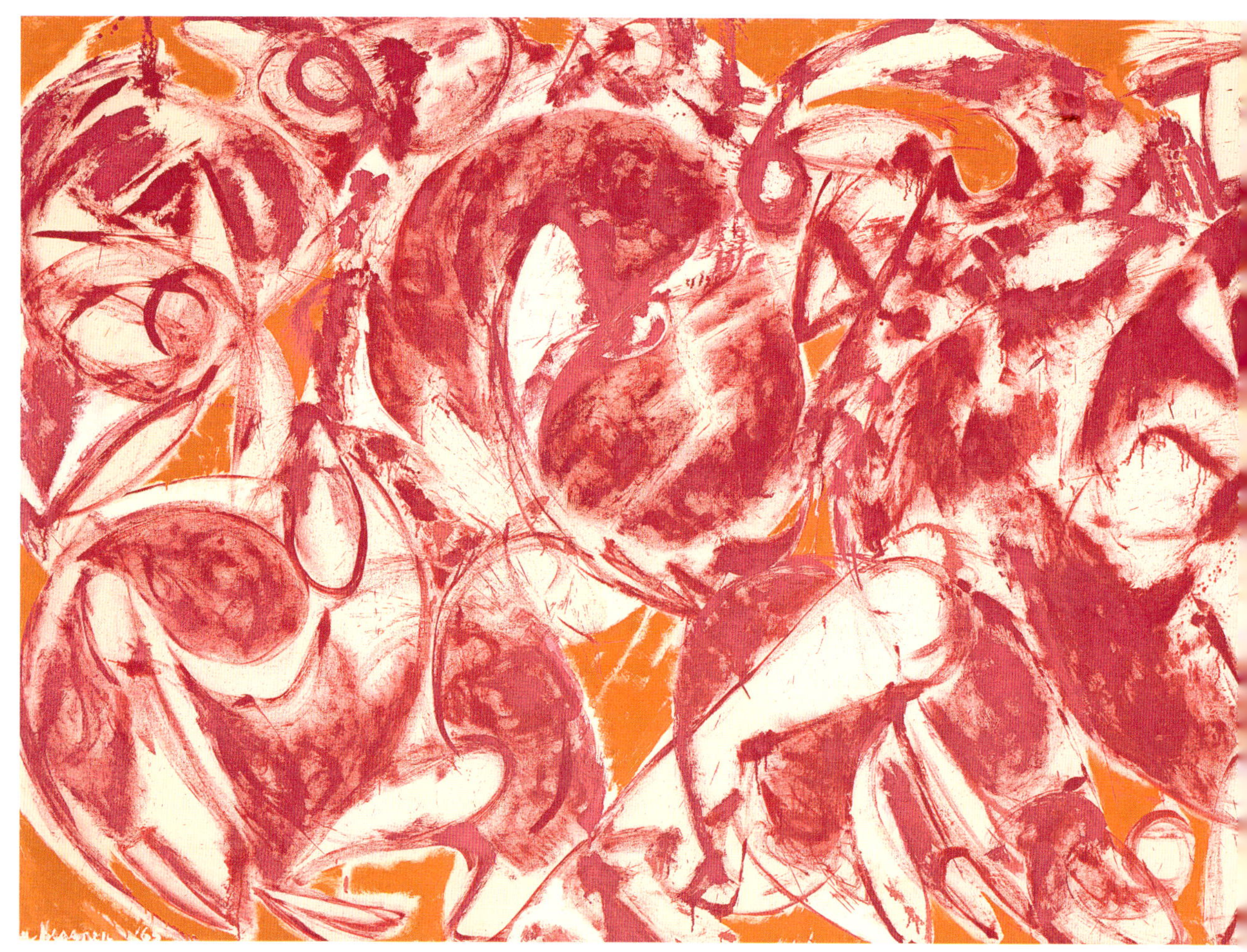

Combat, 1965

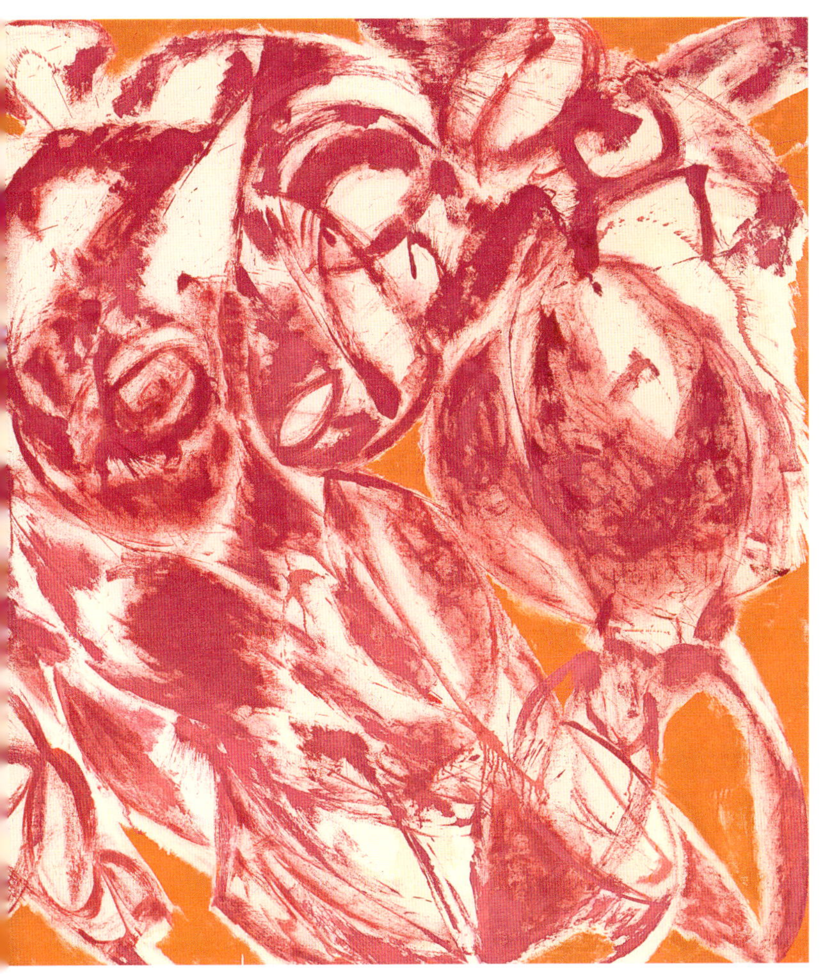

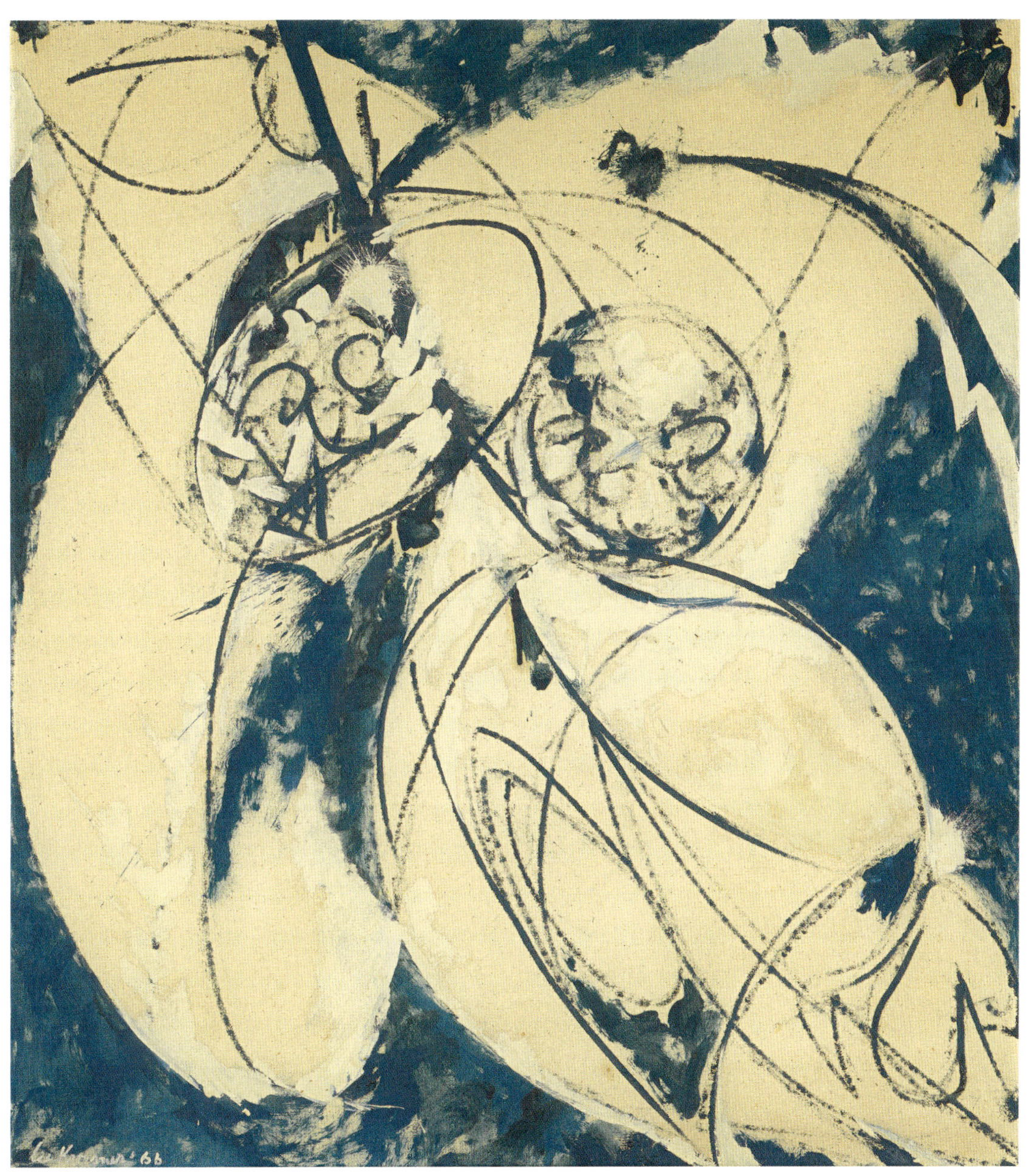

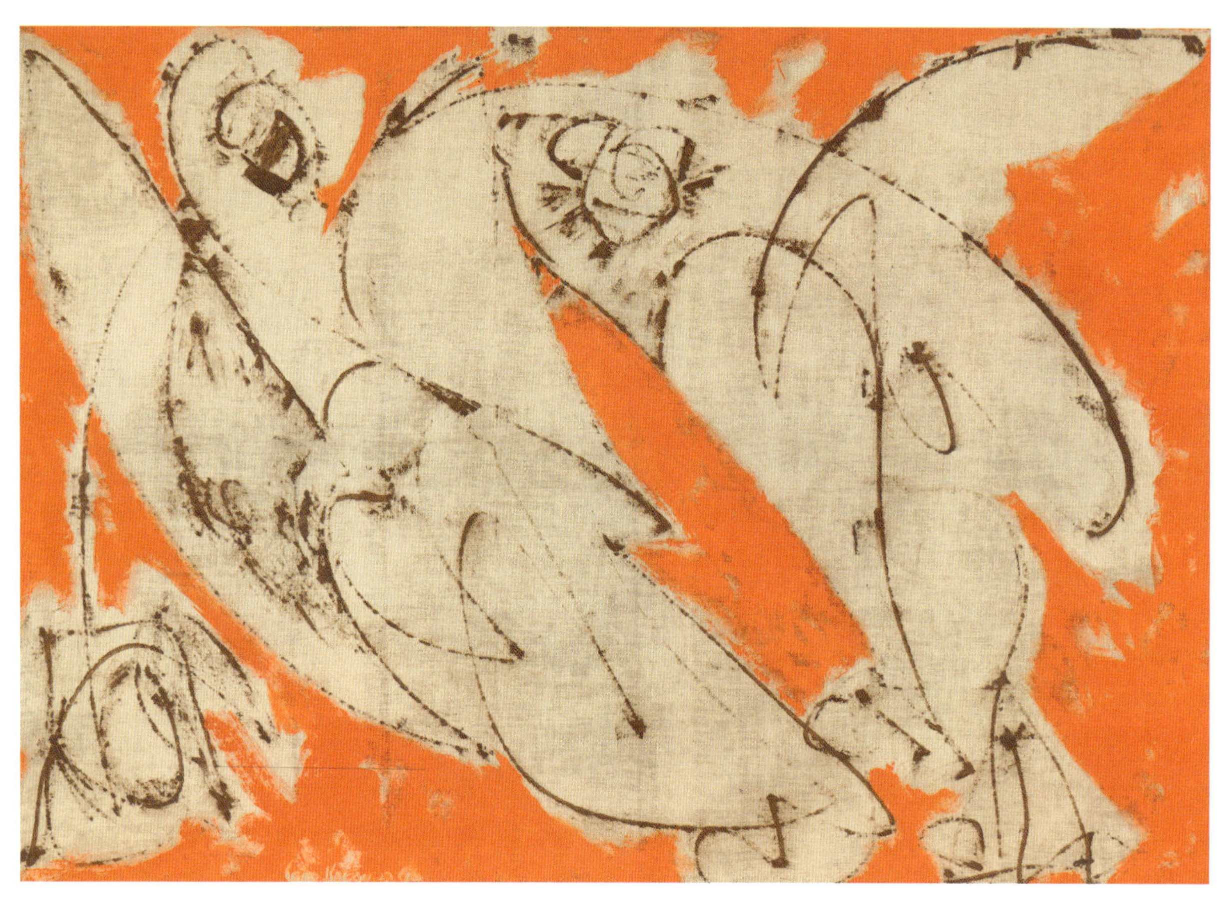

Above: *Courtship*, 1966
Opposite: *Siren*, 1966

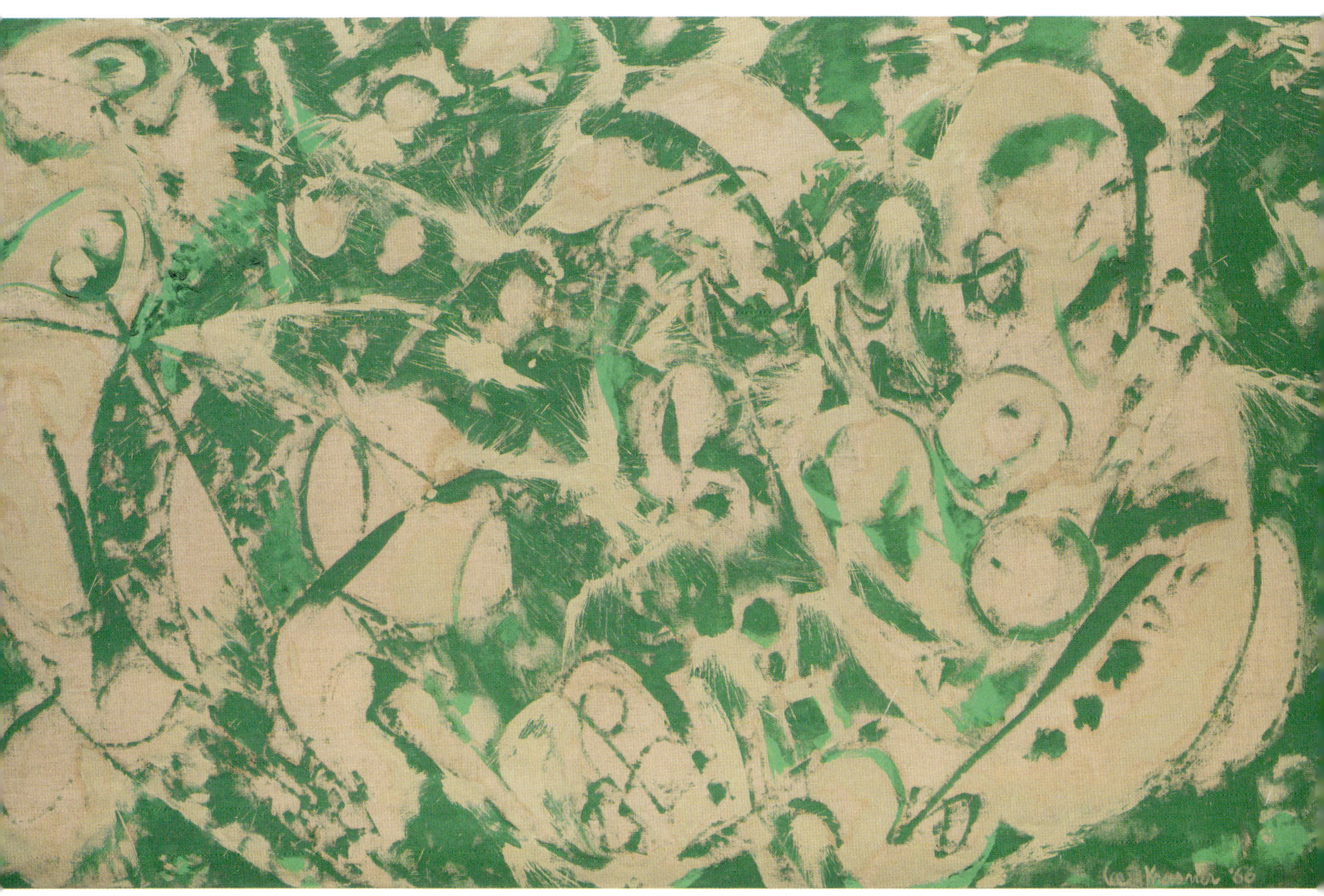

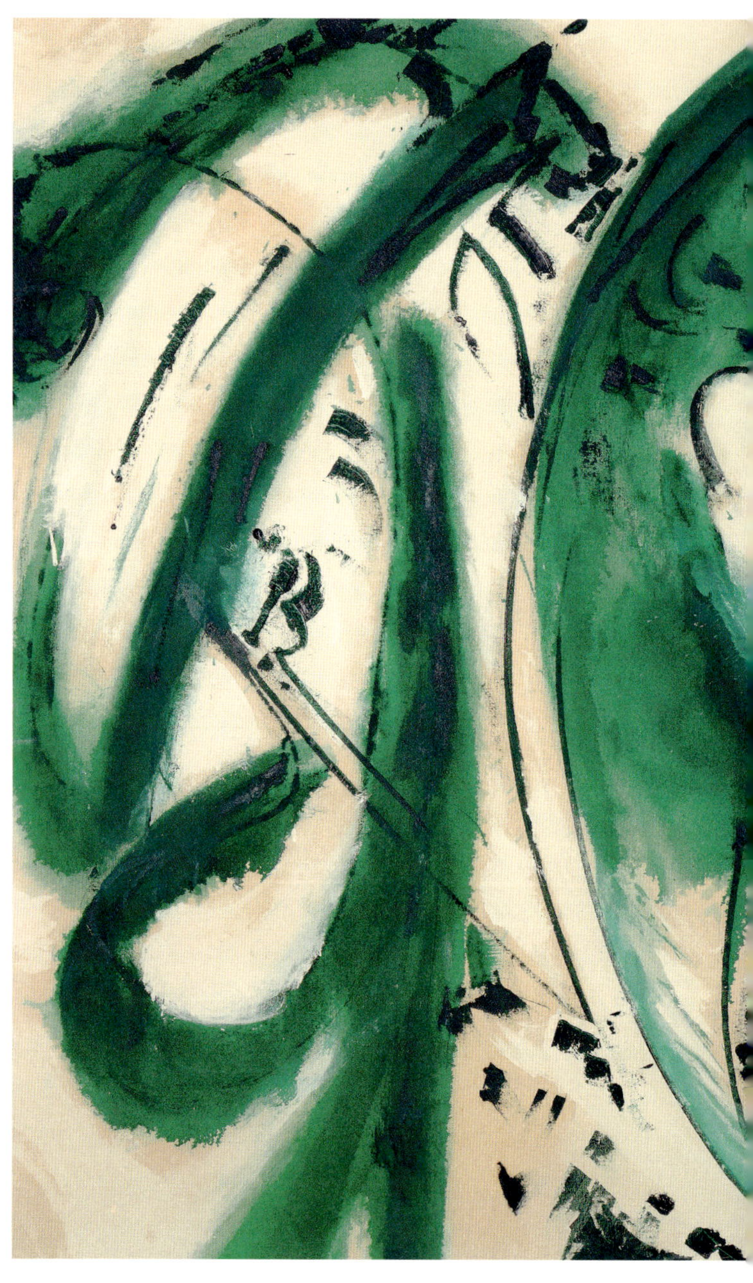

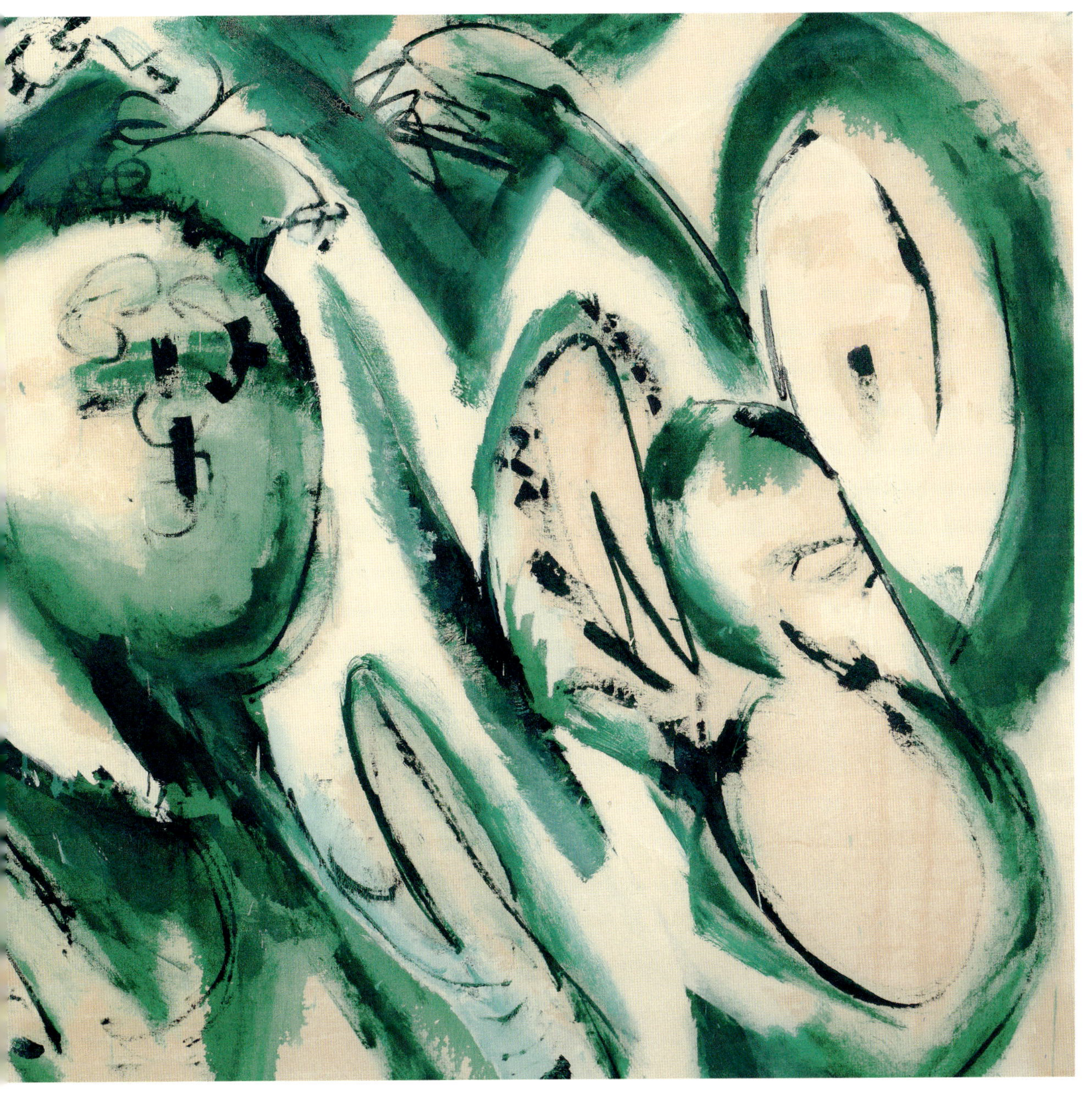

Portrait in Green, 1969

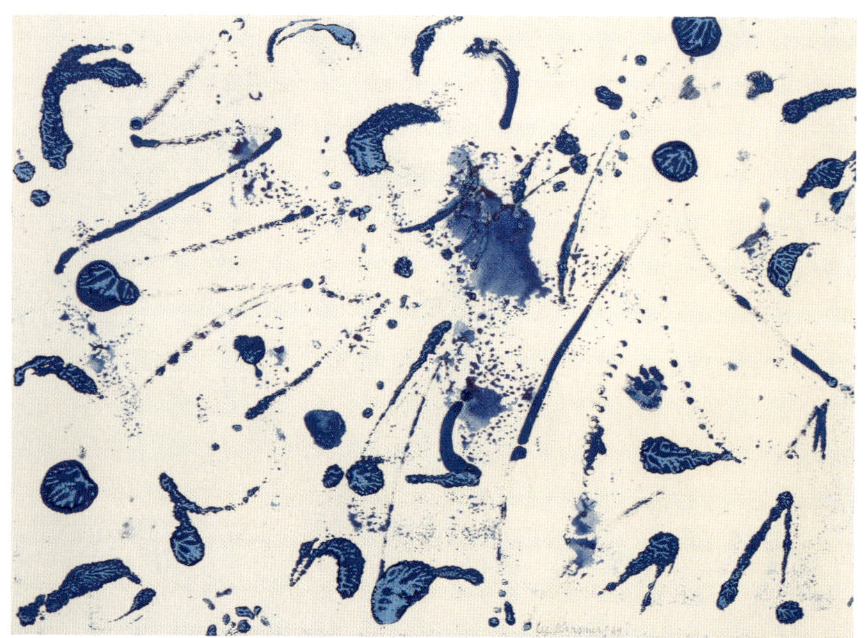

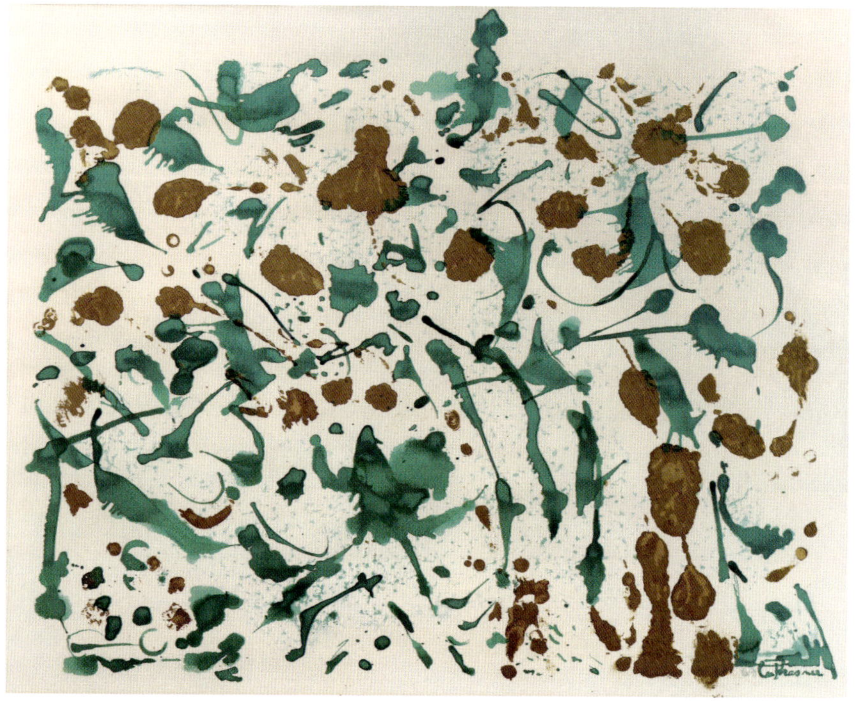

Top: *Seed No. 6,* 1969
Bottom: *Seed No. 4,* 1969

Hieroglyphs No. 18, 1969

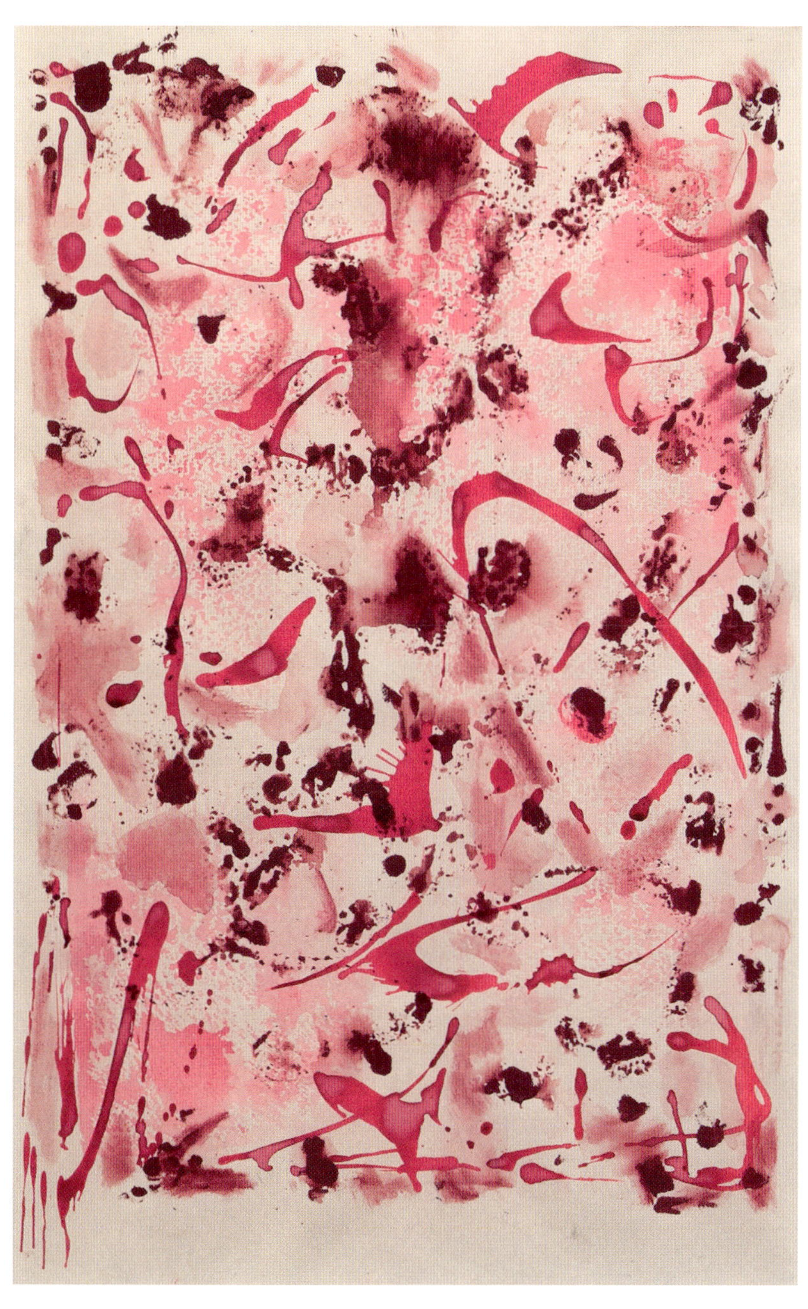

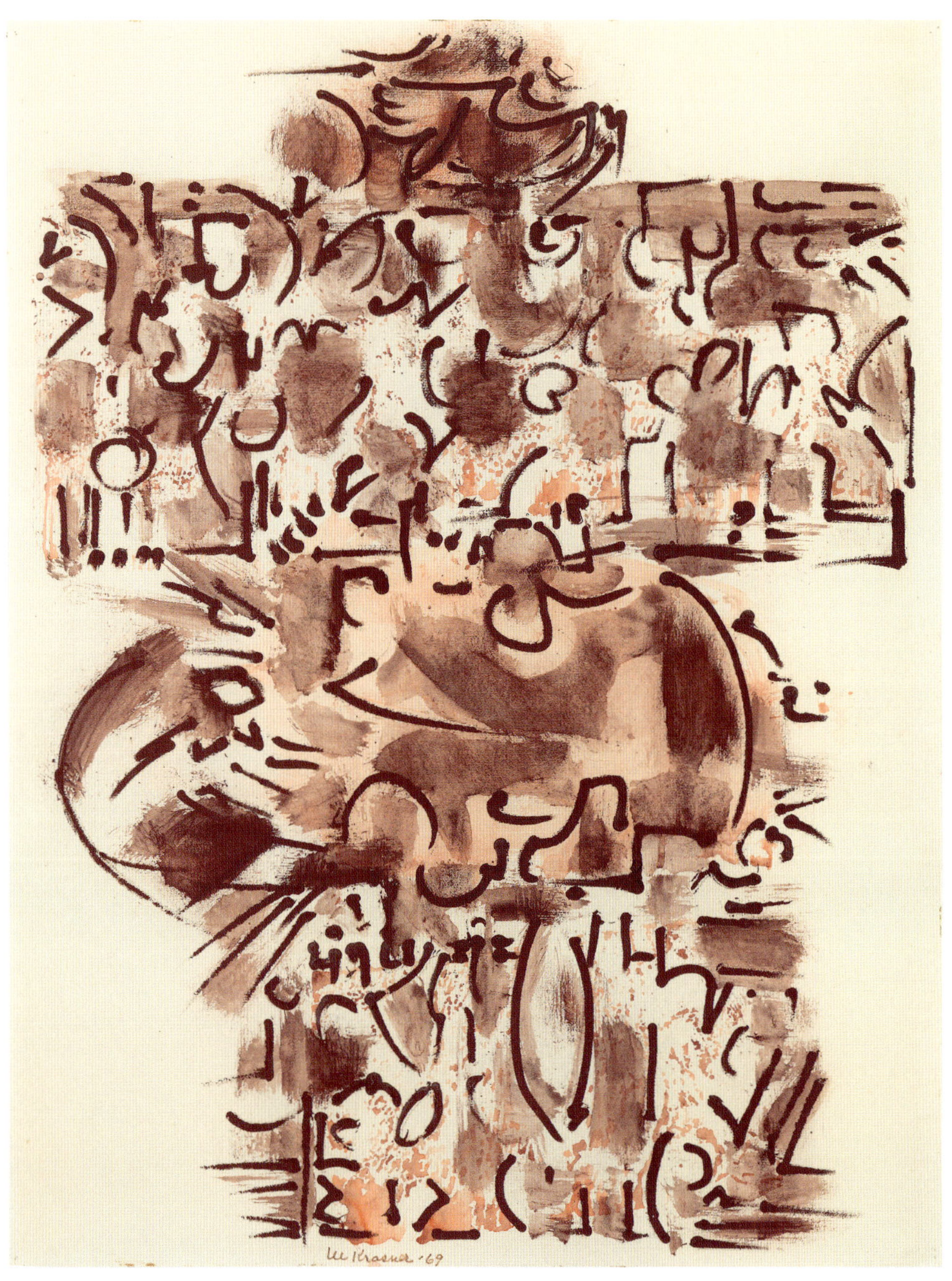

Hieroglyphs No. 4, 1969

Hieroglyphs No. 12, 1969

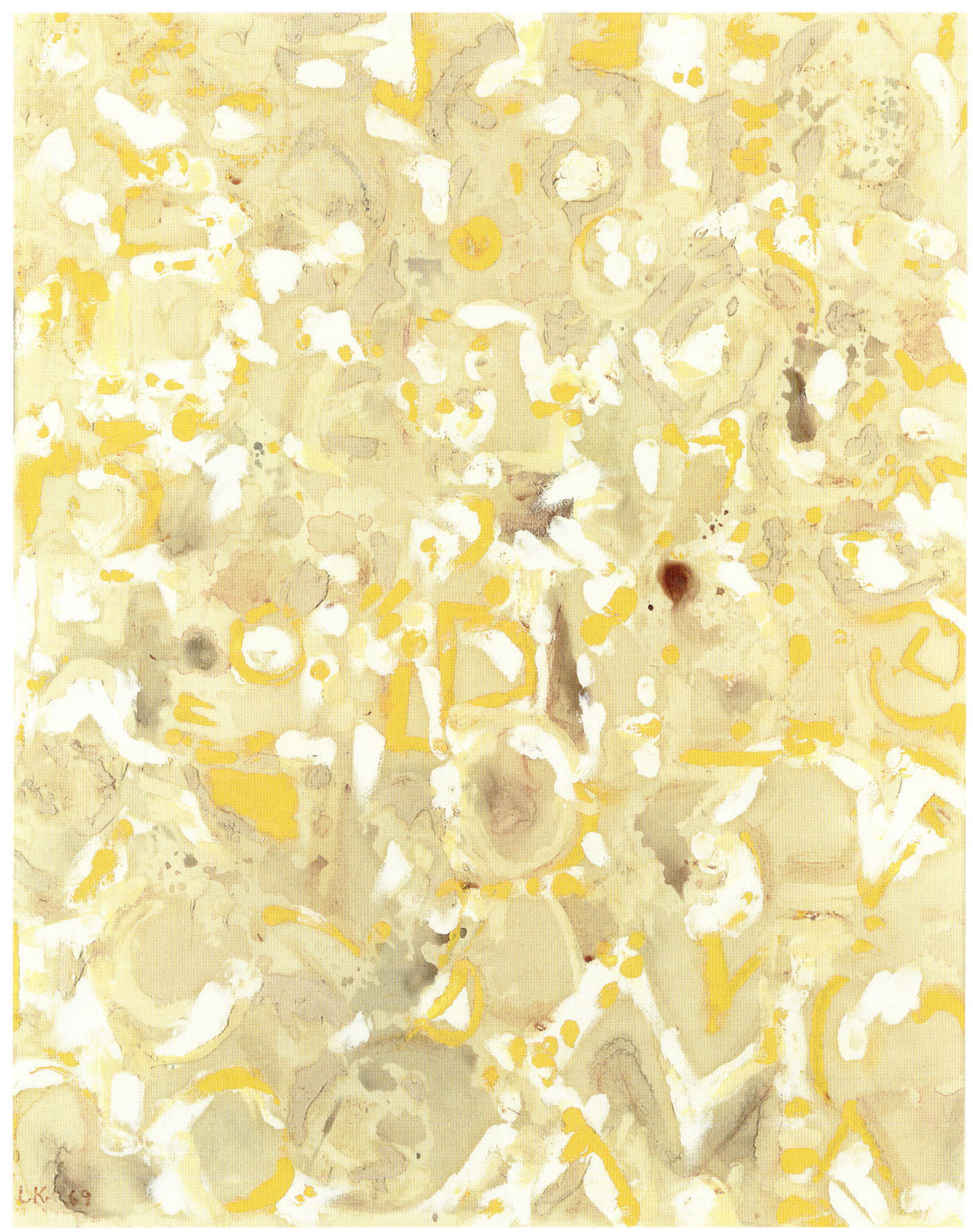

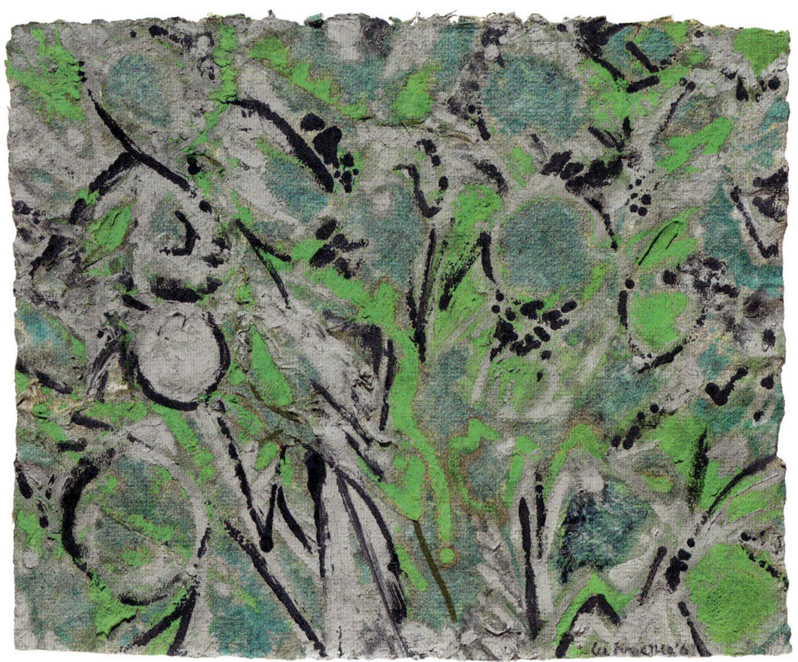

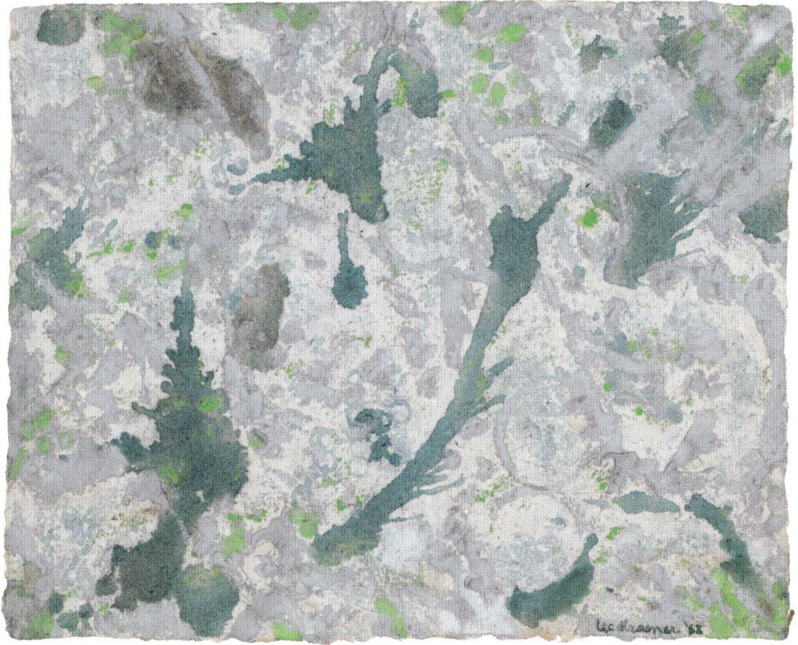

Top: *Earth No. 1*, 1969
Bottom: *Water No. 2*, 1968

Untitled, 1969

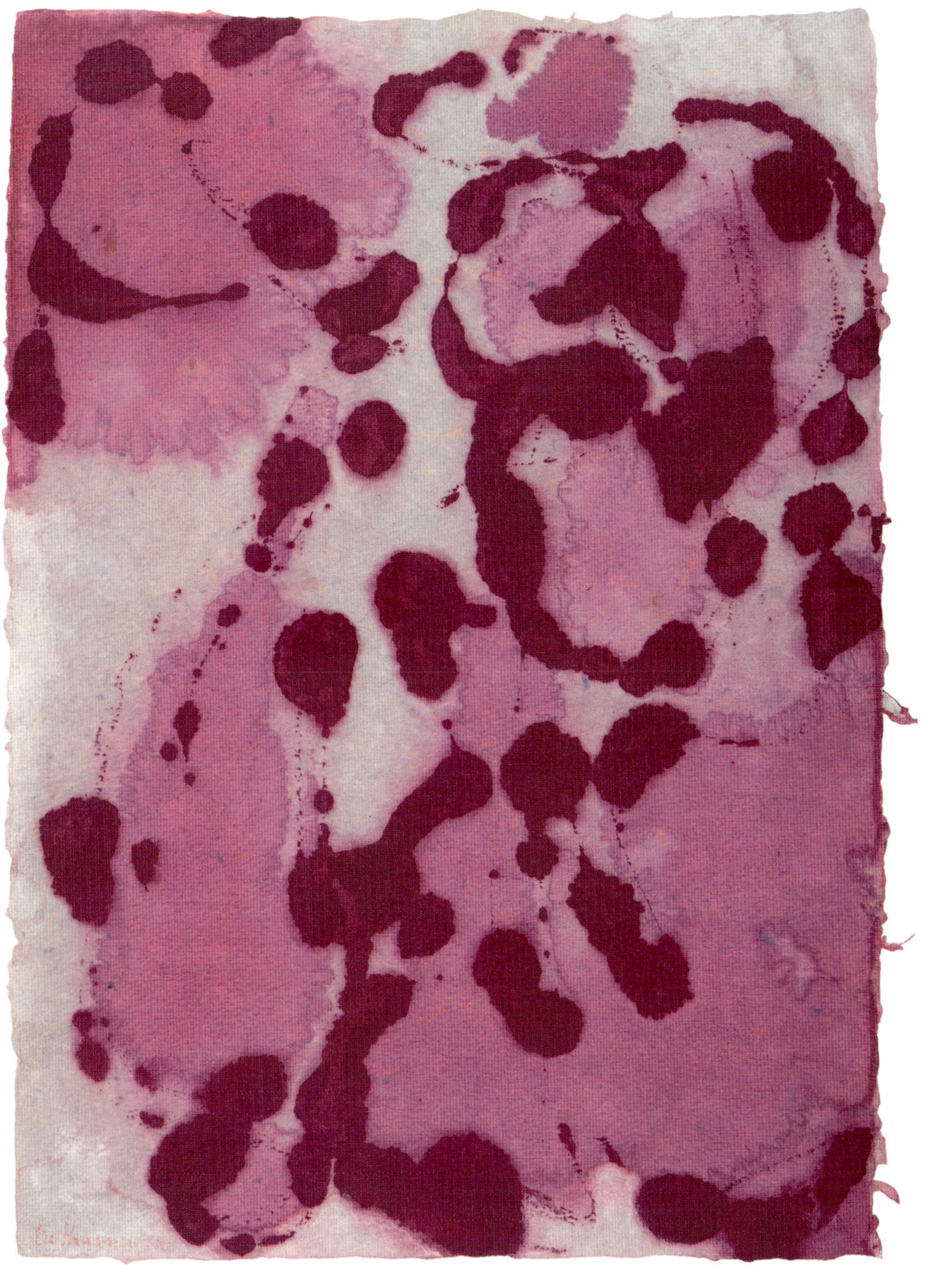

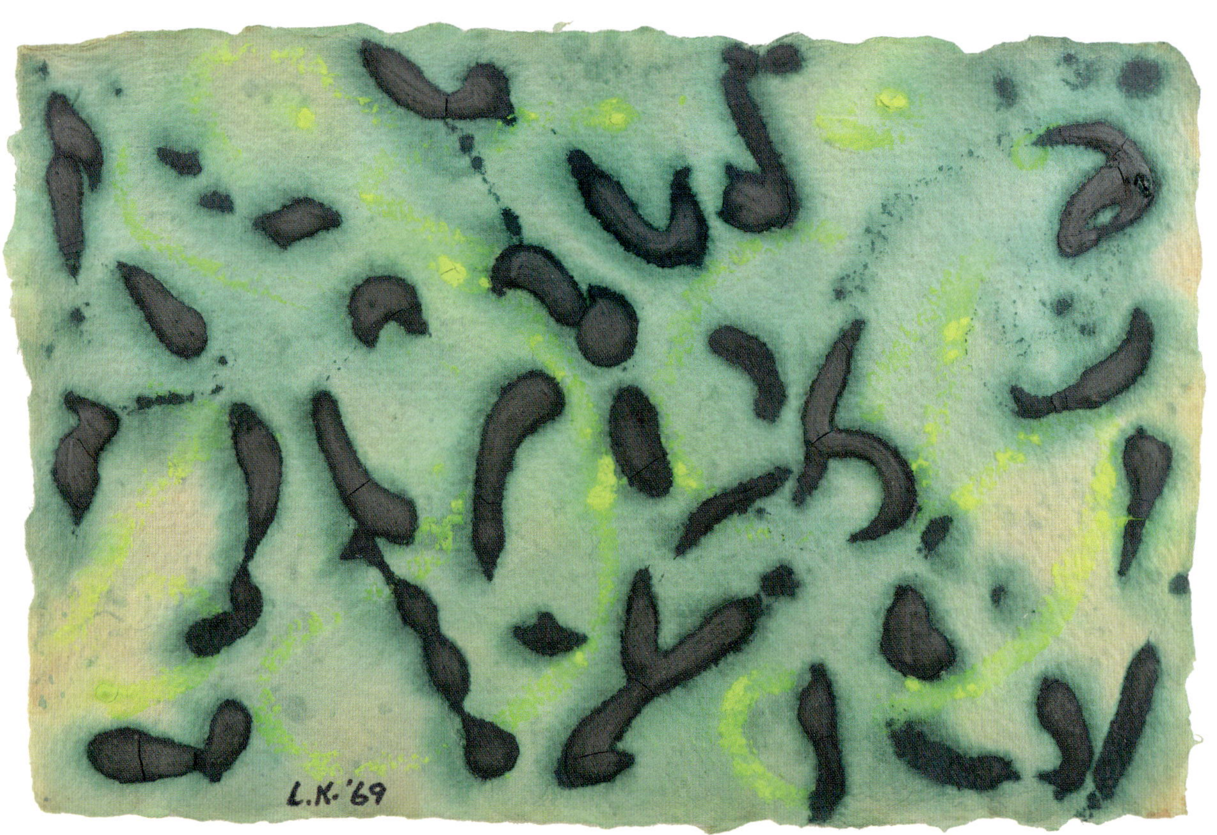

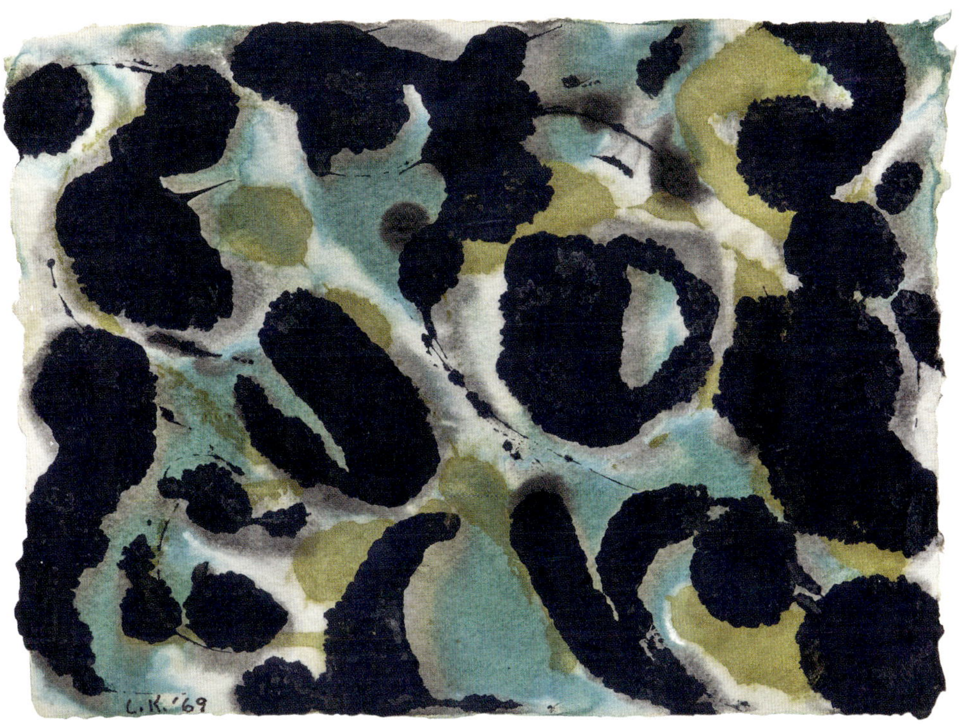

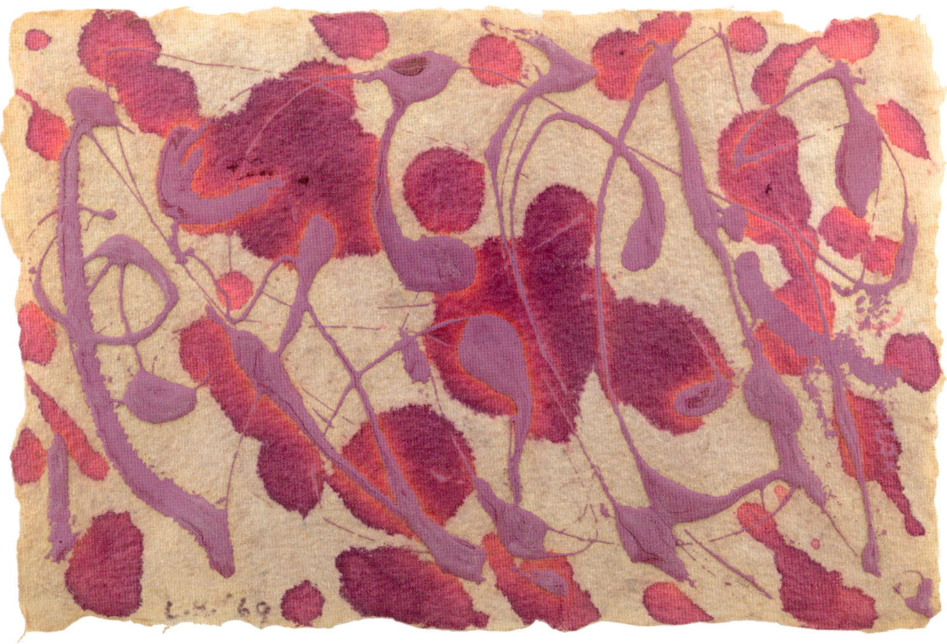

Top: *Water No. 10*, 1969
Bottom: *Water No. 20*, 1969

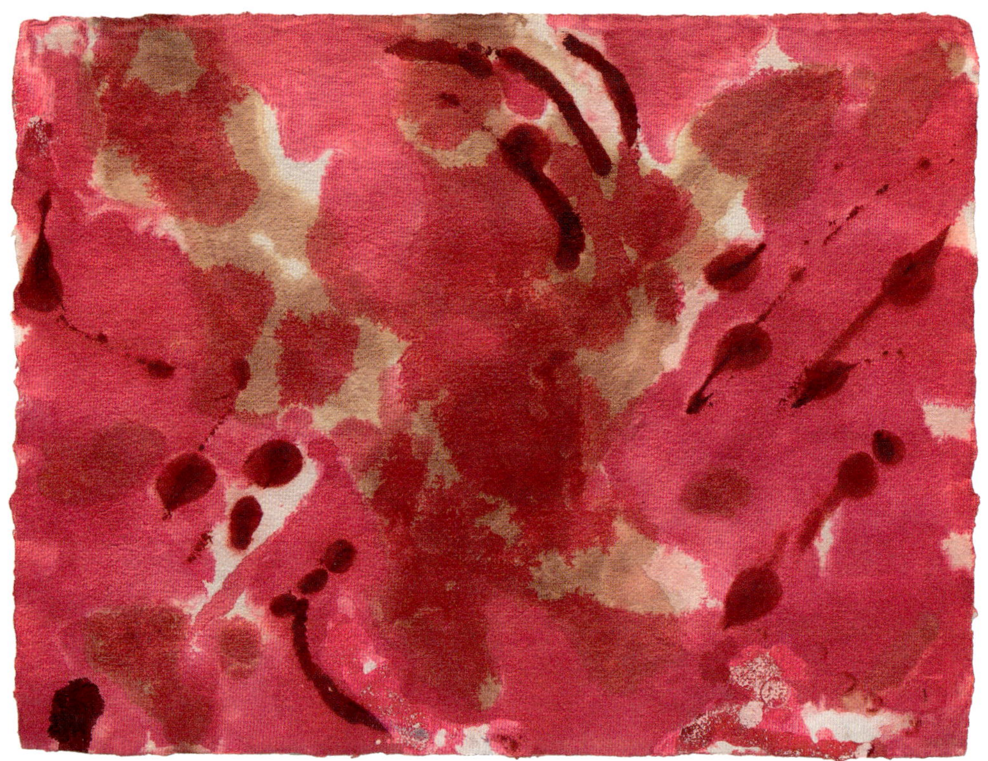

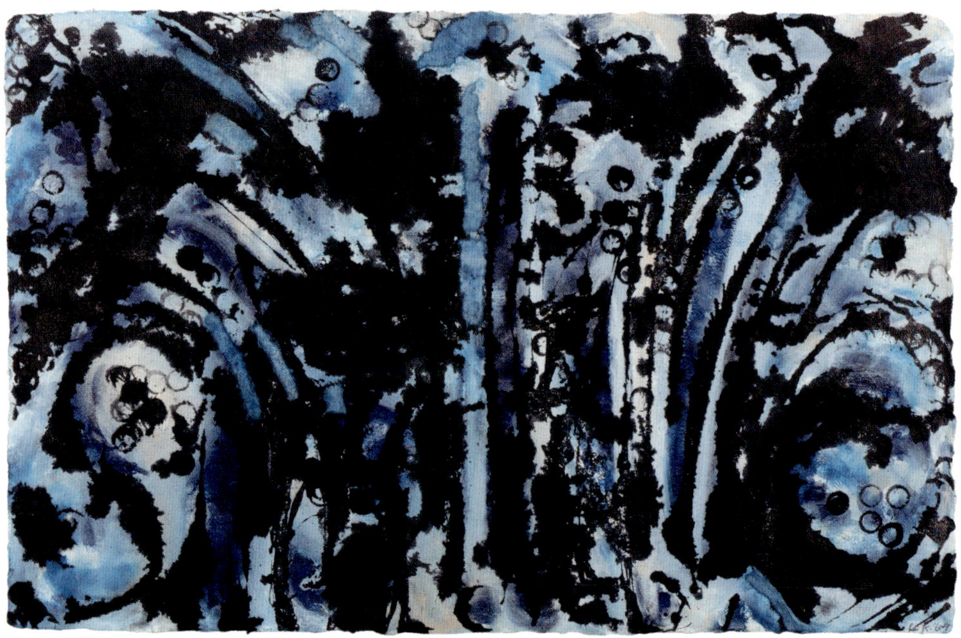

Top: *Seed No. 21, 1969*
Below: *Water No. 14, 1969*

Water No. 18, 1969

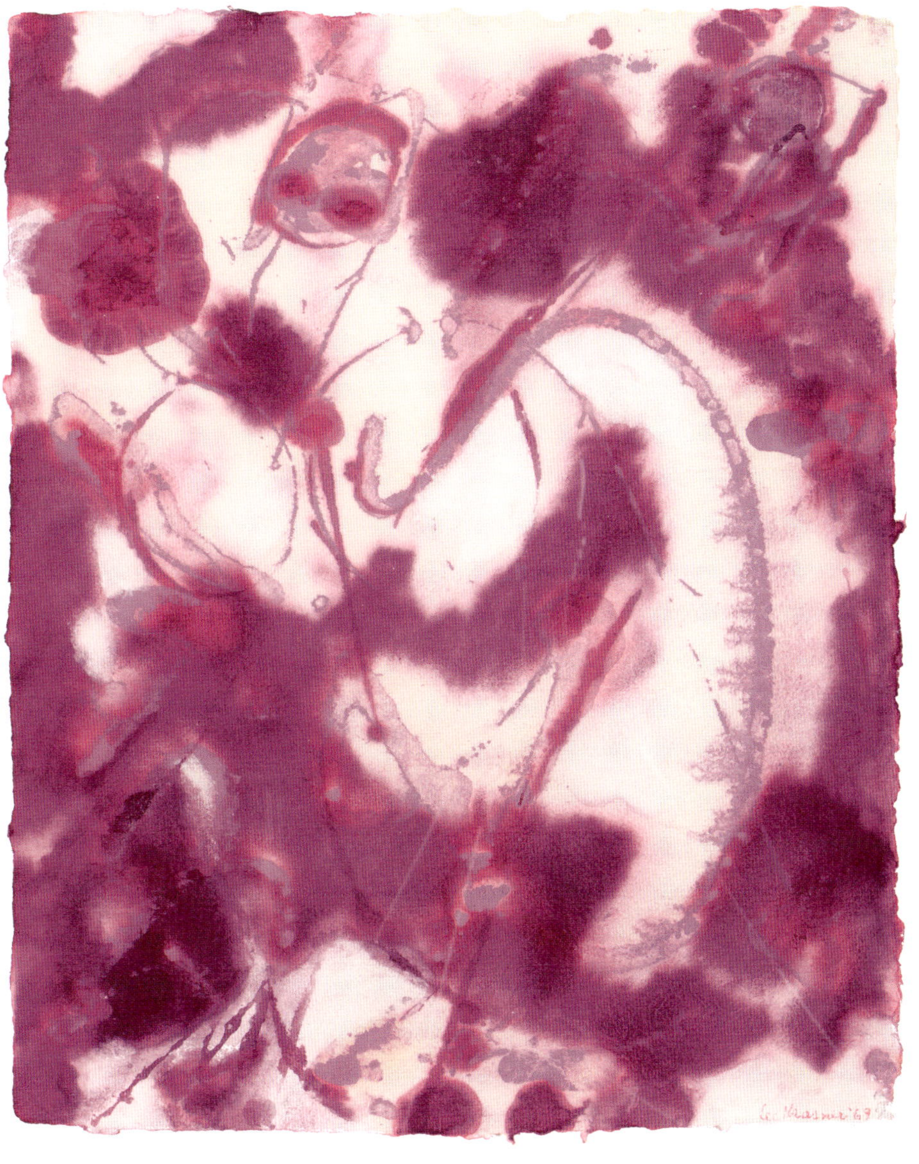

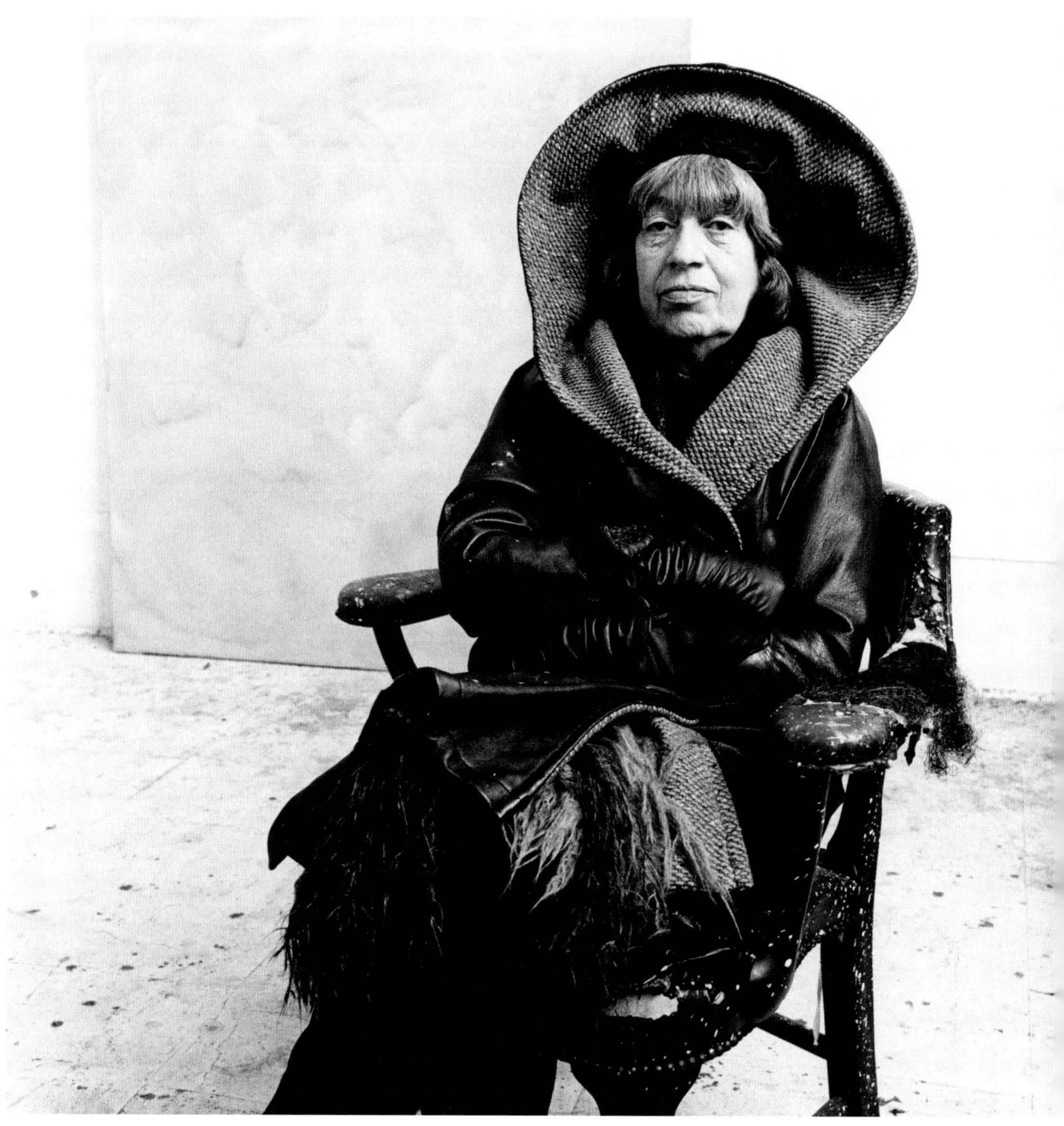

Lee Krasner, Springs, 1972. Photograph by Irving Penn.

PALINGENESIS

In 1973 Krasner presented twelve new paintings at the Marlborough Gallery in New York. The show was met with positive reviews, with the canvases being described as 'her most mature and beautiful [work] to date'.[1] In contrast to the soft, biomorphic shapes undulating across her earlier paintings, a number of hard-edged abstract forms now emerged. The works brimmed with colour – kelly green, carmine red and a fuchsia pink that the critic Robert Hughes described as 'rap[ping] hotly on the eyeball at 50 paces'.[2] Krasner's reputation as a 'good noisy colorist' had been established through her Stable Gallery collages and the monumental 'Primary Series' of the 1960s.[3] This raucous energy, however, was now stilled into a series of quieter geometric forms described by the art historian Cindy Nemser as 'expansive yet contained … stately [and] slow-moving'.[4]

The works shown at Marlborough, which might be compared with colour field painting or what Clement Greenberg called 'post-painterly abstraction', demonstrate Krasner's endless experimentation in the studio and her reluctance to develop a signature style. *Palingenesis* (1971), for example, is a riot of raspberry and green that relates to the Greek term for 'rebirth'. The painting's title has a certain poignancy, given Krasner's thirst for reinvention, which did not lessen as she grew older; indeed, as she explained to Barbara Rose in 1972, 'evolution, growth and change go on. Change is life.'[5]

Krasner's works of the early 1970s formed a prominent part of the exhibition *Lee Krasner: Large Paintings*, curated by Marcia Tucker at the Whitney Museum of American Art, New York, in 1973. The canvases were once again met with glowing reviews, in what would become Krasner's most high-profile show to date. In an essay for the accompanying catalogue, Tucker highlighted the originality of this series and the constantly evolving nature of Krasner's art, saying: 'These are no longer abstract expressionist paintings. They have moved far from the tradition which her earlier work helped to create.'[6]

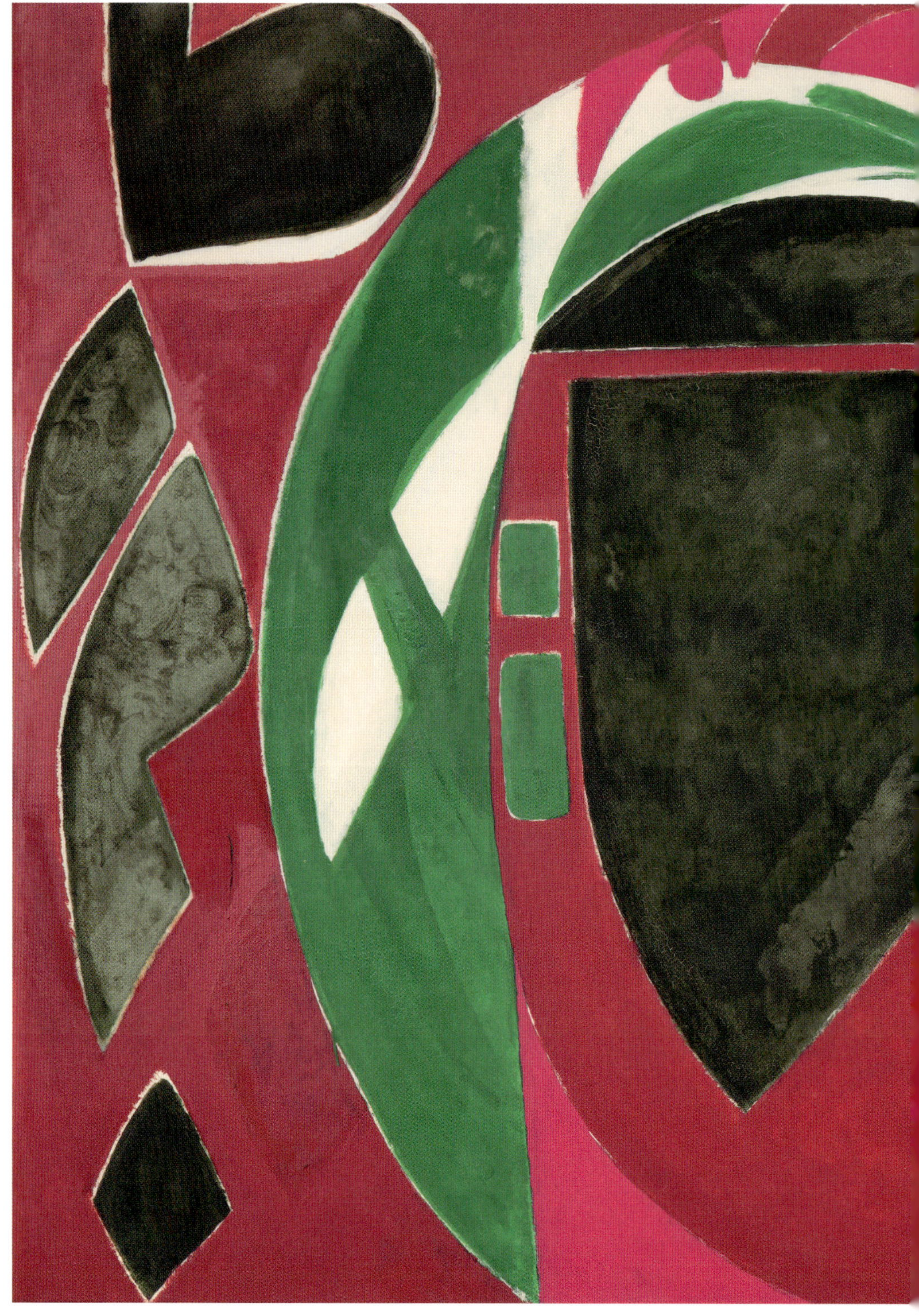

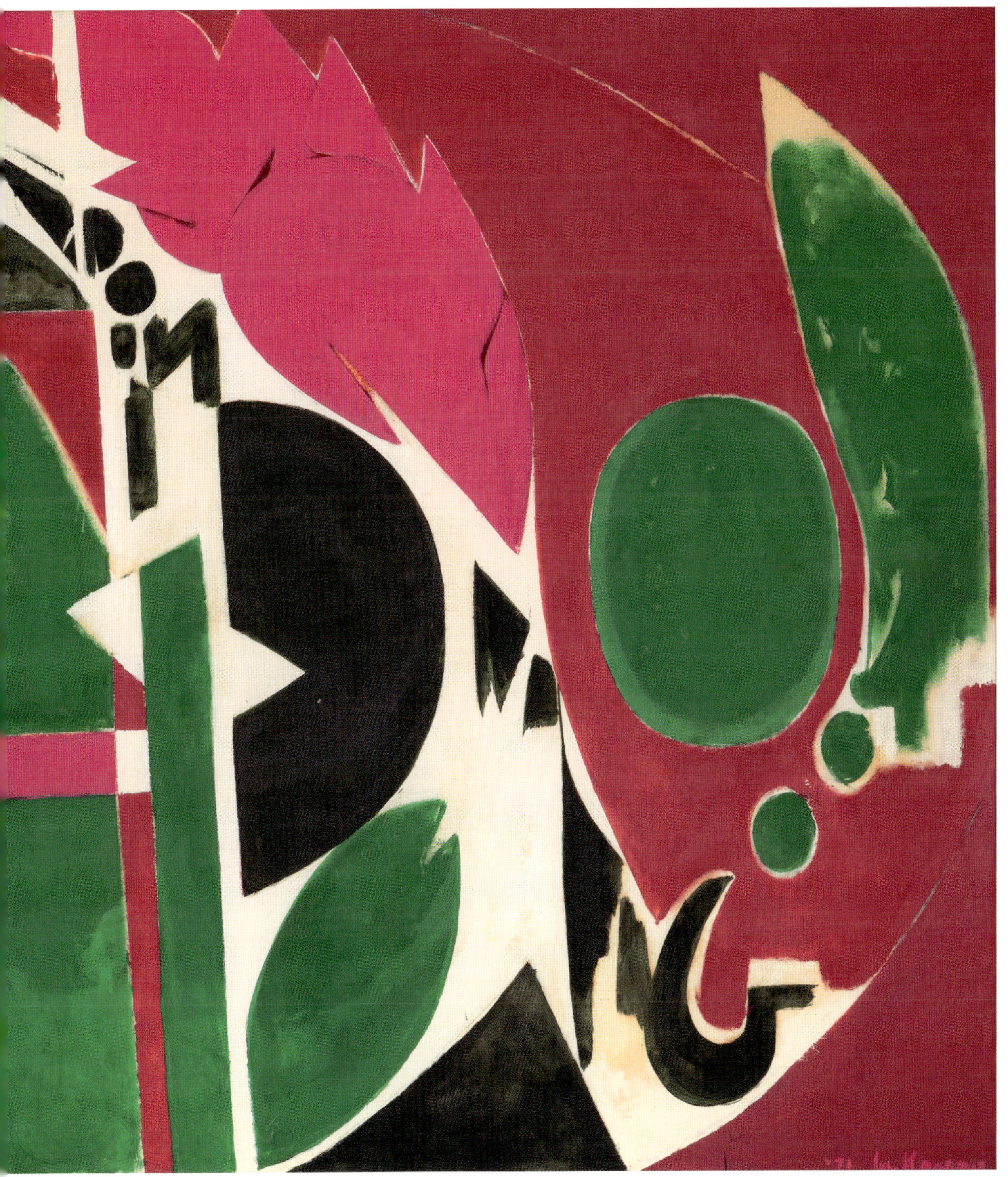

Palingenesis, 1971

Olympic, 1974

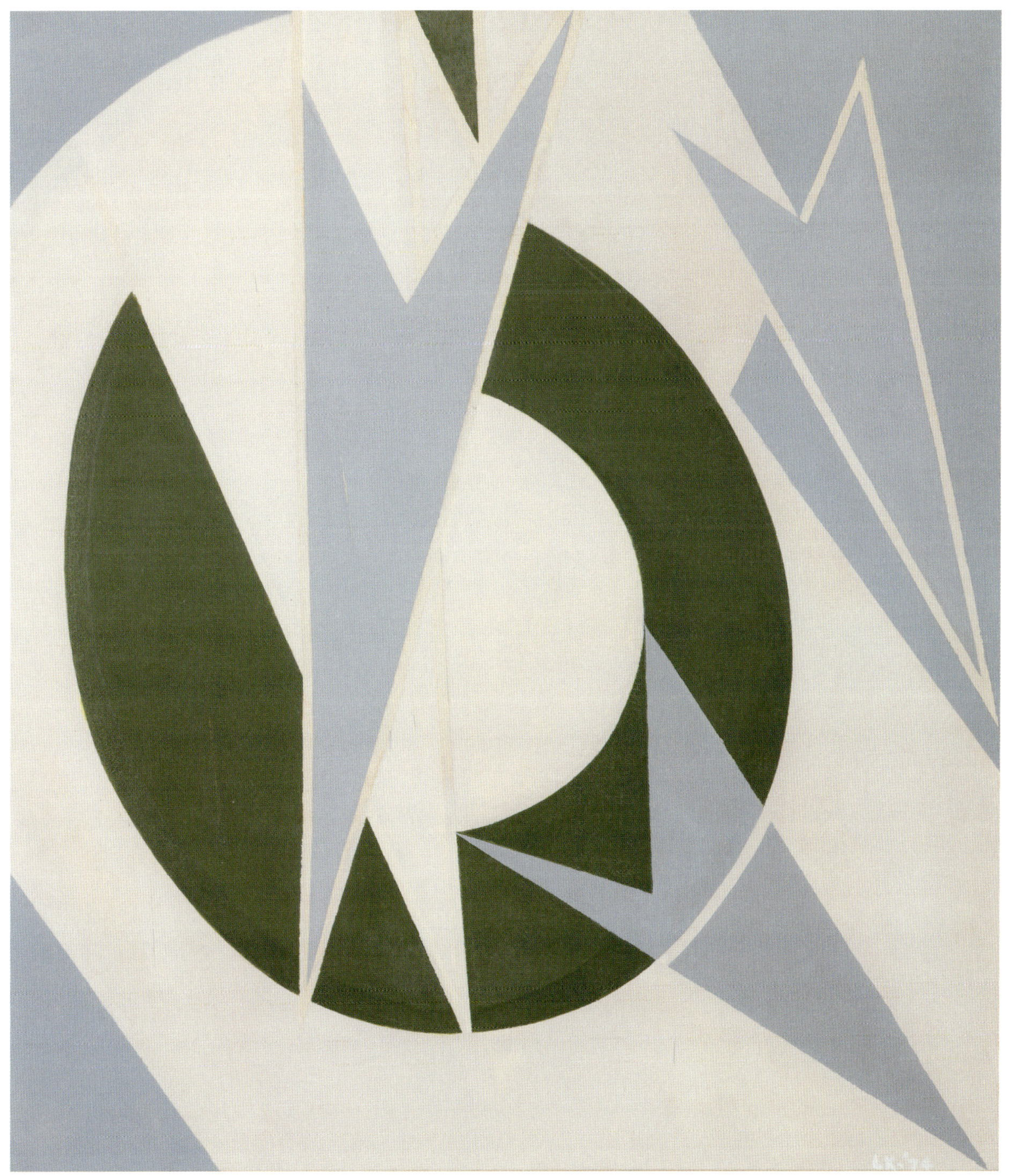

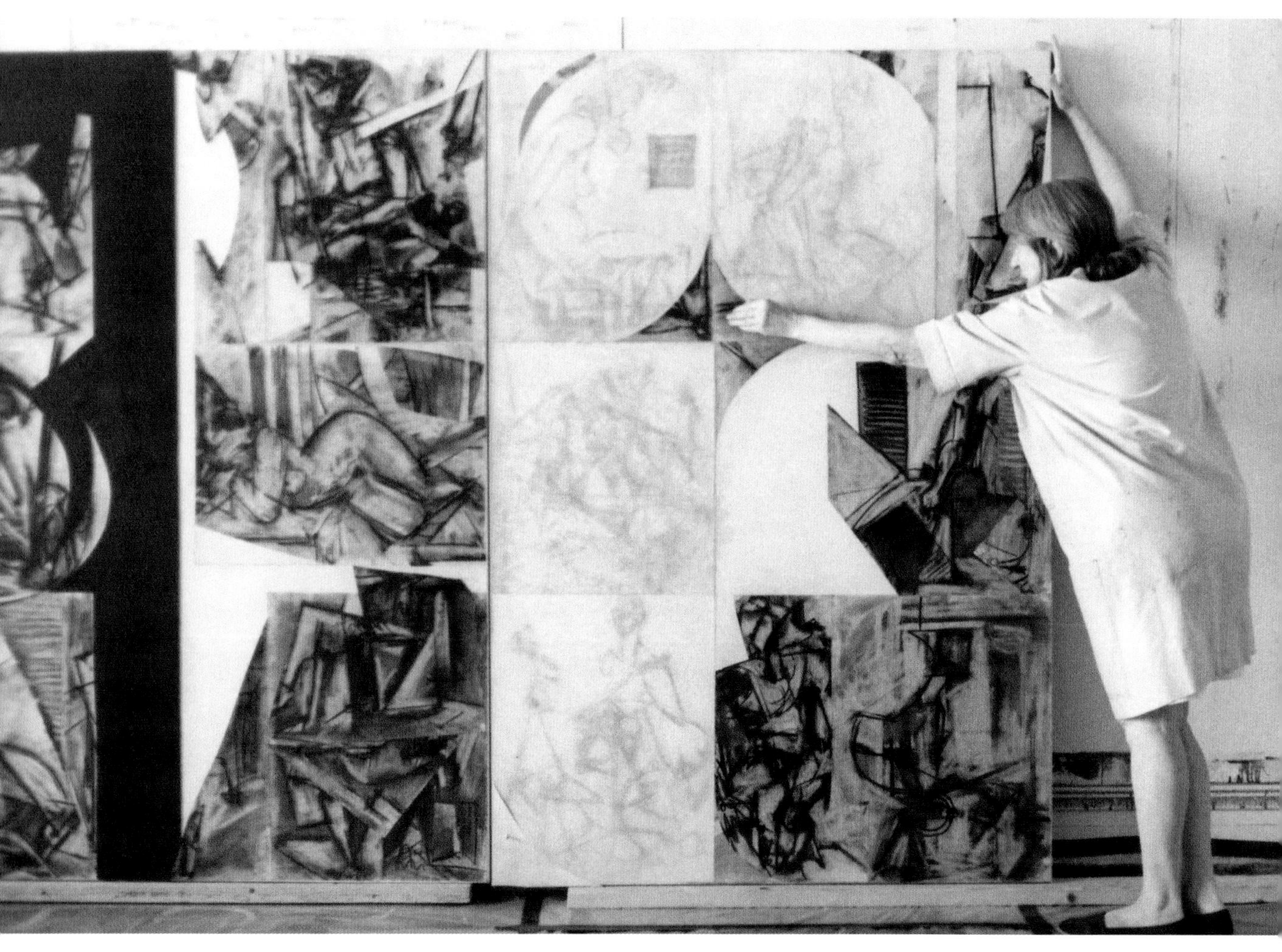

Lee Krasner working on the series 'Eleven Ways to Use the Words to See', 1976.
Photograph by Ray Eames.

ELEVEN WAYS

While visiting Krasner's studio in Springs in 1974, Bryan Robertson discovered a number of old portfolios of her work. Despite Krasner's reservations, Robertson opened the folders to discover a trove of charcoal studies, made during her time at the Hofmann School. Krasner sifted through the drawings, noticing that a number had ghostly charcoal impressions on the reverse because she had not used fixative. She selected a few to be framed and took the rest to her Manhattan apartment, intending to destroy them at a later date. When she came across them again in 1975, she felt impelled to use them as material for a new series of collages.

Rather than tearing the drawings, as she had for her Stable Gallery collages, Krasner took to them with scissors, explaining that 'I wanted precise incision.'[1] This new approach was documented in a series of photographs taken by an old friend of Krasner's from the Hofmann School, the artist and designer Ray Eames. A series of unusual collages began to emerge, the surfaces covered with angular shapes that mirrored the dynamic vectors intersecting the nude figure in her original drawings. Krasner incorporated some of the spectral images from the backs of the drawings and left other areas of the canvas blank – like the empty space around the nude model. In some cases, she attached multiple canvases together to create a diptych or triptych.

The collages were displayed at Pace Gallery, New York, in 1977 under the collective title 'Eleven Ways to Use the Words to See', with each individual work named after a different verb form (*Future Indicative* and *Present Conditional*, for example). Krasner's friend John Bernard Myers recalls her explaining that 'the first collage of the new work is called *Imperative* – [I felt] a peremptory desire to change [the old drawings]; a command, as it were, to make them new.'[2] Numerous reviews focused on the inventive use of such charged earlier work, with *Art in America* noting that the 'energy [of the drawings] is recharged by the energy of this *reworking*, which both idolizes them like so many trophies and dismisses them as a pale past.'[3]

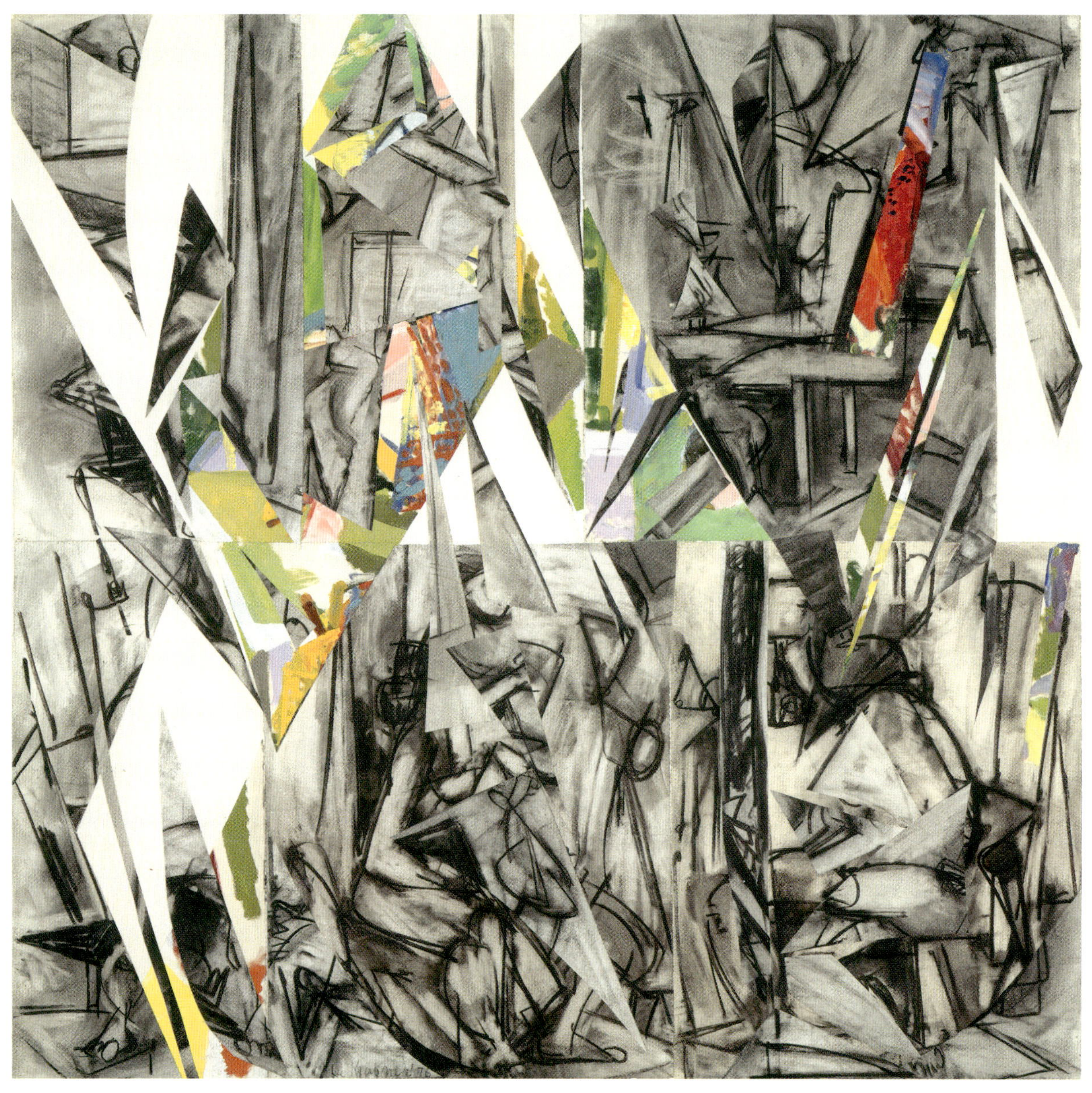

Imperative, 1976

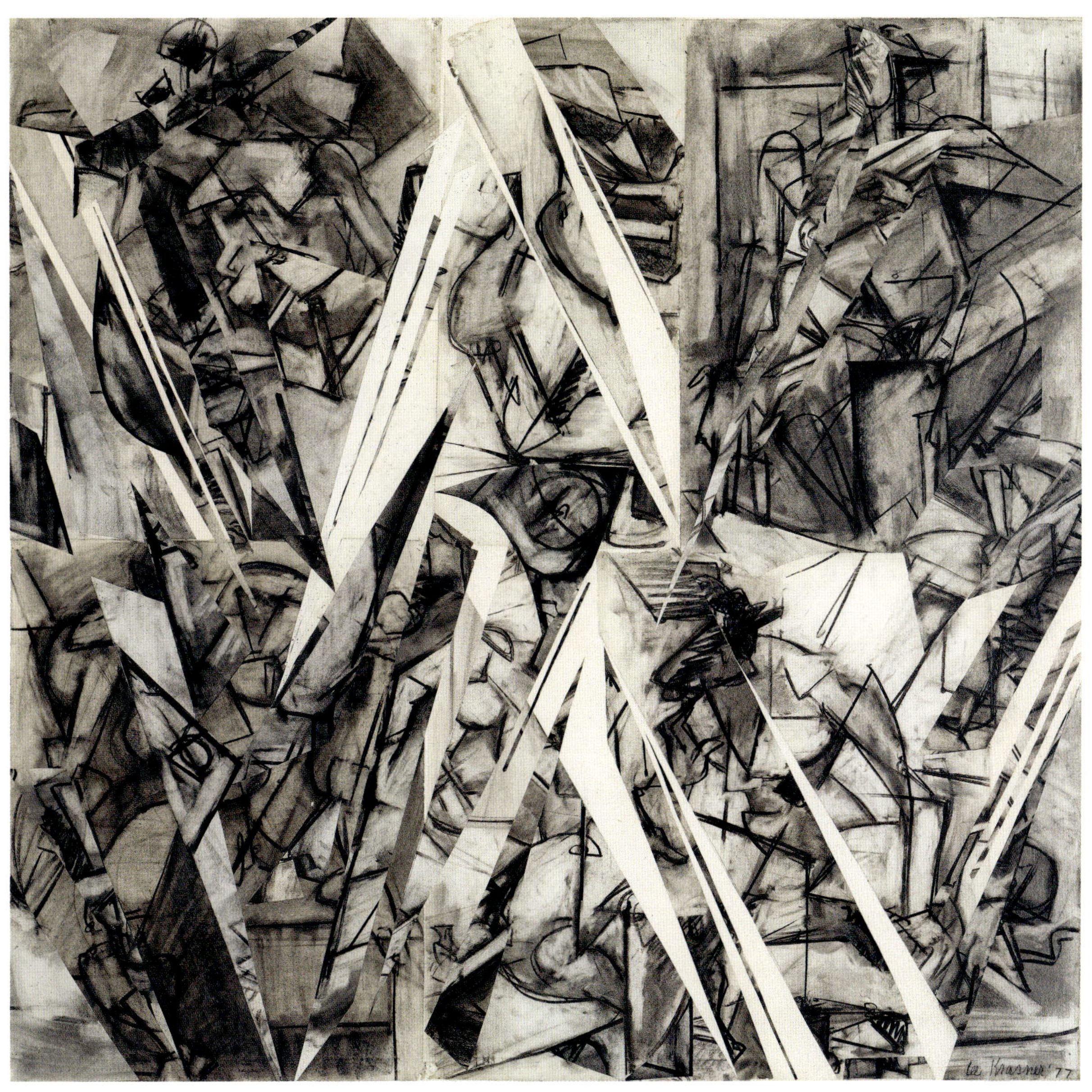

Future Indicative, 1977

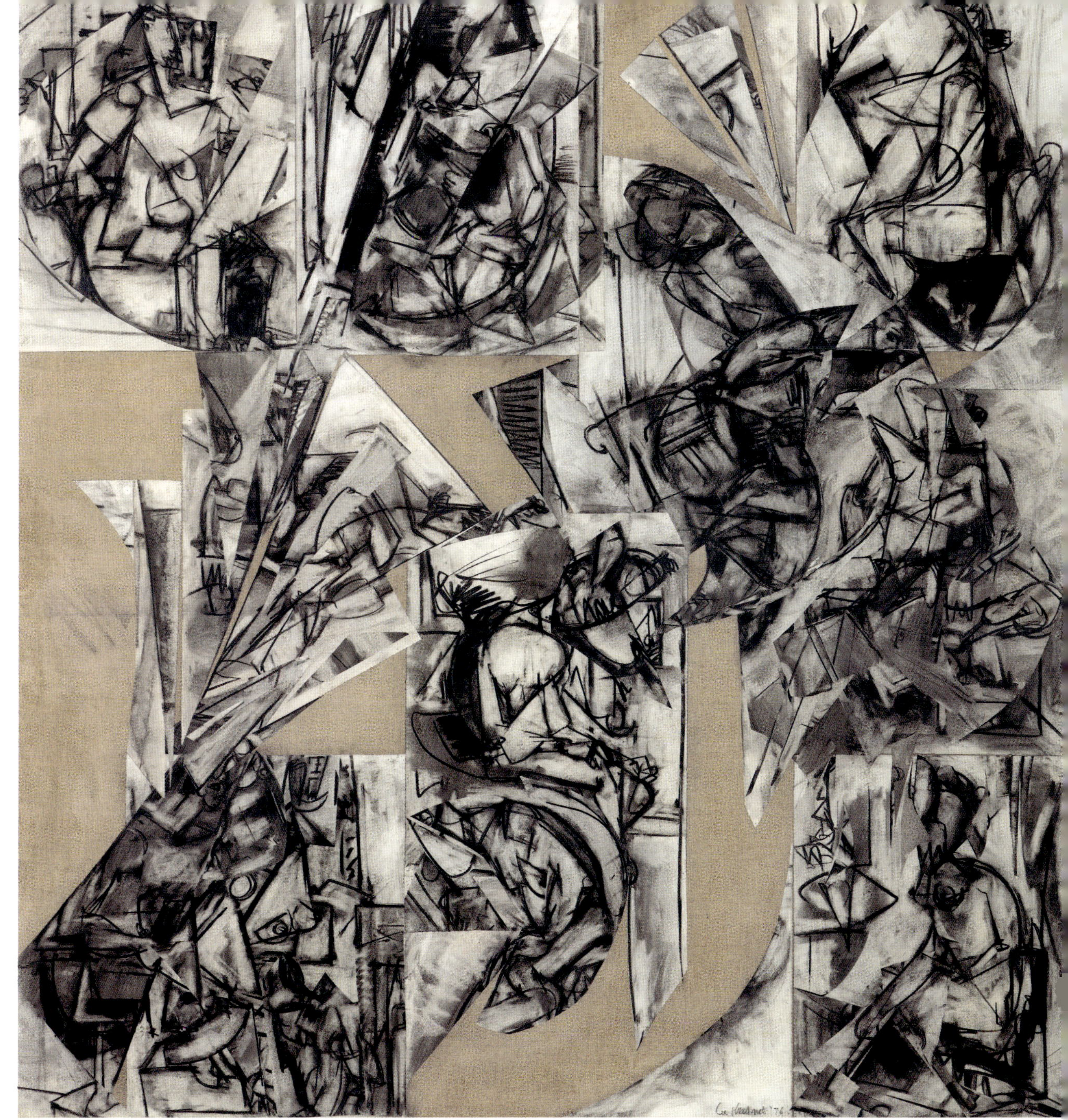

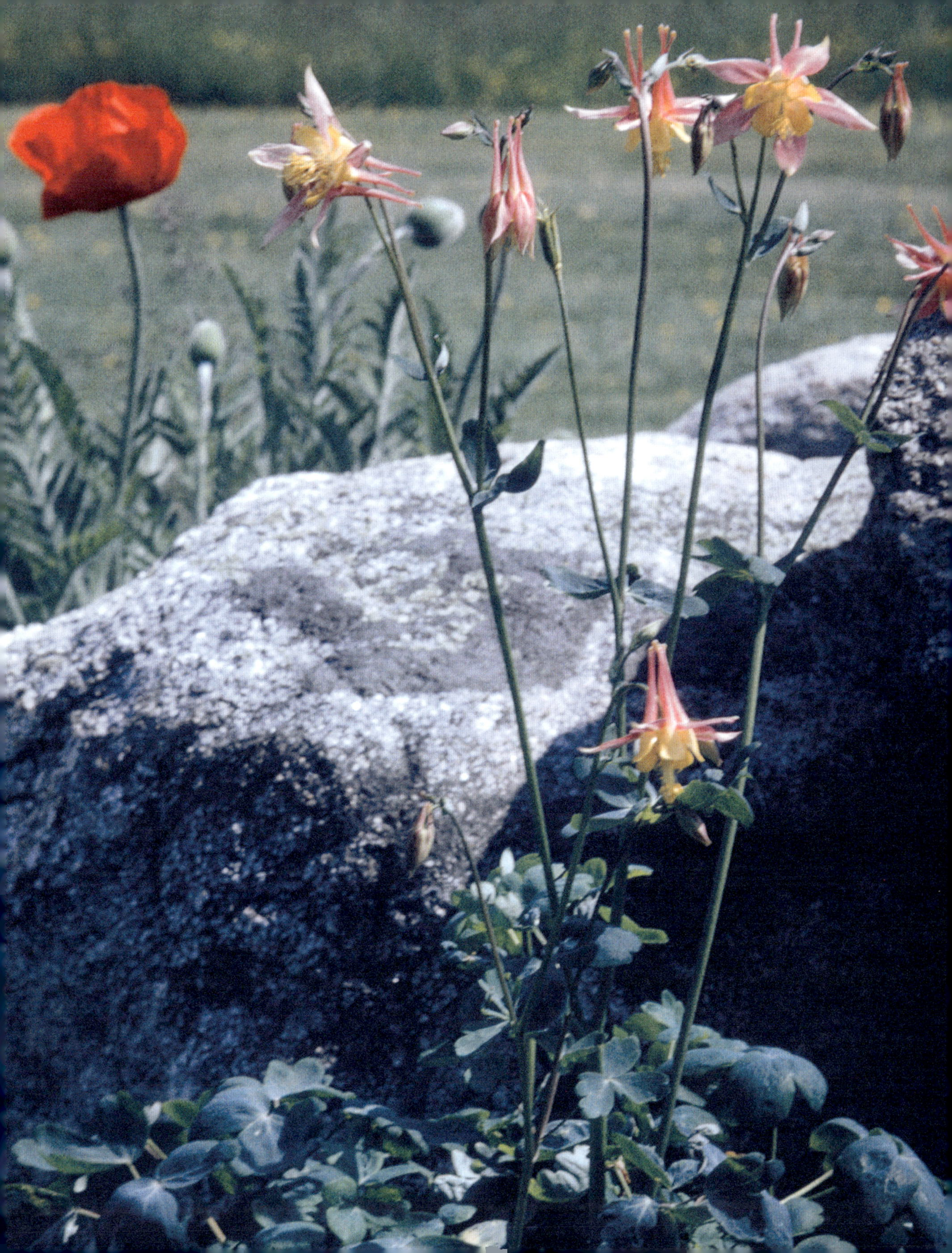

REFLECTIONS

'Why would Lee Krasner give an interview to a twenty-two-year-old?' a colleague once challenged me. I still have the handwritten draft of the letter I sent to Krasner on 2 December 1970: 'I would greatly appreciate an opportunity to speak with you with regard to my doctoral dissertation. I am investigating the artists of the New York School in the 1940s. I am particularly interested in your study with Hans Hofmann and in your recollections and opinions of the artists and events in New York during this period.' I told her that I wanted to see as much as possible of her work and of Pollock's, and that I would be happy to meet with her in East Hampton. A response, dated 15 December 1970, arrived from Donald McKinney of Marlborough Gallery, New York, which at the time represented both Krasner and the Jackson Pollock estate. McKinney wrote: 'Miss Krasner will be happy to give you all the help she can', and instructed me to telephone his secretary to set up a suitable time for an appointment.

When I arrived for the interview, McKinney sat me down and handed me a copy of the catalogue from Krasner's 1965 retrospective at the Whitechapel Gallery in London. I can still recall his words to me: 'Here, she's an artist too.' But then, reviewing my initial request, I see that I already knew that. I had just finished a doctoral-level course on Abstract Expressionism for which we had read Irving Sandler's newly published book, *Abstract Expressionism: The Triumph of American Painting* (1970). Neither Sandler nor my young male professor discussed women artists. In his book, Sandler omitted Krasner from those artists whose work was featured, reproduced and discussed, merely thanking 'Lee Krasner Pollock' in a list of artists who agreed to be interviewed.[1] (Even though, as an artist, she always used her own name, 'Krasner', never with 'Pollock' appended.) Despite such entrenched attitudes – including among the male professors who constituted my doctoral dissertation committee – the feminist movement was reaching young women like me, eager to find women artists and role models.

Krasner, who was sixty-two at the time of our first meeting, showed remarkable patience with my earnest young self. It would have been impossible at the time for either me or her to imagine that I would ever be able to help her career. Yet by 1978, I could insist on including Krasner as the only woman among the so-called 'first generation' in an important exhibition, *Abstract Expressionism: The Formative Years*, at the Whitney Museum of American Art, New York.[2] Nor could either of us have envisaged then that I would one day write her biography.[3]

While I was working on that book, the tapes from this interview disappeared; only later, after it was finished, did they turn up in my basement. So this is the first time that an edited version of our original interview has been published. Looking at our conversation now, I am moved by just how forthcoming Krasner was.

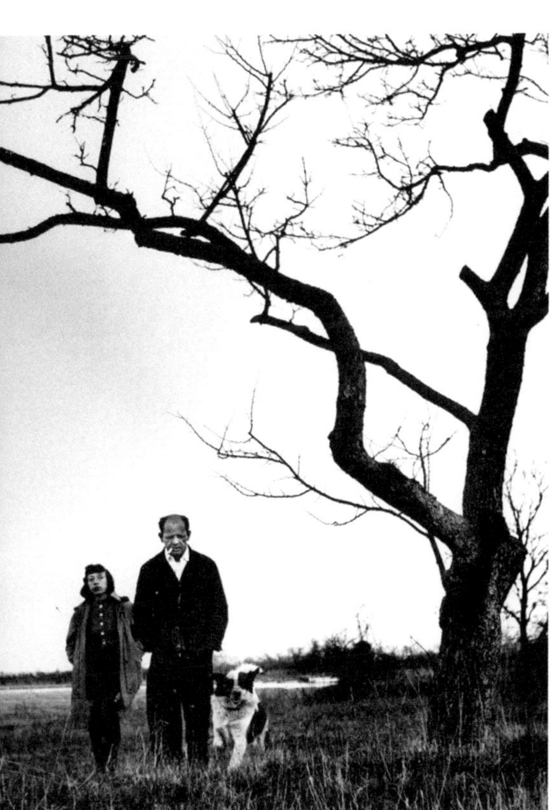

1 Lee Krasner, Jackson Pollock and their dog Gyp walking in a field in Springs, 1949. Photograph by Martha Holmes.

GAIL LEVIN   When did you first meet Pollock?

LEE KRASNER   Well I met Pollock first at a loft party and that's sort of late '30s, let's say about 1936, roughly. I didn't even know his name at the time – just a loft party, where we danced and spoke a while and then there's about a four-year gap before I meet him as Jackson Pollock.

GL   Was this in connection with the McMillen Gallery show?

LK   Yes, we were both exhibiting in that show. And I had never heard of a painter called Jackson Pollock and I looked him up. That's how I met him. And that McMillen show, I can't remember the dates now …

GL   About 1941?

LK   Yes, exactly.

GL   Were there any books that were important to you in the late 1930s, early '40s?

LK   You're asking for quite a bit of recall on my part! … In the past five or six years or something like that, [I have taken] what I have in the way of a library, out in East Hampton, and [have gone] through it very carefully, making notations of which were Pollock's books, at the time I met him, which were my books, and then what we continued as a togetherness collection; so that all that is very definitely recorded and unfortunately in my files someplace.

GL   I read somewhere that Pollock had D'Arcy Thompson's *On Growth and Form* [1917]. Did you have it also?

LK   No, that was his. And that book, if I'm not mistaken, Tony Smith called to his attention, said it was a book that he'd be fascinated by. So it was his book, rather than mine. I glanced through it as well. Pollock wasn't easy; if he read [something] he liked he would not necessarily discuss it. I would assume that he was interested from the number of times that I saw him poking around in the book.

GL   I believe that you both knew John Graham.

LK   That's correct.

GL   Were you familiar with his book *System and Dialectics of Art* [1937]?

LK   I was. And in fact, I was familiar with it before I met Pollock because I knew Graham before I met Pollock. And so I was very much fascinated by that little book of his. My copy unfortunately disappeared many years ago. I feel badly about it, but I still remember it.

GL   Do you think that Pollock might have been familiar with it as well?

LK   That I don't know because the book, if I'm not mistaken, preceded, by quite some time, the relationship between Pollock and Graham.

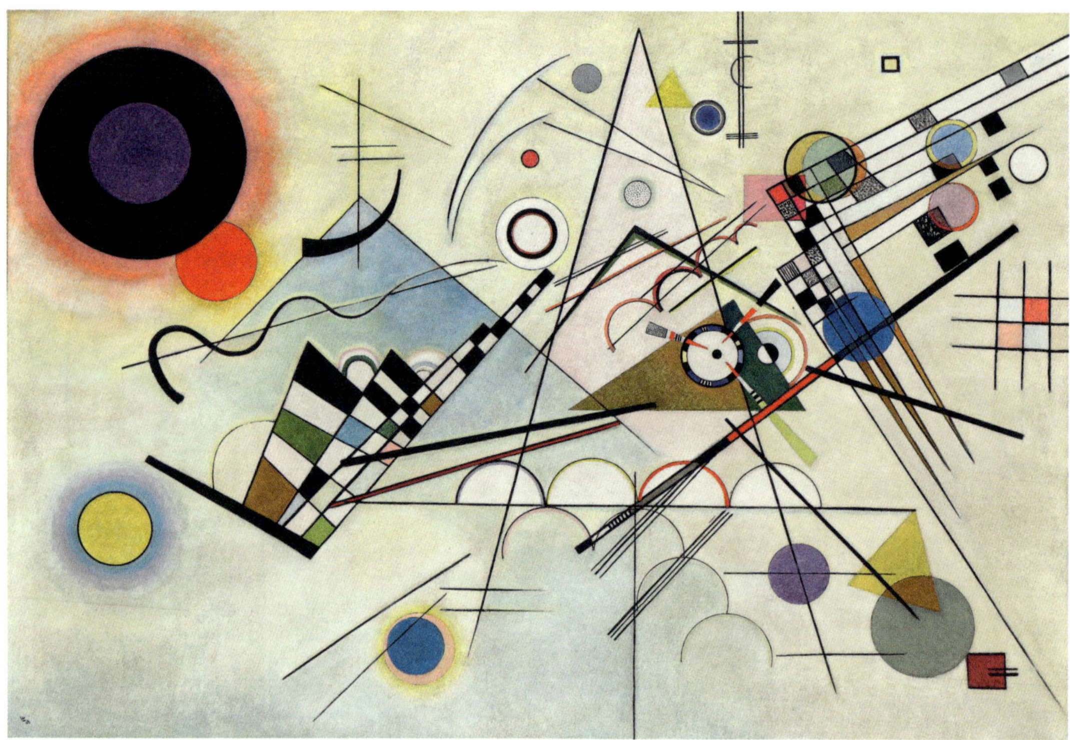

2   Wassily Kandinsky, *Composition 8*, 1923

GL   Kandinsky's own writings – would you have had any like *The Art of Spiritual Harmony* [1914] or *Point and Line to Plane* [1926]? Would Pollock have had them?

LK   No, I wouldn't have had them and I don't think that Pollock had them.

GL   Sometimes Kandinsky's theories appear to me to be applicable.

LK   All I know is that I admired Kandinsky – that is, the early Kandinsky – as a painter. In my relationship with Pollock, I don't remember Kandinsky's name ever coming up by way of certain names that I would hear Pollock discuss.

GL   Do you remember in 1945 at the Museum of Non-Objective Painting, now the Guggenheim Museum, there was a large Kandinsky retrospective?

LK   Oh yes. I saw it when it was held at the Plaza Hotel [in New York] … This was while the Baroness Rebay was heading the museum and it was before they had a definite place. It seems to me that I saw quite an extensive exhibition with a lot of early Kandinsky in it.

GL   Did you see it together with Pollock?

LK   In '45, I wouldn't remember whether we had seen it together or not.

GL   I read in your Whitechapel catalogue about the weekend that you and Pollock went to East Hampton and visited as house guests with the Kadishes. Did you visit Stanley William Hayter?

LK   No. It goes like this. The Kadishes had come from the West Coast and Reuben Kadish had gone to school with Jackson Pollock. He looked Pollock up and I met the Kadishes in New York. And the following summer, they said that they had rented a place in Springs, East Hampton. It was the Hayters, who I believe had stayed there the summer before, that had told them of this place. They invited us to spend a few days with them and that was the first time Pollock or I had been that far out on the island and that led eventually to our move out there.

GL   Am I correct that Pollock worked on some graphics in Hayter's studio? In 1944?

LK   That's correct. That was the atelier on Eighth Street; we lived directly across the street from the atelier. [Pollock] got interested and went over, did a few plates, but never pulled editions of them. It's only the Museum of Modern Art – through Bill Lieberman, who I gave the plates to – that said we can get them pulled into editions. Now we have editions on all but one of the existing plates.

GL   In 1945 Hayter's article 'The Language of Kandinsky' was in the *Magazine of Art*. Did you see it?

LK   I saw the magazine, but I don't remember this particular article. I wouldn't speak for Pollock, whether he read it or not.

GL   How did you begin to study under Hans Hofmann?

LK   Good question. At that time, I was very active in the Artists Union, and the only form of painting was a kind of social realism. The Artists Union was a political group and fighting for the maintenance of jobs on the WPA [Works Progress Administration], but occasionally they did publish something for *Art Front* [magazine]; I don't know if it came out once a month or once in three months. There was a little aesthetic art as well as political purpose.

I was terribly disillusioned on the political front and decided to tackle art seriously all over again. I kept working but was restless and feeling that I needed something else. I'd heard that Hans Hofmann was in New York and teaching, and several people said he's a good person, at least you'll have a model you can work from. So I went to the Hofmann class one day. I had to be interviewed by Mr Hofmann and he asked my background – I had no work with me – which was a women's school, Cooper Union and the National Academy. He said I don't need to see your work, which I thought was a little uppity. We talked for a while and he said OK, I could join the class. I joined the

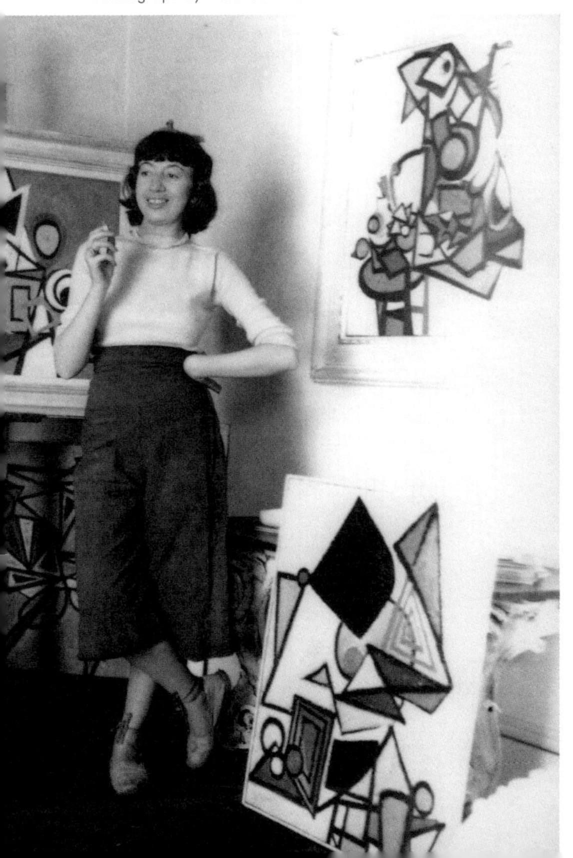

3   Lee Krasner in her New York studio, c.1939.
Photograph by Maurice Berezov.

class in a kind of spirit of 'let's see what this is about'. What Hofmann was teaching at the time was analytical Cubism. I became fascinated; a whole new world had opened up for me. And so I stayed and worked with him some three years. This is prior to my knowing Pollock.

GL Did any of Hofmann's specific theories influence you?

LK Well, that's an interesting thing because to begin with his accent was so heavy. He'd come in twice a week to criticize and he'd work directly on your work, which I found very offensive. However, he'd also keep talking while he was working. The accent was so heavy that I'd say the first six months, I had no idea in the world what this man was saying and was very offended by his going over my drawing. I'd wait until he was through criticism … Then I'd get ahold of the monitor of the class – that was George McNeil – and I'd say, 'Translate what that man said to me.' So in effect, I was getting George McNeil's version of what Hofmann was saying about my work.

GL Did Hofmann talk about other artists, like Matisse and Kandinsky?

LK Yes, a great deal. [That's] my impression through the time I worked with him. Once I got going and got interested and got in the swing of it, I guess I could understand him a little better, [although] possibly when you get very involved in your own work, you're not listening to every syllable and word that's being said, nor are you seeking explanation clearly. So that after I became like a Hofmann student, I was aware that he was perpetually swinging between his god being Picasso or Matisse. Since no student ever saw his work, since he didn't show his own work – religiously didn't, made an issue of it – it had its advantages in so far as you weren't doing Hofmann paintings or drawings.

GL Were you interested in both Matisse and Picasso, before you studied with Hofmann?

LK Yes, indeed. They were both up-top artists for me – and Mondrian as well, really up-top.

GL What were Pollock's interests when you met?

LK Our one strong common factor was Picasso. As for Mondrian, I don't know how he ever felt about Mondrian. And Matisse – possibly my enthusiasm and excitement about Matisse made him, you know, a little more interested in him than he may have been prior.

GL Around 1945 or '46, Pollock seems to have picked up a greater interest in colour. What might account for this?

LK I wouldn't know what accounted for it at that particular moment, probably many factors, but certainly I was interested in Matisse and certainly Matisse is a symbol of colour.

GL Did you have any particular interest in mythology or oriental philosophy? Especially in the early 1940s?

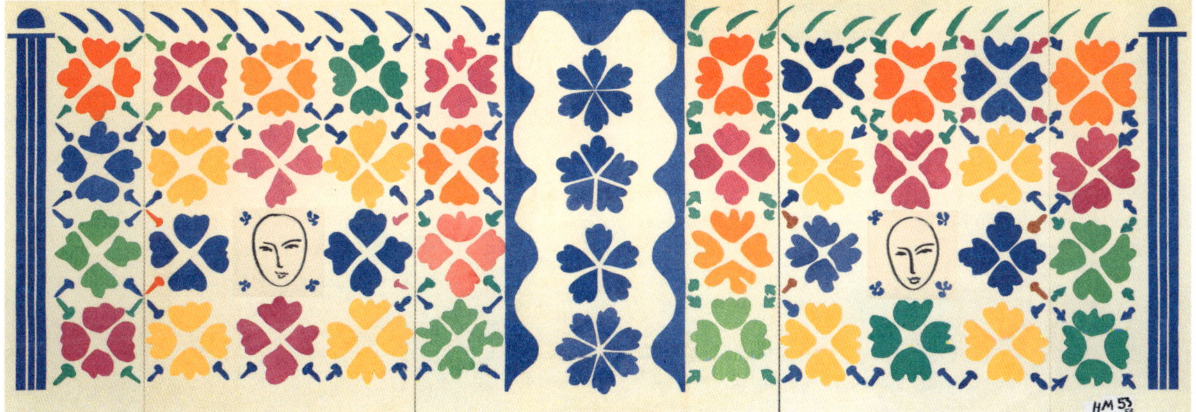

4   Henri Matisse, *Large Decoration with Masks*, 1953

LK   Yes, to both those. In fact, much more so at that point than I might today. Nothing specific. An interest definitely.

GL   And Pollock?

LK   That was one of our common denominators, as was [Herman] Melville, curiously enough. That's one that we both had. So when we acquired one of our dogs, we without hesitancy called him Ahab.

GL   Were either of you interested in James Joyce?

LK   We were both interested in James Joyce, but especially Pollock; I still have the recording of Joyce [reading] 'Anna Livia Plurabelle' [a section from *Finnegans Wake*], which we played 'til we were blue in the face. Tony Smith, who was a great disciple of Joyce, would spend time with us, come out for a weekend. We'd very often have a night, if Tony had had enough to drink, where he'd just recite. And he could go through whole passages of Joyce without even a book in front of him … I'd say that Joyce was a very important figure of interest to Pollock and certainly to myself as well.

GL   Can you express why you found Joyce so appealing?

LK   Why? For me today, he's still one of the writers that interests me most, what he was able to do with the word.

GL   Had Pollock heard lectures by [the Indian philosopher, speaker and writer] Krishnamurti?

LK   This occurred before he came to New York, someplace in California; I don't know specifically where. Certainly this must have occurred while he was in high school. How he got to it was through this teacher he had in high school, [Frederick John de St Vrain] Schwankovsky, who was a special figure for Jackson through his high school period and would have put him in touch.

GL   Were you interested in any specific aspect of psychology in the '40s or late '30s? Did you read any contemporary books?

LK   I was very impressed prior to meeting Pollock with one of Jung's books, *The Integration of the Personality* [1939]. That was my book before I met Pollock.

GL   Did he have any particular books that you recall?

LK   Well, on the subject of books that he had, when I visited his studio – not the first visit but after I visited several times – I said at one point, 'Don't you have any books?' as there were no books visible. And he said, 'I don't believe in putting up what I'm reading; I keep them privately.' And consequently, as I saw him more and knew him better, he had a whole hallway of closets that ran through part of the apartment and all the books were kept in drawers, they were never exposed. So that the first exposure of the books was after we moved to East Hampton, which is '45, and I insisted on bookshelves and we had a long-running battle and he conceded and allowed bookshelves … In some curious way, he was very private about his reading. In fact, I didn't think that he had a book until I got to know him well enough for him to show me where he kept them. But nobody else would know there were books there.

GL   What about poetry? Favourite poets?

LK   My top favourite at the time was Rimbaud; in fact, I had written across a whole wall in the studio a section from *A Season in Hell*. In huge bold writing. One whole wall occupied this prior to my meeting Pollock. One of the things that really moved me.

GL   Did Pollock ever see that in your studio?

LK   Yes, Pollock saw it in my studio and disapproved entirely. I had been very specific about this passage and decided to do it just that way. We had a little battle about it … Tennessee Williams and Fritz Bultman, a painter, came in one day and they went into a harangue, and I kicked them both out of the apartment. I didn't like what they were saying, and how they were dealing with it all, so out they went.

GL   Did you spend an evening writing automatic poetry with Robert Motherwell and his wife?

LK   William Baziotes and his wife, Ethel; Robert Motherwell and his first wife [Maria Emilia Ferreira y Moyeros]; Jackson and I. We may have had dinner together and it was more or less like playing a game [Exquisite Corpse]. You do the head and then fold it over and you do the shoulders, and fold it over, and then the breasts and then fold it over. A few evenings. And Jackson … very often analysed them.

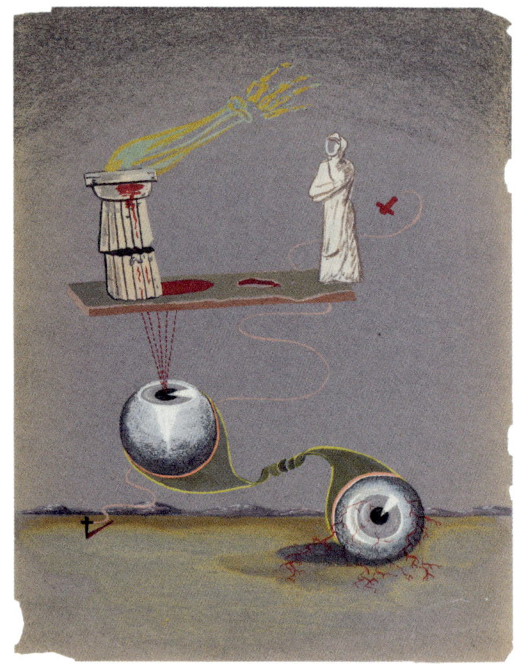

5   *Untitled (Surrealist Drawing)*, c.1935–38

GL   In what way?

LK   In his own peculiar way. His favourite thing was let's do male and female in that manner and then he'd analyse you on the basis of what you did. I'd put that [under] the heading of fun and games, you know, after dinner.

GL   Was Robert Motherwell – or indeed were you – doing this game as a kind of mockery of Surrealism? In terms of psychic automatism?

LK   We didn't set out to do it, so to speak. A lot of people used to do that thing at that point. If there were six of us with that kind of common interest ... It would be a natural thing to do.

GL   Were you interested in Surrealism in the '40s?

LK   I was certainly very aware of it; in that sense, I certainly knew the Surrealist painters and their writings. I was aware of it.

GL   You didn't put the Surrealists in the same category as Matisse and Picasso?

LK   No, not as painters; not that you couldn't find a lot of Surrealism in Picasso. But that was a different thing, because it was in painting. Surrealism interested me less as an idea; only as it became part of painting was it of interest to me.

6   Lee Krasner and Jackson Pollock in the kitchen of their
    home in Springs, 1949. Photograph by Martha Holmes.

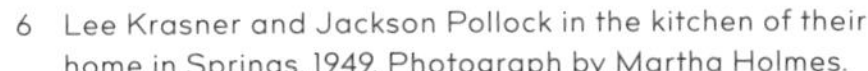

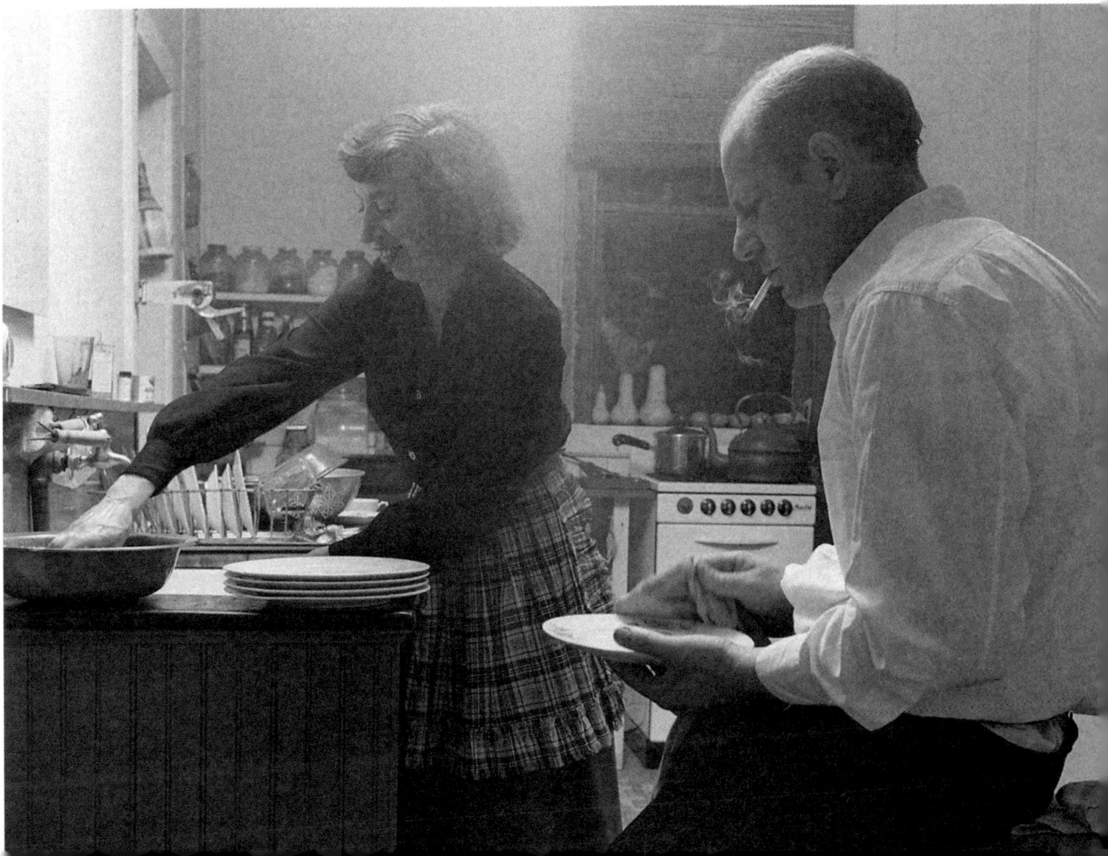

GL   Did you see Surrealist movies?

LK   Yes, I saw some of them. Yes, they impressed me but they were movie[s], and that's a different thing for me.

GL   Were your paintings ever influenced by other media: literature or movies?

LK   When you're painting, it's a total statement of all of your interests, so to speak. I can't say that Surrealist movies affected me in my work or did not affect me in my work. It's pretty hard to know exactly what channels in. If you know it that well, it's no longer an unknown factor; you're conscious there and using something or another.

GL   Did you and Pollock know the European Surrealist painters who were in New York? [André] Masson or [Roberto] Matta?

LK   No. Pollock did visit Matta for a very short time. He'd be the only Surrealist painter that I could point to. I saw painters like [Arshile] Gorky, [John] Graham or [Willem] de Kooning ... I knew Gorky prior to knowing Pollock and saw him very often in cafés and spoke with him a great deal. I also knew de Kooning; I brought Pollock over to meet de Kooning for the first time ... and Hofmann as well ... I did not bring Pollock to Gorky's studio, but they did meet. It would have been very brief ... their meeting was very casual. I had been to [Gorky's] studio many times. He had been to my studio a few times. I was very much interested in what Gorky was doing, but it was so heavily dominated by Picasso at that time; that's all the man was thinking and breathing and feeling. He was beginning to see Matta and other Surrealists, and somewhere in there his transition occurred, and, I might say, to his advantage.

GL   What did you think of [Joan] Miró?

LK   Mad for Miró; I thought he was marvellous! Pollock too – [now] there was a Surrealist who was of interest to both of us! His *painterliness*. There was no separation between idea and painting. My interest in Miró was prior to Pollock. Someplace, in '44, Pollock was interviewed by some magazine and he answered that the two painters that interested him most had never been to this country, Picasso and Miró.

GL   I know that Pollock was working at the Museum of Non-Objective Painting. What did he do?

LK   He ran the elevator for a while. He worked down in the basement, working on frames, that kind of work, and he received a salary for it. He hated it but it was a livelihood; he did not mind the chores, the idea that this is what he had to do because he was an artist.

GL   What about the collection there?

LK   [Pollock's] main interest there was the early Kandinskys ... He did various things [around the same time]; he had been decorating ties and lipsticks [but] he wasn't able to do his own designs. Many years

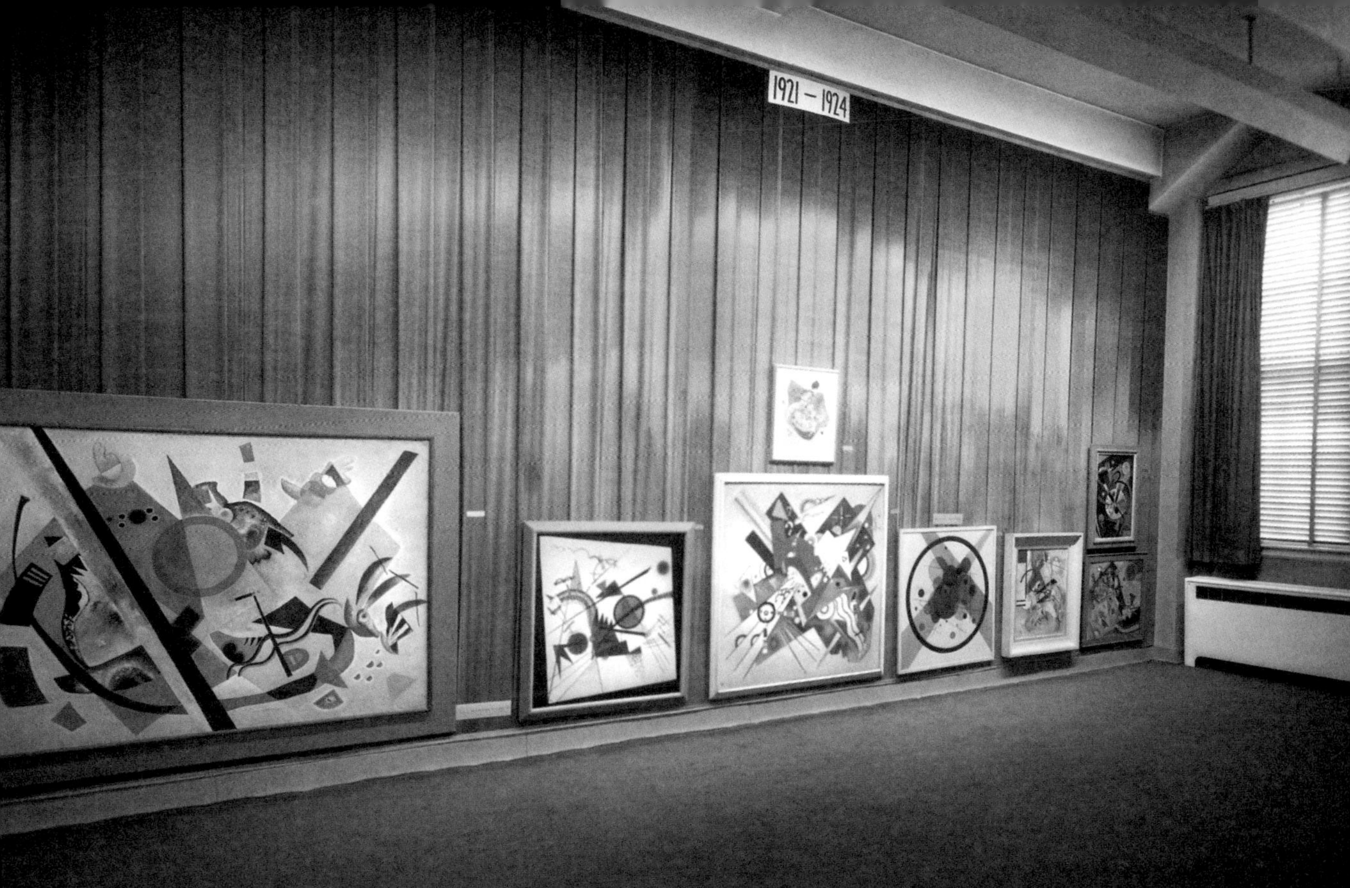

7   Installation view of *Kandinsky Memorial Exhibition* at the Museum of Non-Objective Painting, New York, March 1945.

prior to that he did china and ... he painted some china with his own designs. [Thomas Hart Benton and his wife] have some plates; also [Arloie] McCoy [Sanford McCoy's wife] has a plate or two. This is prior to my knowing him.

GL   How aware of the art world in New York were you? Did you see all of the major shows?

LK   I thought I did.

GL   In 1943 the Museum of Modern Art had a show called *Romantic Painting in America* ...

LK   In '43 the art world was a much smaller art world. It's not likely that any show went on in the art world that we didn't see. We saw any show of any consequence. There were very few galleries showing [contemporary] artists, and if a museum did a show, we would have seen it.

GL   The 1944 book and show, *Abstract and Surrealist Art in America* by Sidney Janis, included you and Pollock, but misspelled your name.

LK   It was like that then. I dropped an 's' because that was enough writing to do [...] Sidney and Harriet Janis came to my studio. I was the one that told him in 1942 to go see a guy called Jackson Pollock and gave the address. That's how he came to Pollock's studio. He acknowledges this.

GL   In December 1944 Kandinsky died and had a big show at Nierendorf Gallery [in New York], followed up in April [1945] by the retrospective at the Museum of Non-Objective Painting.

LK   That one we would have seen.

GL   Were you conscious of newspaper reviews?

LK   Yes, because there was so little you could get ahold of then ... But accepting or rejecting them was another state of affairs! Missed them, no.

GL   During the '40s Harold Rosenberg's wife, May Tabak Rosenberg, was a witness to your wedding. When did you meet?

LK   Many years before, the '30s ... I introduced them to Pollock. Indeed, I introduced [Pollock] to Greenberg as well!

GL   When did you meet Clement Greenberg?

LK   I met Clement Greenberg at the Rosenbergs' house; Harold Rosenberg was not involved with painting at all. He was a writer and so was Clement Greenberg; I don't know what they were working on then. It had nothing to do with art at all ... I knew them socially; not as art critics, as writers.

GL   Was Rosenberg interested in Surrealism as a writer?

LK   I would assume that Rosenberg was interested in Surrealism; he read everything that was ever printed *as a writer*. He's very much in the art world by then and became very interested in what Pollock was doing.

GL   Did you stop painting for a while when you moved to East Hampton?

LK   Only long enough to take care of my wifely duties; the studio set-up and just a little bit to get things settled. A short period, moving into this new situation ... A short period.

I still have my small paintings, what I call my 'Little Image' paintings, that date from 1946–50.

[LK is smoking Gilbert's cigarettes as we talk. Looking at the catalogue of the 1965 retrospective at the Whitechapel Gallery in London, she shows me her self-portrait from the National Academy of Design.]

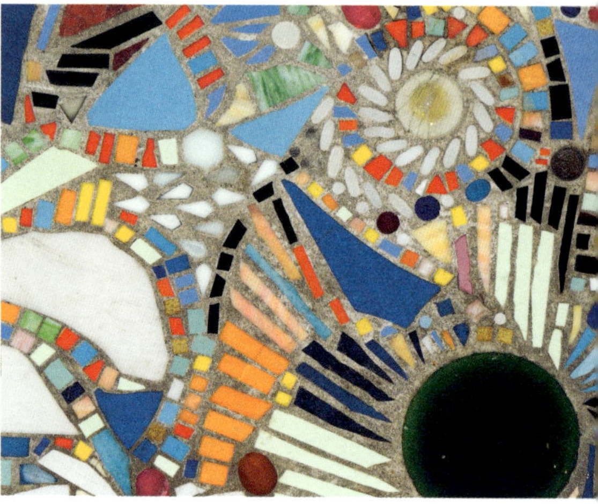

8   Detail from *Mosaic Table*, 1947

GL How did you get into doing mosaics?

LK When we moved out there [to Springs], Pollock worked in one of the bedrooms upstairs, for [an] immediate studio situation. It wasn't until he could get into the barn, which we moved and cleared out, that I could take that over; and in the interim, I had no place to work and had to just take little sections of the house … I did the mosaics because I had to work in the living room and couldn't paint.

GL Do you do your later work [on] stretched or unstretched [canvas]?

LK I work unstretched tacked to the wall, and after it's finished, it's stretched. I don't work on the floor. Pollock very often worked on the floor.

GL If you could sum up important people whom you and Pollock knew in the '40s, who are the key people, artists, critics?

LK For the early '40s, most of the names have been mentioned already, if we're talking about the very early '40s. By the late '40s, we had moved out to the country and maintained our relationships. But the names have come up so far: like Tony Smith, Barnett Newman, Clyfford Still, Bradley [Walker] Tomlin, Alfonso Ossorio, John Little, Jim Brooks, Harold Rosenberg, Clement Greenberg.

9 Detail from *Shellflower*, 1947

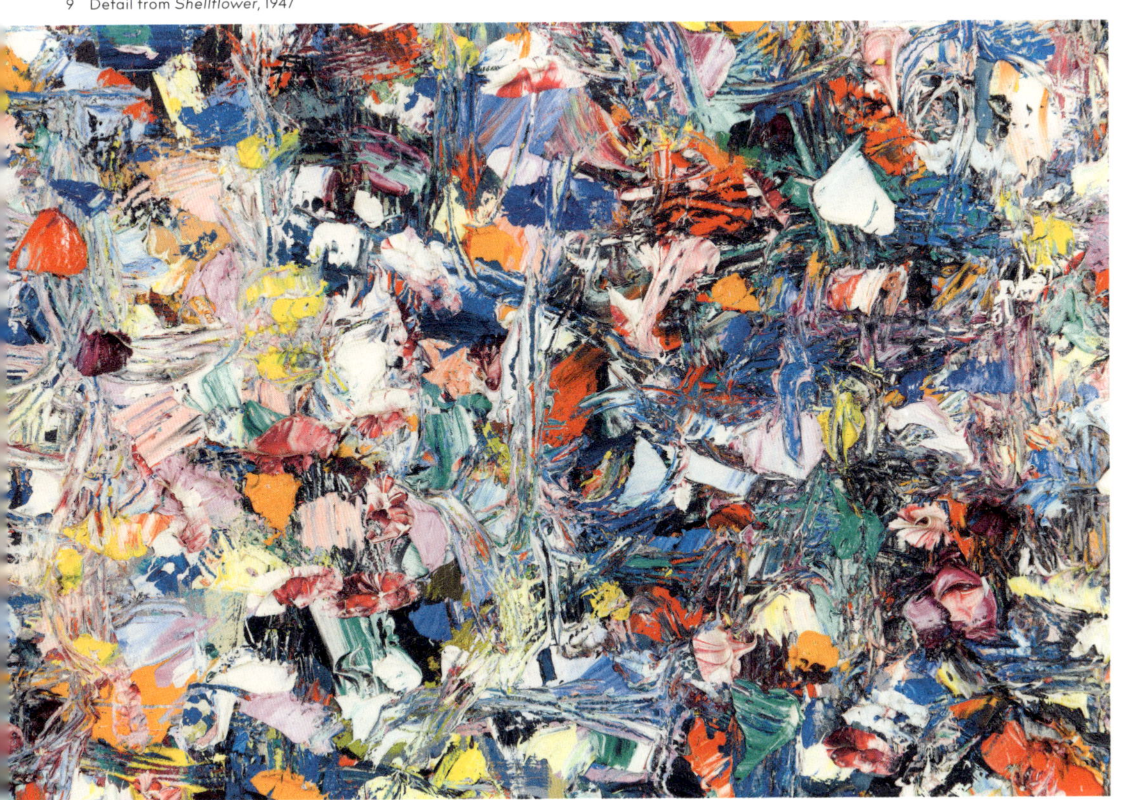

GL   From the Hamptons, did you still come into New York City for shows?

LK   We were very remote. A Pollock show or a show of mine brought us into New York or some very extraordinary show. There was a disconnection with New York, except we had people coming to stay with us. Getting in to what we consider the 'musts only'. By then, it gets a little selective.

GL   Looking back, do you see your studies with Hofmann as very beneficial?

LK   I got a great deal from Hofmann, as a teacher, and his enthusiasm towards painting was marvellous; and then I meet Pollock. So, I'd say for myself, I had two major upheavals in my art life: that is, breaking from the Academy into Cubism, and that would have been Hofmann; then came the second break, after I met Pollock, and that was breaking with Hofmann into whatever it's described as now.

GL   You really broke then from Cubism?

LK   *Oh, oh,* that break was a result of meeting Pollock and seeing his work. I mean, the upheaval and break was even more strenuous from that than it was from breaking with the Academy into Cubism. So those were the two major breaks. And it was Hofmann who was instrumental for me to break with prior painting and then I had to go through that upheaval once more to break away from Cubism via Hofmann to whatever our new aesthetic definition is, and it hasn't been defined. Not as far as I can see. We've used titles and slogans but no definition in aesthetic terms from where I sit.

GL   What about Abstract Expressionism?

LK   By now, you and I know what we mean when we say it. But it certainly hasn't defined anything. If you take the Abstract Expressionists and try to break down the difference between [Barnett] Newman and Pollock, let's say, where are you other than that big loose loophole called Abstract Expressionism? ... We have nothing but phrases to hang on to: first generation, second generation, lost generation, found-now generation. No aesthetic definition!

GL   When you brought Hofmann up to see Pollock, what did they think of each other?

LK   Pretty fiery exchange, there. I brought Hofmann up to see Pollock because I thought he was one of the few people in New York that would dig what was going on. He didn't. He said, 'Ach, you are talented. You should join my class.' ... Pollock, in turn, his response was, 'Your theories in art don't interest me; put up or shut up, where is your art?' Finally, after many fiery exchanges, we were permitted to come to [Hofmann's] studio and look at work. We got Peggy Guggenheim up to the studio, [which] led to the first Hofmann show in New York.

GL   Was this the first time that you had seen Hofmann's work?

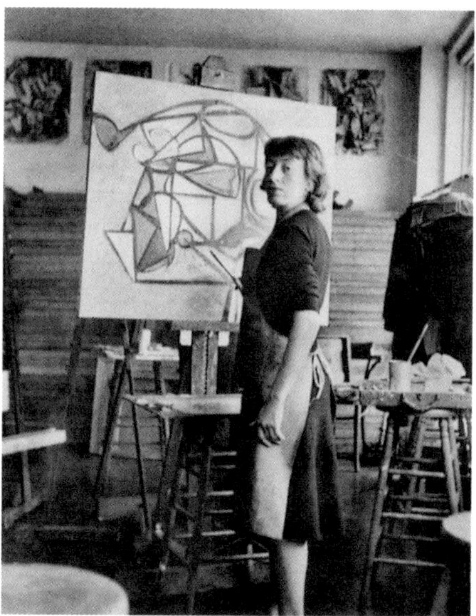

10   Lee Krasner working at the Hans Hofmann School of Fine Arts, c.1940.

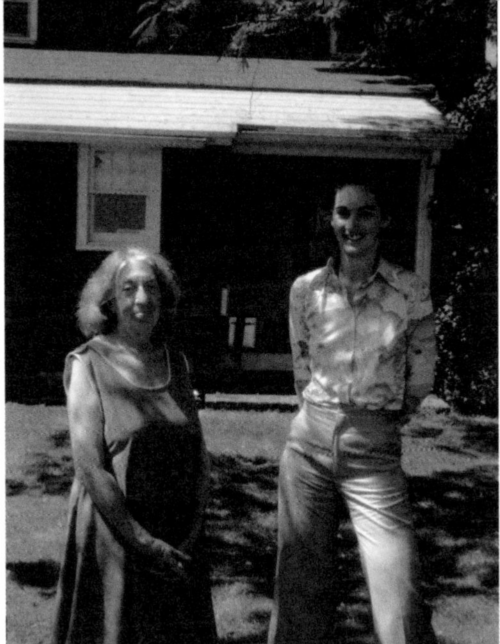

11 Lee Krasner and Gail Levin in Springs, summer 1977.

LK Yes, it's not recorded, but that's what happened. In return, Hofmann took several visits to Pollock's studio before he stopped saying that he was 'talented' and should join his class and began to see and acknowledge the paintings.

GL What about your own aesthetics?

LK By that time, I was in a black–gray period where I painted daily and nothing would come through, and finally, about '46, those first Little Images come through and that's my transition.

GL What about Mark Rothko?

LK I knew Rothko, but so distantly and so remotely it would be unfair to assume that there was a close exchange; we saw a great deal more of Clyfford Still, for instance.

GL: When you saw Tony Smith or [Robert] Motherwell or [William] Baziotes, did you talk to them about art? Or was it just what's going on in the art world?

LK It would depend. It was more art shop-talk; who's in what gallery, and so forth. With Clyfford Still, there was a little more intensity in terms of what was beginning to shape up in the art world and a feeling of what painting is.

GL Pollock never did teach?

LK Pollock was very anti-teaching, and he said that America killed its painters by feeding them into the teaching machine and that America should support the painter. He approved of the WPA.

GL And did you want to teach?

LK I had no desire to teach; and I certainly understood what Pollock was saying.

Reflections: My First Interview with Lee Krasner
Marlborough Gallery, New York, 6 February 1971
Gail Levin

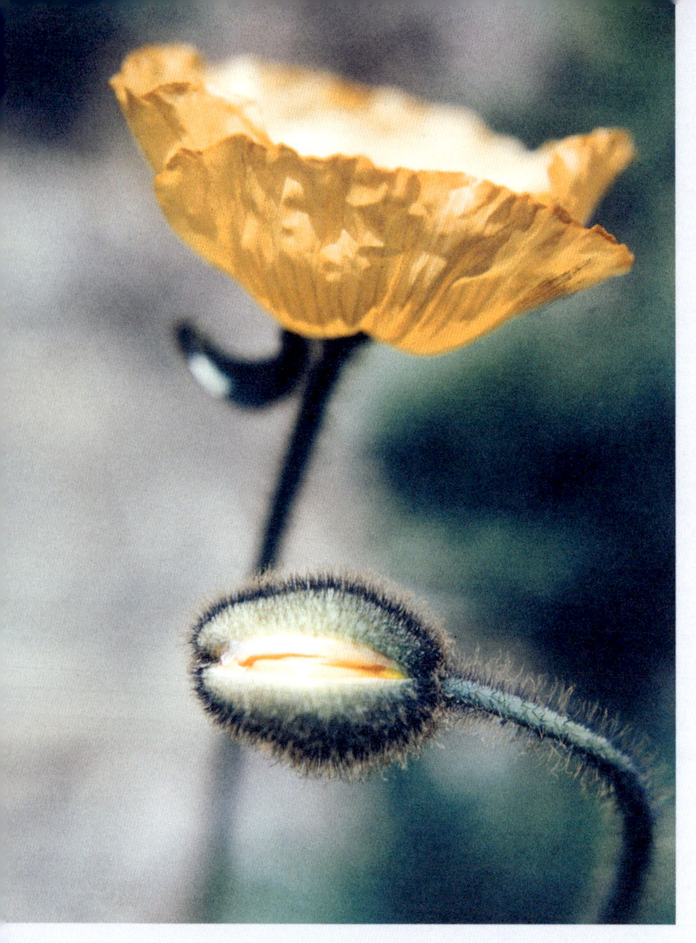
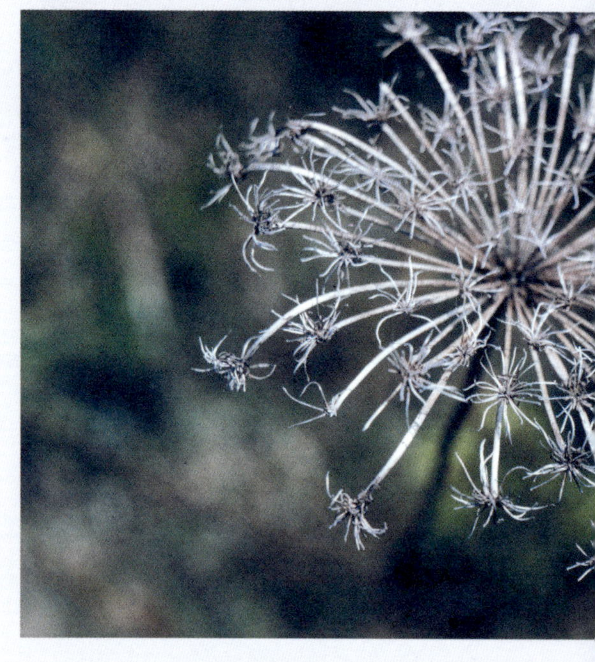
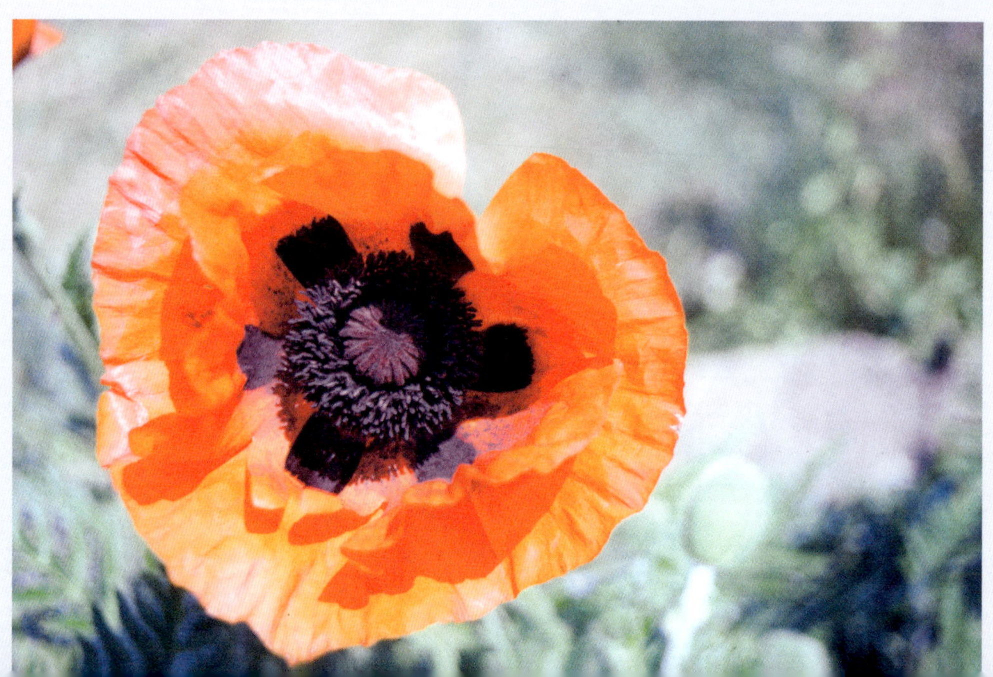

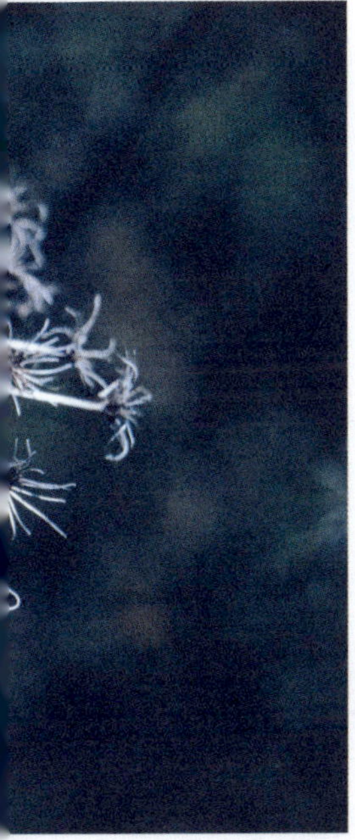
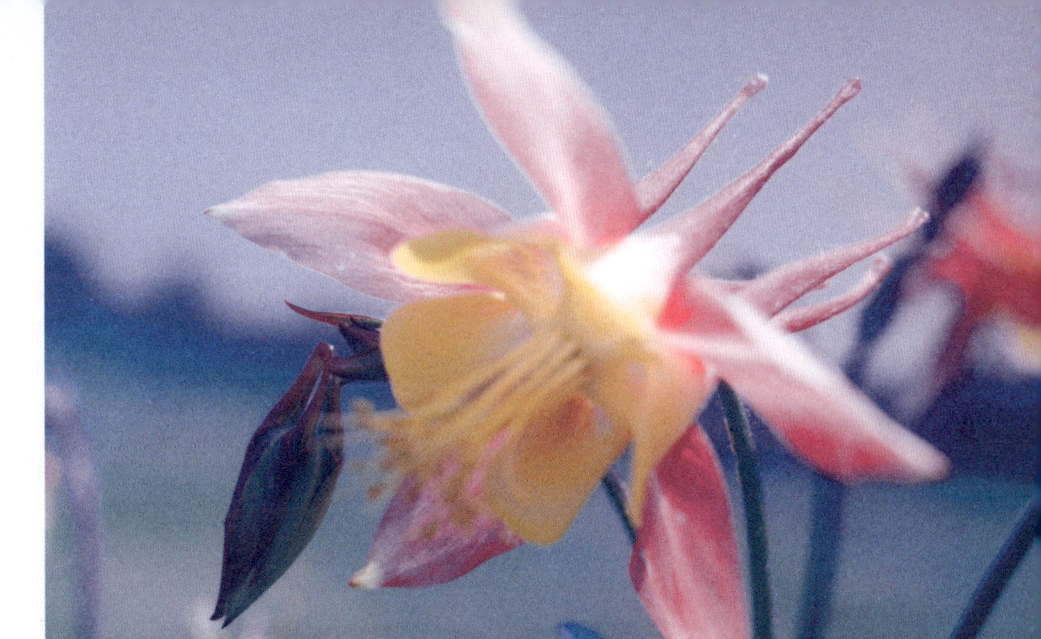
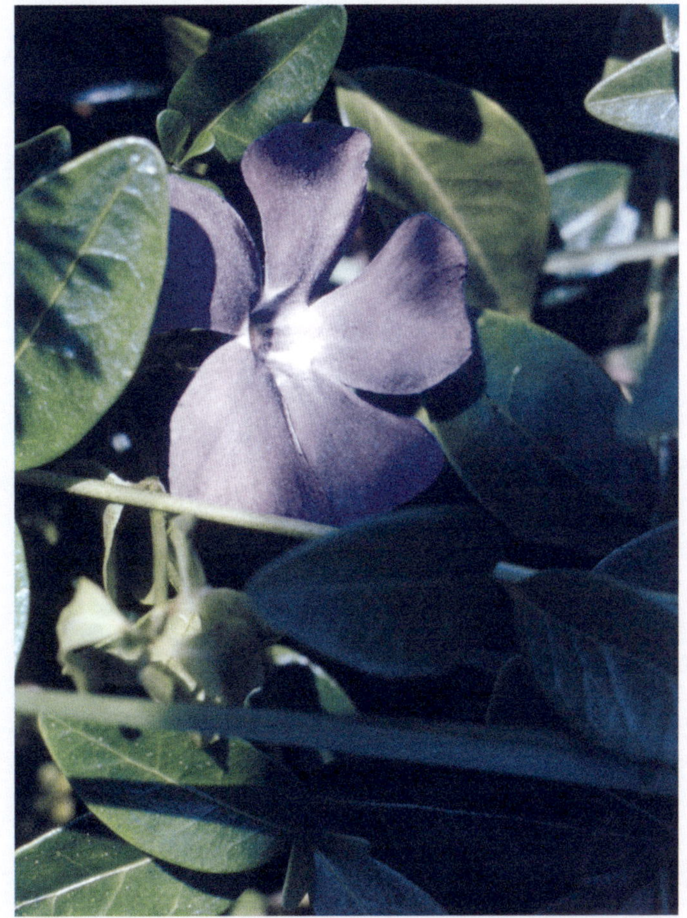

CHRONOLOGY

1908

Lena Krassner is born on 27 October in Brooklyn, New York. She arrives nine months and two weeks after her mother, Chane, is reunited with her husband, Joseph. Three years earlier, Joseph had emigrated to the United States from their small village near Odessa (in what was then Russia and is now central Ukraine), fleeing brutal pogroms and the Russo-Japanese War. The first of the Krassner children to be born in America, Lena joins three sisters – Ides, Esther and Rose – as well as a brother, Isak. Her younger sister, Ruth, is born in 1910 (fig. 1).

1909

Krasner grows up in an Orthodox Jewish household in which her family speak a mixture of Russian, Yiddish and English. Throughout her childhood, she chooses to attend services at the synagogue (unlike her sister Ruth) and takes her religion seriously. 'Yom Kippur. I fasted. I didn't shortcut. I was religious. I observed.'

Her father runs a fruit, vegetable and fish stall at the Blake Avenue Market close to the family home. Krasner later describes the Brooklyn of her childhood as very rural: 'Where I lived there were beautiful flowers. I loved it. A backyard with irises. My fleurs-de-lis – my favourite flower. And wild daisies. Bridal veil. And lilac. And roses on the fences, and in all the back yards.' Her walk to school was 'through the lots filled with buttercups. There was a farm with a pail and cows. Smells. Warm milk in the bucket.'

At the synagogue, Krasner is immersed in literature and music for the first time. She recalls being captivated by the 'mystery' of the Hebrew that she has learned to write but never fully understands. It is only later in life, when reading an English translation of the morning prayer (which she had obediently recited as a child), that she begins to rail against the treatment of women in Jewish scripture: 'If you are a male you say, "Thank you, O Lord, for creating me in your image." If you are a female you say, "Thank you, O Lord, for creating me as you see fit", and that started up a revolution that I have not recovered from.'

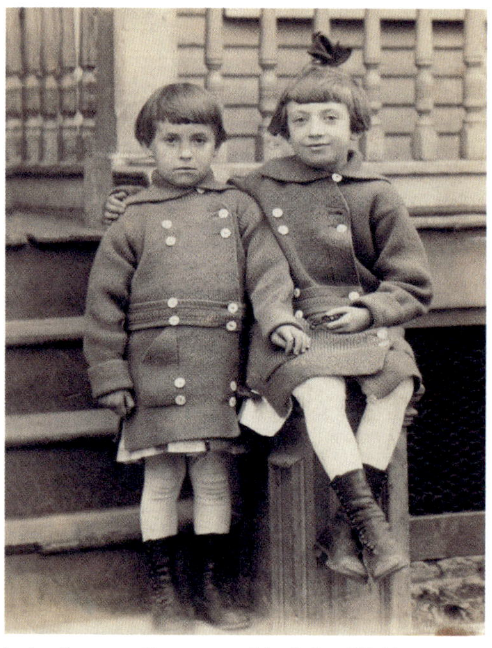

1   Lee Krasner and her younger sister, Ruth, c.1915–16.

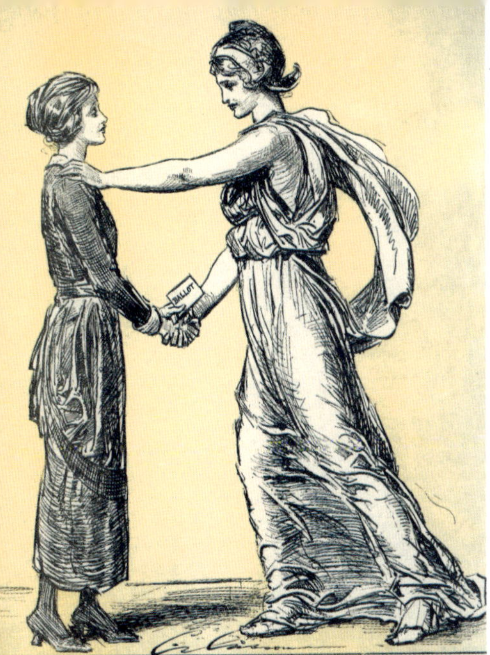

2 Magazine cover commemorating the final ratification of the Nineteenth Amendment to the US Constitution, granting women the right to vote, *Life* magazine, 28 June 1920.

Krasner's brother introduces her to books by prominent Russian authors, including Fyodor Dostoevsky, Nikolai Gogol and Ivan Turgenev.

1920

On 18 August, the Nineteenth Amendment to the United States Constitution comes into force, granting American women the right to vote (fig. 2).

1922

Like many émigrés, Krasner adopts an Americanized version of her name, 'Lenore'. She graduates from P.S. 72 in Brooklyn and applies to Washington Irving High in Manhattan, which at the time was the only public school in Greater New York to offer an art course for girls. Initially she is denied entry and so spends six months at Brooklyn Girls' High.

During this time, she discovers the philosophers Friedrich Nietzsche and Arthur Schopenhauer, whose writings encourage her to rebel against her religious upbringing.

She recalls the uproar provoked by her refusal to sing Christmas carols at school: 'Much to my own astonishment, I got up in the classroom and said, "I refuse to say 'Jesus Christ is my Lord'. He is not my Lord." Now, you can imagine this caused quite a commotion.' She also describes arriving home one Sabbath 'like a charging banshee' and declaring to her parents that she is finished with religion.

1923

On a second attempt, Krasner is accepted by Washington Irving High. This means a daily, two-hour roundtrip to Manhattan, which offers her some of her first experiences of life in the bustling metropolis. She later recalled, 'Not until I went to Washington Irving High School in Manhattan, on the subway, did I have contact with a "city".'

1924

The Best Tales of Edgar Allan Poe is published in New York by Modern Library. Poe would be a great source of inspiration for Krasner, as well as many fellow artists who would congregate in New York, including the Surrealist Max Ernst and the Abstract Expressionist Robert Motherwell. Krasner later recalls that Poe 'had an enormous effect on me in my teens'.

1925

In the spring, Krasner graduates from high school.

1926

In February, Krasner starts at the Cooper Union in Manhattan, studying under Charles Louis Hinton and Victor Semon Pérard. Hinton supervises her studies of hands and feet, the torso, and the full figure from plaster casts – classes that she was required to pass in order to be promoted to life drawing – but she clashes with his traditional teaching methods. 'Mr Hinton ... had a great deal of difficulty with me. Finally, he said that he would promote me to Life drawing not because I deserved it but because he couldn't do anything with me.' Krasner's other courses included costume design and illustration, both with Ethel Traphagen.

In May, Krasner's parents move to Greenlawn in the Huntington area of Long Island.

1927

In January, the Valentine Gallery in New York stages the first US retrospective of Henri Matisse. Arranged by the artist's youngest son, Pierre Matisse, the month-long exhibition includes such works as *White Plumes* (1919) and *Young Woman in Pink* (1923). Matisse goes on to have a powerful impact on Krasner, who comes to consider him as one of her 'gods'.

Around this time, Krasner begins to be called 'Lee' by fellow students.

1928

Victor Semon Pérard commissions Krasner to produce an illustration for his book *Anatomy and Drawing*. The result, 'Studies of Hands, Method of Blocking' (fig. 3), becomes her first piece of paid work.

Krasner leaves the Cooper Union after the spring term, feeling that she 'ought to do something more serious'. That summer, she shares a studio with friends on Fifth Avenue and Fifteenth Street, and earns money by modelling nude for the sculptor Moses Wainer Dykaar, who has a studio in the same building. In July, she registers at the Art Students League and spends a month studying figure drawing with George Bridgman.

On 9 July Krasner's older sister Rose dies suddenly from appendicitis, leaving behind a husband, William Stein, and two young daughters,

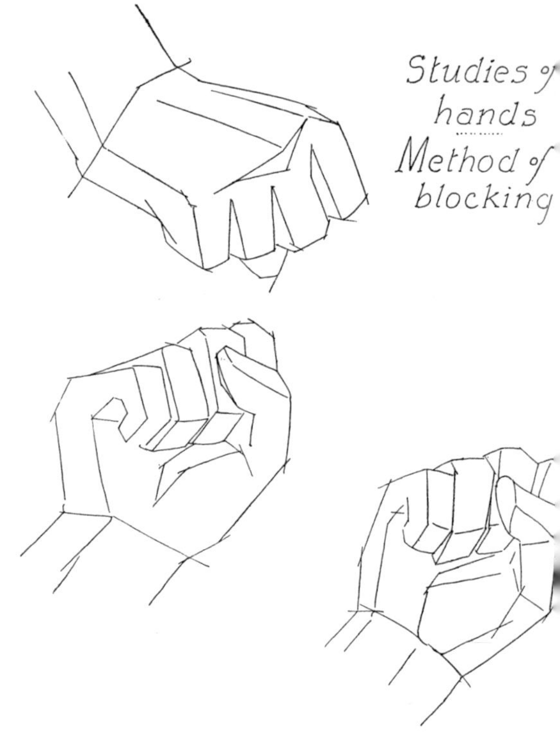

3   'Studies of Hands, Method of Blocking', in Victor Semon Pérard, *Anatomy and Drawing* (New York: Victor Pérard Publisher, 1928).

Muriel and Bernice. Krasner refuses to accept the Old World Jewish custom that the next in line should marry the widow or widower, which forces her younger sister, Ruth, to assume this responsibility.

Krasner spends time at her parents' home in Greenlawn, Long Island, nailing a mirror to a tree in the garden and painting a self-portrait in oil. She hopes the work will qualify her for the course 'Life Drawing from Plaster Casts' at the National Academy of Design in New York, where she is already enrolled. When it is presented to the Academy's committee, they refuse to believe that she could have painted it outside, calling it a 'dirty trick' but promoting her nonetheless.

At the National Academy, Krasner is supervised by Charles Curran, Ivan Olinsky, Leon Kroll, Raymond Nielsen and her old adversary from the Cooper Union, Charles Hinton. For the first time, she is studying art in mixed-gender classes.

1929

On 5 February Ruth Krasner marries William Stein. Lee Krasner lives for a while with the newlyweds and her nieces, who are joined by a brother, Ronald, in 1930. Her niece Muriel later recalls that Krasner was 'like a second mother' to her and her siblings, often taking them to the circus or to films at the local cinema.

On 29 October the US stock market crashes, heralding the Great Depression (1929–39). By 1933, 12.8 million Americans would be out of work, and it would take twenty-three years for the market to recover.

On Friday 8 November the Museum of Modern Art, New York, opens its doors to the public; the inaugural exhibition is *Cézanne, Gauguin, Seurat, Van Gogh*. Founded by Abby Aldrich Rockefeller, Lillie P. Bliss and Mary Quinn Sullivan, the museum begins in a modest set of rented rooms on the twelfth floor of the Heckscher Building, on the corner of Fifth Avenue and Fifty-Seventh Street (fig. 4).

4   Postcard of New York showing the Plaza Hotel (right) and the Heckscher Building (now the Crown Building), where the Museum of Modern Art was initially located, 1923.

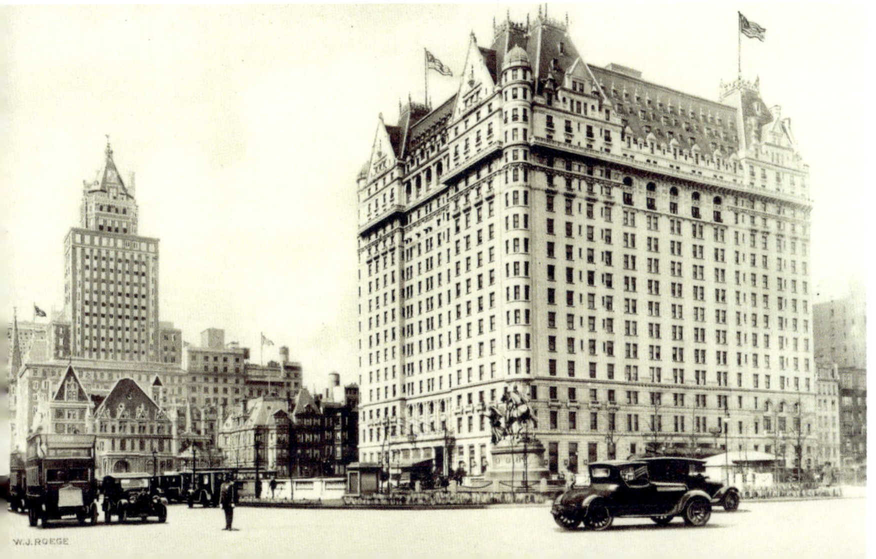

On 7 December Krasner is suspended from the National Academy of Design after venturing with her friend Eda Mirsky into the basement, an area strictly off-limits to women. The rule incensed Krasner: 'It reminded me of being in the synagogue and being told to go up not downstairs.'

At the National Academy, Krasner meets Igor Pantuhoff, a Russian émigré and fellow student. They soon begin living together, forging a relationship that will span most of the 1930s. The two often visit Krasner's nieces and nephew in Brooklyn, as well as spending time during the summers at her parents' house.

Krasner develops a reputation as a brazen student. Her report card from the time reads: 'This student is always a bother … insists upon having her own way despite school rules.'

1930

Krasner's name is listed as 'Lee' in the 1930 US Federal Census. She continues to use a second 's' in 'Krassner'.

In January, the Museum of Modern Art, New York, opens an exhibition titled *Painting in Paris*. Krasner visits the show, and her encounter with 'live Matisses and Picassos' has a profound impact on her. She describes the occasion as 'an upheaval for me … an opening of a door'.

1931

Gertrude Vanderbilt Whitney founds the Whitney Museum of American Art in New York. The Metropolitan Museum of Art, New York, had rejected Whitney's proposed endowment of her collection of more than five hundred works of art, prompting her to establish her own museum devoted exclusively to modern and contemporary American artists.

A fire at Krasner's parents' home destroys most of her early work.

In October, Pierre Matisse opens his own gallery in New York. He will become highly influential in introducing European modern art to America.

In November, the Museum of Modern Art, New York, presents a retrospective of Henri Matisse (3 November – 6 December).

1932

On 6 March a group of artists affiliated with the Unemployed Councils assembles in Union Square, New York, to raise awareness of the widespread unemployment and hardship among artists caused by the Great Depression. This action leads to the establishment of the Artists Union.

5   Franklin D. Roosevelt accepting the presidential nomination at the Democratic National Convention, 2 July 1932. During his speech, Roosevelt promises a 'new deal' for Depression-hit America.

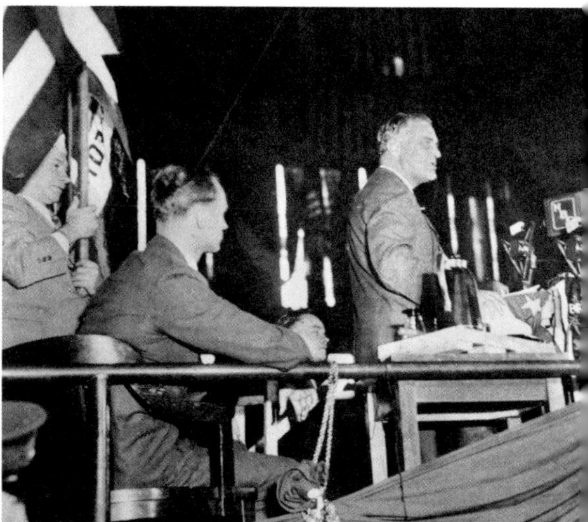

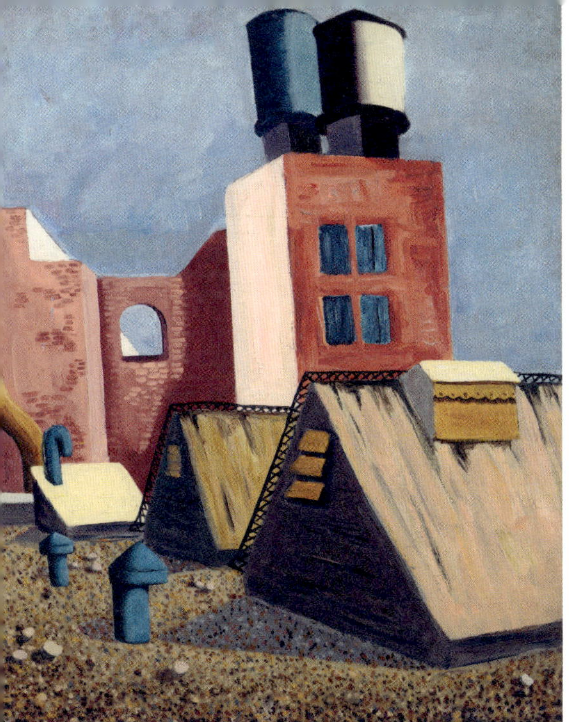

6 *Fourteenth Street*, 1934, painted while Krasner was living with Igor Pantuhoff.

In April, financial difficulties force Krasner to leave the National Academy of Design and sign up to classes at the City College of New York, where tuition is free.

On 2 July, in a speech marking his acceptance of the presidential nomination at the Democratic National Convention, Franklin D. Roosevelt promises to address the suffering caused by the Depression: 'I pledge myself to a new deal for the American people' (fig. 5).

Krasner works as a waitress at the Greenwich Village nightclub Sam Johnson's, an artistic and literary hub. There she meets the writer Harold Rosenberg, the playwright Lionel Abel, the poet Maxwell Bodenheim and the writer and film critic Parker Tyler.

Krasner begins life-drawing classes with the painter Job Goodman at Greenwich House, a community centre in New York.

1933

In December, the Public Works of Art Project (PWAP) is founded as an element of Roosevelt's New Deal. More than 3,700 artists are hired to decorate public buildings.

1934

Krasner is employed by the PWAP from January to March. Her first task is to provide detailed drawings of fossils for a government-subsidized book on rocks.

In the autumn, the German artist Hans Hofmann, who has been teaching in Munich and knows such artists as Picasso and Georges Braque from his time in Paris, opens his modernist School of Fine Arts at 137 East Fifty-Seventh Street.

In December, Krasner marches with workers from Ohrbach's department store, forming a picket line at the branch on East Fourteenth Street to demand union recognition and wage increases.

Around this time, Krasner visits the artist Willem de Kooning in his studio on West Twenty-First Street in Chelsea, Manhattan.

1935

Krasner and Pantuhoff begin sharing an apartment in the East Village with the artists Bob Jonas and Michael Loew.

Following on from the PWAP, Roosevelt's government creates the Works Progress Administration (WPA), which includes the Federal Art

Project (FAP). The FAP becomes an important network for artists, employing many of those who would go on to become significant figures in the New York School, including Stuart Davis and Arshile Gorky.

Hofmann opens his summer school in Provincetown, Massachusetts.

In August, having worked at the Temporary Emergency Relief Administration, Krasner is assigned to the Mural Division of the FAP, where she is supervised by the artist Burgoyne Diller. She is soon asked to assist the muralist Max Spivak.

Krasner finds the WPA remarkably free from discrimination against women: 'There were a lot of us working then – Alice Trumbull Mason, Suzy Frelinghuysen, Gertrude Greene and others. The head of the New York project was a woman, Audrey McMahon.'

1936

Cubism and Abstract Art (2 March – 19 April) opens at the Museum of Modern Art, New York; the curator is the museum's first director, Alfred H. Barr Jr. Krasner attends the exhibition and studies the catalogue carefully.

Krasner is assigned to complete a mural that de Kooning had begun for the WPA (he was unable to complete it because he was not an American citizen). She later explains that he would 'come unofficially into my studio and see what I was doing. It was hard-edged for de Kooning and very abstract.'

Krasner and Pantuhoff begin renting a space in an eight-room apartment at 333 West Fourteenth Street, along with Harold Rosenberg, among others.

On 17 July the Spanish Civil War begins. More than 2,800 Americans, including members of the Artists Union, respond to a call to fight back against the coup led by the military dictator Francisco Franco, who is supported by Adolf Hitler and Benito Mussolini.

In October, Hofmann's School of Fine Arts moves to 52 West Ninth Street.

On 1 December Krasner joins a large group of artists and artists' models in a strike on East Thirty-Ninth Street, protesting the imminent redundancy of 500 workers at the WPA. Following violent clashes with the police, several protesters are arrested, including Krasner, who books herself in as the American Impressionist painter Mary Cassatt. Krasner meets the artist Mercedes Carles (later Mercedes Matter), who has also been detained. Both work in the WPA Mural Division and develop a close friendship.

In December, Krasner meets a man at an Artists Union loft party who she will later realize is the artist Jackson Pollock. Recalling that they danced together, Krasner says: 'He stepped all over my feet!'

Fantastic Art, Dada, Surrealism (9 December – 17 January 1937) opens at the Museum of Modern Art, New York. It is also curated by Barr.

American Abstract Artists (AAA) is established in New York to promote the work of such artists, who receive negligible support from existing institutions.

1937

Krasner enrols in classes at the Hans Hofmann School of Fine Arts. She responds to Hofmann's theories on Cubist abstraction, and he is impressed by the results, famously telling her, 'This is so good you would not know it was painted by a woman.'

Krasner later jokes that, owing to Hofmann's thick German accent, she could not understand what he was saying for the first six months, and had to ask the class monitor, George McNeil, to translate his appraisals of her work. Fellow students at the Hofmann School include Perle Fine, Ray 'Buddha' Kaiser (later Ray Eames), Mercedes Carles, Lillian Olinsey (later Lillian Kiesler), John Little, Fritz Bultman, Wilfrid Zogbaum and George Mercer.

7   Class photo at Hans Hofmann's summer school, including Hofmann (top row, third from left) and Krasner (middle row, second from right), Provincetown, Massachusetts, c.1938.

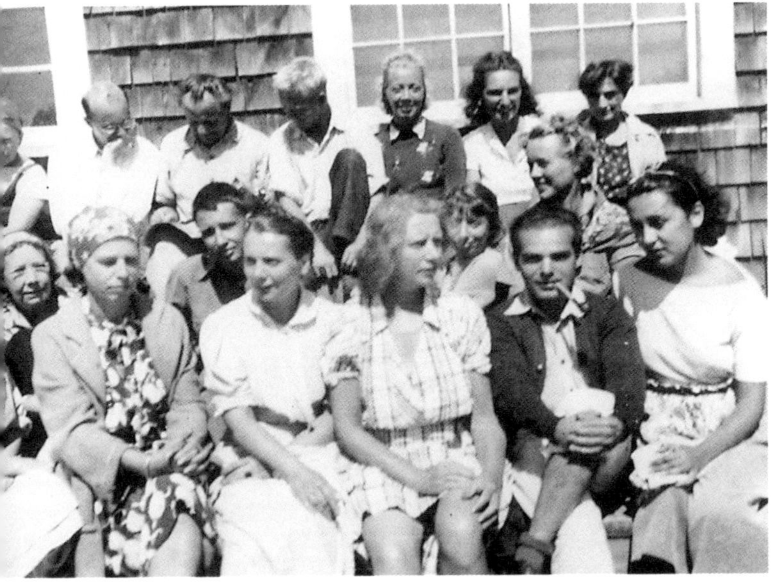

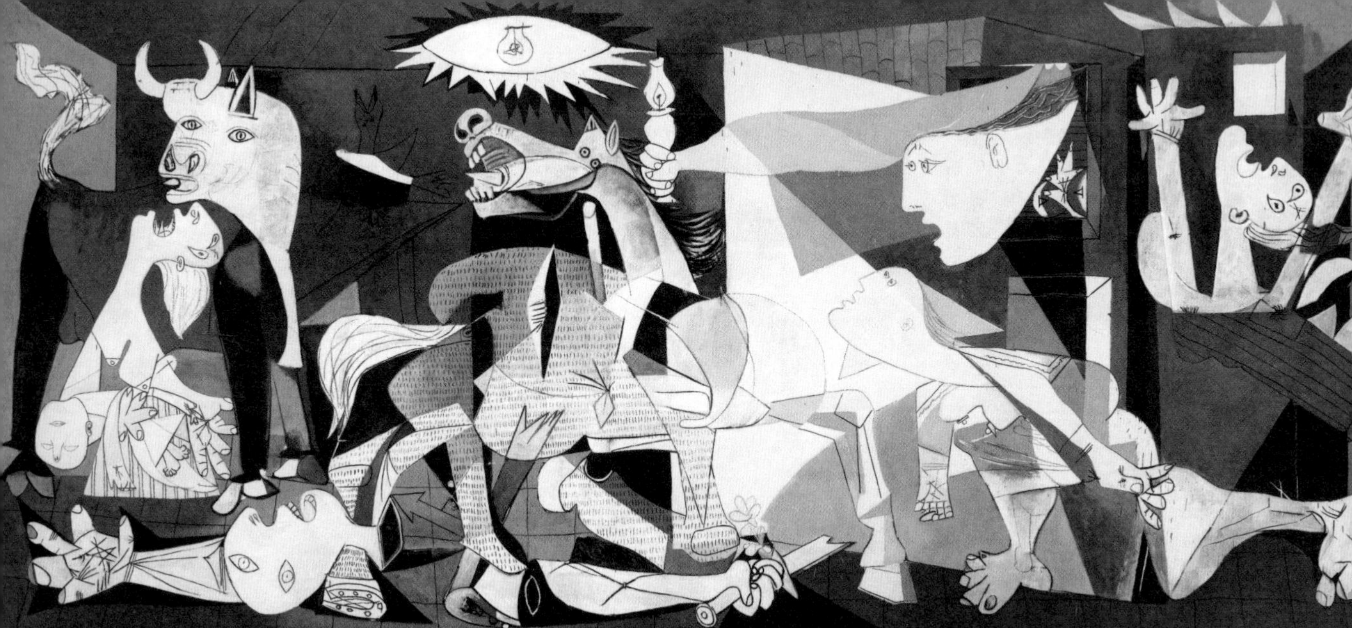

8   Pablo Picasso, *Guernica*, 1937

John Graham's *System and Dialectics of Art* (New York: Delphic Studios) is published, influencing several young Abstract Expressionist artists, including Krasner. Graham writes: 'The purpose of art in particular is to re-establish a lost contact with the unconscious … and develop this contact in order to bring to the conscious mind the throbbing events of the unconscious mind.'

In April, Graham's article 'Primitive Art and Picasso' is published in *Magazine of Art*.

On 16 July Krasner receives a 'pink slip' (a letter of dismissal) from the WPA. She is rehired on 19 August.

Krasner takes part in her first public exhibition: *Pink Slips Over Culture*, held at the ACA Galleries, New York, from 19–31 July. Organized by the Artists Union and the Citizens Committee for the Support of the WPA, the exhibition protests the precarious employment of WPA artists. The accompanying catalogue includes a supporting statement by the novelist Ford Madox Ford and an open letter from the historian Lewis Mumford to President Roosevelt (first published in the *New Republic*), calling for the prevention of further cuts to art projects. Krasner shows a work called *Still Life*.

1938

Harold Rosenberg introduces Krasner to the art critic Clement Greenberg. She encourages Greenberg to attend Hans Hofmann's public lectures each Friday, at which they will often see each other.

Krasner and Pantuhoff spend the summer in Provincetown with a group of fellow artists, among them Arshile Gorky and David Margolis. Krasner attends Hofmann's summer school there (fig. 7).

In December, Barney Josephson opens the nightclub Café Society Downtown at Sheridan Square in Greenwich Village; a sister venue, Café Society Uptown, opens in October 1940. Krasner regularly enjoys dancing at both clubs.

1939

In May, Picasso's *Guernica* is shown at the Valentine Gallery in an exhibition supported by the American Artists Congress to raise money for the Spanish Refugee Relief Fund. Krasner is overwhelmed by the work: 'It knocked me right out of the room. I circled the block four or five times, and then went back and took another look at it' (fig. 8).

On 31 August Krasner is discharged from the WPA again. She has to wait three months before she is rehired, on 29 November.

Krasner joins the executive board of the Artists Union and becomes a member of the AAA.

On 1 September Germany invades Poland, marking the start of the Second World War. European artists, including Max Ernst, Marc Chagall, Salvador Dalí, Fernand Léger and Piet Mondrian, flee to America in the ensuing years.

In its autumn edition, *Partisan Review* publishes Clement Greenberg's essay 'Avant-Garde and Kitsch', in which he interrogates the divisions between high art and popular culture. The text establishes Greenberg as one of the leading critical voices of the New York scene.

In October, Pantuhoff leaves Krasner in New York to stay with his parents in Florida.

Solomon R. Guggenheim opens the Museum of Non-Objective Painting in New York to showcase his collection of American and European abstract artists, including Rudolf Bauer and Alice Mason. Krasner later recalls visiting the museum and seeing an exhibition of the work of the Russian painter Wassily Kandinsky (fig. 9).

On 5 November a new English translation by Delmore Schwartz of Arthur Rimbaud's *Une saison en enfer* (*A Season in Hell*) is published. The work has a profound impact on Krasner, who asks her friend the painter Byron Browne to write out the following passage on the wall of her studio (now at 51 East Ninth Street): 'To whom shall I hire myself out? What beast must one adore? What holy image attack? What hearts shall I break? What lie must I maintain? In what blood must I walk?' As Krasner later explains, 'I experienced it. I identified with it. I knew what he was talking about. How much more reality do you want? Those lines have to do with reality – not lies.' The words are

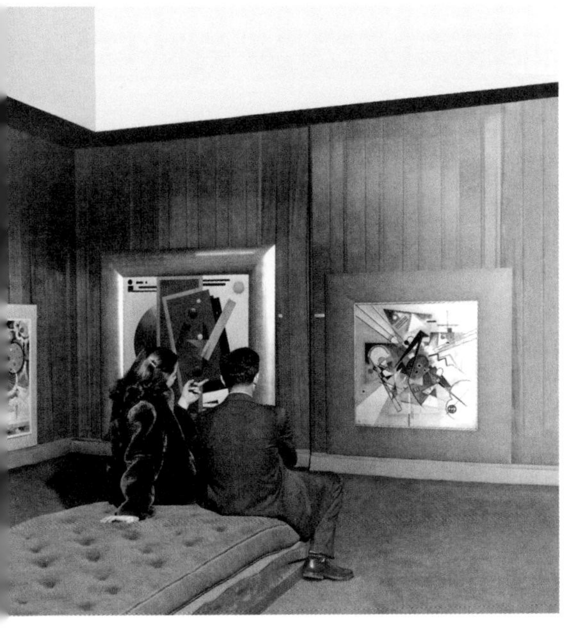

9   The Museum of Non-Objective Painting, New York, February 1946.

painted in black, except the line 'What lie must I maintain?', which is given added emphasis in blue.

On 15 November, *Picasso: Forty Years of His Art* opens at the Museum of Modern Art, New York, running until 7 January 1940.

1940

In February, Pantuhoff writes to Krasner to inform her that he does not intend to return to New York. Krasner is devastated by this news, and is tasked with the burden of returning all his belongings.

On 15 April Krasner participates in a protest at the Museum of Modern Art, New York, organized by the AAA, objecting to the museum's exclusion of abstract art from its programme of exhibitions. The protestors distribute flyers designed by the abstract painter Ad Reinhardt, asking, 'How Modern is the Museum of Modern Art?' – a slogan that the *New York Times* describes as the 'battle cry' of the 'Avant Garde'.

From 5–6 June, Krasner shows her work with the AAA for the first time as part of the *American Abstract Artists Fourth Annual Exhibition* at the American Fine Art Galleries, New York. 'Lenore Krasner' is listed as a participant by Jerome Klein in the *New York Post* – her first mention in a newspaper.

During the summer, Krasner reads Carl Jung's *The Integration of the Personality* (London: Kegan Paul, 1940) and is fascinated by his ideas: 'It was his universality that attracted me, the largeness of his concept, partly because of my very early interest in fairy tales and in the writings of [Maurice] Maeterlinck and Edgar Allan Poe.'

On 20 August the Russian revolutionary Leon Trotsky is assassinated in Mexico by one of Stalin's agents. Krasner was interested in Trotsky's writings and owned copies of *The History of the Russian Revolution* (New York: Simon & Schuster, 1936) and *The Revolution Betrayed: What is the Soviet Union and Where is it Going?* (New York: Doubleday, Doran & Company, 1937).

In November, following a report produced by Krasner with Werner Drewes, Gertrude Greene, Ilya Bolotowsky and George L. K. Morris, the AAA vote to invite Piet Mondrian and Fernand Léger to become members of the group.

The playwright Tennessee Williams visits Krasner's studio with Fritz Bultman. Krasner asks Williams to leave after he insults the lines from Rimbaud's *A Season in Hell* inscribed on her wall. She later recalls, 'They argued so much about [the poem] that I kicked them both out. I didn't like what they were saying so I said, "Out".'

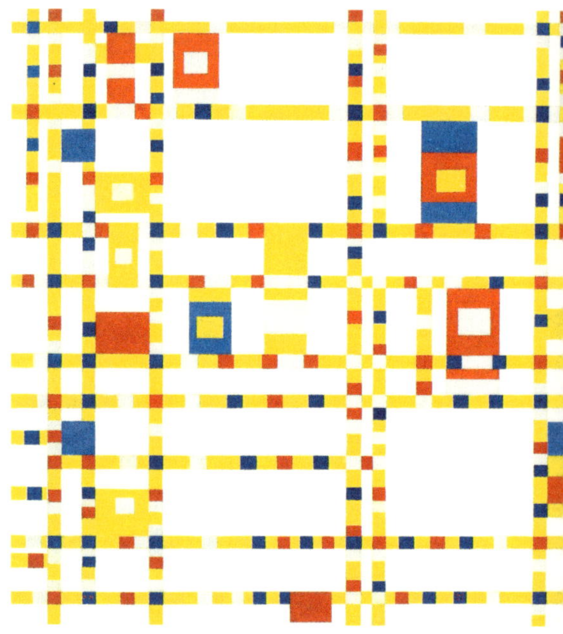

10 Piet Mondrian, *Broadway Boogie Woogie*, 1942–43

At a party held by George L. K. Morris and Suzy Frelinghuysen to celebrate Léger and Mondrian joining the AAA, Krasner meets the latter. The pair discover their shared love of boogie-woogie and go out dancing together. Krasner recalls: 'I loved jazz and he loved jazz, so I saw him several times and we went dancing like crazy.' Mondrian later makes the painting *Broadway Boogie Woogie* (1942–43; fig. 10) as a homage to this style of music.

From 9–23 February Krasner participates in the *Fifth Annual Exhibition of the American Abstract Artists* at the Riverside Museum in New York alongside new AAA members Léger and Mondrian. She is listed as a participant in the *New York Times*. On seeing Krasner's painting in the exhibition, Mondrian tells her, 'You have a very strong inner rhythm. You must never lose it.'

In the spring, Krasner struggles financially and asks Pantuhoff and George Mercer for help.

In early June, André Breton, the French writer and founder of the Surrealist movement, emigrates to New York, where he stays for five years before returning to Paris. Breton becomes an influential figure for many New York artists, including Arshile Gorky.

Krasner submits a successful proposal for an abstract mural to decorate the walls of Studio A at the radio station WNYC. Before she can make a start on the mural, however, she is forced to leave the commission and join other artists working on projects for the war effort.

Towards the end of the year, Krasner meets John Graham, author of *System and Dialectics of Art*. Graham asks to see her work, and on 12 November he sends Krasner a postcard inviting her to participate in a show he is organizing at McMillen Gallery on East Fifty-Sixth Street called *American and French Paintings*: 'Dear Lenore – I am arranging at an uptown gallery a show of French and American paintings with excellent publicity etc. I have Braque, Picasso, Derain, Segonzac, S. Davis, and others. I want to have your last large painting. I will drop at your place Friday afternoon with the manager of the gallery. Telephone me if you can. Ever GRAHAM' (fig. 11).

Krasner later recounts how the only American painter included in Graham's exhibition whose name she did not recognize was Jackson Pollock. She goes to meet him at his studio, which by chance is just one block away from her own (she is on Ninth Street, he on Eighth). She is hugely impressed by his work: 'I was overwhelmed, bowled over, that's all. I saw all those marvellous paintings. I felt as if the floor was sinking … How could there be a painter like that that I didn't know about?' Krasner goes on to introduce Pollock to several other artists, including de Kooning.

On 7 December, in a surprise military strike, the Imperial Japanese Navy Air Service attacks the American naval base at Pearl Harbor, impelling the United States to enter the Second World War.

11   John Graham, postcard to Lee Krasner inviting her to participate in the McMillen Gallery exhibition *American and French Paintings*, 12 November 1941.

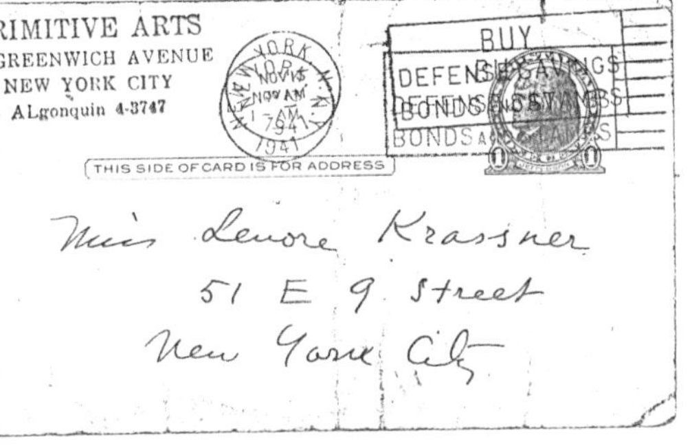

American and French Paintings opens at McMillen Gallery on 20 January. In addition to Pollock, the other American artists in the show include Stuart Davis and de Kooning. Krasner exhibits *Abstraction* (1941), while Pollock shows *Birth* (1941); de Kooning shows *Standing Man* (1942). Krasner later recalls: 'Well, my excitement around it was overwhelming. I found myself flanked by a Matisse on one side and a Braque on the other.' Krasner and Pollock attend the opening together. In a letter dated 11 February 1942, George Mercer enquires, 'What about you? And your co-exhibitor friend that you think you like? Write and let me know.' Krasner later describes the beginnings of her romance with Pollock: 'I resisted at first, but I must admit, I didn't resist very long. I was terribly drawn to Jackson, and I fell in love with him – physically, mentally – in every sense of the word.'

In January, Mondrian's first solo exhibition opens at the Valentine Gallery. Krasner and a group of friends attend a lecture given by the artist on 23 January, called 'Toward the True Vision of Reality'. During the autobiographical talk, which is later published, Mondrian describes how he abandoned a traditional practice: 'The first thing to change in my painting was the colour. I forsook natural colour for pure colour. I had come to feel that the colours of nature cannot be reproduced on the canvas. Instinctively, I felt that painting had to find a new way to express the beauty of nature.'

In March, Clement Greenberg becomes the regular art critic for *The Nation*.

Krasner takes Hans Hofmann to see Pollock's studio. She recalls how the two artists clashed as Hofmann exclaimed, 'You work by heart – that's no good. You must work from nature or you'll repeat yourself', to which Pollock retorted, 'I *am* nature.' This new way of working prompts Krasner to revise her own approach to painting, leading to a long and difficult period during which she produces nothing but 'gray slabs'. These canvases are perpetually painted and repainted, resulting in a dense, amorphous mass of pigment from which she felt 'the image wouldn't emerge'.

The WPA is transformed into the War Services Project. In May, Krasner is chosen to supervise the design and production of a series of large-scale displays for department-store windows throughout New York City, which will promote war training courses being made available at municipal colleges. Her team of assistants includes Pollock. Krasner's designs juxtapose typography with documentary photographs of the courses to create photomontages, reminiscent of the Bauhaus.

Also in May, Krasner signs a petition directed at President Roosevelt, protesting the decline of creative pursuits in the WPA.

In the autumn, Krasner begins living with Pollock at 46 East Eighth Street. She moves into the apartment he has been sharing with his brother Sanford McCoy and his wife, Arloie, after they leave for Connecticut.

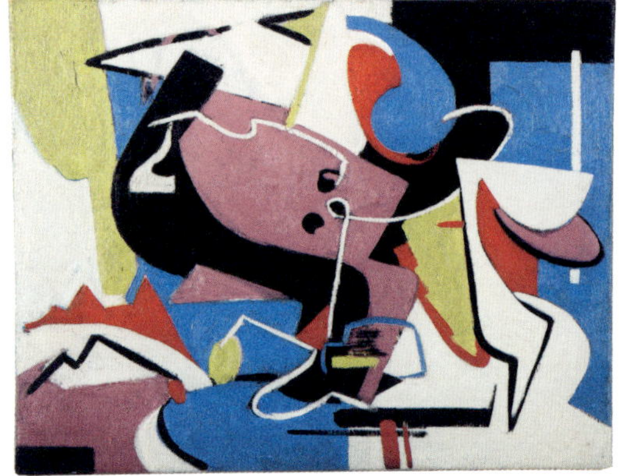

12 *Lavender*, 1942, painted while Krasner was exhibiting with the American Abstract Artists.

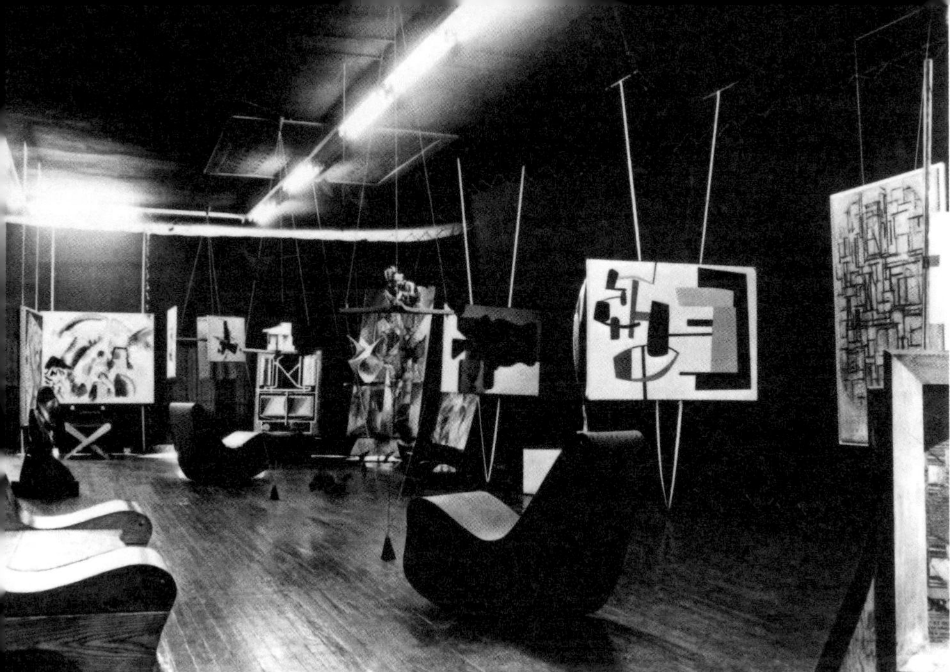

13 Installation view of the Abstract Gallery at Peggy
Guggenheim's gallery Art of This Century, New York,
1942. Photograph by Berenice Abbott.

On 20 October Peggy Guggenheim opens the gallery Art of This Century, designed by the architect, designer and sculptor Frederick Kiesler, at 30 West Fifty-Seventh Street (fig. 13). There she exhibits European Surrealist art, as well as work by such emerging American artists as Pollock, de Kooning, Ad Reinhardt and Robert Motherwell.

On 2 December the first public silence for victims of the Holocaust takes place to raise awareness of the ongoing genocide.

1943

On 2 February the Soviet Union defeats the Nazis in the Battle of Stalingrad.

Both Krasner and Pollock are appointed as trainees in the aviation sheet-metal industry – Pollock to the WPA Project Service Trade Center in Brooklyn, Krasner to the New York Trade School on East Seventh Street.

In March, the 'We Will Never Die' ceremony takes place at Madison Square Gardens, New York. Organized by the screenwriter Ben Hecht, the ceremony is designed to alert the American public to the mass murder of Jews in Europe.

On 6 April Krasner appeals to the City of New York to change the name on her birth certificate from 'Lena Kreisner' to 'Lenore Krassner'.

Beginning on 21 April, Krasner registers 488 hours of training in mechanical drafting. Her instructor later claims that she was 'one of [my] most brilliant students'.

Krasner leaves the AAA, feeling disillusioned: 'The AAA wouldn't allow a Surreal breath to pass the door. They were provincial like any groupie. I tried to keep open. I tried for example to get [Alexander] Calder invited and was told No. Tried to get Hofmann to lecture and was told No.'

On 8 November Pollock's first solo show opens at Art of This Century.

The War Services Project is terminated, leaving many artists without a regular income but with more time to focus on their own work.

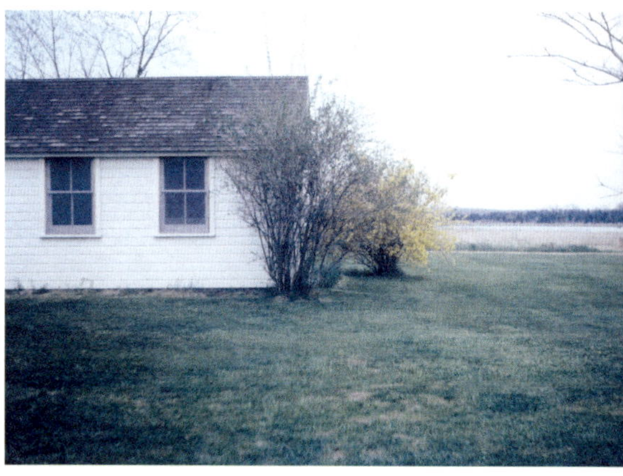

14 One of the outbuildings at the property in Springs, June 1963. Photograph by Ray Eames.

1944

Krasner participates in the exhibition *Abstract and Surrealist Art in America*, organized by the San Francisco Museum of Art, with works selected by Sidney Janis. It opens at the Cincinnati Art Museum on 8 February and tours to three other museums across the United States. Janis's accompanying book includes Krasner's *Composition* (1943). Her work is presented alongside that of other abstract artists, including Hofmann, de Kooning, Stuart Davis and Robert Motherwell.

On 7 March Hofmann's exhibition at Art of This Century opens, running until the end of the month. Krasner and Pollock have been instrumental in introducing Hofmann to Peggy Guggenheim.

On 17 November Krasner's father dies following two years of illness. She is devastated, writing to Mercedes Matter: 'It pretty well tears you to pieces and is like some terrific eruption with everything being torn up ... I must wait until spaces are closed and time changes feeling.'

To avoid having to work in such close quarters with Pollock, Krasner rents a space from the artist Reuben Kadish in the former studio of the Surrealist painter Roberto Matta on Sixth Avenue and Twelfth Street.

1945

Krasner chooses not to participate in a group exhibition called *The Women*, scheduled to open at Art of This Century in June. It is believed she declined the offer because she did not want to be part of a women-only exhibition, and because she disliked Peggy Guggenheim. In a later interview, Krasner states, 'I didn't want to show. [Guggenheim] wasn't friendly to women. She didn't like women.'

In April, Samuel Kootz opens his gallery at 15 East Fifty-Seventh Street with an exhibition of works by Fernand Léger. Later that year, Hofmann, Robert Motherwell and Adolph Gottlieb also sign with Kootz.

Howard Putzel, Guggenheim's former assistant, leaves Art of This Century and opens his own space, Gallery 67. His first exhibition, *A Problem for Critics*, opens on 14 May. Krasner is the only female participant, showing work alongside Pollock, Mark Rothko, Arshile Gorky and Richard Pousette-Dart, as well as Picasso, Jean Arp and Joan Miró, among others.

In the summer, Krasner and Pollock join Reuben and Barbara Kadish on the South Fork of Long Island. After spending several weeks in the area, Pollock and Krasner decide to leave the city and live on Long Island permanently. Their friends Harold and May Rosenberg had recently purchased an old house in the nearby hamlet of Springs.

On 6 and 9 August, the United States drops atomic bombs over the Japanese cities of Hiroshima and Nagasaki. The Second World War comes to an end on 2 September.

On 25 October Krasner and Pollock are married at the Marble Collegiate Church, New York. May Tabak Rosenberg and the church custodian are witnesses, after Peggy Guggenheim turns down Krasner's offer to participate in the ceremony, saying, 'Aren't you already married enough?'

On 5 November, with Guggenheim's financial help, the newlyweds buy a clapboard farmhouse on Fireplace Road in Springs, Long Island, for $5,000. Krasner later remembers how they embraced their new life in the countryside: '[We] cooked, canned, gardened; it was all a beautiful new experience' (figs 14 and 15).

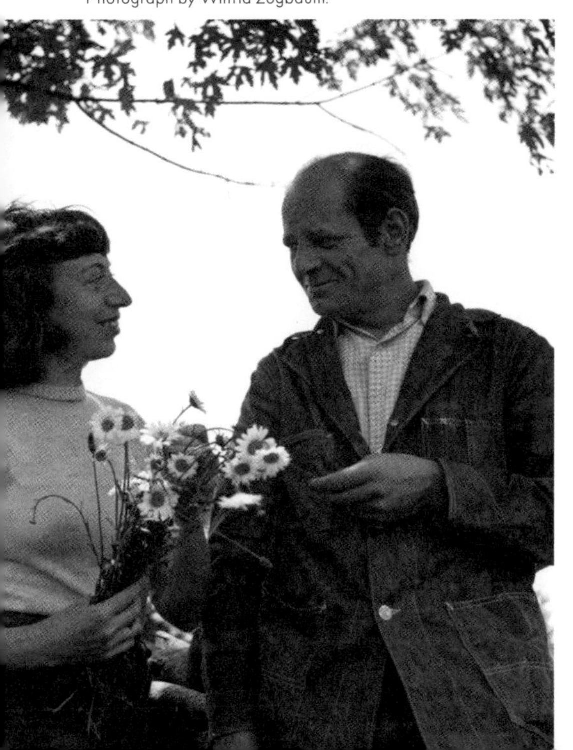

15 Lee Krasner and Jackson Pollock in Springs, 1949. Photograph by Wilfrid Zogbaum.

1946

In the spring, Krasner makes a breakthrough with a new series of works she calls her 'Little Images': 'The grayness of the streets finally began to open up … It was a great change.' Krasner remembers Clement Greenberg seeing an early work in the series and telling her, 'That's hot. It's cooking[!]'

In a review of Hans Hofmann's solo exhibition at Mortimer Brandt Gallery, the art critic Robert Coates uses the phrase 'Abstract Expressionism' in relation to contemporary American abstraction.

Krasner is included in Ad Reinhardt's cartoon *How to Look at Modern Art in America* (fig. 16), which appears in the newspaper *PM* on 2 June. In the widely circulated cartoon, Krasner is placed next to de Kooning, demonstrating the recognition of her work at the time.

The Betty Parsons Gallery opens in New York with the exhibition *Northwest Coast Indian Painting* (30 September – 19 October). Parsons becomes an important supporter of Abstract Expressionist painters, including Pollock, Rothko and Barnett Newman, especially after Peggy Guggenheim moves to Italy.

1947

In the spring, Guggenheim closes Art of This Century and moves permanently to Venice, where she displays her collection.

At the house in Springs, Krasner takes over the upstairs bedroom as her working space, while Pollock begins to use the barn as his studio.

1948

Krasner and Pollock find themselves struggling for money, prompting Betty Parsons to write to Guggenheim to inform her of the 'terrible financial condition of the Pollocks'. James Johnson Sweeney, a curator at the Museum of Modern Art, New York, is able to help by guaranteeing Pollock $1,500 from the Eben Demarest Trust for the advancement of art.

During the summer, Krasner and Pollock invite Elaine and Willem de Kooning to stay with them in Springs.

On 21 July Arshile Gorky, whom Krasner has known since their days working for the FAP, commits suicide. The two had spent a large amount of time together at the Jumble Shop, a popular restaurant in Greenwich Village, debating art, philosophy and, in particular, Picasso. Krasner affectionately said of Gorky, 'I had a great deal of fights with Arshile. Oh yes, it wasn't a relationship which always flowed in glowing terms.'

In the autumn, Krasner begins to be called 'Lee Krasner' in professional and public contexts.

In September, Krasner participates in the exhibition *The Modern House Comes Alive 1948–49* at the Bertha Schaefer Gallery in New York. She exhibits a selection of her Little Images, including *Composition* (1943) and *Abstract No. 2* (1946–48), as well as one of her mosaic tables. Reviewing the exhibition in the *New York Herald Tribune*, Ann Pringle describes Krasner's work as 'magnificent' – the first time that her art has been picked out for critical acclaim.

Also in September, Sidney Janis opens a gallery at 15 East Fifty-Seventh Street with an exhibition of works by Léger. As well as exhibiting American abstract artists, he also shows the work of such European modern painters as Mondrian, Pierre Bonnard and Paul Klee.

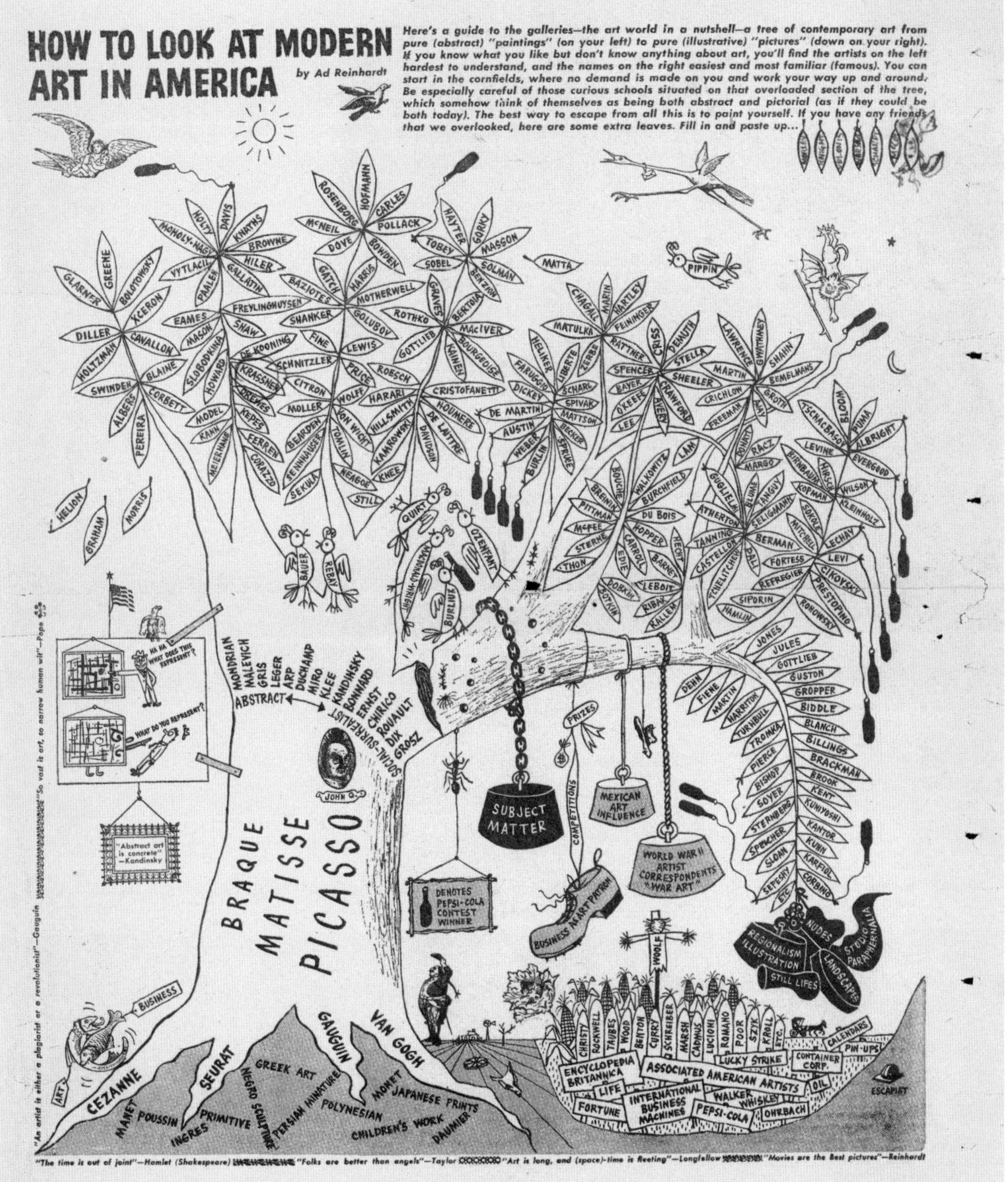

16 Ad Reinhardt, *How to Look at Modern Art in America*, 1946. Krasner has circled her name (top left) on this, her own copy of the cartoon.

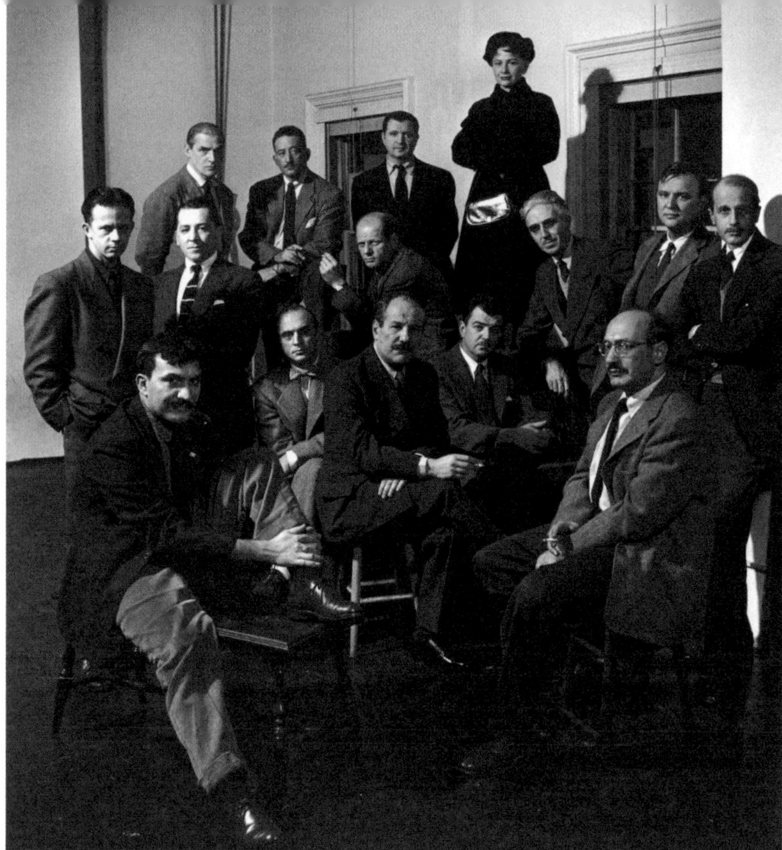

17 'The Irascibles', 24 November 1950. From left: (back row) Willem de Kooning, Adolph Gottlieb, Ad Reinhardt, Hedda Sterne; (middle row) Richard Pousette-Dart, William Baziotes, Jimmy Ernst (seated), Jackson Pollock, James C. Brooks (seated), Clyfford Still, Robert Motherwell, Bradley Walker Tomlin; (front row) Theodoros Stamos, Barnett Newman and Mark Rothko. Photograph by Nina Leen for *Life* magazine, published 16 January 1951.

1949

In March, the Abstract Expressionist painter Grace Hartigan, known for her bold, gestural style, marries the artist Harry Jackson at Krasner and Pollock's home in Springs.

In August, *Life* magazine publishes a feature article titled 'Jackson Pollock: Is He the Greatest Living Painter in the United States?' The article solidifies Pollock's reputation in the New York art scene and contributes greatly to an international awareness of his work.

Krasner and Pollock both take part in *Artists: Man and Wife*, an exhibition held at Sidney Janis's gallery in September. The exhibition features eight other artist-couples, including the de Koonings, Max Ernst and Dorothea Tanning, Picasso and Françoise Gilot, Ben Nicholson and Barbara Hepworth, and Jean Arp and Sophie Taeuber-Arp. Many of the reviews belittle the female artists; a piece in *ARTnews*

18 Franz Kline, poster for the *Ninth Street
Exhibition of Paintings and Sculpture*, 1951

comments, 'Lee Krasner (Mrs. Jackson Pollock) takes her husband's paints and enamels and changes his unrestrained, sweeping lines into neat little squares and triangles.'

In October, 'The Club', an artists' discussion group, is established in a loft at 39 East Eighth Street. Founding members include de Kooning, Franz Kline and Philip Pavia.

1950

During the early months of the year, Krasner and Pollock stay in the home of their friend the painter Alfonso Ossorio at 9 MacDougal Alley in Manhattan while he is away travelling. In March, Krasner and Pollock return to Springs, where Krasner breaks away from her Little Images series as she prepares for her first solo exhibition, at Betty Parsons Gallery. These large-scale works are later repurposed or destroyed.

On 20 May a group of artists writes an open letter to Ronald L. Redmond, president of the Metropolitan Museum of Art, to oppose the conservative slant of the exhibition *American Painting Today – 1950*. The artists, who are photographed by Nina Leen for a feature in *Life* magazine in January 1951, are nicknamed 'The Irascibles' after the photograph's caption (fig. 17). Pollock is positioned in the centre of the group, while Hedda Sterne is the only woman to feature (although the sculptors Louise Bourgeois, Mary Callery and Day Schnabel also signed the letter). Krasner is not invited to participate: 'Barney Newman called and when I answered the phone, he asked for Jackson. He didn't even bother to inform me of the protest.'

In June, Krasner is included in Betty Parsons' exhibition of painters and sculptors. She is one of thirty-three artists, alongside Pollock and her friend Bradley Walker Tomlin.

During the summer, Le Corbusier visits Krasner and Pollock in Springs. The architect is accompanied by their neighbour, the sculptor Costantino Nivola, who later reports Le Corbusier's reaction to Pollock's work: 'This man is like a hunter who shoots without aiming. But his wife, she has talent – women always have too much talent.'

1951

In January, Pollock is in a particularly heavy drinking cycle, writing to Alfonso Ossorio: 'I really hit an all time low – with depression and drinking.' Later, on 9 March, Pollock writes his will, leaving everything to Krasner.

Krasner and Pollock both take part in The Club's *Ninth Street Exhibition*, curated by Leo Castelli in an empty storefront at 60 East Ninth Street, opening on 21 May (fig. 18). The exhibition, which would become legendary in the history of the New York art scene, features work by several influential female artists, including Perle Fine, Helen Frankenthaler, Grace Hartigan, Joan Mitchell and Anne Ryan.

On 15 October Krasner's first solo exhibition, *Paintings 1951, Lee Krasner*, opens at Betty Parsons Gallery. Fourteen canvases are shown, but, as they do not sell, Krasner reuses many of them to create the collages she exhibits at the Stable Gallery in 1955. Writing in the *New York Times*, Stuart Preston describes the 'majestic and thoughtful construction' of one of the works, and goes on to comment on the sense of 'searching for formal and chromatic harmonies rather than a delivery of watertight solutions'.

Encouraged by Krasner and Pollock, Ossorio purchases 'The Creeks', a property in East Hampton formerly owned by the painters Albert and Adele Herter.

Pollock decides to leave the Betty Parsons Gallery because he is not selling enough work. As a result, Parsons asks Krasner to leave as well. Remembering her disappointment, Krasner said: 'It took me almost a year to recover from that shock before I could work again … I was kicked out of the gallery because I was Mrs Jackson Pollock.'

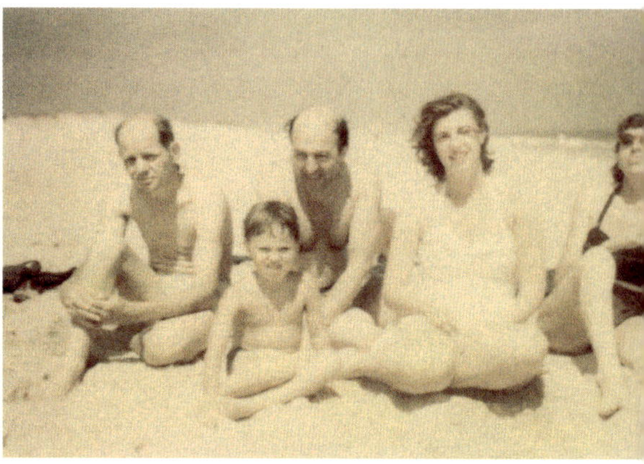

19 From left: Jackson Pollock, Clement Greenberg, Helen Frankenthaler and Lee Krasner at the beach, July 1952.

1952

During the summer, Clement Greenberg and his girlfriend, Helen Frankenthaler, stay with Krasner and Pollock at their house in Springs (fig. 19).

In December, Harold Rosenberg's pivotal article 'The American Action Painters' – in which the term 'action painting' is first used – is published in *ARTnews*. Rosenberg argues that the American abstract painters perceive the canvas 'as an arena in which to act … What was to go on the canvas was not a picture but an event.'

1953

Krasner moves her studio into a small outbuilding, which she and Pollock have transferred to an acre of land they have bought next to the house. For the first time since moving to Springs, Krasner has a studio space of her own.

Krasner embarks on a series of large-scale collages that incorporate fragments of old works, including canvases from her exhibition at Betty Parsons Gallery. She tears the works into shreds and uses them to create dynamic compositions. 'It wasn't a decision. It happened and I observed what I did.' She later tells Barbara Novak that she thinks of her tendency to destroy and then reuse old work as 'a form of clarification … If I'm going back on myself, I'd like to think it's a form of growth.'

Eleanor Ward opens the Stable Gallery in an old livery stable on Seventh Avenue and West Fifty-Eighth Street. The gallery expands on the legacy of the *Ninth Street Exhibition* with an annual exhibition to showcase the best of the contemporary New York art scene. These exhibitions, which continue until 1957, are organized by the participating artists, including de Kooning, Pollock, Franz Kline, Ad Reinhardt and Philip Guston.

Bradley Walker Tomlin dies of a heart attack at the age of fifty-three. He had spent the previous evening at a party thrown by Krasner and Pollock at their home in Springs.

1954

The writer Patsy Southgate, who has recently moved to Long Island, gives Krasner driving lessons in exchange for painting tutorials, resulting in a new lease of independence for the artist.

On 15 August Krasner opens a one-day solo exhibition at the House of Books and Music in East Hampton, run by Donald and Carol Braider. Several of her Little Images are shown for the first time, alongside her new collages.

1955

Clement Greenberg writes an article for the spring edition of *Partisan Review*, challenging Harold Rosenberg's concept of 'action painting' with his own phrase, 'American-Type Painting'. Krasner reacts strongly to Greenberg's terminology: 'It offends me. The minute you send up a slogan, you can put anything in the bag and the slogan carries it. That's boring and provincial in thought and concept, and the antithesis of what I mean by art.'

During the summer, Krasner starts psychoanalysis with Dr Leonard Siegel, a follower of the American psychologist Harry Stack Sullivan.

A series of photographs taken by Hans Namuth in August show Pollock holding Krasner's *Color Totem* (1955), a collage featuring elements not only of her own work but also of Pollock's.

Krasner's solo exhibition at the Stable Gallery opens, running from 26 September to 15 October (fig. 20). The exhibition generates a positive critical response. The painter and critic Fairfield Porter writes in *ARTnews* that 'Krasner's art, which seems to be about nature, instead of making the spectator aware of a grand design, makes him aware of a subtle disorder greater than he might otherwise have thought possible.' Ten years later, in the catalogue for Krasner's 1965 retrospective at the Whitechapel Gallery in London, Clement Greenberg is quoted by Bryan Robertson as describing this exhibition as 'a major addition to the American art scene of that era'.

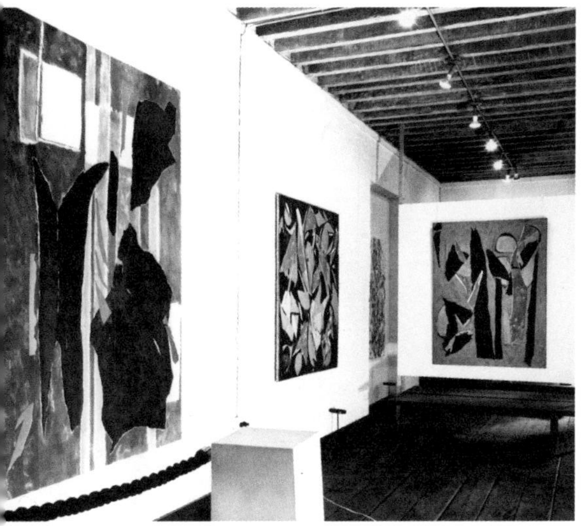

20 Installation view of works by Lee Krasner in her solo exhibition at the Stable Gallery, New York, 26 September – 15 October 1955.

Eleanor Ward later recalls Krasner's audacity in the run-up to the show: 'I told [Lee] that I thought it was a good time for me to select her show. She said, "You select my show? I am selecting my show and I am hanging it on both floors." So I answered, "Lee, then there will be no show, unless it is on one floor and I select it." I realized that if I once let her gain control over me, I would just be putty. [She was] a very strong woman.'

1956

During the summer, Krasner works on a painting she will later call *Prophecy*: 'The painting disturbed me enormously, and I called Jackson to look at it. He assured me it was a good painting, and said not to think about it, just continue – do another one.'

Pollock's alcoholism worsens, and he begins an affair with Ruth Kligman. In July, Krasner gives him an ultimatum, telling him that she will be going on their planned three-week trip to Europe to visit their friends Paul and Esther Jenkins alone.

In Paris, Krasner visits a number of old friends, including John Graham and Betty Parsons, as well as meeting the dealers Charles Gimpel, René Drouin and Michel Tapié. Krasner later recalls the impact of seeing Chartres Cathedral and the Old Masters in the Louvre, saying that the three paintings that 'stopped me dead in my tracks' were Paolo Uccello's *The Battle of San Romano* (c. 1435–40), Andrea Mantegna's *St Sebastian* (c. 1480) and Francisco Goya's *The Countess del Carpio, Marquesa de La Solana* (1794–95). She travels to the home of Charles and Kay Gimpel in Ménerbes and finds Helen Frankenthaler there. Krasner also goes to see the British art historian Douglas Cooper in Menton on the French Riviera.

On Sunday 12 August, soon after Krasner's return to Paris, Clement Greenberg telephones with news of Pollock's death. On the evening of 11 August, Pollock had been driving with Ruth Kligman and her friend Edith Metzger, and had crashed his car while speeding on Fireplace Road. Only Kligman had survived. Krasner flies to New York that night and is met at the airport by Barnett Newman and his wife, Annalee. Pollock's funeral takes place on 15 August at Springs Chapel. He is buried in Green River Cemetery, Springs.

In October, two of Krasner's friends, the artist couple Charlotte Park and James Brooks, stay with her in Springs. After their departure, she lives with Fritz and Jeanne Bultman in their house on East Ninety-Fifth Street in Manhattan for a few months before staying with the art critic B. H. Friedman and his wife, Abby. Krasner spends New Year's Eve there, with Helen Frankenthaler, Betty Parsons, Robert Motherwell, and Philip Guston and his wife, Musa.

Pollock's memorial retrospective at the Museum of Modern Art, New York, opens on 19 December and closes on 3 February the following year. Krasner is heavily involved in its organization.

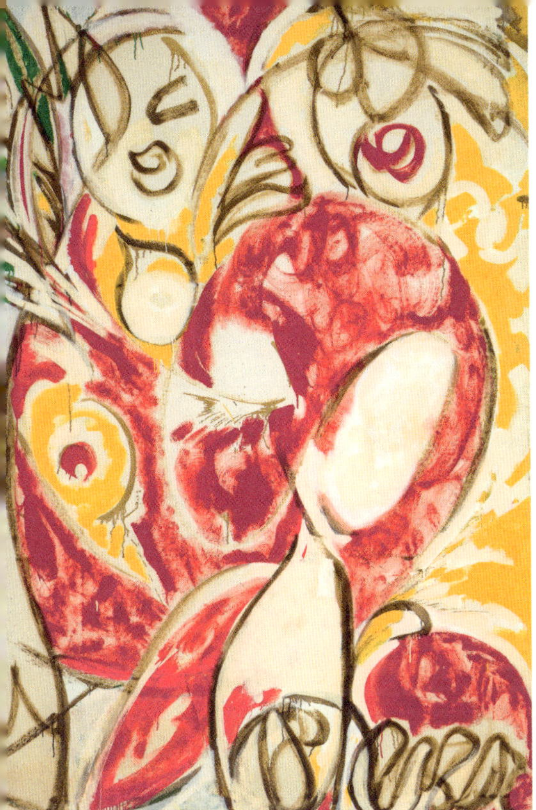

21 *Sun Woman I*, 1957

1957

During the summer, Krasner takes over Pollock's studio in the barn in Springs.

Unable to tolerate living alone in Springs, Krasner returns to Manhattan in the autumn and decides to divide her time between the countryside and the city, signing a two-year lease on an apartment at 147 East Seventy-Second Street.

Alfonso Ossorio, John Little and Elizabeth Parker open the Signa Gallery in East Hampton, the first commercial gallery in the area to show contemporary artists at the forefront of the New York art scene. The inaugural exhibition features the work of twenty-nine artists, including Krasner.

1958

In February, Krasner's recent paintings are exhibited in a solo exhibition at the Martha Jackson Gallery in New York. The seventeen works shown, all dating from either 1956 or 1957, include *Listen*, *Earth Green*, *Spring Beat*, *Upstream*, *Sun Woman I* (fig. 21), *The Seasons*, *Embrace* and *Birth*. *Time* magazine quotes Krasner as saying: 'These are special paintings to me. They come from a very trying time, a time of life and death.' The show receives considerable attention from the press, including a review by Stuart Preston in the *New York Times*: 'The bravado of Lee Krasner's recent and huge abstract paintings … presents a raw challenge to the eye … Sensuous, sensual and aggressively decorative, these paintings compel attention to the fact that the artist is directing her compositions, not just submitting to her material, or giving free rein to automatism.'

In April, Krasner's work is included in *International Art of a New Era*, an exhibition organized by Michel Tapié at the Gallery of Takashimaya for the Osaka Art Festival in Japan. Krasner chooses to show *The Seasons* (1957) and *Rose Red* (1958).

B. H. Friedman, at that time vice president of Uris Buildings Corporation (a real estate business owned by his uncles Percy and Harold Uris), commissions Krasner to design two large-scale mosaic panels for the company's headquarters in downtown Manhattan (fig. 22). Krasner is assisted by her nephew, Ronald Stein, although the mural is executed by workmen under her supervision owing to union regulations. She already has experience of working at a monumental scale from her days at the WPA: 'By the time I came to do a mosaic in the Uris Brothers building in downtown Manhattan, eighty-six feet long, that scale was nothing new to me. Long before I met Pollock, too, I had been working that large.'

That summer, Friedman's novelist brother, Sanford, and Sanford's partner, the poet Richard Howard, live in the small barn at Springs, which now functions as a guesthouse.

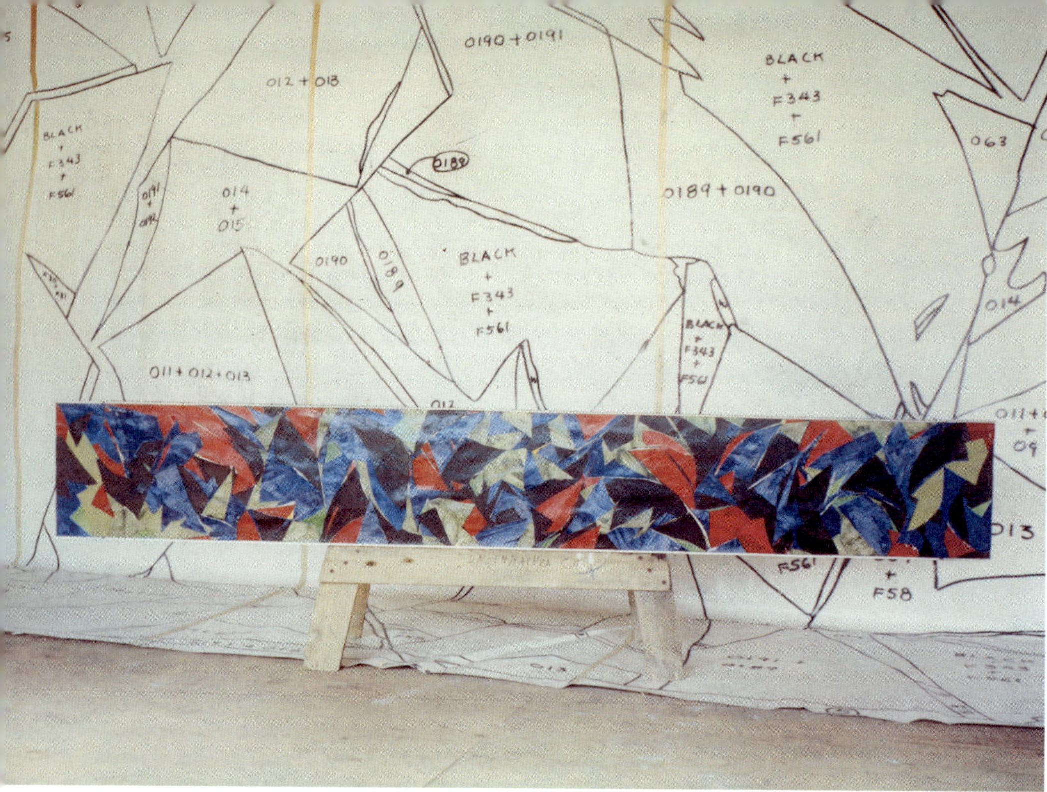

22 Krasner's original collage sketch (scaled 1 inch to 1 foot) for one of two glass mosaic
panels for the headquarters of the Uris Buildings Corporation, Manhattan, c. 1958–59.
The sketch is pictured in front of a full-scale positive cartoon. The mosaic craftsmen
used the cartoon to estimate the quantities of material needed, while Krasner used
it to simplify her design. From the positive cartoon, a negative in reverse was made,
to which the glass tesserae were adhered. Photograph by Walter Silver.

1959

Krasner's mother dies. Her death, coming so soon after Pollock's,
plunges Krasner into a deep depression. 'I wasn't allowed to mourn
at my own tempo', she later reflects.

Krasner begins a new body of work referred to as the 'Umber' series.
Some of the paintings are created in the barn at Springs, others in
New York City. All are done at night, under artificial light, as Krasner
is suffering from chronic insomnia. Richard Howard describes them
as 'mourning' pictures, each generated by a 'night journey'.

Clement Greenberg, who dislikes the direction of Krasner's new work,
falls out with her, leading to the cancellation of the solo exhibition
of her work that he was planning for the gallery French & Company.
As she later recalls, 'I was going down deep into something which
wasn't easy or pleasant ... Well, there was so much taking place. My
mother dies at this time. A lot happens aside from my grief for Jackson.
There are many elements. I cancel my show with Greenberg – a show
scheduled at French & Co. And these paintings are already underway.'

Krasner signs a contract with the Howard Wise Gallery in New York.

On 18 July Jack Kerouac turns up at a party Krasner is giving in Springs, accompanied by an entourage. He exclaims, 'I thought this was an open party', to which Krasner responds, 'It's not that open.'

Lee Krasner Paintings: 1947–59 opens at Signa Gallery (24 July – 20 August). The exhibition includes a selection of Little Images alongside *Cornucopia* (1958) and *Breath* (1959).

In the summer, Krasner meets the gallerist and art dealer David Gibbs, whom she subsequently asks to help administer Pollock's estate.

1960

In the summer, Krasner gives her first interview, to Louise Elliott Rago, a secondary school teacher writing for *School Arts* on the subject of 'Why People Create'. Krasner states: 'I am preoccupied with trying to know myself in order to communicate with others. Painting is not separate from life. It is one. It is like asking – do I want to live? My answer is yes – and I paint.'

Exhibition of Recent Paintings by Lee Krasner opens at the Howard Wise Gallery (15 November – 10 December). Krasner shows paintings from the Umber series.

1961

John Graham, Krasner's old friend, dies in London.

1962

New Work by Lee Krasner opens at the Howard Wise Gallery (6–30 March). The exhibition includes paintings from the Umber series.

On Christmas evening, while having dinner with Ronald Stein and his wife, Frances, in East Hampton, Krasner suffers a brain haemorrhage. Following surgery at Saint Luke's Hospital, New York, Krasner recuperates at the Hotel Adams on the Upper East Side.

1963

Hans Hofmann and His Students opens on 6 May at International House in Denver, Colorado, and travels across America until 11 April 1965.

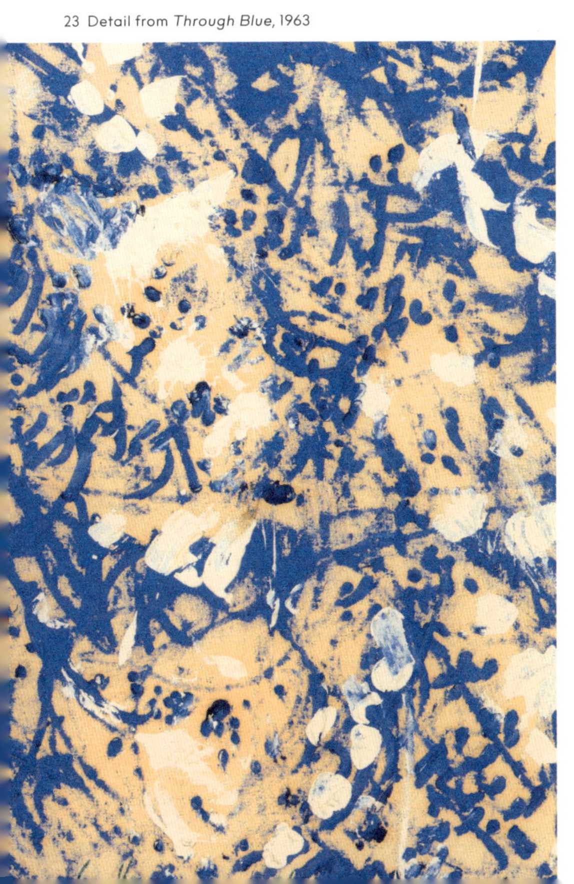

23 Detail from *Through Blue*, 1963

In June, Krasner is released from her contract with the Howard Wise Gallery. She questions Wise's commitment to her career after he refuses to cover shipping costs for her upcoming London retrospective.

Krasner moves back to Springs for the summer. While walking down Main Street in East Hampton, she becomes dizzy and falls, breaking her right arm. Although her dominant arm is now set in a cast, she continues to work, applying paint directly to the canvas from the tube, and using the fingertips of her right hand to guide the movements of her left. These canvases contribute to her new 'Primary Series', in which colour bursts back into her painting (fig. 23).

Continuing a long-running argument about the role of women in Judaism, Barnett Newman asks Krasner if she has seen his design for a synagogue, exhibited at the Jewish Museum in *Recent American Synagogue Architecture* (6 October – 8 December). He claims that this will settle the dispute. Krasner recalls their exchange: '"Well, where are the women in your synagogue?" I asked. "You'll see! You'll understand!" he said. "Right on the altar!" And I said, "Never. You can sit on the altar and get yourself slaughtered. I want the first empty seat on the aisle."'

24 Installation view of works by Lee Krasner in her retrospective at the
    Whitechapel Gallery, London, 22 September – 31 October 1965.

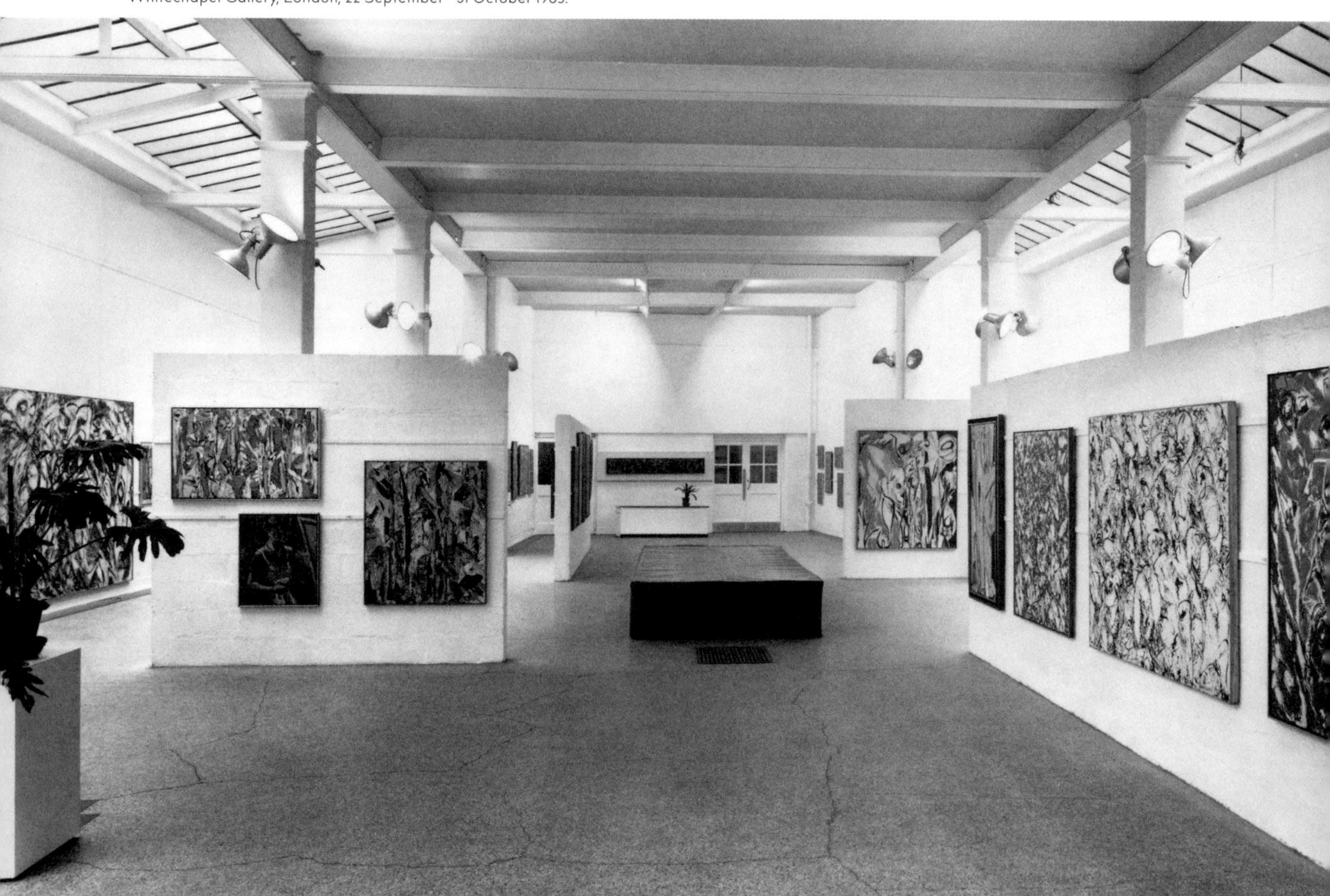

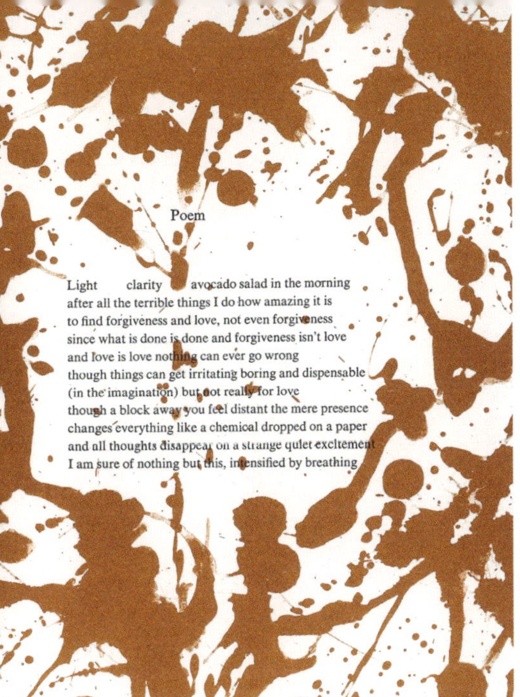

25 Frank O'Hara's 'Poem', illustrated by Lee Krasner for
*In Memory of My Feelings: A Selection of Poems by
Frank O'Hara* (New York: Museum of Modern Art, 1967).

1965

In September, Krasner's retrospective *Lee Krasner: Paintings, Drawings and Collages*, curated by Bryan Robertson, opens at the Whitechapel Gallery in London (fig. 24). The Arts Council of Great Britain takes the exhibition on tour: Ferens Art Gallery, Hull; Victoria Street Gallery, Nottingham; City Art Gallery, Manchester; Arts Council Gallery, Cardiff; and City Art Gallery, York. In the Paris edition of the *Herald Tribune*, Sheldon Williams writes that the exhibition 'awards [Krasner] the stature she deserves', adding that 'at a time when the British public has been gradually conditioned to expect pop or stain hard-edge from the United States, it is good to find an artist as good as Lee Krasner continuing along the tachist road undismayed.' John Russell calls the retrospective an 'exhilarating experience'.

Lee Krasner, Gouaches and Drawings opens at the Franklin Siden Gallery in Detroit (8–27 November).

1966

Krasner joins the Marlborough-Gerson Gallery, New York.

1967

Paintings by Lee Krasner, a solo exhibition of twenty-three large canvases at the University of Alabama, Tuscaloosa, opens in February. Krasner spends a week living on campus as artist-in-residence.

Krasner spends an increasing amount of time in Manhattan, buying an apartment at 180 East Seventy-Ninth Street with a huge bedroom, which she turns into a studio.

Krasner contributes to the book *In Memory of My Feelings: A Selection of Poems by Frank O'Hara* (fig. 25). Published by the Museum of Modern Art, New York, and edited by the poet Bill Berkson, the book commemorates O'Hara – the poet, art critic and Museum of Modern Art curator who had died in an accident the year before – by inviting thirty artists he knew to illustrate a selection of his poems.

Ad Reinhardt dies on 30 August and is buried in Green River Cemetery. Krasner organizes a wake for him at her home in Springs.

1968

In March, Krasner has her first exhibition of new work at Marlborough-Gerson Gallery: *Lee Krasner Recent Paintings*. This is the first exhibition of Krasner's to be widely reviewed in the context of the emerging feminist movement.

In April, Krasner hears Jorge Luis Borges reading from his work at the YM-YWHA, an important poetry venue in New York. His books *Ficciones* and *Labyrinths* had recently been published in America (New York: Grove Press, 1962). 'I went to hear Borges the other night. Well, this is sheer joy. I don't find new truths, but it's nice to hear truths restated again. And it gives beautiful confirmation – beautiful.'

Krasner's interest in calligraphy and illuminated manuscripts leads her to attend a series of lectures on the *Book of Kells* at the Morgan Library in New York by the art historian Meyer Schapiro.

1969

Krasner produces four series of small, calligraphic colour experiments in gouache on paper handmade by the local Long Island artist Douglass Morse Howell. The series are named 'Earth', 'Water', 'Seed' and 'Hieroglyphs'.

Krasner is the only female artist to be featured in *The New American Painting and Sculpture: The First Generation* (18 June – 5 October), an exhibition staged by the curator William Rubin at the Museum of Modern Art, New York.

In the summer, Mark Patiky, the younger brother of Frances Stein, takes the first photographs of Krasner painting in her studio at Springs. Patiky captures her working on what will become *Portrait in Green* (fig. 31).

Lee Krasner: Recent Gouaches opens at Marlborough-Gerson Gallery on 27 September, running until 18 October. The exhibition tours to the Reese Palley Gallery in San Francisco. In the *San Francisco Chronicle*, Alfred Frankenstein writes: '[Krasner's] work … has such force, richness and individuality as to set one wondering just who, in this instance, influenced whom.'

1971

Linda Nochlin's groundbreaking essay, 'Why Have There Been No Great Women Artists?', is published in the January edition of *ARTnews*. The essay seeks to expose the hidden institutional barriers faced by female artists throughout history. It has a profound impact on the art world and feminist art history.

1972

On 12 April Krasner joins a group called Women in the Arts and pickets the Museum of Modern Art, New York, to protest against its neglect of female artists (fig. 26). The group of around three hundred

26　*Attention! Women Artists and Feminists!*, poster designed by Women in the Arts for a protest at the Museum of Modern Art, New York, 12 April 1972.

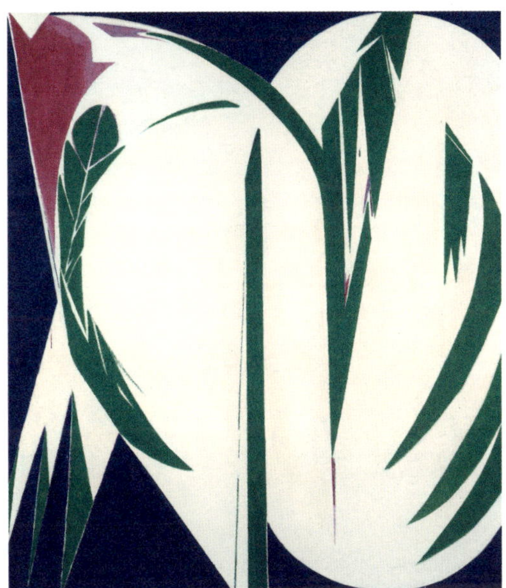

27 *Rising Green*, 1972

demonstrators calls for an exhibition of the work of female artists to take place at the Brooklyn, Metropolitan, Whitney and Guggenheim museums, as well as the Museum of Modern Art. Among the protestors are Louise Bourgeois and the Greek-born artist Chryssa.

Krasner hands over Pollock's estate and archives to the collector and dealer Eugene Victor Thaw. (Following Krasner's death, Thaw becomes the executor of her estate as well; he also helps establish the Pollock-Krasner Foundation.) 'Now I can once again concentrate on being Lee Krasner the painter.'

In June, the curator Barbara Rose publishes a landmark interview, 'American Great: Lee Krasner', in *Vogue* magazine. Krasner counters the popular stereotype of Pollock as a dominating, overbearing figure, discussing the admiration and respect they had for each other during their relationship. She states: 'I'm an artist – not a "woman artist"; not an "American artist".'

1973

In April, the Marlborough Gallery (formerly the Marlborough-Gerson Gallery) opens *Lee Krasner: Recent Paintings* (19 April – 12 May), the first public viewing of Krasner's new canvases. She shows twelve paintings from the last two years, including *Palingenesis*, *Majuscule* and *Rising Green* (fig. 27). The exhibition is well received by critics. In the *New York Times*, Hilton Kramer describes it as 'by far the finest exhibition of Miss Krasner's work I have seen', while Barbara Rose calls the canvases a 'breakthrough'.

Twenty-One Over Sixty opens at the Guild Hall in East Hampton (21 July – 12 August). Although it was Krasner who had initially suggested the concept for the exhibition, she later expressed doubts about the notion: 'Now I wish I never got the idea to begin with. It's just that one gets a little bored with the American youth image. It's suburbia and Hollywood all in one. It started in the '60s, which I call the Sterile '60s. If you haven't had a major show by the time you're thirty-five, you're nothing.'

In November, the Whitney Museum of American Art presents *Lee Krasner: Large Paintings* (13 November – 6 January 1974; fig. 28). This is Krasner's first solo show at a major New York museum. Curated by Marcia Tucker, it features eighteen works from the past twenty years, including *The Seasons* (1957) *Polar Stampede* (1960) and *Gaea* (1966).

1974

In March, Krasner is asked by Miriam Schapiro's students on the Feminist Art Program at the California Institute of the Arts to write a letter to a 'young woman artist'. Krasner responds with a quotation adapted from an interview with Cindy Nemser in 1973: 'If you think

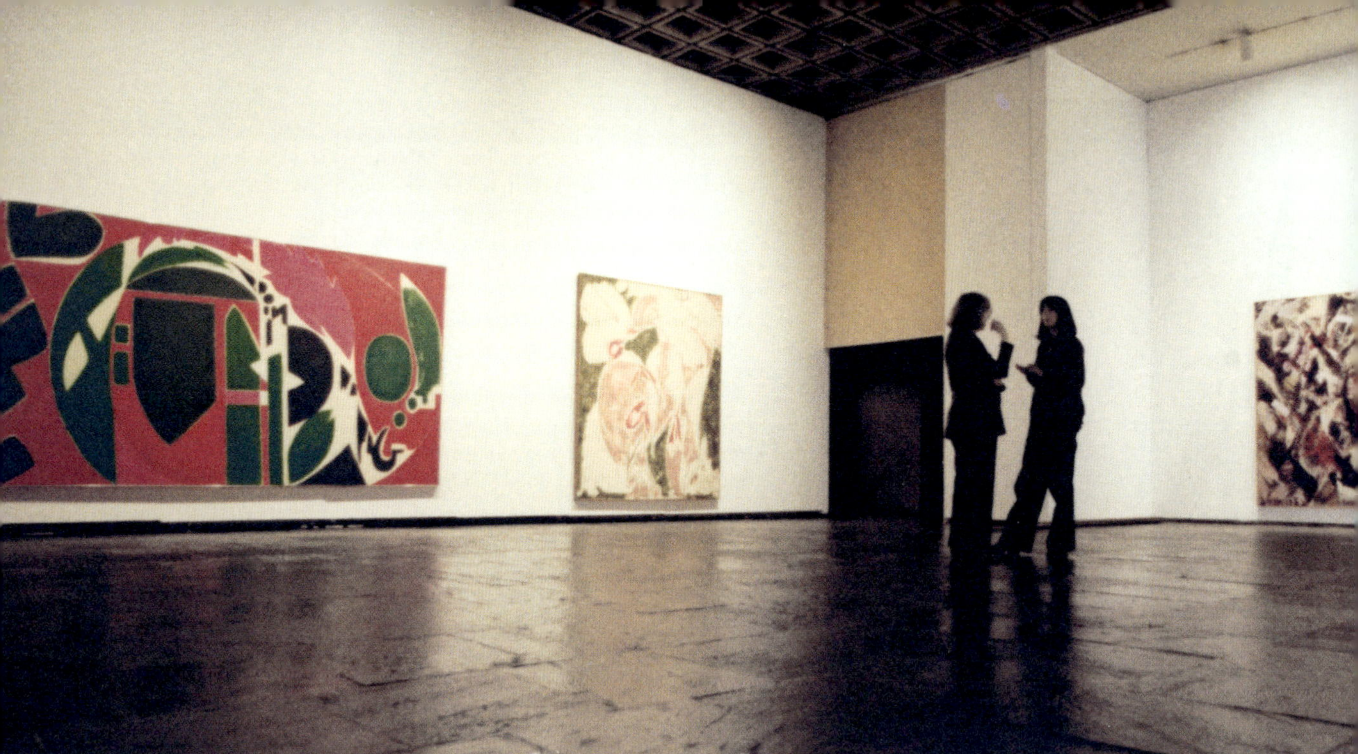

28 Installation view of the exhibition *Lee Krasner: Large
Paintings* at the Whitney Museum of American Art,
New York, 13 November 1973 – 6 January 1974.

of it in terms of time, in relation to past, present and future, and
think of them all as a oneness, you will find that you swing the pen-
dulum constantly to be with now ... I think there is an order, but it isn't
better, better, best. I don't believe in that kind of scaling.'

Also in March, the Miami-Dade Community College presents *Lee
Krasner, Selections from 1946–1972*. The exhibition travels to Beaver
College in Glenside, Pennsylvania, and Gibbes Art Gallery in Charleston,
South Carolina.

1975

Lee Krasner: Collages and Works on Paper, 1933–1974, organized
by the art critic Gene Baro, opens in January at the Corcoran Gallery
of Art in Washington DC. The exhibition tours to the Pennsylvania
State University Museum of Art and the Rose Art Museum at Brandeis
University in Massachusetts.

In July, Krasner undertakes a residency at Marge Schilling's artists'
conference at Dune Hame Cottage, Rhode Island.

Krasner declines an invitation to participate in a group exhibition, *Women Artists Here and Now*, at Ashawagh Hall, Springs. During the exhibition's run, Carolee Schneemann, the feminist performance artist, stages her landmark work *Interior Scroll* on 29 August.

Marlborough Prints and Drawings Gallery, New York, opens *Works on Paper: 1937–39*, which runs until 1 November.

1976

In June, Krasner leaves Marlborough Gallery to join Pace Gallery, New York. She becomes the third woman to be represented by Pace, alongside the monochromatic sculptor Louise Nevelson and the abstract painter Agnes Martin.

Krasner participates in the exhibition *Women Artists: 1550–1950* (21 December – 13 March 1977), curated by Linda Nochlin and Ann Sutherland Harris at Los Angeles County Museum of Art. The exhibition travels to the University Art Museum, University of Texas, Austin; the University of Pittsburgh; and the Brooklyn Museum.

1977

In February, Pace Gallery opens *Eleven Ways to Use the Words to See* (19 February – 19 March). The eleven large-scale collages presented in the show are the result of Bryan Robertson's serendipitous discovery of a stack of Krasner's 1937–40 Hofmann School charcoal drawings while he was visiting her studio in Springs. Krasner decided to cut up and reuse these drawings, a strategy described by the *New York Times* critic Grace Glueck as 'the present ingesting the past'.

Krasner is included in *Extraordinary Women* at the Museum of Modern Art, New York (22 July – 20 September). The exhibition also features works by Hannah Höch, Sonia Delaunay, Sophie Taeuber-Arp, Natalia Goncharova and Suzanne Valadon.

Krasner visits the exhibition *Henri Matisse: Paper Cut-Outs* at the Detroit Institute of Arts (23 November – 8 January 1978), on tour from the National Gallery of Art, Washington DC, where it had run from 10 September to 23 October.

1978

Abstract Expressionism: The Formative Years, curated by Gail Levin and Robert Hobbs, opens at the Herbert F. Johnson Museum, Cornell University, Ithaca, New York (30 March – 14 May). Krasner's Little Images and works made between 1934 and 1941 feature prominently. The exhibition travels to Seibu Museum, Tokyo (17 June – 12 July),

and the Whitney Museum of American Art, New York (5 October
–3 December). It is the first major show not only to recognize Krasner's
importance as a first-generation Abstract Expressionist, but also to
emphasize that she was one of the only artists in New York working
abstractly before the war. Hilton Kramer later remarks: '[It] was one
of the first surveys of the subject to accord her an honored place
in its history.'

Barbara Rose's documentary, *Lee Krasner: The Long View*, is released.
The film is screened during *Abstract Expressionism: The Formative
Years* at the Whitney Museum.

On 23 September the exhibition *Lee Krasner: Works on Paper, 1938
to 1977* opens at the Janie C. Lee Gallery in Houston.

1979

Krasner is included in *Hans Hofmann as Teacher: Drawings by His
Students* at the Metropolitan Museum of Art, New York (23 January
–4 March). The exhibition travels to Provincetown Art Association
and Museum in Massachusetts (1 August 1980–12 October 1980).

On 3 February Pace Gallery opens *Lee Krasner Paintings 1959–1962*,
which runs until 10 March. The exhibition features works from Krasner's
Umber series, as exhibited at Howard Wise Gallery in the early 1960s.

On 28 November Krasner receives a letter from Lee Anne Miller,
president of the Women's Caucus for Art, informing her that she has
been chosen to receive its Outstanding Achievement in the Visual Arts
award, celebrating her 'extraordinary contributions as a painter'. Fellow
recipients include Anni Albers and Louise Bourgeois. In her acceptance
speech (delivered by Gail Levin), Krasner states: 'I am really very
pleased – honored – to receive this award from the Women's Caucus
for Art. However, I hope for the day when such an award could be
a joint acknowledgment from men and women. The belated recognition
that I have recently received is largely due to consciousness-raising
by the feminist movement, which I consider the major revolution of our
time. Thank you.'

1980

In March, the Stony Brook Foundation grants Krasner its Distinguished
Contributions to Higher Education award. The citation reads: 'Scores
of prominent lay artists have learned from you. The critics here finally
caught up to you. And now, Lee Krasner, the painter, is established
as a prestigious and original artist in her own right as well as the
strong and dedicated executor of the estate of the late, great Jackson
Pollock ... All of this achievement called for a single-minded devotion
to art.'

Lee Krasner, Recent Works on Paper opens at Tower Gallery in Southampton, New York (16–29 August).

1981

On 7 February Janie C. Lee Gallery opens *Lee Krasner: Paintings 1956–1971*.

Pace Gallery stages *Lee Krasner / Solstice* (20 March – 18 April).

In September, the Guild Hall opens *Krasner / Pollock: A Working Relationship*, curated by Barbara Rose (8 September – 4 October). The exhibition tours to Grey Art Gallery and Study Center, New York University (3 November – 12 December). Krasner acknowledges that '[the show] could be a terrible pitfall for me as an artist. I'm aware of that. I've been around. But I couldn't give two hoots about that. I want to see it with my eye for myself – because I've never seen it visually, and until I see it visually, I don't know what they're talking about. And because I have an endless curiosity above and beyond the mob, I couldn't care less about what their reaction is.' The critical response is in fact positive, with one reviewer, William Pellicone, writing: 'The revelation exposed is the fact that Lee Krasner gave Pollock everything because of her superior talent and he eventually destroys her true path with his superior barbaric, macho strength ... The Guild Hall show calls for a completely new evaluation of the Krasner–Pollock link.'

Towards the end of the year, Krasner leaves Pace Gallery, stating: 'We never had a fight. We are still friends. But I remember the dealer Pierre Matisse saying, "It's the artists who've made my gallery." Arne

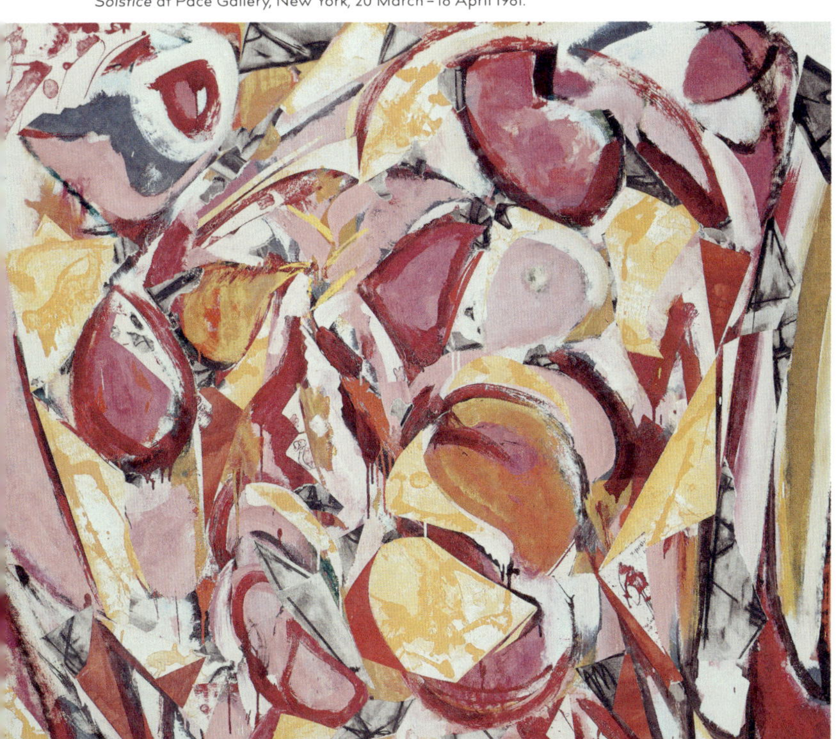

29 *Vernal Yellow*, 1980. The work was included in *Lee Krasner / Solstice* at Pace Gallery, New York, 20 March – 18 April 1981.

[Glimcher], on the other hand, feels the gallery made his artists, and this is a serious disturbance. I wasn't comfortable there.'

Krasner joins Robert Miller Gallery in New York. Robert Miller is an old friend, having worked as Krasner's studio manager in the past.

1982

On 11 January Krasner receives the Chevalier de l'Ordre des Arts et des Lettres (fig. 30). The award is presented by the French minister of culture, Jack Lang, just a few days before the opening of Pollock's retrospective at the Musée National d'Art Moderne at the Centre Pompidou, Paris, an exhibition that Krasner made possible with considerable loans from the estate.

In October, Robert Miller Gallery opens its inaugural Krasner exhibition, *Lee Krasner: Paintings from the Late Fifties* (26 October – 20 November). Works on view include *Thaw* (1957), *Cornucopia* (1958) and *The Bull* (1959).

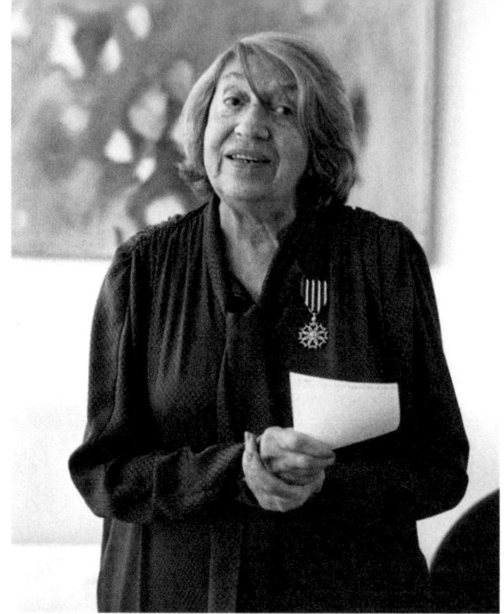

30 Lee Krasner giving her acceptance speech after receiving the Chevalier de l'Ordre des Arts et des Lettres at the Centre Pompidou, Paris, 11 January 1982.

1983

On 27 October, the day of Krasner's seventy-fifth birthday, *Lee Krasner: A Retrospective* opens at the Museum of Fine Arts, Houston, running until 8 January 1984. Curated by Barbara Rose, and featuring 152 paintings and drawings, the exhibition travels to the San Francisco Museum of Modern Art; the Chrysler Museum of Art, Norfolk, Virginia; Phoenix Art Museum, Arizona; and the Museum of Modern Art, New York.

1984

Krasner is not well enough to attend the opening of her retrospective at the San Francisco Museum of Modern Art (16 February – 14 April).

Charcoal Drawings from 1938–1940 opens at Robert Miller Gallery (5–30 March).

On 20 May Krasner is awarded an Honorary Doctorate of Fine Arts in absentia by the State University of New York, Stony Brook.

On 14 June a Women Artists Visibility Event brings together around four hundred demonstrators to protest against the extreme under-representation of female artists in *An International Survey of Painting and Sculpture*, the exhibition marking the expansion of the Museum of Modern Art, New York. The demonstrators' posters and badges parody the museum's own rhetoric for the grand re-opening: 'Museum of Modern Art Opens but Not to Women Artists'.

On 19 June Krasner dies in New York Hospital, Manhattan. Her funeral, organized by her younger sister, Ruth, takes place on 25 July in Sag Harbor, Long Island. She is buried in Green River Cemetery in Springs, next to Pollock. Their gravestones are fashioned from the same rough stone that lay on the salt marshes in front of their Springs home.

On 17 September a commemorative service is organized by the prominent curator William Lieberman in the Metropolitan Museum of Art's Medieval Sculpture Court. Speakers include the writer Susan Sontag, the art critic Robert Hughes and the playwright Edward Albee. Sontag describes Krasner's 'talent for friendship, her genuine vitality and openness to experience'.

On 19 December *Lee Krasner: A Retrospective* opens at the Museum of Modern Art, New York, where it runs until 12 February 1985. Krasner becomes one of the few female artists to be given a solo exhibition at the museum.

To coincide with this retrospective, exhibitions open at the Brooklyn Museum (*Lee Krasner, Works on Paper*, 20 December – 25 February 1985) and at Krasner's alma mater, the Cooper Union (*Lee Krasner: The Education of an American Artist*, opened 16 January 1985).

1985

On 23 June, in accordance with Jewish tradition, Krasner's headstone is unveiled one year after her death.

Jessica Freeman-Attwood

31 Lee Krasner painting *Portrait in Green* in her studio
    in Springs, 1969. Photograph by Mark Patiky.

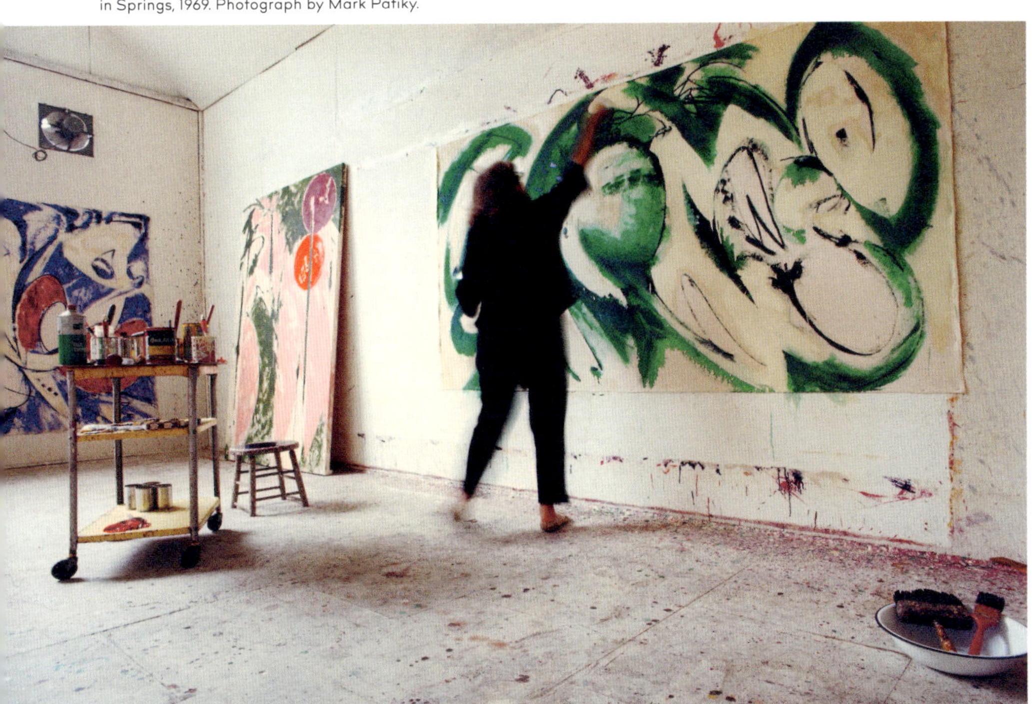

FOREWORD

1   Richard Howard, 'Lee Listening', *Grand Street*, vol. 4, no. 1, Autumn 1984, pp. 183–86. Emphasis in original.
2   *Ibid.*, p. 186.
3   See Bryan Robertson, *Lee Krasner: Paintings, Drawings and Collages*, exhib. cat. (London: Whitechapel Gallery, 1965).
4   Howard, 'Lee Listening', p. 183.

TO BREATHE AND BE ALIVE

Epigraph: Lee Krasner, quoted in Dorothy Seckler, 'Oral History Interview with Lee Krasner', Session Three, 11 April 1968, Archives of American Art, Smithsonian Institution, Washington DC (hereafter 'AAA'), np.
1   Copy of tribute given by Edward Albee at the memorial service for Lee Krasner, sent to Jason McCoy on 4 October 1984, p. 1. Archives of the Library of Congress, Washington DC.
2   In his introductory essay to the catalogue for Lee Krasner's retrospective at the Whitechapel Gallery in London in 1965, B. H. Friedman wrote that 'Lee Krasner is a woman – in a field which still, even now in 1965, barely tolerates women, condescends to them with the phrase "woman painter," as odious and pejorative as "woman writer" or "woman driver."' Bryan Robertson, *Lee Krasner: Paintings, Drawings and Collages*, exhib. cat. (London: Whitechapel Gallery, 1965), p. 5.
3   Anonymous [Dorothy Seiberling], 'Jackson Pollock: Is He the Greatest Living Painter in the United States?', *Life*, 8 August 1949, pp. 42–45.
4   Albee tribute, p. 1.
5   Lee Krasner, quoted in Cindy Nemser, 'A Conversation with Lee Krasner', *Arts Magazine*, April 1973, p. 47.
6   Anne Wagner considers this remark to be 'edged with the mixture of aggression and abnegation, bravado and aggrievedness typical of Krasner's conversational style'. In her thoughtful and timely essay, Wagner analyses the many personae that Krasner adopted and the impossibility of locating a 'self' within her work as easily as Krasner suggests. While I agree that all selves, and particularly those constructed by artists in the public sphere, are necessary fictions, I feel more confident of the productivity of considering Krasner's work and life in dialogue (especially if the temptation to romanticize is avoided). See Wagner, 'Krasner's Fictions', in *Three Artists (Three Women): Modernism and the Art of Hesse, Krasner, and O'Keeffe* (Berkeley: University of California Press, 1996), pp. 105–90.
7   Lee Krasner, quoted in Marcia Tucker, *Lee Krasner: Large Paintings*, exhib. cat. (New York: Whitney Museum of American Art, 1973), p. 8.

8   Krasner's earliest work dates to *c.* 1928, but it was not until 1960 that she conducted her first interview, with Louise Elliott Rago.
9   The impression of Lee Krasner's life given in this essay is hugely enriched by Gail Levin's biography of the artist. Likewise, the Barbican exhibition that this catalogue accompanies is the first major show to be able to benefit from Levin's forensic research for her biography.
10 Gail Levin, *Lee Krasner: A Biography* (New York: William Morrow, 2011), pp. 15–16.
11 Lee Krasner, quoted in Barbara Novak, 'Lee Krasner Interview', WGBH-TV, 1979, p. 4. Lee Krasner Papers, AAA (hereafter 'LK Papers').
12 Other émigré artists who changed their names include Mark Rothko, who was born Markus Yakovlevich Rothkowitz and emigrated from Russia to the United States in 1913, and Arshile Gorky, who was born Vostanik Manoug Adoian and arrived in America in 1920 after fleeing the Armenian Genocide.
13 John Berger, 'A Kind of Sharing', *Keeping a Rendezvous* (New York: Pantheon Books, 1991), p. 109. Originally published in *The Guardian*, 23 November 1989.
14 At the time, students at the National Academy had to paint a self-portrait in order to qualify for admission to the academic life-drawing class. See Barbara Rose, *Lee Krasner: A Retrospective*, exhib. cat. (Houston and New York: Museum of Fine Arts and Museum of Modern Art, 1983), p. 15. Many artists who would become associated with the so-called New York School experimented with this form, which made for a fascinating opening room in the recent *Abstract Expressionism* exhibition at the Royal Academy in London (2016–17), co-curated by David Anfam and Edith Devaney.
15 Lawrence Campbell, 'Of Lilith and Lettuce', *ARTnews*, 67, March 1968, p. 63.
16 Lee Krasner, quoted in John Bernard Myers, 'Naming Pictures: Conversations between Lee Krasner and John Bernard Myers', *Artforum*, vol. 23, no. 3, November 1984, p. 71. This is an imagined interview written by Myers after Krasner's death, based on conversations they had had, and is therefore not a direct quotation from Krasner. The words echo Pollock's famous line, 'Every good artist paints what he is', but given that Krasner often articulated ideas on Pollock's behalf, she may have originated the phrasing. Selden Rodman, *Conversations with Artists* (New York: Capricorn Books, 1961), pp. 84–85.
17 Although she did obtain her certificate, she abandoned the idea of teaching. As she explained in an interview with Dorothy Seckler, 'I got my pedagogy and decided the last thing in the world that I wanted to do was to teach art so I tore that up.' Dorothy Seckler, 'Oral History Interview with Lee Krasner', Session One, 2 November 1964, AAA, np.

18 Photographs show Krasner posing nude on the beach in Cape Cod, where she holidayed with Pantuhoff in 1938, along with a group of artist friends that included Arshile Gorky and David Margolis.
19 Lee Krasner, quoted in Esphyr Slobodkina, *Notes of a Biographer*, 3 vols (Great Neck, NY: Urquart-Slobodkina Inc., 1976–83), vol. 2, p. 242, quoted in Levin, *Lee Krasner*, p. 54.
20 Hofmann's 'push and pull' theories related to how to create the impression of movement and depth to a work through creating contrasts in form, colour and space.
21 Ellen G. Landau, *Lee Krasner: A Catalogue Raisonné* (New York: Harry N. Abrams, 1995), p. 93.
22 In 1942, after the United States had joined the Second World War, Roosevelt converted the Works Progress Administration into the War Services Project. The assignments given to artists now had to focus on supporting the war effort. Krasner's window displays were to advertise training courses offered in municipal colleges to educate people in wartime skills. The subjects offered included cryptography, map-making, meteorology, optics, metallurgy, industrial chemistry and mechanical drawing. See Landau, *A Catalogue Raisonné*, p. 93.
23 The course was taught by Professor Burtell. Levin, *Lee Krasner*, p. 189.
24 Eleanor Munro, *Originals: American Women Artists* (New York: Simon & Schuster, 1979), p. 112.
25 Barbara Rose states that Krasner 'saw and studied both show and catalogue intently'. Rose, *Lee Krasner*, p. 18.
26 Interview with Dorothy Seckler, 2 November 1964, transcript, LK Papers, np. Krasner was not shy about acknowledging Pollock's influence on her as an artist, and she often said that his biggest contribution to her work was to encourage her to abandon Hofmann's insistence on working from a model in favour of drawing from internal sources. When Krasner brought Hofmann to visit Pollock's studio, Pollock famously declared, 'I *am* nature.'
27 Lee Krasner, quoted in George Mercer, letter to Krasner, 24 April 1945, Pollock-Krasner House and Study Center. Quoted in Levin, *Lee Krasner*, p. 219.
28 Lee Krasner, quoted in Nemser, 'A Conversation', p. 44.
29 Quoted in Landau, *A Catalogue Raisonné*, p. 106.
30 In her interview with Barbara Novak, Krasner discussed her early study of Hebrew: 'Visually I loved it. I didn't know what it meant.' Novak, 'Lee Krasner Interview', p. 50. There was a widespread interest in hieroglyphs and written codes among artists at the time. In *System and Dialectics of Art*, which Krasner had read soon after it was published in 1937, John Graham

insisted that 'The difficulty in producing a work of art lies in the fact that the artist has to unite at one and the same time three elements: thought, feeling and "*automatic écriture*".' John Graham, *System and Dialectics of Art* (New York: Delphic Studios, 1937), p.55. In 1944 the painter Mark Tobey, who was likely also familiar with Graham's theories of *écriture*, presented his new technique of 'white writing' in his solo exhibition at the Willard Gallery, New York.

31 Sigmund Freud, quoted in Richard H. Armstrong, *A Compulsion for Antiquity: Freud and the Ancient World* (Ithaca, NY: Cornell University Press, 2005), p.110.

32 Stuart Preston, 'Among One-Man Shows', *New York Times*, 21 October 1951, p.105; Robert Goodnough, 'Lee Krasner', *ARTnews*, November 1951, p.59.

33 Lee Krasner, quoted in Phyllis Braff, 'From the Studio', *East Hampton Star*, 21 August 1980, clipping in LK Papers, Box 13, Folder 1, np.

34 Lee Krasner, quoted in Braff, 'From the Studio'.

35 Fairfield Porter, 'Lee Krasner', *ARTnews*, November 1955, p.66; Clement Greenberg, comment to Bryan Robertson, quoted in Robertson, *Lee Krasner*, p.4.

36 Krasner would probably have seen this new body of 'découpages' when they were first shown at Pierre Matisse Gallery in 1949.

37 Stuart Preston, 'Modern Work in Diverse Shows', *New York Times*, 2 October 1955, p.15; Matisse's studio colleagues, quoted in T. J. Clark, 'Madame Matisse's Hat', *London Review of Books*, vol.30, no.16, 14 August 2008, pp.29–32. In an interview with Barbara Rose in 1972, Krasner explained that 'my pull towards Matisse dates way back, and if I had to point to one colorist today, he would still be the one.' Barbara Rose, interview transcript, 1972, LK Papers, Box 9, Folder 47, np.

38 Pollock made very few paintings after 1954. Francis Valentine O'Connor and Eugene Victor Thaw (eds) *Jackson Pollock: A Catalogue Raisonné of Paintings, Drawings, and Other Works* (London and New Haven, CT: Yale University Press, 1978), p.199.

39 Lee Krasner, quoted in Richard Howard, 'A Conversation with Lee Krasner', 1978, in Howard, *Lee Krasner: Paintings 1959–1962*, exhib. cat. (New York: Pace Gallery, 1979), np.

40 *Ibid.*

41 Quoted in O'Connor and Thaw (eds), *Jackson Pollock: A Catalogue Raisonné*, p.276.

42 Lee Krasner, quoted in Louise Elliott Rago, 'We Interview Lee Krasner', *School Arts*, 60, September 1960, p.32.

43 The floor of Pollock's studio was immortalized by the photographer Hans Namuth in a series of photos first published in *Portfolio* magazine in 1951. These photographs offered the first glimpse of Pollock's radical painting technique.

44 Amei Wallach, 'Lee Krasner: Out of Jackson Pollock's Shadow', *Newsday*, 1981, quoted in Levin, *Lee Krasner*, p.331. It is worth noting that both of their beloved dogs, the Border collie Gyp and the chocolate poodle Ahab (a gift from their friend Alfonso Ossorio), also died around this time.

45 Krasner emphasized the exertion required to make these works in her interview with Richard Howard: 'These are physical paintings. The gesture is a thrust – I don't generally do that.' Howard, 'A Conversation', 1978, np.

46 Ralph Waldo Emerson, 'Circles', 1841, quoted in Levin, *Lee Krasner*, p.351.

47 Emily Genauer, 'Artists Turning to Dark Myths', *New York Herald Tribune*, 20 November 1960, p.21; Stuart Preston, 'Art: Allusive Portraits', *New York Times*, 19 November 1960, p.43.

48 Although Krasner did not create the large paintings commonly associated with Abstract Expressionism until relatively late in her career, it is worth remembering that her work for the Mural Division of the WPA had included some enormous pieces. She described one mural that 'seemed to be two or three miles wide. I worked from the original small sketch and blew it up … Long before I met Pollock, too, I had been working that large.' Munro, *Originals*, p.108.

49 Lee Krasner, quoted in Andrew Forge, 'Interview between Lee Krasner and Andrew Forge', 13 October 1965, LK Papers, Box 9, Folder 45.

50 Bryan Robertson was the director of the Whitechapel Gallery from 1952 to the end of 1968, during which time he curated a truly extraordinary run of exhibitions, making the Whitechapel *the* place to see American art in particular. Other highlights of his programme include exhibitions by Mark Tobey (1962), Philip Guston (1963), Robert Rauschenberg (1964), Jasper Johns (1964), Morris Louis (1965) and Robert Motherwell (1966). He also curated a number of important exhibitions of women artists, including Barbara Hepworth (1954 and 1962), Ida Kar (1960) and Prunella Clough (1960).

51 John Russell, 'Germany's Other Man of Iron', *Sunday Times*, 3 October 1965, np; Nigel Gosling, 'A Portent from Brooklyn', *The Observer*, 26 September 1965, np.

52 Lee Krasner, quoted in Cindy Nemser, *Art Talk: Conversations with 12 Women Artists* (New York: Scribner, 1975), p.98.

53 Robert Hughes, 'Bursting Out of the Shadows', *Time*, 14 November 1983, p.93.

54 Clement Greenberg, 'Post Painterly Abstraction', 1964, in John O'Brian (ed.), *Clement Greenberg: The Collected Essays and Criticism*, vol.4, *Modernism with a Vengeance, 1957–1969* (Chicago: University of Chicago Press, 1993), p.196.

55 Presumably Krasner wanted to avoid what Hilton Kramer called 'that bright, dead look we have become inured to since the advent of acrylics and other plastic pigments'. Hilton Kramer, 'Making Vivid the Spirit of the New York School', *New York Times*, 16 April 1978, p. D26, clipping in the Pollock-Krasner House and Study Center Archives.

56 Hilton Kramer, '2 Displays Honor Photographer, 90', *New York Times*, 28 April 1973, p.20.

57 Lee Krasner, quoted in Nemser, *Art Talk*, p.105.

58 Robertson had discovered the portfolios in the summer of 1974. See Bryan Robertson, *Lee Krasner: Collages*, exhib. cat. (New York: Robert Miller Gallery, 1986), np.

59 Lee Krasner, quoted in Landau, *A Catalogue Raisonné*, p.278.

60 Hofmann's method of tearing up his students' work is described in Lillian Orlowsky, *The Provocative Years, 1935–1945: The Hans Hofmann School and Its Students in Provincetown*, exhib. cat. (Provincetown, MA: Provincetown Art Association and Museum, 1990), p.4.

61 This complicated system was apparently proposed by her friend Saul Steinberg, which would explain the sharp deviance from her preference for more terse, enigmatic titles (often suggested by friends or even their children), such as *Combat* or *Rising Green*.

62 Lee Krasner, quoted in Jerry Tallmer, 'Scissors, Paste & Bits of Survival', *New York Post*, February 1977, LK Papers, Box 12, Folder 32.

63 In a 1980 interview with Barbara Cavaliere for the journal *Flash Art*, Krasner reflected on her career: 'Not having been a giant success in my life has been, in the end, a blessing. I can afford now to do as I wish.' Quoted in Robert Hobbs, *Lee Krasner*, exhib. cat. (New York: Independent Curators International in association with Harry N. Abrams, 2001), p.112.

64 Lee Krasner, quoted in David Bourdon, 'Lee Krasner: I'm Embracing the Past', *Village Voice*, 7 March 1977, p.57, cited in Levin, *Lee Krasner*, p.410.

65 Gail Levin highlights Krasner's fondness for this line; see Levin, *Lee Krasner*, p.404. The extract comes from T. S. Eliot's 'Little Gidding', the fourth of the *Four Quartets*, first published in 1942.

NOTHING OUTSIDE NATURE

Epigraph: Richard Howard, interview with the author, August 2018. Howard spent the summers of 1958–60 with Krasner on Long Island, and they remained friends until her death, seeing each other in New York City. I would like to thank Richard Howard for his generosity in speaking to me; Helen Harrison for the benefit of her counsel and long experience with Krasner studies; and my graduate assistant Erin Kimmel, for her diligent research support. Gail Levin's carefully researched biography of the artist was also an important resource; Levin, *Lee Krasner: A Biography* (New York: William Morrow, 2011). Finally, my thanks to Eleanor Nairne, for her incisive thinking and exchanges on the subject of Lee Krasner.

1 There are many historiographic accounts of this debate. Among the most useful are Ernst Mayr, 'What is Life?', in Mayr, *This is Biology: The Science of the Living World* (Cambridge, MA, and London: Harvard University Press, 1997), pp.1–23; and Donna Jeanne Haraway, *Crystals, Fabrics, and Fields: Metaphors of Organicism in Twentieth-Century Developmental Biology* (New Haven, CT: Yale University Press, 1976).

2 Geoffrey Grigson, 'Comment on England', *Axis*, no.1, 1935, p.8; Alfred H. Barr Jr, *Cubism and Abstract Art*, exhib. cat. (New York: Museum of Modern Art, 1936). The concept would be revived by Lawrence Alloway (whose perspective included London's Independent Group and also gestural painting in the US) in his article 'The Biomorphic '40s', *Artforum*, vol.4, no.1, September 1965, pp.18–22. Important secondary accounts include Jennifer Mundy, 'Form and Creation: The Impact of the Biological Sciences on Modern Art', in *Creation: Modern Art and Nature*, exhib. cat. (Edinburgh: Scottish National Gallery, 1984), and Mundy, 'The Naming of Biomorphism', in Oliver A. I. Botar and Isabel Wünsche (eds), *Biocentrism and Modernism* (Farnham: Ashgate, 2011); the entire volume is illuminating.

3   Many of these artists have been somewhat
    stranded in terms of art history, since their work
    either precedes or refuses such critical stylistic
    categories as Abstract Expressionism – even
    that of those artists later labelled as such,
    including Adolph Gottlieb and Mark Rothko.
    A few prescient curators cast the work in
    organicist terms, most notably Howard Putzel
    (former advisor to Peggy Guggenheim), who
    essayed the term 'new metamorphism' in the
    statement for his 1945 exhibition *A Problem
    for Critics*, reprinted in Edward Alden Jewell,
    'Toward Abstract or Away', *New York Times*,
    1 July 1945, p.2; the exhibition included a work
    by Krasner.
4   Dorothy Seckler, 'Oral History Interview with
    Lee Krasner', Session One, 2 November 1964,
    Archives of American Art, Smithsonian
    Institution, Washington DC (hereafter 'AAA').
5   This seems as good a place as any to note the
    almost singular phenomenon associated with
    Krasner scholarship: the strong women claiming
    a polemical interpretation of her nature as an artist
    and as a woman, a wife and a widow – a rejoinder
    to other writers, including the other female and
    feminist scholars. Primarily Barbara Rose (curator
    of Krasner's first retrospective in 1983–85), Gail
    Levin (Krasner's biographer) and Ellen G. Landau
    (author of the Krasner catalogue raisonné), whose
    scholarly relations are sometimes conflicted; and
    also those mainly addressing the historiography
    of Krasner's reception, Anna C. Chave and Anne
    M. Wagner, among the foremost feminist scholars
    of their generation. This itself is an enormous
    tribute to the artist. Wagner, 'Lee Krasner as
    L.K.', *Representations*, no. 25, Winter 1989,
    pp.42–57; Chave, 'Pollock and Krasner: Script
    and Postscript', *RES: Anthropology and
    Aesthetics*, vol. 24, Autumn 1993, pp.95–111.
6   Later, there seemed to be both a change of heart
    on the part of Hofmann himself and an attempt
    to recuperate him to the more contemporary
    attitude. In an essay on Joan Mitchell's 1974
    exhibition at the Whitney Museum of American
    Art, Harold Rosenberg wrote of Hofmann that
    'instead of copying nature, he saturated himself
    with it … "I bring the landscape home in me" was
    his way of describing his approach.' Instead of
    seeing the older artist as amending his views,
    Rosenberg (ever the sexist) is at pains to cast him
    as the predecessor to Mitchell, who was much
    more deeply engaged in the internalization of the
    landscape. Rosenberg, 'Artist Against Background',
    New Yorker, 29 April 1974, p.76.
7   Edward Weston, entry for 24 April 1930, in Nancy
    Newhall (ed.), *The Daybooks of Edward Weston*,
    vol. 2, *California* (New York: Horizon, 1966), p.154.
8   Lee Krasner, quoted in Cindy Nemser, *Art Talk:
    Conversations with 12 Women Artists* (New York:
    Scribner, 1975), p.90.
9   Some have seen D'Arcy Wentworth Thompson's
    Growth and Form (a gift from the artist Tony
    Smith, and still resident on the Pollock-Krasner
    bookshelves) as an influence following a reference
    by B. H. Friedman, much as it was in England
    for Henry Moore and Richard Hamilton. Neither
    Pollock nor Krasner were readers; both were
    interested in the big ideas shared at the time
    and may have browsed the volume. Friedman,
    Jackson Pollock: Energy Made Visible (New York:
    Da Capo Press, 1995), pp.91–92.

10 Krasner discusses the move to Springs as
    immediately productive for Pollock, and in
    a delayed fashion for herself. Grace Glueck,
    'Scenes from a Marriage: Krasner and Pollock',
    ARTnews, vol. 80, no. 10, December 1981, p.60;
    Barbara Rose, *Krasner/Pollock: A Working
    Relationship*, exhib. cat. (New York: Grey Art
    Gallery and Study Center, 1981), np.
11 Eleanor Munro, *Originals: American Women
    Artists* (Boulder, CO: Da Capo Press, 2000),
    p.103.
12 Ellen G. Landau, 'Lee Krasner's Early Career,
    Part Two: The 1940s', *Arts Magazine*, vol. 56,
    no. 3, November 1981, p.80.
13 David Bourdon, 'The Driftwood Aesthetic',
    Art Journal, vol. 25, no. 1, 1965, p.31.
14 Ellen G. Landau, *Lee Krasner: A Catalogue
    Raisonné* (New York: Harry N. Abrams, 1995),
    p.106. In a statement, Pollock discussed using
    'sand, broken glass, or other foreign matter';
    Pollock, 'My Painting', *Possibilities*, vol. 1, no. 1,
    Winter 1947–48, p.79.
15 As Ossorio told Ellen G. Landau in a 1979
    interview, cited in Landau, 'Alfonso Ossorio:
    Beyond the Congregations', in Klaus Kertess,
    Alfonso Ossorio: Congregations, exhib. cat.
    (Southampton, NY: Parrish Art Museum, 1997),
    p.27 n.20.
16 For a thorough exploration of this topic, see
    Eileen Elizabeth Costello, 'Beyond the Easel:
    The Dissolution of Abstract Expressionist Painting
    into the Realm of Architecture', unpublished
    dissertation, University of Texas, 2010.
17 See Trisha Laughlin, 'Lee Krasner and the
    Decorative Impulse in Modern Art', *Art Criticism*,
    vol. 10, no. 2, 1995, p.37.
18 See Mayr, *This is Biology*, p.22. For a historical
    discussion of this view of organism, see Gillian
    Barker et al. (eds), *Entangled Life: Organism
    and Environment in the Biological and Social
    Sciences* (Dordrecht: Springer, 2014).
19 Lee Krasner, quoted in Barbara Novak, 'Excerpts
    from an Interview with Lee Krasner' [Boston,
    October 1979], in *Lee Krasner, Recent Work*,
    exhib. cat. (New York: Pace Gallery, 1981), np.
20 *Ibid.*
21 Jean Arp, 'Concrete Art' [1944], in Arp, *Arp:
    On My Way: Poetry and Essays 1912–1947*
    (New York: Wittenborn, Schulz, 1948), p.70.
22 For an extended discussion of 'unfinishedness',
    see Katy Siegel, *Since '45: America and the
    Making of Contemporary Art* (London: Reaktion
    Press, 2011), pp.25–29.
23 Most notably, Bryan Robertson, 'The Nature
    of Lee Krasner', *Art in America*, vol. 61, no. 6,
    November – December 1973, pp.83–87; and
    Robertson, 'Krasner's Collages', in *Lee Krasner,
    Collages*, exhib. cat. (New York: Robert Miller
    Gallery, 1986), np.
24 Krasner discusses the genesis of these first
    collages in her dissatisfaction with/destruction
    of her own work in Dorothy Seckler, 'Oral
    History Interview with Lee Krasner', Session
    Two, 14 December 1967, AAA, np; and Nemser,
    Art Talk, pp.93–94. Jean Arp, 1950 statement,
    cited in Astrid von Asten, '"We want to produce
    like a plant that produces a fruit": Hans Arp and
    the "Nature Principle"', in Paul Crowther and
    Isabel Wünsche (eds), *Meanings of Abstract Art:
    Between Nature and Theory* (London: Routledge,
    2012), pp.88–89.

25 For an extended discussion of Krasner's and
    Ryan's collages, see Daniel Haxall, 'Cut and
    Paste Abstraction: Politics, Form, and Identity
    in Abstract Expressionist Collage', unpublished
    dissertation, Pennsylvania State University, 2009.
26 Ellen G. Landau, 'Lee Krasner's Early Career,
    Part One: Pushing in Different Directions', *Arts
    Magazine*, vol. 56, no. 2, 1981, pp.110–22; see
    also Barbara Rose, *Lee Krasner: A Retrospective*,
    exhib. cat. (Houston and New York: Museum of
    Fine Arts and Museum of Modern Art), 1983, p.86.
27 Richard Howard, interview with the author.
28 John Bernard Myers, 'Naming Pictures:
    Conversations between Lee Krasner and John
    Bernard Myers', *Artforum*, vol. 23, no. 3,
    November 1984, p.71.
29 A. N. Whitehead, *The Concept of Nature*
    (Cambridge: Cambridge University Press, 1920),
    p.185.
30 Lee Krasner, quoted in Novak, 'Excerpts from
    an Interview with Lee Krasner'.

WRITING RIMBAUD ON THE WALL

1   Lee Krasner, quoted in Gail Levin, *Lee Krasner: A
    Biography* (New York: William Morrow, 2011), p.31.
2   Montrose J. Moses, 'Foreword', in Maurice
    Maeterlinck, *On Emerson and Other Essays*,
    trans. Montrose J. Moses (New York: Dodd,
    Mead, 1912), p.13
3   Maeterlinck, *On Emerson*, p.30.
4   Allen Tate, 'The Angelic Imagination: Poe and
    the Power of Words', *Kenyon Review*, vol. 14,
    no. 3, Summer 1952, p.461
5   Ralph Waldo Emerson, *Self-Reliance, the
    Over-Soul, and Other Essays* (Claremont,
    CA: Coyote Canyon Press, 2010), p.21.
6   Hans Hofmann, quoted in Levin, *Lee Krasner*,
    p.129.
7   Emily Wasserman, 'Lee Krasner in Mid-Career',
    Artforum, vol. 6, no. 7, March 1968, p.39.
8   Arthur Rimbaud, *A Season in Hell*, trans.
    Delmore Schwartz (Norfolk, CT: New Directions,
    1939), p.15.
9   Levin, *Lee Krasner*, p.138.
10 *Ibid.*, pp.138–39.
11 Wyatt Mason, 'Introduction', in Arthur Rimbaud,
    Rimbaud Complete, vol. 1, *Poetry and Prose*,
    trans., ed. and intro. Wyatt Mason (New York:
    Modern Library, 2003), p.xxxv.
12 *Ibid.*
13 *Ibid.*, p.xxix.
14 Lee Krasner, quoted in Gaby Rodgers, 'She Has
    Been There Once or Twice: An Interview with Lee
    Krasner', 1977, Lee Krasner Papers, Archives
    of American Art, Smithsonian Institution,
    Washington DC (hereafter 'LK Papers'),
    microfilm 3774.
15 Arthur Rimbaud, letter to Paul Demeny, 15 May
    1871, in *Rimbaud: Complete Works, Selected
    Letters*, trans., intro. and notes Wallace Fowlie
    (Chicago: University of Chicago Press, 1966),
    p.307.
16 Arthur Rimbaud, letter to Georges Izambard,
    13 May 1871, cited in Wyatt Mason (ed.), *I Promise
    to be Good: The Letters of Arthur Rimbaud*
    (New York: Modern Library, 2003), p.28.
17 Lee Krasner, quoted in Barbara Novak, 'Excerpts
    from an Interview with Lee Krasner' [Boston,
    October 1979], in *Lee Krasner: Recent Work*,
    exhib. cat. (New York: Pace Gallery, 1981), np.

18 Lee Krasner, interview with John Post Lee, East Hampton, New York, 28 November 1981, in 'Lee Krasner and "Eleven Ways to Use the Words to See"', unpublished senior thesis, Vassar College, 4 December 1981, p.36.

19 Dorothy Seckler, 'Oral History Interview with Lee Krasner', Session One, 2 November 1964, Archives of American Art, Smithsonian Institution, Washington DC.

20 Levin, *Lee Krasner*, p.290.

21 Lee Krasner, quoted in Phyllis Braff, 'From the Studio', *East Hampton Star*, 21 August 1980, clipping in LK Papers, Box 13, Folder 1, np.

22 John Bernard Myers, 'Naming Pictures: Conversations Between Lee Krasner and John Bernard Myers', *Art Forum*, November 1984, p.71.

PRESENT CONDITIONAL

1 Lee Krasner, quoted in Barbara Rose, 'Lee Krasner – American Great', *Vogue*, June 1972, p.118.

2 Barbara Rose, *Lee Krasner: A Retrospective*, exhib. cat. (Houston and New York: Museum of Fine Arts and Museum of Modern Art, 1983), p.157.

3 *Ibid.*

4 This was also the year in which Harold Rosenberg published *The Tradition of the New* (New York: Horizon, 1959), from which Krasner is notably absent – something that, given that she and Rosenberg had known each other since the 1930s, must have felt like a slap in the face.

5 Cindy Nemser, 'A Conversation with Lee Krasner', *Arts Magazine*, April 1973, p.47; Lee Krasner, quoted in Rose, *Lee Krasner*, p.155.

6 Anne M. Wagner, 'Lee Krasner as L.K.', *Representations*, no.25, Winter 1989, p.45.

7 Regarding the point of the preceding sentence, Robert Hobbs reminds us that following Pollock's death, Krasner 'elaborates on her signature so that it expands to become the armature for the entire painting [*Listen*, 1957] ... Far more than the simple act of affixing her name to a work of art, the umber-colored signature and its extension into the painting come at a time when Krasner was forging a separate identity from Pollock and a period when many Abstract Expressionists had already settled on self-defining schemas known as their 'signature images,' including Pollock's drips, [Mark] Rothko's veils, [Barnett] Newman's zips, [Clyfford] Still's rugged patchwork of stalactitic and stalagmitic forms, [Robert] Motherwell's ripped and torn edges, [Adolph] Gottlieb's primordial Bursts, and Willem de Kooning's women. Whether Krasner chose to be a maverick or accepted this default role as her path, her prominent signature and its underlying and unifying role in *Listen* can be considered a parody of one-image art.' Robert Hobbs, 'Krasner, Mitchell, and Frankenthaler: Nature as Metonym', in Joan Marter (ed.), *Women of Abstract Expressionism* (Denver, CO: Denver Art Museum in association with Yale University Press, 2016), p.61.

8 Ellen G. Landau, *Lee Krasner: A Catalogue Raisonné* (New York: Harry N. Abrams, 1995), p.10. She continues: 'Krasner felt so strongly about her self-image that, in 1943, she actually filed a petition to amend her birth certificate. In later life, with a peremptory wave of her hand, she dismissed as "mistakes" official evidence

of former personas found in extant library and school records.'

9 Ellen G. Landau also cites the 1936 Dada show at the Museum of Modern Art, New York, Surrealism and Russian avant-garde films as points of reference. See Landau, *Catalogue Raisonné*, p.94.

10 Barbara Rose goes so far as to characterize the shapes she would apply as 'left-overs' kept from 'her periodic bouts of artistic housekeeping'. Rose, *Lee Krasner*, p.76.

11 Lee Krasner, quoted in Phyllis Braff, 'From the Studio', *East Hampton Star*, 21 August 1980, clipping in Lee Krasner Papers, Archives of American Art, Smithsonian Institution, Washington DC, Box 13, Folder 1, np.

12 Lee Krasner, quoted in Barbaralee Diamonstein, *Inside New York's Art World* (New York: Rizzoli, 1979), p.205. Before the Stable Gallery show in 1955, some of the collages were shown in 1954 on Main Street in East Hampton, at the House of Books and Music, the bookstore-gallery run by Krasner and Pollock's Springs neighbours Carol and Donald Braider.

13 That size was linked to – or wholly delimited by – the studio space is a fallacy that might be corrected for Pollock too. In 1950 Pollock mounted an exhibition at the Betty Parsons Gallery, hanging more than a dozen paintings measuring 56 centimetres (22 in.) square in stacks alongside his heroically scaled canvases. In these small paintings, the artist dripped enamel across Masonite panels, creating his familiar lustrous skeins. While we are accustomed to understanding Pollock's accomplishments through the mural-like dimensions of his larger works, their diminutive complements recount cause and effect just as expediently. Even more, it is in relation to one another that they mutually articulate themselves, or such is T. J. Clark's point when he writes: 'Bigness needed smallness to register as such.' If size is literal (albeit referential, since inevitably it relates to the body measuring it), scale is metaphorical. T. J. Clark, 'Pollock's Smallness', reprinted in Kirk Varnedoe and Pepe Karmel (eds), *Jackson Pollock: New Approaches* (New York: Museum of Modern Art, 1999), p.21.

14 Rose, *Lee Krasner*, p.86.

15 Lee Krasner, quoted in Cindy Nemser, 'The Indomitable Lee Krasner', *Feminist Art Journal*, Spring 1975, p.7.

16 Lee Krasner, quoted in John Bernard Myers, 'Naming Pictures: Conversations between Lee Krasner and John Bernard Myers', *Artforum*, November 1984, p.71.

17 Hobbs, 'Krasner, Mitchell, and Frankenthaler', p.88.

18 Hilton Kramer, 'Two New Shows – Lee Krasner and Mary Frank', *New York Times*, 6 March 1977, p.87.

19 Paul Brach, 'Lee Krasner: Front and Center', *Art in America*, February 2001, p.98.

20 Lee Krasner, quoted in Myers, 'Naming Pictures', p.71.

BECOMING LEE

Epigraph: From Lee Krasner, National Academy of Design Report Card, 1928–29, quoted in Ellen G. Landau, *Lee Krasner: A Catalogue Raisonné* (New York: Harry N. Abrams, 1995), p.302.

1 Lee Krasner, quoted in Deborah Daw, 'Lee Krasner: On Climbing a Mountain of Porcelain', 1979, p.14. Lee Krasner Papers, Archives of American Art, Smithsonian Institution, Washington DC, Box 10, Folder 9.

2 Lee Krasner, quoted in Esphyr Slobodkina, *Notes of a Biographer*, 3 vols (Great Neck, NY: Urquart-Slobodkina Inc., 1976–83), vol.2, p.242, quoted in Gail Levin, *Lee Krasner: A Biography* (New York: William Morrow, 2011), p.54.

LIFE DRAWING

Epigraph: Lee Krasner, quoted in *Lee Krasner: The Long View*, dir. Barbara Rose, American Federation of Arts, New York, 1978, colour, 30 minutes.

1 Gail Levin, *Lee Krasner: A Biography* (New York: William Morrow, 2011), pp.121–22.

2 Lee Krasner, quoted in Barbara Novak, 'Lee Krasner Interview', WGBH-TV, 1979, p.25. Lee Krasner Papers, Archives of American Art, Smithsonian Institution, Washington DC.

3 Ellen G. Landau, 'Lee Krasner's Early Career, Part One: "Pushing in Different Directions"', *Arts Magazine*, October 1981, p.113.

4 *Ibid.*, pp.113–14; Micheal Cannell, 'An Interview with Lee Krasner', *Arts Magazine*, September 1984, vol.59, no.1, p.87.

WAR SERVICE WINDOWS

Epigraph: Lee Krasner, quoted in Barbara Rose, 'Tape-recorded Interview with Lee Krasner', 31 July 1966, p.17. Barbara Rose Papers, Archives of American Art, Smithsonian Institution, Washington DC.

1 Barbara Rose, *Lee Krasner: A Retrospective*, exhib. cat. (Houston and New York: Museum of Fine Arts and Museum of Modern Art, 1983), p.45.

2 Ellen G. Landau, 'Lee Krasner's Early Career, Part One: "Pushing in Different Directions"', *Arts Magazine*, October 1981, p.118.

3 Lee Krasner, quoted in Anne Bowen Parsons, 'Interview with Lee Krasner', 23 August 1967, p.1. Archives of American Art, Smithsonian Institution, Washington DC.

4 Francis O'Connor, quoted in Parsons, 'Interview with Lee Krasner', p.1.

LITTLE IMAGES

Epigraph: Lee Krasner, quoted in Deborah Daw, 'Lee Krasner: On Climbing a Mountain of Porcelain', 1979, p.4. Lee Krasner Papers, Archives of American Art, Smithsonian Institution, Washington DC, Box 10, Folder 9.

1 Lee Krasner, quoted in Cindy Nemser, 'Lee Krasner', *Art Talk: Conversations with 12 Women Artists* (New York: Scribner, 1975), p.89.

2 Ann Pringle, 'Modern Houses Inside and Out', *New York Herald Tribune*, 20 September 1948, quoted in Ellen G. Landau, 'Lee Krasner's Early Career, Part Two: The 1940s', *Arts Magazine*, November 1981, p.83.

STABLE GALLERY

Epigraph: Lee Krasner, quoted in Ellen G. Landau, *Lee Krasner: A Catalogue Raisonné* (New York: Harry N. Abrams, 1995), p.146.

1   Lee Krasner, quoted in Cindy Nemser, 'A Conversation with Lee Krasner', *Arts Magazine*, vol. 47, no. 6, April 1973, p.45.
2   Clement Greenberg, quoted in Bryan Robertson, *Lee Krasner: Paintings, Drawings and Collages* (London: Whitechapel Art Gallery, 1965), p.4.
3   Stuart Preston, 'Modern Work in Diverse Shows: Contemporary American and Italian Work in New Displays', *New York Times*, 2 October 1955, p.15.
4   *Ibid.*
5   Lee Krasner, quoted in Gaby Rodgers, 'She Has Been There Once or Twice: An Interview with Lee Krasner', 1977, p.4. Lee Krasner Papers, Archives of American Art, Smithsonian Institution, Washington DC, Box 9, Folder 48.

PROPHECY

Epigraph: Lee Krasner, quoted in Eleanor Munro, *Originals: American Women Artists* (New York: Simon & Schuster, 1979), p.116
1   Lee Krasner, quoted in Gail Levin, *Lee Krasner: A Biography* (New York: William Morrow, 2011), p.305.
2   Lee Krasner, letter to Jackson Pollock, 21 July 1956, quoted in Levin, *Lee Krasner*, p.309.
3   Lee Krasner, quoted in Louise Elliott Rago, 'We Interview Lee Krasner', *School Arts*, 60, September 1960, p.32.

NIGHT JOURNEYS

Epigraph: Lee Krasner, quoted in Richard Howard, 'A Conversation with Lee Krasner', December 1978, p.1. Lee Krasner Papers, Archives of American Art, Smithsonian Institution, Washington DC (hereafter 'LK Papers'), Box 10, Folder 3.
1   Lee Krasner, quoted in Eleanor Munro, *Originals: American Women Artists* (New York: Simon & Schuster, 1979), p.116.
2   Lee Krasner, quoted in Cindy Nemser, 'A Conversation with Lee Krasner', *Arts Magazine*, vol. 47, no. 6, April 1973, p.47.
3   *Ibid.*
4   Lee Krasner, quoted in Deborah Daw, 'Lee Krasner: On Climbing a Mountain of Porcelain', 1979, p.27. LK Papers, Box 10, Folder 9.

PRIMARY SERIES

Epigraph: Lee Krasner, quoted in Louise Elliott Rago, 'We Interview Lee Krasner', *School Arts*, 60, September 1960, p.32.
1   Henri Matisse, quoted in Hilary Spurling, *The Unknown Matisse: A Life of Henri Matisse – The Early Years, 1869–1908* (Berkeley: University of California Press, 1998), p.322.

2   Lee Krasner, quoted in Emily Wasserman, 'Lee Krasner in Mid-Career', *Artforum*, vol. 6, no. 7, March 1968, p.42.
3   Lee Krasner, quoted in Cindy Nemser, 'A Conversation with Lee Krasner', *Arts Magazine*, April 1973, p.48.

PALINGENESIS

Epigraph: Lee Krasner, quoted in Emily Wasserman, 'Interview with Lee Krasner Pollock', January 1968, p.3. Lee Krasner Papers, Archives of American Art, Smithsonian Institution, Washington DC (hereafter 'LK Papers'), Box 9, Folder 46.
1   Phyllis Dressler, 'New York Letter', *Art International*, vol. 17, no. 41, September 1973, p. 41.
2   Robert Hughes, 'Bursting Out of the Shadows', *Time*, 14 November 1983, p.93.
3   Stuart Preston, 'Modern Work in Diverse Shows: Contemporary American and Italian Work in New Displays', *New York Times*, 2 October 1955, p.15.
4   Cindy Nemser, 'A Conversation with Lee Krasner', *Arts Magazine*, vol. 47, no. 6, April 1973, p.48.
5   Barbara Rose, 'Interview with Lee Krasner', March 1972, np. LK Papers, Box 9, Folder 47.
6   Marcia Tucker, *Lee Krasner: Large Paintings*, exhib. cat. (New York: Whitney Museum of American Art, 1973), p.17.

ELEVEN WAYS

Epigraph: Lee Krasner, quoted in Eleanor Munro, *Originals: American Women Artists* (New York: Simon & Schuster, 1979), p.119.
1   Lee Krasner, quoted in Gail Levin, *Lee Krasner: A Biography* (New York: William Morrow, 2011), p.412.
2   Lee Krasner, quoted in John Bernard Myers, 'Naming Pictures', *Art Forum*, vol. 23, no. 3, November 1984, p.71.
3   Donald B. Kuspit, 'Lee Krasner at Pace', *Art in America*, 1977, p.136.

REFLECTIONS

1   Irving Sandler, *Abstract Expressionism: The Triumph of American Painting* (New York: Praeger, 1970), p.vi. Krasner belonged in this book on the movement's first generation.
2   *Abstract Expressionism: The Formative Years*, co-curated by Gail Levin and Robert C. Hobbs, was shown at the Herbert F. Johnson Museum at Cornell University and the Whitney Museum of American Art, New York. It also travelled to the Seibu Museum of Art in Tokyo, Japan.
3   See Gail Levin, *Lee Krasner: A Biography* (New York: William Morrow, 2011).

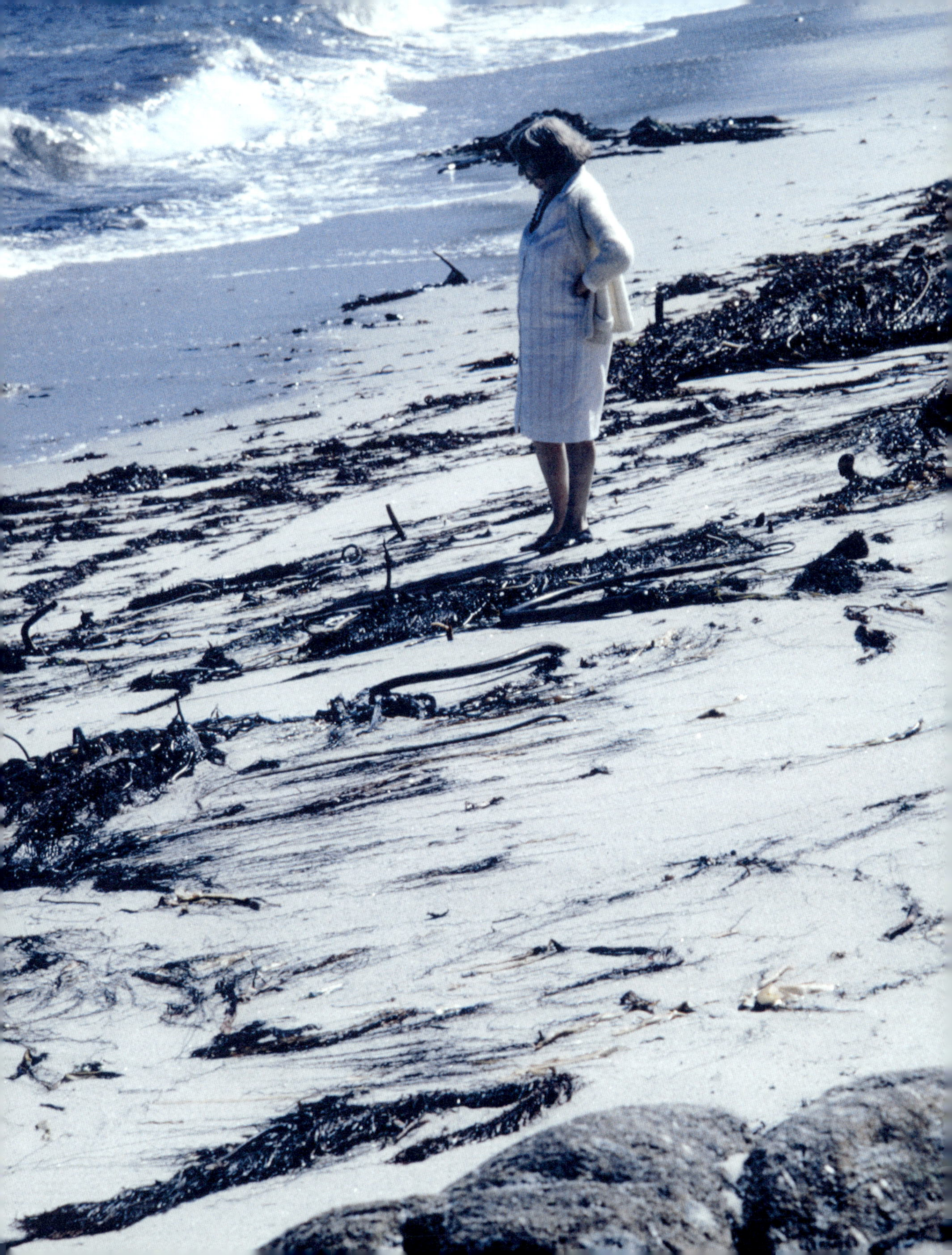

AAA   Archives of American Art,
           Smithsonian Institution,
           Washington DC
LK Papers Lee Krasner Papers

INTERVIEWS

Barbara Cavaliere, 'Interview with Lee Krasner',
LK Papers, AAA, Box 9, Folder 43, undated

Bruce Glaser, 'An Interview with Lee Krasner: An
Inquiry into the Background of the New American
Painting', LK Papers, AAA, Box 9, Folder 42, undated

Bruce Glaser, 'Interview with Lee Krasner', *Artforum*,
LK Papers, AAA, Box 9, Folder 42, undated

Louise Elliott Rago, 'We Interview Lee Krasner',
School Arts, 60, September 1960, pp.31–32

Dorothy Seckler, 'Oral History Interview with
Lee Krasner', Session One, 2 November 1964,
AAA

Andrew Forge, 'Interview between Lee Krasner
and Andrew Forge', *Insert for New Comment*,
LK Papers, AAA, Box 9, Folder 45, 13 October 1965

Barbara Rose, 'Tape-recorded Interview with Lee
Krasner', Barbara Rose Papers, AAA, 31 July 1966

Bruce Glaser, 'Jackson Pollock: An Interview with
Lee Krasner', *Arts Magazine*, vol. 41, no. 6, April
1967, pp.36–39

Francine du Plessix and Cleve Gray, 'Who Was
Jackson Pollock?', *Art in America*, May–June 1967,
pp.48–59

Anne Bowen Parsons, 'Interview with Lee Krasner',
AAA, 23 August 1967

Dorothy Seckler, 'Oral History Interview with
Lee Krasner', Session Two, 14 December 1967,
AAA

Emily Wasserman, 'Interview with Lee Krasner
Pollock', LK Papers, AAA, Box 9, Folder 46,
9 January 1968

Dorothy Seckler, 'Oral History Interview with
Lee Krasner', Session Three, 11 April 1968,
AAA

B. H. Friedman, 'An Interview with Lee Krasner
Pollock', in *Jackson Pollock: Black and White*,
exhib. cat. (New York: Marlborough-Gerson Gallery,
1969), pp.7–9

Doloris Holmes, 'Interview with Lee Krasner',
LK Papers, AAA, Box 15, Folder 12, 1972

Barbara Rose, 'Interview with Lee Krasner',
LK Papers, AAA, Box 9, Folder 47, March 1972

Barbara Rose, 'American Great: Lee Krasner',
Vogue, June 1972, pp.118–21, cont. p.154

Cindy Nemser, 'A Conversation with Lee Krasner',
Arts Magazine, April 1973, pp.43–48

Judy Seigel, 'Women's Panels at the CAA', *Feminist
Art Journal*, Spring 1973, pp.10–15

Roberta Brandes Gratz, 'Daily Closeup: After
Pollock', *New York Post*, 6 December 1973

Cindy Nemser, 'Lee Krasner', in *Art Talk:
Conversations with 12 Women Artists* (New York:
Scribner, 1975), pp.80–111

Cindy Nemser, 'The Indomitable Lee Krasner',
Feminist Art Journal, Spring 1975, pp.4–9

Eleanor Munro, untitled manuscript, LK Papers,
AAA, Box 10, Folder 8, c. 1977

Gaby Rodgers, 'She Has Been There Once or
Twice: An Interview with Lee Krasner', LK Papers,
AAA, Box 9, Folder 48, 1977

David Bourdon, 'Lee Krasner: I'm Embracing the
Past', *Village Voice*, 7 March 1977, p.57

Barbara Cavaliere, 'Interview with Lee Krasner',
LK Papers, AAA, Reel 3774, c. 1978

Barbaralee Diamonstein, 'Inside New York's Art
World: Lee Krasner', LK Papers, AAA, Box 9, Folder
49, 16 February 1978

Barbara Rose, 'Interview with Lee Krasner',
LK Papers, AAA, Box 10, Folder 1, 21 June 1978

Unknown interviewer [B. R.], 'Pollock's Studio:
Interview with Lee Krasner', LK Papers, AAA,
27 June 1978

Helen Weinberg, 'Interview with Lee Krasner',
LK Papers, AAA, Box 10, Folder 2, Summer 1978

Unknown interviewer, 'Lee Krasner in Her Studio,
New York', LK Papers, AAA, Box 9, Folder 44, 21
September 1978

Richard Howard, 'A Conversation with Lee
Krasner', LK Papers, AAA, Box 10, Folder 3,
December 1978

Richard Howard, 'A Conversation with Lee Krasner',
in *Lee Krasner: Paintings 1959–1962*, exhib. cat.
(New York: Pace Gallery, 1979), np

Eleanor Munro, *Originals: American Women Artists*
(New York: Simon & Schuster, 1979), pp.100–19

Ellen G. Landau, 'An Interview with Lee Krasner
about John Graham', LK Papers, AAA, Box 10,
Folder 4, 28 February 1979

Flora Lewis, 'Two Paris Shows à la Pollock',
New York Times, October 1979, p.C21

Barbara Novak, 'Lee Krasner Interview', WGBH
New Television Workshop Videotape Archive of
the Arts, AAA, October 1979

Barbara Rose, 'Jackson Pollock at Work: An Interview
with Lee Krasner', *Partisan Review*, vol. 47, no. 1,
1980, pp.82–92

Barbara Cavaliere, 'An Interview with Lee Krasner',
Flash Art, January–February 1980, pp.14–16

Richard Lorber, 'Women Artists on Women in Art',
Portfolio, February–March 1980, pp.68–69

Phyllis Braff, 'From the Studio', *East Hampton
Star*, LK Papers, AAA, Box 13, Folder 1, 21 August
1980, np

Barbara Delatiner, 'Lee Krasner: Beyond Pollock',
New York Times, 9 August 1981

Grace Glueck, 'Scenes From a Marriage: Krasner
and Pollock', *ARTnews*, December 1981, pp.57–61

Michael Cannell, 'An Interview with Lee Krasner',
Arts Magazine, September 1984, pp.87–89

John Bernard Myers, 'Naming Pictures:
Conversations between Lee Krasner and John
Bernard Myers', *Artforum*, vol. 23, no. 3, November
1984, pp.69–73

EXHIBITION CATALOGUES

Alfonso Ossorio, *Exhibition of Recent Paintings by
Lee Krasner* (New York: Howard Wise Gallery, 1960)

Bryan Robertson, *Lee Krasner: Paintings, Drawings
and Collages* (London: Whitechapel Art Gallery, 1965)

Lee Krasner (New York: Marlborough-Gerson
Gallery, 1968)

Lee Krasner: Recent Gouaches (New York:
Marlborough-Gerson Gallery, 1969)

Jason McCoy and Carol Lindsley, *Lee Krasner: Recent Gouaches* (San Francisco: Gallery Reese Palley, 1969)

Lee Krasner: Recent Paintings (New York: Marlborough Gallery, 1973)

Marcia Tucker, *Lee Krasner: Large Paintings* (New York: Whitney Museum of American Art, 1973)

Lee Krasner: Collages and Works on Paper, 1933–1974 (Washington DC: Corcoran Gallery of Art, 1975)

Gene Baro, *Twelve Americans: Masters of Collage* (New York: Andrew Crispo Gallery, 1977)

Lee Krasner: Eleven Ways to Use the Words to See (New York: Pace Gallery, 1977)

Linda L. Cathcart, *American Painting of the 1970s* (Buffalo, NY: Albright-Knox Art Gallery, 1978)

Robert Hobbs and Gail Levin, *Abstract Expressionism: The Formative Years* (Ithaca, NY: Cornell University Press, 1978)

Lee Krasner: Works on Paper, 1938 to 1977 (Houston: Janie C. Lee Gallery, 1978)

5 Action Painters of the 50s: Willem de Kooning, Franz Kline, Lee Krasner, Robert Motherwell, Jackson Pollock (New York: Pace Gallery, 1979)

Lee Krasner/Solstice (New York: Pace Gallery, 1981)

Barbara Rose, *Krasner/Pollock: A Working Relationship* (New York: Grey Art Gallery and Study Center, 1981)

Constance Schwartz, *The Abstract Expressionists and Their Precursors* (Roslyn, NY: Nassau County Museum of Fine Art, 1981)

Gene Baro, *Carnegie International* (Pittsburgh: Carnegie Institute, Museum of Art, 1982)

June Blum, *Women's Art: Miles Apart* (New York: Aaron Berman Gallery, 1982)

Linda L. Cathcart, *The Americans: The Collage* (Houston: Contemporary Arts Museum, 1982)

Lee Krasner: Paintings from the Late Fifties (New York: Robert Miller Gallery, 1982)

Barbara Rose, *Lee Krasner: A Retrospective* (Houston and New York: Museum of Fine Arts and Museum of Modern Art, 1983)

Collage Expanded (New York: Visual Arts Museum, 1984)

Sam Hunter (ed.), *An American Renaissance: Painting and Sculpture Since 1940* (Fort Lauderdale, FL: Museum of Art, 1986)

Bryan Robertson and Robert Hughes, *Lee Krasner, Collages* (New York: Robert Miller Gallery, 1986)

Sandor Kuthy and Ellen G. Landau, *Lee Krasner, Jackson Pollock: Künstlerpaare, Künstlerfreunde = Lee Krasner, Jackson Pollock: Dialogues d'artistes, résonances* (Bern: Kunstmuseum Bern, 1989)

Lilian Orlowsky, *The Provocative Years, 1935–1945: The Hans Hofmann School and Its Students in Provincetown* (Provincetown, MA: Provincetown Art Association & Museum, 1990)

Edward Albee, Lisa Liebmann and Stephen Westfall (eds), *Lee Krasner: Paintings from 1965–1970* (New York: Robert Miller Gallery, 1991)

John Cheim (ed.), *Lee Krasner: Umber Paintings, 1959–1962* (New York: Robert Miller Gallery, 1993)

Ellen G. Landau, *Lee Krasner: Collages, 1953–1955* (New York: Jason McCoy Inc., 1995)

Lee Krasner: The Nature of the Body, Works from 1933 to 1984 (East Hampton, NY: Guild Hall Museum, 1995)

Edward Albee, *Lee Krasner: Collages and Paintings* (Los Angeles: Tasende Gallery, 1998)

Robert Hobbs, *Lee Krasner* (New York: Independent Curators International in association with Harry N. Abrams, 1999)

Abstrakter Expressionismus in Amerika: Lee Krasner, Hedda Sterne, Elaine de Kooning, Joan Mitchell, Helen Frankenthaler (Kaiserslautern: Pfalzgalerie, 2001)

Barbara Rose, *Dialogue: Lee Krasner and Jackson Pollock* (New York: Robert Miller Gallery, 2005)

Katy Siegel (ed.), *High Times, Hard Times: New York Painting, 1967–1975* (New York: Distributed Art Publishers, 2006)

Gail Levin, *Lee Krasner: Little Image Paintings 1946–1950* (East Hampton, NY: Pollock-Krasner House and Study Center, 2008)

Norman L. Kleeblatt and Stephen Brown, *From the Margins: Lee Krasner/Norman Lewis, 1945–1952* (New York: Jewish Museum, 2014)

David Anfam (ed.), *Abstract Expressionism* (London: Royal Academy of Arts, 2016)

Lee Krasner (New York: Robert Miller Gallery, 2016)

Joan Marter (ed.), *Women of Abstract Expressionism* (Denver, CO: Denver Art Museum in association with Yale University Press, 2016)

PRESS & REVIEWS

Patricia C. Johnson, 'On Her Own', *Houston Chronicle*, date unknown

Alex Beard, 'Alex Rosenberg on Lee Krasner', *Hamptons*, 26 July [year unknown], p.25

Stuart Preston, 'Among One-Man Shows', *New York Times*, 21 October 1951, p.105

Robert Goodnough, 'Lee Krasner', *ARTnews*, November 1951

Stuart Preston, 'A Melange of Summer Shows; East Hampton Abstraction – Silvermine Guild – Local Shows', *New York Times*, 2 August 1953, p.7

Stuart Preston, 'Modern Work in Diverse Shows; Contemporary American and Italian Work in New Displays', *New York Times*, 2 October 1955, p.15

Fairfield Porter, 'Lee Krasner', *ARTnews*, November 1955

B. H. Friedman, 'Mrs Jackson Pollock', *Time*, 17 March 1958, p.67

Stuart Preston, 'Art: Allusive Portraits', *New York Times*, 19 November 1960, p.43

Emily Genauer, 'Artists Turning to Dark Myths', *New York Herald Tribune*, 20 November 1960, p.21

Vivien Raynor, 'Lee Krasner' [Wise Gallery], *Arts Magazine*, vol.35, January 1961, p.54

Vivien Raynor, 'Lee Krasner' [Wise Gallery], *Arts Magazine*, May–June 1962, pp.100–01

'The Abstract Art of Lee Krasner', *The Times*, September 1965

Nigel Gosling, 'A Portent from Brooklyn', *The Observer*, 26 September 1965

John Russell, 'Germany's Other Man of Iron', *Sunday Times*, 3 October 1965

Sheldon Williams, 'London Retrospective for Abstract Pioneer', *Herald Tribune* (Paris edition), 4 October 1965

Lawrence Campbell, 'Of Lilith and Lettuce', *ARTnews*, March 1968, pp.42–43, 61–64

Emily Wasserman, 'Lee Krasner in Mid-Career', *Artforum*, vol.6, no.7, March 1968, pp.38–43

Grace Glueck, '… And Mr Kenneth Does Her Hair', *New York Times*, 17 March 1968, p.34

C. N. [Cindy Nemser?], 'Lee Krasner at Marlborough-Gerson', *Arts Magazine*, April 1968, p.57

Grace Glueck, 'Women Artists Charge Bias at Modern Museum', *New York Times*, 13 April 1972, p.36

Hilton Kramer, 'Lee Krasner', *New York Times*, 28 April 1973, p.20

Unknown author, '"21 Over 60" Show Talent Is Ageless', *New York Times*, 29 July 1973, p.86

Phyllis Dressler, 'New York Letter', *Art International*, vol.17, no.41, September 1973

A. T. Baker, 'Out of the Shade', *Time*, 19 November 1973, pp.76–77

Bryan Robertson, 'The Nature of Lee Krasner', *Art in America*, November–December 1973, pp.83–87

Barbara Rose, 'The Best Midwestern Museum in New York?', *New York Magazine*, December 1973, p.102

Emily Genauer, 'Art & the Artist', *New York Post*, 1 December 1973

'Lee Krasner, The Whitney Museum', *Artforum*, vol.12, no.2, 1974, pp.72–73

Al Brunelle, 'Lee Krasner: Large Paintings', *ARTnews*, no.73, January 1974

Griffin Smith, 'Lee Krasner – A Re-evaluation at Last', *Miami Herald*, 17 March 1974

Griffin Smith, 'A New Bass?', *ARTnews*, vol.73, no.54, May 1974, p.54

Barbara Rose, 'Lee Krasner and the Origins of Abstract Expressionism', *Arts Magazine*, February 1977, pp.96–100

Jerry Tallmer, 'Scissors, Paste & Bits of Survival', *New York Post*, 19 February 1977, p.10

Hilton Kramer, 'Two New Shows – Lee Krasner and Mary Frank', *New York Times*, 6 March 1977, p.87

Barbara Cavaliere, 'Lee Krasner Pace [Gallery]', *Arts Magazine*, April 1977, p.26

Donald B. Kuspit, 'Lee Krasner at Pace', *Art in America*, November–December 1977, pp.135–36

Hilton Kramer, 'Making Vivid the Spirit of the New York School', *New York Times*, 16 April 1978, p.D26

Barbara Cavaliere, 'Five Action Painters of the Fifties', *Arts Magazine*, vol.54, no.21, 1979, p.21

Hilton Kramer, 'Art: Elegiac Works of Lee Krasner', *New York Times*, 9 February 1979, p.25

Eleanor Munro, 'Krasner in the Sixties Free for the Big Sixties', *Art World*, vol.3, no.6, February–March 1979, pp.1, 6

Helen A. Harrison, 'Artists Find a Special Light on LI', *New York Times*, 15 February 1981

Barbara Cavaliere, 'Lee Krasner Pace [Gallery]', *Arts Magazine*, vol.55, June 1981, p.34

John Russell, 'Lee Krasner and Jackson Pollock Painting Show in Hamptons', *New York Times*, 14 August 1981

Ann Pringle, 'Modern Houses Inside and Out', *New York Herald Tribune*, 20 September 1948

Amei Wallach, 'Lee Krasner: Out of Jackson Pollock's Shadow', *Newsday*, 23 September 1981

Carter Ratcliff, 'Lee Krasner at Pace', *Art in America*, October 1981, p.139

Hilton Kramer, 'Art View: Social Art and the Pollock Krasner Connection', *New York Times*, 15 November 1981

Paul Brach, 'Tandem Paint: Krasner/Pollock', *Art in America*, March 1982, pp.92–95

Michael Kohn, 'Lee Krasner: Paintings from the Fifties' [Robert Miller Gallery], *Flash Art*, January 1983, p.62

Stephen Westfall, 'The Expressionist Image', *Arts Magazine*, January 1983, p.39

Barbara Gallati, 'Lee Krasner' [Robert Miller Gallery], *Arts Magazine*, February 1983, pp.33–34

Lawrence Campbell, 'Lee Krasner at Robert Miller', *Art in America*, March 1983, pp.150–51

Amei Wallach, 'Krasner's Triumph', *Vogue*, November 1983, pp.442–45, cont. 501–02

Robert Hughes, 'Bursting Out of the Shadows', *Time*, 14 November 1983, pp.92–93

Susie Kalil, 'Lee Krasner: A Life's Work', *Artweek*, vol.14, no.42, 10 December 1983, pp.1, 20

Ellen G. Landau, 'Lee Krasner's Past Continuous', *ARTnews*, vol.83, February 1984, pp.68–76

Ed Hill and Suzanne Bloom, 'Lee Krasner, Museum of Fine Arts, Houston', *Artforum*, vol.22, May 1984, p.93

Marcia E. Vetrocq, 'An Independent Tack: Lee Krasner', *Art in America*, May 1984, pp.136–45

Richard Howard, 'Lee Listening: Lee Krasner Pollock', *Grand Street*, vol.4, no.1, Autumn 1984, pp.183–86

Kay Larson, 'Lee Krasner's Enduring Gestures', *New York Magazine*, 14 January 1985, pp.48–49

Arthur C. Danto, 'Lee Krasner: A Retrospective', *The Nation*, February 1985, pp.219–22

Kathleen Paradiso, 'Lee Krasner: A Retrospective', *Women Artists News*, Spring 1985, pp.10–11

Jane Bell, 'Lee Krasner: Robert Miller', *ARTnews*, March 1987, p.147

Robert Hobbs, 'Lee Krasner: A Retrospective', *Woman's Art Journal*, vol.8, no.1, Spring–Summer 1987, pp.43–45

Stephen Polcari, 'Lee Krasner and Abstract Expressionism', University Gallery, State University of New York at Stony Brook, 1988, pp.3–7

Jennifer Donelan, 'With Splatters, Dribbles and History, Pollock/Krasner', *Village Times*, July 1988, pp.L6–L7

'Krasner and Pollock in Bern', *Flash Art*, January–February 1990, p.151

Stephen Polcari, 'In the Shadow of an Innovator', *Art International*, Autumn 1990, pp.105–07

Robert G. Edelman, 'Lee Krasner at Robert Miller', *Art in America*, July 1991, pp.118–19

Michael Kimmelman, 'Lee Krasner: Umber Paintings 1952–1962', *New York Times*, 15 January 1993, p.C22

John Ash, 'Lee Krasner: Robert Miller', *Artforum*, May 1993, pp.102–03

'Lee Krasner: Robert Miller, New York', *Flash Art*, May–June 1993, p.125

Helen A. Harrison, 'The Roof, the Leak, the Guest and His Lover', *Hamptons*, June 1995, p.160

Phyllis Braff, 'Lee Krasner's Use of Figure and Her Treatment of Nature', *New York Times*, 27 August 1995, p.16

M. G. Lord, 'Lee Krasner, Before and After the Ball was Over', *New York Times*, 27 August 1995, pp.31–32

Lee Siegel, 'Lee Krasner at Jason McCoy', *ARTnews*, May 1996, pp.134–35

Joan Marter, 'Lee Krasner: A Catalogue Raisonné by Ellen G. Landau', *Art Journal*, vol.55, no.3, Autumn 1996, pp.88–89

Martica Sawin, 'Reviews of R. Hobbs, "Lee Krasner" (1993), E. G. Landau, "Lee Krasner: A Catalogue Raisonné" (1995), and M. Luyekx, R. Slivka, "Elaine de Kooning: The Spirit of Abstract Expressionism, Selected Writings" (1994)', *Woman's Art Journal*, vol.18, no.2, Fall 1997 – Winter 1998, pp.31–33

Suzanne Muchnic, 'Lee Krasner, Tasende', *ARTnews*, May 1998, p.178

Kenneth Baker, 'More than Mrs Pollock: Considering the Many Sides of Lee Krasner', *ARTnews*, September 1999, pp.132–33

Hilton Kramer, 'Pollock's Widow Krasner is no Postmodernist', *The Observer*, 11 June 2000

Michael Brenson, 'Natural Woman', *New York Magazine*, 10 October 2000, pp.100–01

Greta Berman, 'Lee Krasner and the Brooklyn Museum of Art', *Julliard Journal*, December 2000 – January 2001, p.14

Phong Bui, 'Lee Krasner at the Brooklyn Museum of Art', *Brooklyn Rail*, no.43–44, December 2000 – January 2001, pp.12–13

Barbara Pollack, 'Lee Krasner', *ARTnews*, January 2001, p.150

David Anfam, 'Lee Krasner: Brooklyn', *Burlington Magazine*, vol.143, no.1,177, April 2001, pp.243–44

Ann Landi, '"Dialogue: Lee Krasner and Jackson Pollock" Robert Miller', *ARTnews*, April 2006, p.140

Jonathan Gilmore, 'Pollock & Krasner at Robert Miller; Pollock at Washburn; Pollock & Louis Comfort Tiffany at Tilton', *Art in America*, September 2006, pp.167–68

Robert G. Edelman, 'Krasner's "Little Image" Paintings', *Artnet*, September 2008

Karen Rosenberg, 'Lee Krasner and Norman Lewis at the Jewish Museum', *New York Times*, 11 September 2014, p.C30

ARTICLES & BOOKS

Aleisha E. Barton, '"Fuchsia Lipstick": The Domestication of Lee Krasner in Post-War Criticism', paper given at the Richard A. Harrison Symposium, Lawrence University, Appleton, WI, 2015

John Berger, 'A Kind of Sharing', in *Keeping a Rendezvous* (New York: Pantheon Books, 1991), first published in *The Guardian*, 23 November 1989

John Berger, *Portraits: John Berger on Artists* (London: Verso Books, 2015)

Paul Brach, 'Lee Krasner: Front and Center', *Art in America*, February 2001, pp.91–99

Marcia Brennan, *Modernism's Masculine Subjects: Matisse, the New York School and Post-Painterly Abstraction* (Cambridge, MA: MIT Press, 2004)

Anna C. Chave, 'Pollock and Krasner: Script and Postscript', *RES: Anthropology and Aesthetics*, no. 24, Autumn 1993, pp.95–111

Deborah Daw, 'Lee Krasner: On Climbing a Mountain of Porcelain', LK Papers, AAA, Box 10, Folder 9, 1979

Ines Janet Engelmann, *Jackson Pollock and Lee Krasner* (Munich: Prestel, 2007)

Elsa Honig Fine, *Women & Art: A History of Women Painters and Sculptors from the Renaissance to the 20th Century* (Montclair, NJ, and London: Allanheld & Schram/Prior, 1978)

B. H. Friedman, 'Manhattan Mosaic', *Craft Horizons*, vol. 19, no. 1, January/February 1959, pp.25–29

Mary Gabriel, *Ninth Street Women: Lee Krasner, Elaine de Kooning, Grace Hartigan, Joan Mitchell, and Helen Frankenthaler – Five Painters and the Movement that Changed Modern Art* (Boston, MA: Little Brown and Company, 2018)

Ann Eden Gibson, *Abstract Expressionism: Other Politics* (New Haven, CT: Yale University Press, 1997)

Ann Gibson, 'Lee Krasner and Women's Innovations in American Abstract Painting', *Woman's Art Journal*, vol. 28, no. 2, Fall–Winter 2007, pp.11–19

Uta Grosenick (ed.), *Women Artists in the 20th and 21st Century* (Cologne and New York: Taschen, 2001)

John Gruen, *The Party's Over Now: Reminiscences of the Fifties – New York's Artists, Writers, Musicians, and Their Friends* (New York: Viking Press, 1972)

Andrew Hardman, 'Studio Habits: Francis Bacon, Lee Krasner, Jackson Pollock and Agnes Martin', unpublished PhD thesis, University of Manchester, 2014

Helen A. Harrison, *An Exquisite Corpse: Death in Surrealist New York* (Mira Digital Publishing, 2016)

Daniel L. Haxall, 'Collage and the Nature of Order: Lee Krasner's Pastoral Vision', *Woman's Art Journal*, vol. 28, no. 2, Fall–Winter 2007, pp.20–27

Daniel L. Haxall, 'Cut and Paste Abstraction: Politics, Form, and Identity in Abstract Expressionist Collage', unpublished doctoral thesis, Pennsylvania State University, May 2009

Barbara Hess, *Abstract Expressionism* (Cologne: Taschen, 2016)

Robert Hobbs, *Lee Krasner* (New York: Abbeville Press, 1993)

Robert Hobbs, 'Lee Krasner's Skepticism and Her Emergent Postmodernism', *Woman's Art Journal*, vol. 28, no. 2, Fall–Winter 2007, pp.3–10

Robert Hughes, *Nothing if Not Critical* (London: Penguin, 1992)

'Jackson Pollock: Is He the Greatest Living Painter in the United States?', *Life*, 8 August 1949, pp.42–45

Sidney Janis, *Abstract and Surrealist Art in America* (New York: Reynal & Hitchcock, 1944)

Pepe Karmel (ed.), *Jackson Pollock: Key Interviews, Articles, and Reviews* (New York: Museum of Modern Art, 1999)

Ellen G. Landau, 'Lee Krasner's Early Career, Part One: "Pushing in Different Directions"', *Arts Magazine*, October 1981, pp.110–22

Ellen G. Landau, 'Lee Krasner's Early Career, Part Two: The 1940s', *Arts Magazine*, November 1981, pp.80–89

Ellen G. Landau, *Lee Krasner: A Catalogue Raisonné* (New York: Harry N. Abrams, 1995)

Ellen G. Landau, 'Channeling Desire: Lee Krasner's Collages of the Early 1950s', *Woman's Art Journal*, vol. 18, no. 2, Autumn 1997 – Winter 1998, pp.27–30

Ellen G. Landau (ed.), *Reading Abstract Expressionism: Context and Critique* (New Haven, CT: Yale University Press, 2005)

Trisha Laughlin, 'Lee Krasner and the Decorative Impulse in Modern Art', *Art Criticism*, vol. 10, no. 2, 1995, pp.32–54

Gail Levin, 'Beyond the Pale: Lee Krasner and Jewish Culture', *Woman's Art Journal*, vol. 28, no. 2, Fall–Winter 2007, pp.28–34

Gail Levin, *Lee Krasner: A Biography* (New York: William Morrow, 2011)

Gail Levin, 'The Extraordinary Interventions of Alfonso Ossorio, Patron and Collector of Jackson Pollock and Lee Krasner', *Archives of American Art Journal*, vol. 50, no. 1/2, Spring 2011, pp.4–19

Joan Marter, 'Negotiating Abstraction: Lee Krasner, Mercedes Carles Matter, and the Hofmann Years', *Woman's Art Journal*, vol. 28, no. 2, Fall–Winter 2007, pp.35–39

Cindy Nemser, 'Lee Krasner's Paintings 1946–49', *Artforum*, December 1973, pp.61–65

Francis V. O'Connor and Eugene V. Thaw (eds), *Jackson Pollock: A Catalogue Raisonné of Paintings, Drawings and Other Works* (New Haven, CT: Yale University Press, 1978)

Griselda Pollock, 'Cockfights and Other Parades: Gesture, Difference, and the Staging of Meaning in Three Paintings by Zoffany, Pollock, and Krasner', *Oxford Art Journal*, vol. 26, no. 3, 2003, pp.143–65

Jeffrey Potter, *To a Violent Grave: An Oral Biography of Jackson Pollock* (Wainscott, NY: Pushcart Press, 1987)

Françoise S. Puniello and Halina R. Rusak, *Abstract Expressionist Women Painters: An Annotated Bibliography* (London: Scarecrow Press, 1996)

Mark Stevens, 'The American Masters', *Newsweek*, 2 January 1984, pp.66–68

Anne M. Wagner, 'Lee Krasner as LK', *Representations*, no. 25, Winter 1989, pp.42–57

Anne M. Wagner, *Three Artists (Three Women): Modernism and the Art of Hesse, Krasner, and O'Keeffe* (Berkeley: University of California Press, 1996)

Reba White Williams, 'The Prints of Lee Krasner', *Print Quarterly*, vol. 18, no. 4, December 2001, pp.396–41

Compiled by Saskia Flower

Page 52: *Self-Portrait*, 1929–30
Oil and graphite on paper, 16.5 × 13.3 cm
(6 ½ × 5 ¼ in.), The Metropolitan Museum of Art,
New York, gift of the Pollock-Krasner Foundation,
1997 (1997.403.2)

Page 53: *Self-Portrait*, c. 1928
Oil on linen, 76.5 × 63.8 cm (30 ⅛ × 25 ⅛ in.),
The Jewish Museum, New York. Purchase: Esther
Leah Ritz Bequest; B. Gerald Cantor, Lady Kathleen
Epstein, and Louis E. and Rosalyn M. Schecter
Gifts, by exchange; Fine Arts Acquisitions Committee
Fund; and Miriam Handler Fund, 2008-32

Page 54: *Self-Portrait*, c. 1931–33
Oil on linen, 45.7 × 40.6 cm (18 × 16 in.),
Pollock-Krasner Foundation, New York

Page 55: *Self-Portrait*, c. 1929
Oil on canvas, 76.2 × 81.6 cm (30 × 32 ⅛ in.),
The Metropolitan Museum of Art, New York,
gift of Eda Mirsky Mann, 1988 (1988. 119.3)

Page 58: *Study from the Nude*, 1933
Conté crayon on paper, 53 × 40 cm (20 ⅞ × 15 ¾ in.),
Pollock-Krasner Foundation, New York

Page 59: *Study from the Nude*, 1933
Conté crayon on paper, 51.4 × 37.7 cm
(20 ¼ × 14 ⅞ in.), Pollock-Krasner Foundation,
New York

Page 60: *Study from the Nude*, 1933
Conté crayon on paper, 52.9 × 40.6 cm
(20 ⅞ × 16 in.), Pollock-Krasner Foundation,
New York

Page 61: *Study from the Nude*, 1933
Conté crayon on paper, 60.3 × 44.4 cm
(23 ¾ × 17 ½ in.), Pollock-Krasner Foundation,
New York

Page 62: *Untitled*, 1940
Charcoal on paper, 63.5 × 48.3 cm, Pollock-Krasner
Foundation, New York

Page 63: *Nude Study from Life*, 1938
Charcoal on paper, 64.8 × 50.8 cm (25 ½ × 20 in.),
Pollock-Krasner Foundation, New York

Page 64: *Nude Study from Life*, 1940
Charcoal on paper, 62.9 × 48.3 cm (24 ¾ × 18 ⅞ in.),
Pollock-Krasner Foundation, New York

Page 65: *Nude Study from Life*, 1940
Charcoal on paper, 62.9 × 48 cm (24 ¾ × 18 ⅞ in.),
Pollock-Krasner Foundation, New York

Page 66: *Nude Study from Life*, 1940
Charcoal on paper, 62.2 × 47.6 cm (24 ½ × 18 ¾ in.),
Pollock-Krasner Foundation, New York

Page 67: *Nude Study from Life*, 1940
Charcoal on paper, 62.9 × 47.9 cm (24 ¾ × 18 ⅞ in.),
The Metropolitan Museum of Art, New York, gift
of Mr and Mrs Jason McCoy, 1978 (1978.446)

Pages 70–81:
Photographs of designs for War Service
Window Displays (original collages lost), 1942
Photomontage and collage, dimensions unknown,
Jackson Pollock and Lee Krasner Papers,
Archives of American Art, Smithsonian Institution,
Washington DC

Page 85: *Untitled*, 1946
Oil on linen, 70.5 × 76.8 cm (27 ¾ × 30 ¼ in.),
Collection of Bobbi and Walter Zifkin

Page 86: *Abstract No. 2*, 1946–48
Oil on canvas, 52 × 59 cm (20 ½ × 23 ¼ in.), IVAM,
Institut Valencià d'Art Modern, Generalitat, Spain.

Page 87: *Untitled*, 1947
Oil on canvas, 55.9 × 40.6 cm (22 × 16 in.), Munson-
Williams-Proctor Arts Institute, Utica, New York

Page 88: *Shattered Colour*, 1947
Oil on canvas, 53.3 × 66 cm (22 × 26 ⅛ in.), Guild
Hall Museum, East Hampton, New York

Page 89: *Mosaic Table*, 1947
Mosaic and mixed media on wood, 116.8 cm (46 in.)
diameter, private collection

Page 90: *Composition*, 1949
Oil on canvas, 96.7 × 70.6 cm (38 ⅛ × 27 ¾ in.),
The Philadelphia Museum of Art, gift of the Aaron
E. Norman Fund Inc., 1959, 1959-31-1

Page 91: *Stop and Go*, 1949–50
Oil and enamel on panel, 116.2 cm (54 ¾ in.)
diameter, private collection

Page 92: *Black and White Squares No. 1*, 1948
Oil and enamel on linen, 61.3 × 76.2 cm (24 ⅛ × 30 in.),
private collection

Page 93: *Untitled*, c. 1948–49
Oil on canvas, 61 × 76.3 cm (24 × 30 in.),
private collection

Page 94: *Night Light*, 1949
Oil on linen, 101.6 × 63.5 cm (40 ¼ × 27 in.),
private collection, Dallas, Texas

Page 95: *Untitled (Little Image)*, 1950
Oil on canvas, 114.3 × 27.9 cm (45 × 11 in.),
Collection of halley k harrisburg and Michael
Rosenfeld, New York

Pages 98–99: *Shattered Light*, 1954
Oil and paper collage on Masonite, 86.4 × 121.9 cm
(34 × 48 in.), private collection

Page 100: *Forest No. 2*, 1954
Collage and oil on panel, 152 × 61 cm (59 ⅞ × 24 in.),
Kunstmuseum Bern, Switzerland, 1993.3

Page 101: *Untitled*, 1954
Oil, glue, canvas and paper collage on Masonite,
121.9 × 101.6 cm (48 × 40 in.), private collection,
New York

Page 103: *Burning Candles*, 1955
Oil, paper, cloth and canvas collage on linen,
147.6 × 99.1 cm (58 × 39 in.), Collection Neuberger
Museum of Art, Purchase College, State University
of New York, gift of Roy R. Neuberger

Page 104: *Bird Talk*, 1955
Oil, paper and canvas on cotton duck,
147.3 × 142.2 cm (58 × 56 in.), private collection,
New York

Page 105: *Bald Eagle*, 1955
Oil, paper and canvas collage on linen,
195.6 × 130.8 cm (77 × 51 ½ in.), Collection
of Audrey Irmas, Los Angeles

Page 106: *Milkweed*, 1955
Oil and paper collage on canvas, 209.6 × 146.7 cm
(82 3/8 × 57 ¾ in.), Collection Albright-Knox
Art Gallery, Buffalo, New York, gift of Seymour
H. Knox Jr, 1976

Page 107: *Desert Moon*, 1955
Collage of oil on paper on canvas, and oil on
canvas, 147.3 × 108 cm (58 × 42 ½ in.), Los Angeles
County Museum of Art, purchased with funds
provided by Jo Ann and Julian Ganz Jr, Robert
F. Maguire III, Leslie and John Dorman, Betty
and Brack Duker, John and Joan Hotchkis, Mr
and Mrs H. Tony Oppenheimer / Oppenheimer
Brothers Foundation, Lynda and Stewart Resnick,
Sheila and Wally Weisman, Marilyn B. and Calvin
B. Gross, Judith and Steaven K. Jones, Myron
Laskin, Tally and Bill Mingst, and Irene Christopher
through the 2000 Collectors Committee, Director's
Discretionary Fund, Judith and Richard Smooke,
and two anonymous donors

Page 109: *Blue Level*, 1955
Oil, paper and burlap collage on canvas,
208.9 × 147.3 cm (87 ¼ × 58 in.), private collection

Page 113: *Prophecy*, 1956
Oil on cotton duck, 147.6 × 86.4 cm (58 1/8 × 34 in.),
private collection

Page 114: *Birth*, 1956
Oil on canvas, 209.6 × 121.9 cm (82 ½ × 48 in.),
Reynolda House Museum of American Art,
Winston-Salem, North Carolina, gift of Barbara
B. Millhouse, 2014.1.1

Page 115: *Embrace*, 1956
Oil on canvas, 162.6 × 144.8 cm (64 × 57 in.),
private collection

Page 117: *Three in Two*, 1956
Oil on canvas, 190.5 × 147.3 cm (75 × 58 in.),
private collection, San Francisco

Page 121: *Triple Goddess*, 1960
Oil on canvas, 218.4 × 147.3 cm (86 × 58 in.),
private collection

Pages 122–23: *The Eye is the First Circle*, 1960
Oil on canvas, 235.6 × 487.4 cm (92 ¾ × 191 ⅞ in.),
private collection

Page 124: *Assault on the Solar Plexus*, 1961
Oil on cotton duck, 205.7 × 147.3 cm (81 × 58 in.),
Suzanne Deal Booth

Page 125: *The Guardian*, 1960
Oil on canvas, 134.9 × 147.6 cm (53 × 58 in.),
Whitney Museum of American Art, New York,
purchase, with funds from the Uris Brothers
Foundation Inc., 60.61

Pages 126–27: *Polar Stampede*, 1960
Oil on canvas, 243.8 × 412.4 cm (96 × 162 ⅜ in.),
The Doris and Donald Fisher Collection at the
San Francisco Museum of Modern Art

Pages 130–31: *Another Storm*, 1963
Oil on canvas, 238.8 × 447.7 cm (94 × 176 ¼ in.),
private collection, courtesy of Nevill Keating Pictures

Page 132: *Happy Lady*, 1963
Oil on canvas, 147.3 × 192.4 cm (58 × 75 ¾ in.),
Collection of the Flint Institute of Arts, Michigan;
purchased with funds from the National Endowment
for the Arts Museum Purchase Grant and the
Samuel and Alma Catsman Foundation, 1978.59

Page 133: *Through Blue*, 1963
Oil on canvas, 191.8 × 147.3 cm (75 ½ × 58 in.),
private collection, New York

Page 134: *Chrysalis*, 1964
Oil on cotton duck, 112 × 117.2 cm
(44 ⅛ × 46 ⅛ in.), Thomson Family Collection,
New York

Page 135: *Icarus*, 1964
Oil on canvas, 116.8 × 175.3 cm (46 × 69 in.),
Thomson Family Collection, New York

Pages 136–37: *Kufic*, 1965
Oil on canvas, 205.7 × 325.1 cm (81 × 128 in.),
Pollock-Krasner Foundation, New York

Pages 138–39: *Combat*, 1965
Oil on canvas, 179 × 410.4 cm (70 ½ × 161 in.),
National Gallery of Victoria, Melbourne, Felton
Bequest, 1992 (IC1-1992)

Page 141: *Mister Blue*, 1966
Oil on canvas, 132 × 114.3 cm (52 × 45 in.),
Collection of Ron Delsener

Page 142: *Courtship*, 1966
Oil on canvas, 129.5 × 180.3 cm (51 × 71 in.),
Collection of David Dechman and Michel Mercure

Page 143: *Siren*, 1966
Oil on canvas, 128.6 × 206.1 cm (51 5/8 × 81 ⅛ in.),
Hirshhorn Museum and Sculpture Garden,
Washington DC, The Joseph H. Hirshhorn Bequest,
1981, 86.2768

Pages 144–45: *Portrait in Green*, 1969
Oil on canvas, 140.3 × 239.8 cm (55 × 94 in.),
Pollock-Krasner Foundation, New York

Page 146, top: *Seed No. 6*, 1969
Gouache on Howell paper, 56.5 × 76.2 cm
(22 ¼ × 30 in.), Pollock-Krasner Foundation,
New York

Page 146, bottom: *Seed No. 4*, 1969
Gouache on Howell paper, 56.5 × 76.2 cm
(22 ¼ × 30 in.), Pollock-Krasner Foundation,
New York

Page 147: *Hieroglyphs No. 18*, 1969
Gouache on Howell paper, 1969, 48.3 × 38.1 cm
(19 × 15 in.), private collection

Page 148: *Hieroglyphs No. 4*, 1969
Gouache on Howell paper, 76.2 × 55.9 cm
(30 × 22 in.), Pollock-Krasner Foundation, New York

Page 149: *Hieroglyphs No. 12*, 1969
Gouache on Howell paper, 61 × 48.2 cm
(24 × 19 in.), private collection, United States

Page 150, top: *Earth No. 1*, 1969
Gouache on collage on Howell paper, 45.7 × 54.6 cm
(18 × 21 ½ in.), Dr Greg Shannon and family

Page 150, bottom: *Water No. 2*, 1968
Gouache on Howell paper, 44.1 × 54.3 cm
(17 ⅜ × 21 ⅜ in.), courtesy of James Barron Art
LLC, Kent, CT, and Michael Rosenfeld Gallery LLC,
New York, NY

Page 151: *Untitled*, 1969
Gouache on Howell paper, 45.7 × 31.8 cm
(18 × 12 ½ in.), Pollock-Krasner Foundation,
New York

Page 152: *Untitled*, 1969
Gouache on Howell paper, 17.1 × 25.4 cm
(6 ¾ × 10 in.), Pollock-Krasner Foundation,
New York

Page 153, top: *Water No. 10*, 1969
Gouache on Howell paper, 22.2 × 29.2 cm
(9 × 11 ½ in.), private collection

Page 153, bottom: *Water No. 20*, 1969
Gouache on Howell paper, 17.1 × 25.4 cm
(6 ¾ × 10 in.), Pollock-Krasner Foundation,
New York

Page 154, top: *Seed No. 21*, 1969
Gouache on Howell paper, 38.1 × 48.9 cm
(15 × 19 in.), private collection

Page 154, bottom: *Water No. 14*, 1969
Gouache on Howell paper, 55.2 × 83.8 cm
(21 ¾ × 33 in.), Pollock-Krasner Foundation,
New York

Page 155: *Water No. 18*, 1969
Gouache on Howell paper, 48.3 × 38.1 cm
(19 × 15 in.), Gusford Collection

Pages 158–59: *Palingenesis*, 1971
Oil on canvas, 208.3 × 340.4 cm (82 × 134 in.),
Pollock-Krasner Foundation, New York

Page 161: *Olympic*, 1974
Oil on canvas, 209.6 × 179 cm (82 ½ × 70 ½ in.),
Pollock-Krasner Foundation, New York

Page 164: *Imperative*, 1976
Oil, charcoal and paper on canvas, 127 × 127 cm
(50 × 50 in.), National Gallery of Art, Washington
DC, gift of Mr and Mrs Eugene Victor Thaw, in
honour of the 50th anniversary of the National
Gallery of Art

Page 165: *Future Indicative*, 1977
Collage on canvas, 127 × 127 cm (50 × 50 in.),
private collection

Page 167: *Imperfect Indicative*, 1976
Collage on canvas, 198.1 × 182.9 cm (78 × 72 in.),
Pollock-Krasner Foundation, New York

CONTRIBUTORS

ELEANOR NAIRNE

Eleanor Nairne is Curator at Barbican Art Gallery, London, where her exhibitions include *Basquiat: Boom for Real* (2017) and *Imran Qureshi: Where the Shadows Are So Deep* (2016). She was previously Curator of the Artangel Collection at Tate, working with such artists as Francis Alÿs, Yael Bartana, Jeremy Deller, Mike Kelley, Tony Oursler and Catherine Yass. She is a regular catalogue essayist, a writer for *frieze* magazine and a previous Jerwood Writer in Residence.

KATY SIEGEL

Katy Siegel is the Eugene V. and Clare E. Thaw Endowed Chair at Stony Brook University, New York, and Senior Curator of Research and Programming at the Baltimore Museum of Art, Maryland. Her recent exhibitions include *Odyssey: Jack Whitten Sculpture, 1963–2017* (2018); *Postwar: Art between the Pacific and the Atlantic, 1945–65* (2017); and Mark Bradford's presentation in the US Pavilion at the Venice Biennale (2017). Her retrospective exhibition of the work of Joan Mitchell will open in 2020.

JOHN YAU

John Yau is Professor of Critical Studies at Mason Gross School of the Arts, Rutgers University, New York, and lives in New York City. A poet and critic, he has written monographs on Richard Artschwager, Jasper Johns, Catherine Murphy, Thomas Nozkowski, A. R. Penck, Philip Taffe and William Tillyer. In 2018 he was the winner of the Jackson Poetry Prize, which is awarded annually to an exceptional American poet who deserves wider recognition.

SUZANNE HUDSON

Suzanne Hudson is Associate Professor of Art History and Fine Arts at the University of Southern California. An art historian and critic, her scholarship has focused on abstraction, painting and American philosophy. Her writing has appeared in *Parkett*, *Flash Art*, *Art Journal* and *October*, and she is a regular contributor to *Artforum*. She is the author of *Robert Ryman: Used Paint* (2009), *Painting Now* (2015) and *Agnes Martin: Night Sea* (2017).

GAIL LEVIN

Gail Levin is Distinguished Professor of Art History, American Studies and Women's Studies at the City University of New York, and the biographer of Lee Krasner (2011), who was her mentor. Acknowledged as the authority on the American painter Edward Hopper, Levin is the author of his catalogue raisonné, a biography and other Hopper-related publications. The institutional destruction of most of the canvases by Jo Hopper, Edward's wife, prompted Levin to write a biography of the feminist artist Judy Chicago.

CHARLOTTE FLINT

Charlotte Flint is Exhibition Assistant at Barbican Art Gallery, where she has worked on *Another Kind of Life: Photography on the Margins* (2018), as well as the accompanying catalogue and public programme. Prior to joining the Barbican, she worked at the Victoria and Albert Museum, London, as Assistant Curator, and at the Hayward Gallery, London. Her writing has been published in *ARC* and *Eye* magazines.

JESSICA FREEMAN-ATWOOD

Jessica Freeman-Attwood, who worked as a research assistant on *Lee Krasner: Living Colour*, is a curator and writer based in London. She has previously managed the studio of the Turner Prize-nominated artist Michael Dean, and has worked at London's Herald St gallery on exhibitions by Ida Ekblad, Jessi Reaves, Klaus Weber and Christina Mackie. She is a writer for *Hyperallergic* and holds an MA from the Courtauld Institute of Art, London, completed under the supervision of Professor Sarah Wilson.

SASKIA FLOWER

Saskia Flower, who worked as a research assistant on *Lee Krasner: Living Colour*, is a London-based researcher and curator. In 2018 she co-curated *There Not There*, an exhibition of contemporary art at the Courtauld Gallery, London, and has worked at Blain Southern and Timothy Taylor galleries, also in London. She has an MA in 'Curating the Art Museum' from the Courtauld Institute of Art.

Page numbers in *italic* indicate illustrations.

Front cover: *Desert Moon* (detail), 1955.
Back cover: Lee Krasner, *c.* 1938. Photographer unknown.

Section dividers: Ray Eames, a close friend of Krasner's from their Hofmann School days, visited the house at Springs numerous times over the years, photographing Krasner's home, her studio and her idyllic natural environment. We have included these photographs at intervals throughout the catalogue, to offer an intimate view into Krasner's life, her studio practice and the surrounding nature that inspired her work.

First published in the United Kingdom in 2019 by
Thames & Hudson Ltd, 181A High Holborn, WC1V 7QX,
in association with Barbican Art Gallery

First published in 2019 in the United States of America by Thames & Hudson Inc., 500 Fifth Avenue, New York, New York 10110

Published on the occasion of the exhibition *Lee Krasner: Living Colour*, curated by Eleanor Nairne, 30 May–1 September 2019

Barbican Art Gallery, Barbican Centre
Silk Street, London EC2Y 8DS
barbican.org.uk

This paperback edition first published in 2024 by
Thames & Hudson Ltd in association with Barbican Art Gallery

EDITED BY   Eleanor Nairne
DESIGNED BY   A Practice for Everyday Life

British Library Cataloguing-in-Publication Data
A catalogue record for this book is available from the British Library

Library of Congress Control Number 2018956163

ISBN 978-0-500-29758-2

Printed and bound in Italy by Printer Trento SrL

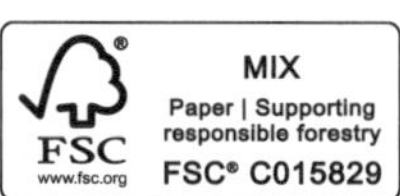

Be the first to know about our new releases, exclusive content and author events by visiting
thamesandhudson.com
thamesandhudsonusa.com
thamesandhudson.com.au

LEE KRASNER: LIVING COLOUR

Barbican Art Gallery, London: 30 May–1 September 2019
Schirn Kunsthalle Frankfurt: 11 October 2019–12 January 2020
Zentrum Paul Klee, Switzerland: 7 February–10 May 2020
Guggenheim Museum Bilbao, Spain: 29 May–6 September 2020

EXHIBITION CURATOR   Eleanor Nairne
EXHIBITION ASSISTANT   Charlotte Flint
RESEARCH ASSISTANTS   Jessica Freeman-Atwood and Saskia Flower
CURATORIAL TRAINEE   Amrita Dhallu

EXHIBITION DESIGN   David Chipperfield Architects
EXHIBITION GRAPHIC DESIGN   A Practice for Everyday Life

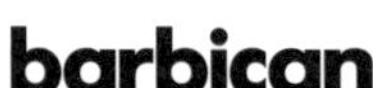
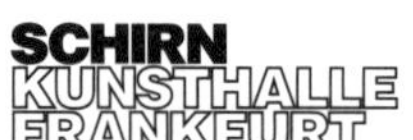
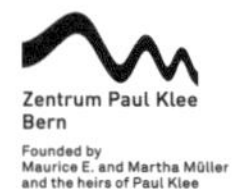

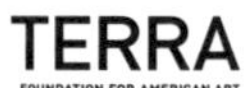
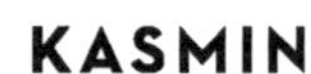
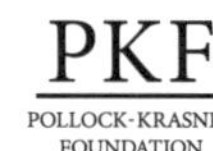
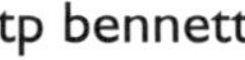